Professional Studies in Primary Education

2nd Edition

Professional Studies in Primary Education

Edited by Hilary Cooper

SAGE

Los Angeles | London | New Delhi
Singapore | Washington DC

SAGE

Los Angeles | London | New Delhi
Singapore | Washington DC

SAGE Publications Ltd
1 Oliver's Yard
55 City Road
London EC1Y 1SP

SAGE Publications Inc.
2455 Teller Road
Thousand Oaks, California 91320

SAGE Publications India Pvt Ltd
B 1/I 1 Mohan Cooperative Industrial Area
Mathura Road
New Delhi 110 044

SAGE Publications Asia-Pacific Pte Ltd
3 Church Street
#10-04 Samsung Hub
Singapore 049483

Editor: James Clark
Editorial assistant: Rachael Plant
Production editor: Nicola Marshall
Project manager: Jeanette Graham
Copyeditor: Rosemary Campbell
Proofreader: Sharon Cawood
Indexer: Hilary Cooper
Marketing manager: Catherine Slinn
Cover designer: Naomi Robinson
Typeset by: C&M Digitals (P) Ltd, Chennai, India
Printed and bound in Great Britain by Ashford Colour Press Ltd

MIX
Paper from responsible sources
FSC
www.fsc.org
FSC® C011748

First edition published in 2011
Second edition published in 2014

Library of Congress Control Number: 2013947930

British Library Cataloguing in Publication data

A catalogue record for this book is available from the British Library

ISBN 978-1-4462-8075-1
ISBN 978-1-4462-8076-8

CONTENTS

ABOUT THE EDITOR

Hilary Cooper is Professor Emeritus of History and Pedagogy at the University of Cumbria. After many years teaching in London primary schools and undertaking her doctoral research on child development using data collected as a class teacher, she lectured in Education at Goldsmiths' College, London University. In 1993 she became Director of Professional Studies in the Department of Education at Lancaster University, then Reader, and later Professor of Education at St Martin's College, now the University of Cumbria. She has published widely and has an international reputation.

ABOUT THE CONTRIBUTORS

Jan Ashbridge is Subject Leader and Senior Lecturer in Early Childhood Education at the University of Cumbria. She was a Foundation Stage Teacher for 12 years and also a senior advisory teacher for the Foundation Stage with Cumbria Local Education Authority. Jan has been involved in planning and delivering training sessions to students and early years educators across the north-west of England in all aspects of young children's learning and the skills adults need to support this. She has published a number of book chapters on this subject.

Pete Boyd is Reader in Professional Learning at the University of Cumbria and works in Educational Development. He taught in high schools for 15 years before moving to an academic post in teacher education and development. His current role as research coordinator is focused on building the research capacity of lecturers and teachers based in universities and in partnership organisations. He supervises teachers and lecturers in educational research at Masters and Doctoral level and supports collaborative research in development projects with teachers in Partnership schools. His doctoral research is focused on the workplace learning of educational professionals including teacher educators based in universities and in schools. He has also coordinated a text on assessment in Higher Education and published research concerning how lecturers learn to grade and give feedback on coursework.

Nerina Díaz has had extensive teaching experience in primary schools throughout the world. She has worked as a Senior Lecturer at the University of Cumbria, teaching Education Studies and tutoring students who are completing school placements. Her research interests lie with students' perceptions of the academic requirements and assessments for Higher Education. She is currently working as an Education Consultant, her latest assignment being to develop the Diploma in Education for Bangladesh.

Sally Elton-Chalcraft is Reader in Education at the University of Cumbria. She is also Equality and Diversity Officer for Cumbria QTS programmes. She has published numerous articles in the areas of research methods, creative teaching and learning, children's spirituality and teaching for diversity. Her book publications include *It's Not Just About Black and White Miss: Children's Awareness of Race* (Trentham Books, 2009) from her PhD research, and *Doing Classroom Research: A Step-By-Step Guide for Student Teachers* (Open University Press, 2008) with A. Hansen and S. Twiselton. She is currently working on the book *Teaching RE Creatively* for a series with Routledge. She lives on the edge of the Lake District with her husband, three children and cat.

Kim Harris is Senior Lecturer in Education at the University of Worcester. Her background is in primary teaching and initial teacher education. Previously, she worked for eight years as a Senior Lecturer in Music Education at the University of Cumbria and taught as a Primary School Class Teacher in Berkshire and Cumbria, working across both KS1 and 2. Her particular areas of interest are music and mathematics initial teacher education. Her research interests focus on teacher development in primary music education and the induction and professional development of academic staff in teacher education within the Higher Education sector.

Donna Hurford was until recently a Principal Lecturer in the Faculty of Education, University of Cumbria with a specialism in Education Studies and Global Citizenship. After teaching in KS1 and KS2 classes in Lancashire schools with an ICT responsibility, Donna moved to Higher Education, initially specialising in ICT education. Donna has been involved in a variety of research projects on aspects of Assessment for Learning (AfL), criticality in Global Citizenship and collaborative research. Her doctoral research is focused on student teacher responses to Assessment for Learning. Currently she is working abroad as an educational consultant.

Jo Josephidou is a Senior Lecturer at the University of Cumbria. She works predominantly within the early years team but also teaches inclusion modules and Modern Foreign Languages (MFL) on the primary programmes. She came to the university as a teacher fellow after many years teaching in the primary school where she was Foundation Stage leader and SENCO. Her particular interests are early years education and inclusion.

Verna Kilburn is a Senior Lecturer in Inclusion and Special Educational Needs at the University of Cumbria. Previously, she taught in primary schools in London, Newcastle and Jamaica.

Suzanne Lowe is a Senior Lecturer, teaching Education Studies, Inclusion and Science modules to ITE students at the University of Cumbria. Previously she has been a primary school class teacher working across both KS1 and KS2 for 10 years. She was a Leading Teacher of Mathematics within Cumbria for four years. Suzanne has also been involved in education in local museums. Her particular area of interest is inclusion and her MA examined aspects of educational leadership, curriculum development and children's cognitive processes and learning.

Kären Mills is a Senior Lecturer in the Faculty of Education at the University of Cumbria. After teaching across the key stages in schools in both Lancashire and a London borough, Kären moved to Higher Education to teach on ITE courses, particularly Education and Primary Mathematics. More recently, she has contributed to the SEN specialism offered to undergraduates. Her research interests include approaches to blended learning and students' perceptions of assessment, both peer and self. She is passionate about preparing ITE students to look at the holistic development of the child, as well as curriculum development and is shaping her ITE programme around this.

Andrew Read is Head of Primary Initial Teacher Education at the University of East London. After teaching in schools in Tower Hamlets, East London, Andrew moved into Higher Education, initially as an English specialist, later moving into the field of Educational Studies. Working in collaboration with Donna Hurford, Andrew has been involved in research projects on aspects of Assessment for Learning (AfL), criticality in Global Citizenship and collaborative research. His current research focuses on 'good practice' in supporting learners with English as an additional language.

Anne Renwick is a Senior Lecturer at the University of Cumbria, teaching across the full range of early years programmes. She has worked in a number of primary schools in the north-east and Cumbria, teaching Nursery, Reception and Key Stage 1 children. Before joining the university, Anne was employed as a Senior Early Years

Advisory teacher for Cumbria Children's Services, supporting practitioners in a range of early years schools and settings. Anne has developed her own research on the subject of professional development for the children's workforce and her Master's dissertation focused on support for teachers working in children's centres. Her current research centres on transition into Higher Education and the development of teacher identity in undergraduate QTS students.

Chris Rowley was Senior Lecturer in Environmental and Geographical Education at the University of Cumbria until his recent retirement. He taught at a variety of schools before joining Charlotte Mason College of Education in 1987. He was a member of the SAPERE Committee (Society to Advance Philosophical Enquiry in Education) from 1997 to 2003. An interest in children's understanding of the environment led him to work with teachers around Morecambe Bay between 2003 and 2004 to co-produce *Thinking on the Edge* (Lewis and Rowley, 2004). In 2004, Chris was co-editor of *Geography 3–11* (Fulton) and in 2010 of *Cross-curricular Approaches to Teaching and Learning* (SAGE).

Lin Savage was a Principal Lecturer at the University of Cumbria with responsibility for early years programmes between 2009 and 2013. Previously, Lin had over 25 years of experience teaching early years and primary children in Cumbria and London. She was an Advanced Skills teacher and worked as an Early Years Advisory Teacher and Area SENCO for Cumbria Local Education Authority, supporting practitioners and delivering professional training for leaders and practitioners. Lin is interested in all aspects of early years education. Her Master's research focused on early years students' experience of joining the workforce. Recent research has included a consideration of the professional status of early years educators and analysis of practitioners' conversations with young children. Lin retired from the University of Cumbria in April 2013.

Deborah Seward graduated from St Martin's College and taught for many years in a range of primary schools. She completed her MA, 'Developing Teacher Expertise', whilst working as a Senior Lecturer in History Education for St Martin's College, Carlisle campus, before becoming the head teacher of a small primary school in North Cumbria. As a head teacher, she was particularly interested in cross-curricular teaching and the development of creative approaches to learning and teaching, successfully leading a Creative Futures project within the school. She has a wide range of experience in mentoring students and Newly Qualified Teachers, and has recently returned to a Senior Lecturer role at the University of Cumbria where she works on the early years programmes as a module and cohort leader and is undertaking doctoral research.

Susan Shaw is Primary Programme Leader at Edgehill University. Previously she was Principal Lecturer in the Faculty of Education at the University of Cumbria. She spent 20 years in primary schools, with positions ranging from class teacher to head teacher before becoming a lecturer. She has an NPQH and is a Fellow of the Higher Education Academy. She is passionate about preparing ITE students to understand the holistic development of the child as well as curriculum development, and is shaping her ITE programme around this.

Andrew Slater taught for many years, working both in primary and secondary schools. Whilst working in the Higher Education sector, he has maintained a particular interest in urban education and strategies to enhance community cohesion. His doctoral study focused upon pupil interaction. Wider interests include citizenship education and the use of story within training.

Diane Vaukins is a Senior Lecturer and Director of School Engagement Partnership at the University of Cumbria London Campus and the Module Leader for the three-year BA/QTS mathematics specialist course. Prior to lecturing in Higher Education, she was a primary school teacher and deputy head teacher. She has a keen interest in working with schools to encourage creativity in mathematics.

Diane Warner is a Senior Lecturer at the University of Cumbria, working with undergraduate student teachers and also teaching on the MA in Education programme. Her professional areas of interest and study are English Education and developing English specialist knowledge, such as teaching Shakespeare in the Primary School. Her doctoral study focused on Black and Minority student experiences in teacher training. Previously she worked in an inner-city school, with a high percentage of Asian Muslim children.

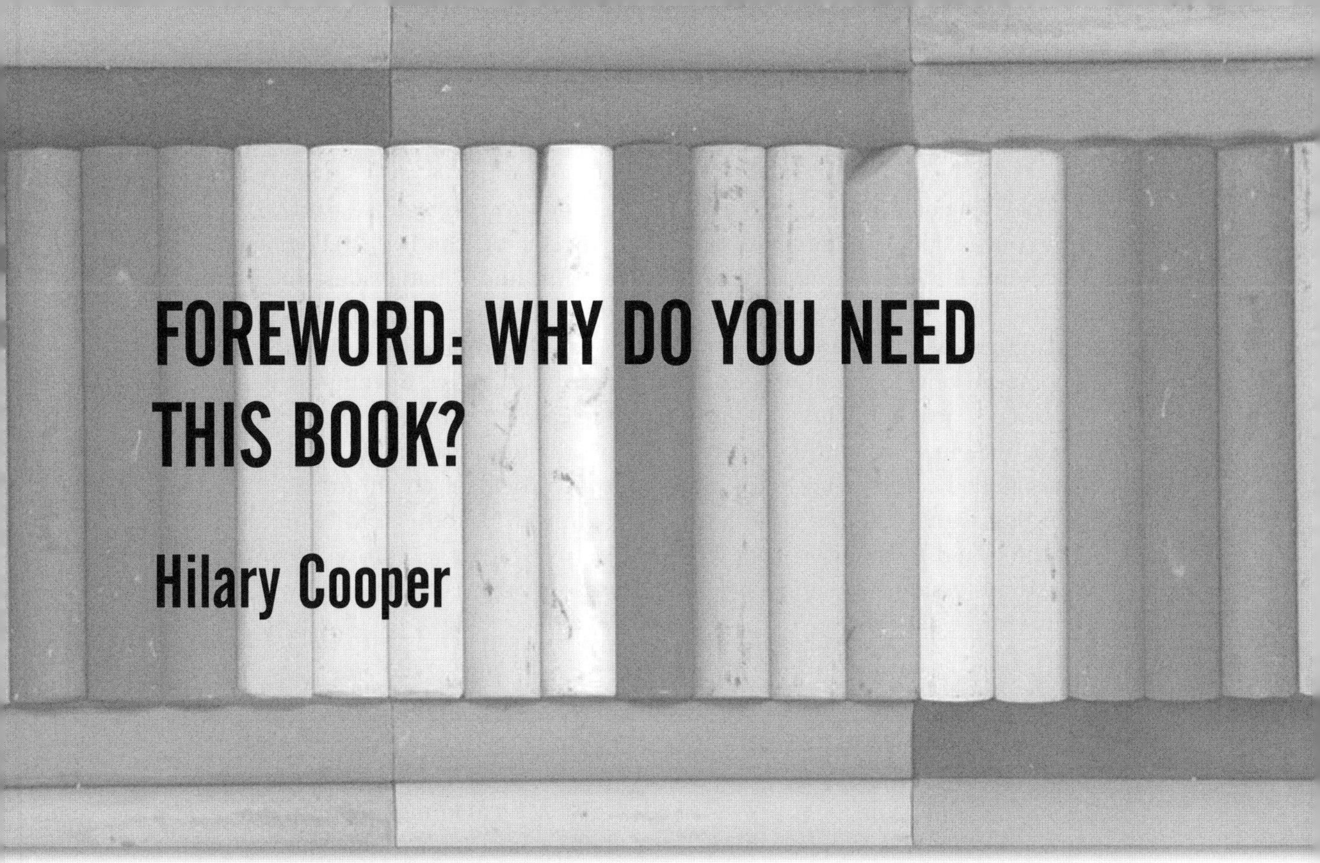

FOREWORD: WHY DO YOU NEED THIS BOOK?

Hilary Cooper

Many of us wanted to be teachers in order to be different from some of the teachers we had known and to be inspiring, as some of our teachers were. At a time of continuously changing expectations and prescriptions, often politically driven, how free are we to do this? The answer is, remarkably free, if we have a confident and secure understanding of the professional choices we are able to make.

Making professional choices

It sometimes seems that, because everyone has been to school, they all feel entitled to a valid opinion about how children should be taught. This can be very frustrating! I recently read a letter in *The Spectator* (22.06.13: 29) in which a former PGCE student argued that studying education was a waste of time and described how he fell asleep during a seminar on, 'How psychological theory can optimise motivation in the classroom'. By the end of this book you should be able to give him a confident and well-informed response! The ability to make informed professional choices is what gives you the authority to be a teacher.

This will enable you to make decisions about how to teach, based on personal and professional judgements about the needs of children, recognising their different, individual needs, what excites them and what makes them want to learn. You will become a teacher who understands children's different backgrounds, difficulties, local and personal environments, and that emotional and social development are an integral part of cognitive development. You will become a teacher who enjoys exploring learning *with* children, who fosters their imagination and curiosity, who works in partnership with children's parents and carers, who helps children to be articulate about and evaluate their learning. You will be confident in working with others to plan children's learning and to monitor it in skilful and sensitive ways. You will learn how to make professional judgements about classroom organisation and how to manage behaviour effectively.

What, exactly, are 'professional studies'?

When, in a previous post, I was asked at a social gathering, what my role was in my university and I replied, 'Director of Professional Studies', this was met with a wry laugh, accompanied by, 'Whatever are Professional Studies?' (I felt that no answer was expected.) Professional Studies courses educate you to make professional judgements, based on the knowledge you have about the ways in which children learn and the things that stop them reaching their potential. This knowledge is based on your familiarity with the rich body of literature relating to child development and creating classrooms which are safe, exciting and inclusive learning environments, negotiated environments for which you and the children both take responsibility and share the excitement of learning. Your judgements are also based on a combination of what you know from your reading and the way you relate this to, and interpret it in terms of, your own experience of working with children, colleagues and parents in schools. Professional judgement is not static; it grows, develops and changes as you grow and as society changes. Above all, this book shows you how to interpret the ever-changing demands made on teachers by continually changing curriculum requirements, assessment requirements, reports and recommendations, with imagination and integrity, so that you can interpret the agendas of politicians and other stakeholders with confidence, articulate your ideas and explain and justify your practice. There are many otherwise good teachers who cannot explain the complexity of their practice to others; this undermines their status and also prevents them analysing and developing their practice. This book aims to enable you to meet current and future government requirements within a broad and deep interpretation of the concept of 'professional studies'.

ACKNOWLEDGEMENTS

SAGE would like to thank the following reviewers whose comments have helped shape this second edition:

Elizabeth Broad – University of Roehampton
Sally Howard – University of Warwick
Phil Jefferies – University of Greenwich
Mark Jenkins – University of Winchester
Sarah Martin-Denham – Sunderland University

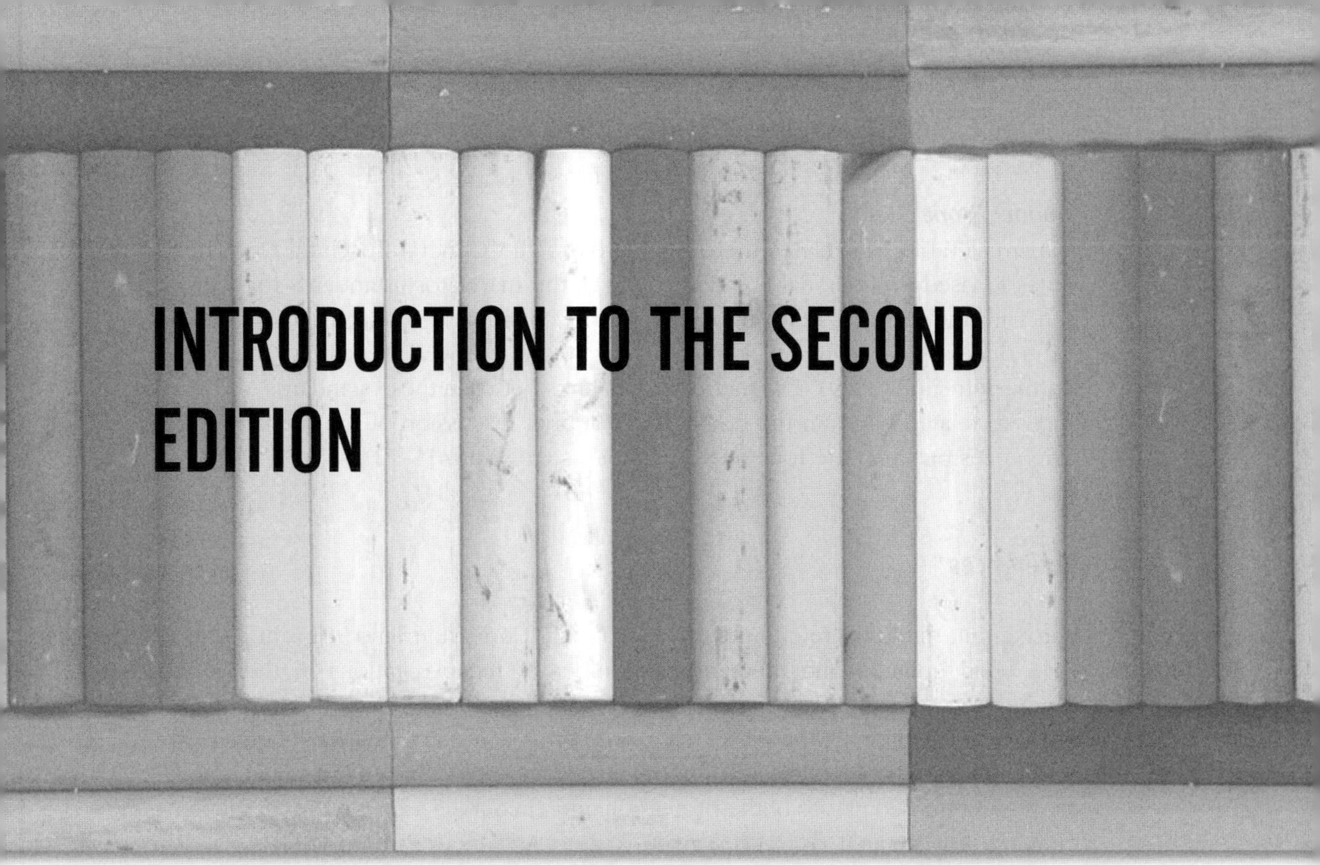

INTRODUCTION TO THE SECOND EDITION

Why is a second edition of *Professional Studies in Primary Education* necessary?

The central thesis of the first edition of the book was that, paradoxically, the only constant in education is change, and the need to interpret changes in a professional way. So it is not surprising that, after two years of changes, particularly in government policies, it is appropriate to weave these into a new edition. This second edition does this in the following ways.

Teachers' Standards

The *Teachers' Standards* have been updated throughout to the Standards applicable since May 2012 (DfE 2013).

Broader Scope

A matrix (Table I.1) relates these Standards to the General Teaching Council for Wales Revised Professional Standards (2011), the mandatory standards for registration with the General Teaching Council for Scotland (2013) and the Competences for trainees and newly qualified teachers at the General Teaching Council for Northern Ireland (2009). The matrix makes links between these standards and references to related pages in the book. There is brief discussion of the similarities and differences between the four sets of Standards (p. 5; pp. 11–12).

References

Throughout the book references to the National Curriculum and relevant literature have been updated and there are a number of recent citations in the Further Reading section at the end of each chapter, with reasons why each will extend your thinking. One or more of these references is to a research paper related to the chapter, which will be of interest and relevance to readers, in order to make explicit the research-based nature of the profession and encourage a continuum in reflective thinking. Any general references given (e.g. to Alexander 2010) now have a clear focus within them.

Policy update

Throughout the book any policy-dependent advice has been updated to reflect the most recent guidance.

Clearer school-based focus

The second edition has a clearer school-based focus, engaging with the greater schools-based focus in Initial Teacher Education, given the shift to more time in schools on Primary PGCE courses and the rise in School Direct. Integrated into each chapter is a box titled 'Work in school', which has a 'student teacher voice'. In the box a number of comments from students working in schools or referring to experiences in school, which are relevant to the chapter, are quoted. These are followed by analytical comments from the chapter author, discussing the quotation. There is also an additional chapter at the beginning of Part 3 focusing on situated learning in school and early years settings, exploring different ways of learning in school and related issues.

Greater focus on planning and assessment

A separate chapter has been allocated to planning and assessment in this edition, given their importance in underpinning effective teaching, learning and progression.

Early years/primary links

While recognising the distinctive nature of early years education, it is also important to perceive this as part of a continuum in primary education. Therefore, brief comments at the beginning of chapters indicate ways in which the chapter is relevant across the primary age phase.

Website material

Website material has been updated where appropriate. It can be found at www.sagepub.co.uk/cooper

Chapters

Modifications have been made in response to constructive feedback from users of the first edition.

The second edition is longer than the first, in order to accommodate these changes, without losing essential material from the first edition.

The structure of the book

Recurring chapter features

Each chapter has consistent features. At the beginning of each chapter, there are statements about the learning which you should acquire through engaging with the chapter, and an introduction outlining the content of the chapter. Embedded in each chapter are activities which will help you to consider, or if possible discuss with others, the issues raised within the chapter. The dialogues in the sections headed 'Work in school' in chapters are fictitious, but based on questions which the experienced tutors and mentors who wrote them were frequently asked during discussions in schools. At the end of each chapter, there is a summary of the content which enabled you to engage with the learning objectives at the beginning of the chapter, followed by questions for discussion of the issues raised and a summary of the chapter content. Finally, there are suggestions for further reading and reasons why this may be of interest.

Parts 1–3

The book is organised into three parts. Part 1 introduces you to the philosophy which underpins the book: the range of professional issues about which teachers have to make judgements and decisions in interpreting statutory frameworks. It does so in the context of what we might call the foundations of Professional Studies, that is the generic professional knowledge, skills and understanding which underpin the curriculum. These chapters outline the history of state primary education in England and of educational philosophy, and show how understanding of these areas helps you to make judgements about implementing the basic components of professional studies, planning, assessment and managing the learning environment.

Part 2 is concerned with different aspects of inclusion, the need to take into account children's varied individual needs, and strategies for doing this, in order to provide equal educational opportunities.

Part 3 deals with strategies for critical thinking about educational issues and reminds you of the statutory requirements you will need to take into account in doing so. It begins with a new chapter specifically focusing on the learning you can acquire while teaching in school. It concludes with a review of the increasingly sophisticated understanding you should have, after engaging with the previous chapters, and suggests networks which will support you in continuing to develop as an imaginative, exciting and inspiring teacher.

Using the book

The three sections are essentially sequential, each deepening your thinking about the educational decisions and judgements required and how to engage with them. However, the book can be used in flexible ways. You may read a chapter before a related teaching session, in order to discuss the questions and issues it poses, on the basis of colleagues' contrasting experiences – for there are often many different and equally valid answers. You may want to follow the session up by dipping into the suggestions for further reading – which will give you more information and further food for thought. You may want to skim read the whole book to 'get the feel of it', then return to specific chapters in connection with seminars or to throw light on your work in school and find ideas for discussions with teachers and mentors or reread certain chapters when you find yourself teaching a different age group or in a different type of school. You may well find it useful to keep ongoing notes in relation to the Teachers' Standards (Table I.1 below) as evidence of your developing philosophy, reading and practice. And you may well find it helpful for your continuing professional development, in preparation for postgraduate study.

Many chapters have website material which extends the chapter content. This may include additional material which space limitations prevented including in the book, references to further reading or to related web links, or further activities for exploring questions raised in the chapter. The companion website for the book can be found at www.sagepub.co.uk/cooper

Teachers' Standards: England, Wales, Scotland, Ireland

Table I.1 analyses the professional attributes addressed throughout the book. It shows how the Standards for both trainee and experienced teachers in England (DfE 2012) can be linked to The Standards for Qualified Teacher Status in Wales (2009), the Standards for Registration in Scotland (2013) and the Professional Competences for Teaching in Northern Ireland (2009). These standards are not discrete but are referred to throughout the book. The final column shows the pages in this book which refer to each of the Standards.

The four sets of standards address this continuum in different ways. In England the Standards apply to all trainees and teachers, interpreted according to their role and context. In Wales the standards referred to in the table are those for practising teachers. There are also Standards for Higher Level Teaching Assistants, and for leadership. In Scotland there are Standards for Initial Teacher Education, for Full Registration as a qualified teacher (given in Table I.1) and Standards for Headship. In Northern Ireland each competence statement is supported by exemplars of how it should be interpreted for Initial Teacher Education, Induction, Early Professional Development and Continuing Professional Development (see also Chapter 3, pp. 60–1 and Chapter 4, p. 86).

Constructing this table was an interesting, although time-consuming exercise. Each of the English Standards in column one cross-refers with parts of statements in the other three sets of Standards. The four sets of Standards are basically homogenous, but are developed more specifically in some cases (which accounts for a lot of the overlap). The main differences are specific references to each country's National Curriculum. It is not possible here to give a detailed analysis of other differences in emphasis which distinguish them but only to point out some interesting differences. There is detailed information about differences in legislation on education in England, Wales, Scotland and Ireland in Chapter 15.

Table I.1 This table links the Teachers' Standards for England (DfE 2013) with the standards for Wales, Scotland and Northern Ireland and shows the pages in this book which are related to them

Standard for trainees and teachers (DfE 2013)	Brief description (DfE 2013)	Practising Teacher Standards	QTS Registration	Competences for trainees and NQT teachers	Pages in this book referring to the competence
		GTC Wales (2011)	GTC Scot. (2013)	GTC N. Ireland (2009)	
Preamble	First concern is the education of their pupils	1. 5.			Throughout
	Are accountable for achieving the highest possible standards in work and conduct	3. 24. 26. 27.	2.1.4.	PC15	Throughout
	Act with honesty and integrity			PC1	65–6, 167, 276, 324
	Have strong subject knowledge	16.			65–6, 272, 274
	Keep their knowledge and skills as teachers up to date and are self-critical	9. 10. 15. 16.	2.4.1.	PC3i	75–6, 90, 283–4, 324–6
			2.4.3.	PC3ii	98, 157, 269, 271, 307, 309
			3.2,	PC11	322–3, 339–40, 369, 373–80
	Positive professional relationships	8. 28. 54.	2.1.5.	PC1 PC10	279–80
	Work with parents (carers) in the best interests of their pupils	4. 6. 32. 39.	2.1.5. 3.3.		25, 62, 82
PART 1 Teaching 1 Set high expectations which inspire, motivate and challenge pupils	Establish a safe and motivating environment for pupils, rooted in mutual respect	2. 21. 40. 32. 40. 48.	2.2.1	PC19	104–7 191 360–1
	Set goals which motivate and challenge pupils of all backgrounds	3. 16. 21. 24. 26. 27. 46.	2.1.4.	PC5 PC10 PC15 PC20	72, 87 94, 248
	Demonstrate consistently the positive attitudes, values and behaviour which are expected of pupils	32.	2.2.1.		122, 199–200, 299
Teaching 2 Promote good progress and outcomes by pupils	Be accountable for pupils' attainment and outcomes		2.3.2. 2.4.1.	PC15	55–99

Standard for trainees and teachers (DfE 2013)	Brief description (DfE 2013)	Practising Teacher Standards	QTS Registration	Competences for trainees and NQT teachers	Pages in this book referring to the competence
		GTC Wales (2011)	GTC Scot. (2013)	GTC N. Ireland (2009)	
	Be aware of pupils' capabilities and their prior knowledge and plan teaching to build on these	21. 24. 26. 46.	2.1.1. 2.1.4.	PC5 PC14 PC15	64–5, 68, 72 86–7
	Guide pupils to reflect on the progress they have made and their emerging needs	5. 21. 24. 26. 36. 46.	2.1.2. 2.1.4.	PC10 PC15 PC24	72, 82, 87–8
	Demonstrate knowledge and understanding of how pupils learn and how this impacts on teaching	14. 15. 16.	2.1.1.	PC6	41–51, 56, 104, 107–8, 108–12, 272–4, 231–3
	Encourage pupils to take a responsible and conscientious attitude to their own work and study	5. 21. 24. 26. 36. 46.	2.1.2. 2.1.4.	PC15	72, 82, 87–8, 91, 94, 111–5, 133, 197, 236
Teaching 3 Demonstrate good subject and curriculum knowledge	Have a secure knowledge of the relevant subject(s) and curriculum areas, foster and maintain pupils' interest in the subject and address misunderstandings	16. 21. 24. 26. 27.	2.1.1. 2.1.3. 2.4.3.	PC3ii PC15 PC25	65, 145, 272, 238
	Demonstrate a critical understanding of developments in the subject and curriculum areas and promote the value of scholarship	9. 10. 14.15. 16.	2.4.1. 2.4.3. 3.2.	PC3ii PCxi	95, 148–9, 154–9, 152–4, 150–2 Web 2, 8
	Demonstrate an understanding of and take responsibility for promoting high standards of literacy, articulacy and the correct use of standard English, whatever the teachers' specialist subject	17.		PC3i	153, 198 Web 2

(Continued)

Table I.1 (Continued)

Standard for trainees and teachers (DfE 2013)	Brief description (DfE 2013)	Practising Teacher Standards	QTS Registration	Competences for trainees and NQT teachers	Pages in this book referring to the competence
		GTC Wales (2011)	GTC Scot. (2013)	GTC N. Ireland (2009)	
	If teaching early reading demonstrate a clear understanding of appropriate teaching strategies	14. 17.		PC3i	154–5, 159 Web 8
Teaching 4 Plan and teach well-structured lessons	Impart knowledge and develop understanding through effective use of lesson time	21. 25. 31. 47.		PC5	71–2, 95
	Promote a love of learning and children's intellectual curiosity	5. 16. 21. 27. 46. 53.		PC15 PC17 PC20	67, 72, 191, 230–6 Web 11
	Set homework and plan other out-of-class activities to consolidate and extend the knowledge and understanding pupils have acquired				72–3
	Reflect systematically on the effectiveness of lessons and approaches to teaching	10. 21. 24. 25.	2.3.2. 2.3.2. 2.4.1.	PC3i PC20	75–6, 236–8 Throughout 270, 296–8, 289–91, 292–3, 301
	Contribute to the design and provision of an engaging curriculum within the relevant subject area(s)	16. 21. 25. 27.	2.1.2. 2.1.3. 2.4.3. 3.3.	PC5 PC20	275–7, 284, Web 11, 12
Teaching 5 Adapt teaching to respond to the strengths and needs of all pupils	Know when and how to differentiate properly, using approaches which enable pupils to be taught effectively	14. 15. 16. 19. 21. 24. 26. 35. 42.	2.1.1. 2.1.3. 2.1.4. 3.1.	PC6 PC8 PC9 PC15	72–4, 86, 93–4, 96, 131, 145, 176, 181–2
	Have a secure understanding of how a range of factors can inhibit pupils' ability to learn and how best to overcome these	14. 15. 16. 19. 21. 24. 26. 35. 42.	2.1.1. 2.1.3. 3.1.	PC6 PC8 PC9 PC15	49, 181–2, 248

Standard for trainees and teachers (DfE 2013)	Brief description (DfE 2013)	Practising Teacher Standards GTC Wales (2011)	QTS Registration GTC Scot. (2013)	Competences for trainees and NQT teachers GTC N. Ireland (2009)	Pages in this book referring to the competence
	Demonstrate awareness of the physical, social and intellectual development of children and how to adapt teaching to support pupils' education at different stages of development	14. 15. 16. 19. 21. 24. 26. 35. 42. 42.	2.1.1. 2.1.2. 2.1.3. 2.1.4. 3.1.	PC6 PC8 PC9 PC15	115, 131, 132, 151, 209, 221
	Have a clear understanding of the needs of all pupils, including those with special educational needs; those of high ability; those with English as an additional language; those with disabilities and be able to use and evaluate distinctive teaching approaches to engage and support them	14. 15. 16. 19. 21. 24. 26. 35.	2.1.1. 2.1.2. 2.1.3. 2.1.4. 3.1.	PC6 PC8 PC9 PC15 PC21	131, 146 164–85, 245, 248 365 Web 2, 8, 12
Teaching 6 Make accurate and productive use of assessment	Know and understand how to assess the relevant subject and curriculum areas, including statutory assessment requirements	14. 16. 25. 26. 33. 34.	2.3.1.	PC24 PC25 PC26	96–8
	Make use of summative and formative assessment to secure pupils' progress				68, 84–5, 94–5, 146
	Use relevant data to monitor progress and plan subsequent lessons	21. 25. 26. 33. 36.	2.3.1.	PC24 PC26	75–6, 97–8 83, 88
	Give pupils regular feedback	5. 21. 24. 26. 33. 36. 38.	2.1.2. 2.1.4. 2.3.1.		88–92, 231
Teaching 7 Manage behaviour effectively	Have clear rules and routines for behaviour in classrooms and take responsibility for promoting good and courteous behaviour, both in classrooms and around the school, in accordance with the school's behaviour policy	2. 21. 40. 49.	2.2.1. 2.2.2.	PC6 PC19 PC7 PC15 PC22	113–5, 182, 192–3

(Continued)

Table I.1 (Continued)

Standard for trainees and teachers (DfE 2013)	Brief description (DfE 2013)	Practising Teacher Standards	QTS Registration	Competences for trainees and NQT teachers	Pages in this book referring to the competence
		GTC Wales (2011)	GTC Scot. (2013)	GTC N. Ireland (2009)	
	Have high expectations of behaviour and establish a framework for discipline, with a range of strategies, using praise, sanctions and rewards consistently and fairly	21. 49.		PCvi PCvii PC15 PC22	113, 191, 200–2
	Manage classes effectively, using approaches which are appropriate to pupils' needs, in order to involve and motivate them	46.	2.1.2. 2.2.1. 2.2.2.	PC6 PC7 PC21	104–18, 284
	Maintain good relationships with pupils, exercise appropriate authority and act decisively when necessary	2. 21.	2.2.1. 2.2.2.	PC6 PC7 PC15 PC22	121–2, 195, 197–8 252
Teaching 8 Fulfil wider professional responsibilities	Make a positive contribution to the wider life and ethos of the school	7. 30.	3.3.	PC12 PC17	276–7, 284
	Develop effective professional relationships with colleagues, knowing how and when to draw on specialist advice and support	8. 20. 28. 32. 54.	2.1.5. 2.2.2. 2.4.2.	PC1 PC3i	126–30, 136, 176, 275–6 276–7, 283–4, 308
	Deploy support staff effectively	8. 28. 29.	2.1.5.	PC10 PC16	108, 122, 176 179–80
	Take responsibility for improving teaching through appropriate professional development, responding to advice and feedback from colleagues	9. 10. 16.	2.4.1. 2.4.3. 3.2.	PC3i PC3ii PC10 PC11	275–8
	Communicate effectively with parents with regard to pupils' achievements and well-being	4. 6. 39.	2.1.5. 3.3.	PC1 PC10 PC27	25, 62, 82, 84–5, 123, 193

Standard for trainees and teachers (DfE 2013)	Brief description (DfE 2013)	Practising Teacher Standards	QTS Registration	Competences for trainees and NQT teachers	Pages in this book referring to the competence
		GTC Wales (2011)	GTC Scot. (2013)	GTC N. Ireland (2009)	
PART 2 Personal and Professional Conduct	1. Treat pupils with dignity, building relationships based on mutual respect, observing proper boundaries appropriate to a teacher's professional position	2.		PC19	88–9, 103–7, 195, 197, 199, 203, 364–5
	2. Safeguard pupils in accordance with statutory provisions	48.		C 1 C 9 C13 C14 C 22	194, 197, 360–1
	3. Show tolerance and respect for the rights of others				Throughout
	4. Not undermine fundamental British values, including democracy, the rule of law, individual liberty and mutual respect and tolerance of those with different faiths and beliefs				249, 308–9, 316 Throughout
	5. Ensure that personal beliefs are not expressed in ways which exploit pupils' vulnerability or might lead them to break the law				Throughout
	6. Have proper and professional regard for the ethos, policies and practices of the school in which they teach and maintain high standards in their attendance and punctuality		1.2.2.	C22	88–9, 249, 276–7, 322
	7. Have an understanding of and always act within the statutory frameworks set out in their professional duties and responsibilities	12. 13. 22.	1.2.1. 1.2.2.	C22	249, 266–7

Theory, research and debate

The English Standards require teachers to take responsibility for their professional development, and to 'understand how children learn'. Part 3 of the English Standards stresses the importance of working within school policies and statutory frameworks and maintaining 'British values'. This contrasts significantly with the aims and aspirations of the Irish Competences which are embedded in an inspiring document, *Teaching: The Reflective Profession* (GTCNI 2009). This stresses the importance of developing a professional identity in order to exercise professional autonomy, in a constantly changing educational context, and the importance of professional dialogue. It talks about vision and moral purpose, creativity, and value-based practice. It describes teachers as characterised by concerns for the purposes and consequences of education, prepared to experiment with the unfamiliar and learn from it, by openness and wholeheartedness. Such teachers act as activist pedagogues and are experts in teaching and learning, reflective and critical problem solvers, researchers and change agents, creators of knowledge and builders of theory. The Scottish Standards refer specifically to 'relevant principles, perspectives and theories to inform professional values and practices' (1.3.1) and 'an understanding of research and its contribution to education' (1.3.2), accessing and evaluating professionally relevant literature (2.4.1) and to constructing and sustaining reasoned arguments (2.4.2) about educational matters and professional practices. The Welsh Standard 9 requires teachers to 'share and test understandings with colleagues through active involvement in professional networks and learning communities'.

Social justice and the community

The English Standards refer to making a positive contribution to the life and ethos of the school and to working with parents, while The Scottish Standards refer to a commitment to social justice (3.1) and to valuing, respecting and showing commitment to the communities in which teachers work (3.3). Professional values and personal commitment include: values of sustainability, equality and justice and demonstrating a commitment to engaging learners in real-world issues to enhance learning experiences and outcomes, and to encourage learning our way to a better future, critically examining the connections between personal and professional attitudes and beliefs, values and practices to effect improvement and, when appropriate, bringing about transformative change in practice. One of the Welsh Standards (7) refers to celebrating the contribution children and young people make in their communities.

Teaching is a complex and serious and important business. There are always some lows to overcome for all of us. But it is also satisfying and rewarding – and it is fun!, For if you are not enjoying yourself, how can you expect that the children are? We hope this book will help you to always want to know more, to teach better and to enjoy your work with confidence.

References

Department for Education (DfE) (2013) *Teachers' Standards,* www.education.gov.uk

Department for Education and Skills, Welsh Government (2011) *Revised Professional Standards for Education Practitioners in Wales,* www.cymru.gov.uk

General Teaching Council for Northern Ireland (GTCNI) (2009) *Teaching: The Reflective Profession*, www.gtcni.org.uk

General Teaching Council for Scotland (GTCS) (2013) *Standards for Registration*, www.gtcs.org.uk/standards

Part 1

INTRODUCTION TO PROFESSIONAL STUDIES

The first six chapters of this book introduce readers to the philosophy which underpins the book and establish what we might call the foundations of professional studies in primary education. The philosophy of the book aims to show that, within statutory requirements, teachers are nevertheless responsible for constantly making professional decisions and judgements in all aspects of teaching and learning, interpreted through the qualities and skills of confident professional integrity. In Part 1 you will read about the history of primary education so that you can take an objective and long-term view of the present and of future changes. You will learn, through philosophical enquiry, how to ask questions about, debate and challenge educational theories, practices and policies. And you will begin to see how there are complex decisions and judgements to make and evaluate, in planning and assessment, in creating an effective learning environment and in your interactions with children and adults in school. You will begin to develop your own educational philosophy, which will enable you to become a teacher who is capable of managing change with integrity.

CHAPTER 1

HISTORY OF EDUCATION

Susan Shaw

By the end of this chapter, you should:

- have knowledge of the education system from 1870 onwards
- have an understanding of changes in the philosophy, curriculum, management and accountability in primary schools
- be able to speculate about the future of education
- begin to form your own professional philosophy and values
- understand the need to respond to changes with professional integrity.

Introduction

In order to fully appreciate and understand the education system that will be in place once you qualify, it is necessary to have an insight into the influences and decisions that have taken place in the past to form and develop the current system of primary education. The norm today is for all children aged 5 years to attend primary school. However, compulsory primary education in England did not begin until 1880. Before this, there were many types of formal and informal schooling. This chapter will highlight some key dates, people and events that have contributed to the current education system and the primary curriculum.

It considers the impact of legislation on teaching and learning (for example, the curriculum and the effects of increasing centralisation, testing and league tables) and the advantages claimed for this legislation (that is, the values underpinning the National Curriculum). It shows how an informed educational philosophy helps us respond to centralised changes and considers the development of new curricula.

1870: the beginning of compulsory state education

Rationale

By 1870 England was a largely industrial rather than an agricultural society. Conditions in many of the rapidly expanding cities were often very bad. Compulsory schooling was introduced, partly to provide the labour force with the basic skills and routines necessary in an industrial society and also to attempt to prevent civil unrest, which people feared as a very real possibility.

Church and state

The Education Act of 1870, known as the 'Forster Act', laid down the requirement to establish compulsory, elementary education in England. It recognised a dual education system consisting of both voluntary denominational schools and non-denominational state schools. These were intended to supplement rather than replace schools already run by the churches, guilds and private individuals or organisations. In other countries, the church was less involved in state education but in Britain, as a result of the 1870 Act the church has continued to play a substantial part in the education of young children.

School Boards

School districts were formed throughout the country and where there was not enough educational provision for the children in a district, School Boards were formed. They set up schools which became known as Board Schools. These had to be non-denominational. The School Boards could charge a weekly fee if there were insufficient funds, but the fee was not allowed to be more than 9 pence. The School

Boards had to ensure that children between the ages of 5 and 13 attended the schools in their districts and this was enforced by an Attendance Officer.

The curriculum

The curriculum in the 1870s mainly consisted of the 3 Rs (reading, writing and 'rithmetic) and religious instruction, which was an integral part of the school curriculum but was not actually compulsory. There were some additional aspects, for example drill and 'object lessons'. Object lessons involved the study of an artefact. Needlework was an extra for girls and carpentry an extra for boys. Her Majesty's Inspectors visited the schools to test children's skills in the '3 Rs' and teachers' payment was based on the children's attainment, i.e. it was 'payment by results'.

In some respects, as we shall see, primary education remains tied to its Victorian roots. The exceptionally early start for formal schooling, the generalist primary school teacher, the separation of 'infants' and 'juniors', the focus on the basics at the expense of a broader curriculum remain and have not been seriously questioned. But the Victorian Elementary School was intended to prepare the poor for their 'station' in life rather than to broaden their opportunities.

1902–1944

There were three developments in education during this period: the Balfour Act (1902) which created Local Education Authorities, the Fisher Act (1918) which raised the school leaving age from 12 to 14, and the Hadow Reports (1923–31), one of which recommended school transfer at 11, so creating the idea of the primary school.

Reflective task

Read *Children, their World, their Education*, Chapter 13 (Alexander 2010), which compares the curriculum past and present. In groups, compare the curriculum in the late 1800s with the curriculum of today. Compare similarities and differences. To what extent are the external forces which influence the content of the curriculum the same or different today? If you could put together a primary curriculum, what would your priorities be?

Post World War II: primary schools and three types of secondary school

The Butler Education Act of 1944

The tripartite system for secondary education

The education system offered primary education, secondary education and further education. The tripartite system of secondary education, implemented in the 1944 Act, offered three types of education after the age of 11: grammar schools for the most able, based on 'intelligence tests', secondary modern schools for most pupils, and secondary technical schools for those perceived to have technical or scientific ability. This was intended to increase opportunities for all.

Church schools

After the 1944 Act, the Church of England still had control of most rural schools and many urban ones. The 1944 Act put church schools into two categories: 'voluntary aided' (where the church had greater control) and 'voluntary controlled' (where the Local Education Authority had greater control), and this is still the case. This control is in regard to buildings, staffing and the religious curriculum and worship.

Local Education Authorities

Primary education and secondary education became free for all children up to the age of 15. The Local Education Authorities (LEAs) took more responsibility and there was a rise in their status. They had to ensure that there was sufficient provision for the educational needs of pupils in their geographical area. Through the provision LEAs offered, they had to make sure that pupils had an effective education which contributed to their spiritual, moral, mental and physical development, but they were not responsible for the more detailed curriculum.

The curriculum

The Act gave head teachers, in consultation with governors, control of the school curriculum and resourcing. The Act said very little about the curriculum, apart from religious education. Teachers were left to decide what to teach and how to teach it. Religious education and collective worship were to take place in all schools, and if you worked in an aided school you could be dismissed by the governors if you did not deliver religious instruction 'efficiently and suitably'. It is quite clear at this point that there was no expectation that the national government would ever have control of the curriculum.

Special Educational Needs provision

The 1944 Act included provision for Pupils with Special Educational Needs. If pupils were deemed to be unable to profit from being educated in a mainstream school, their education had to be provided in a special school. At this time, the types and degrees of disability were named and this was the case until 1981, when it was agreed that these labels were inappropriate.

Effects of the 1944 Education Act

The selection process, rather like SATs (Standardised Attainment Tests), had an effect on primary education. The need to 'get children through' the eleven plus had the same effect as the need to get Level 4 or 5 at age 11. There were also large classes through the late 1940s and 1950s and a shortage of teachers. Whole-class teaching continued and the curriculum emphasised basic literacy and numeracy. 'Writers looking back at the early curriculum saw that, in fact, the tradition derived from 1870 was still dominant' (Galton et al. 1980 p. 36). It was not until the 1960s that more formal class teaching gave way to new ideas. In 1964 the Schools Council was formed and the partnership between LEAs, schools and universities led to more experiments with the curriculum.

The Plowden Report: a new philosophy of education?

There had not been a specific review of primary education since the Hadow report of 1931. The context of the time in which the Plowden Report (1967) was written was one of a liberal view of education and society. The emphasis of the Plowden Report could be encapsulated in the phrase 'at the heart of the educational process lies the child' (Plowden 1967 p. 9). Plowden advocated experiential learning, increased parental involvement, universal pre-school education and opportunities for the less privileged. It highlighted firmly the need for differentiation and supported the requirement for personalisation when saying 'individual differences between children of the same age are so great that any class … must always be treated as a body of children needing individual and different attention' (Plowden 1967 p. 25). Chapter 2 also discusses testing, and the use of IQ (Intelligence Quotient) tests in eleven-plus selection tests in the 1950s and 1960s. Plowden says that they 'should not be treated as infallible predictors. Judgements which determine careers should be deferred as long as possible'. It was the Labour government of this time that almost removed all eleven-plus tests at the end of primary schooling, but since it lost the election in 1970, it failed to quite eradicate all testing at 11. There are many aspects of the Plowden Report that most primary teachers would agree with.

> One of the main educational tasks of the primary school is to build on and strengthen children's intrinsic interest in learning and lead them to learn for themselves rather than from fear of disapproval or desire for praise. (Plowden 1967 p. 532)

The persistent acknowledgement of individual learning, flexibility in the curriculum, use of the environment, learning by discovery and the importance of the evaluation of children's progress have a certain resonance, not only with educational theory but in the philosophy of many teachers.

The Plowden Report endorsed the move away from formal class teaching to group work, projects and learning through play and creativity. Chapters of the report challenged the existing aims of primary education, classroom organisation and the curriculum and supported 'child-centred' primary schools. It was a real attempt to enlarge the concept of primary education.

Nevertheless, most schools changed very little. The HMI primary survey (DES 1978) reported that only 5 per cent of primary schools was 'exploratory' and three-quarters still used 'didactic' methods.

Back to basics, market forces and increasing centralisation

Economic recession led to cutbacks in educational expenditure and was partly blamed for the series of 'Black Papers' written by right-wing educationalists. The first paper was published in 1969. Specifically focusing on the 'progressive education' being developed in the primary schools, the writers challenged the figures on reading standards and accused teachers of neglecting basics and concentrating too much on informality. The years 1992 and 1998 also saw a return of the 'back to basics' theme and a desire to challenge 'progressive' ideas in education.

Her Majesty's Inspectorate 1975

In 1975 Her Majesty's Inspectors (HMI) began a survey of the primary curriculum. This included assessments of children's work at 7, 9 and 11. The report was not published until 1978. It criticised teachers' underestimation of children's abilities and noted the lack of specialist teachers. The questioning of teacher assessment, which later resulted in Standardised Attainment Tests (SATs), and the content of the curriculum are recurring themes for both Conservative and Labour governments and successive Secretaries of State for Education.

Callaghan's Ruskin Speech – Great Debate on Education 1976

Labour Prime Minister, James Callaghan, 'brought comfort to his Tory enemies ... schools were convenient scapegoats, education a scarecrow...'. This was 'the impression conveyed by the Prime Minister' (Morris 1988 p. 7). He argued that not just teachers and parents but also government and industry had an important part to play in formulating the aims of education.

In his historic speech, Callaghan spoke about:

- a public debate on education: employers, trade unions, parents, teachers and administrators were to make their views known
- a curriculum which paid too little attention to the basic skills of reading, writing and arithmetic
- how teachers lacked adequate professional skills, could not discipline children or teach them good manners and did not manage to instil in them the need for hard work
- the underlying reason for all this which was that the education system was out of touch with the fundamental needs of the country.

This Great Debate on Education seems to have been ongoing since 1976 and consecutive governments have increasingly tightened their grip on education. Whether 'progressive education' was slowed down by James Callaghan's speech or by the next 18 years of Conservative rule and education policy is debatable.

The 1979 Education Act

Margaret Thatcher was Education Secretary before becoming Prime Minister. She overturned Labour's 1976 Act and gave back to LEAs the right to select pupils for secondary education at 11. However, comprehensive secondary education was popular and reversal did not gain the backing expected.

A framework for the curriculum 1980

This was the first of a long series of reports about what the curriculum should contain: *Framework for the School Curriculum* (HMI 1980a), *A View of the Curriculum* (HMI 1980b), *The School Curriculum* (DES 1981a), Circular 6/81 (DES 1981b). *The School Curriculum 1981* encouraged putting a high priority on English and mathematics:

> It is essential that the early skills in reading, writing and calculating should be effectively learned in primary schools, since deficiencies at this stage cannot easily be remedied later and children will face the world seriously handicapped. (DES 1981a para 35)

However, schools also had to provide a 'wide range of experience, in order to stimulate the children's interest and imagination and fully to extend pupils of all abilities' (DES 1980 p. 10). Religious Education, Topic Work, Science, Art and Craft, Physical Education, Music and French were all mentioned in this report, alongside personal and social development. From 1981 to 1986, Sir Keith Joseph had responsibility for implementing education policies, right down to everyday practice.

The Curriculum from 5 to 16 (HMI 1985)

This was a forward-looking document talking about 'areas of learning and experience'. This concept was developed in the introduction of a National Curriculum, in the Education Reform Act 1988. The curriculum of all schools had to provide pupils with the following areas of learning and experience: aesthetic and creative, human and social, linguistic and literary, mathematical, moral, physical, scientific, spiritual and technological.

Work in school

Student A: From what I have read about the history of primary education it seems to be swings and roundabouts – one step forward, one step back – teachers having to respond to constant policy changes. Am I right about this?

Mentor: It can seem like that, but there are underlying developments I think. Why don't you look at the 1967 Plowden Report. It talks about experiential learning through the environment, evaluating progress, parental involvement, differentiation and personalised learning, a flexible curriculum and a philosophy in which the child is at the heart of educational processes. Inspectors found that it hadn't had much impact by 1978. But I suggest you note, under these headings, evidence you find of its influence in the 2013 National Curriculum and in this school today. You may be surprised.

Student B: In recent years there seems to have been increasing emphasis on reading, writing and arithmetic. I agree that these are essential skills. But I also think music, art, history – all the rest of the curriculum – is very important and that children should enjoy learning. How can I combine these beliefs?

Mentor: Well, there are two questions to think about here. First let's think of all the ways in which 'the basics' can be taught in ways the children enjoy . . . And also think about how you can teach literacy and maths across the curriculum . . . Note down some ideas to discuss before our planning meeting – and have a look at what Alexander (2010) says about primary schools being seen as happy places, which nevertheless do not neglect the 3 Rs.

Parent power

Successive governments had tried to get parents to engage with education. The Conservative government of the 1980s saw parents as consumers and clients. The 1980 Education Act gave more power to parents. Parents were encouraged to serve on governing bodies. Growing parental choice meant that parents had the right to choose their children's schools and could appeal if they were not accepted by the school they chose. The forerunner of league tables began when exam and test results were published. The Warnock Report (1978) gave parents new rights in relation to Special Educational Needs. LEAs identified the needs of children with learning difficulties but also had to produce 'statements' for parents on how these needs would be met. Parent power was increased in the 1984 Green Paper, *Parental Influence at School* (HMI 1984), which reiterated the role and responsibilities of parents and the vital role parents have to play in the education system.

The 1986 Education Act

The 1986 (1) Education Act introduced the requirement that the LEAs had to give governors financial information on the financing of schools. The 1986 (2) Education Act adopted the proposals in the 1985 White Paper, *Better Schools*, arguing yet again for breadth, balance and progression in order to achieve standards in literacy and numeracy; a close throwback to comments by HMI in 1978. *Better Schools* opened with: 'The Government will: take the lead in promoting national agreement about the purposes and the content of the curriculum ...' (DES 1985 p. 1).

The Education Reform Bill 1988

The Great Education Reform Bill (generally known as Gerbil) was seen as the most important Education Act since the 1944 Act which aimed to give more power to schools. However, from the LEAs' point of view, it was taking power from them and giving it to the Secretary of State.

A National Curriculum

The Act had significant implications for primary schools. The government proposed a common curriculum for pupils aged 5 to 16, a National Curriculum. This was a shift away from teachers deciding what was taught to central government having control. The curriculum was divided into discrete subjects and there were three core subjects

(English, mathematics and science) and seven 'foundation subjects'. Prior to this, teachers wrote schemes of work they considered appropriate for their pupils.

Written by a government 'quango' of subject specialists and with a substantial content base, teachers were hardly involved in the development of the National Curriculum and felt they were deliverers of a curriculum rather than designers and pace-setters. The National Curriculum had three main aims: the school curriculum had to provide opportunities for all pupils to learn and to achieve; pupils across the country were entitled to the same broad curriculum; and the curriculum should aim to promote pupils' spiritual, moral, social and cultural development and prepare all pupils for the opportunities, responsibilities and experiences of life (DES 1988).

The 'Three Wise Men Report' (DES 1992) was a government-commissioned report which emphasised the need for a return to quality in primary school pedagogy. 'Whatever the mode of curriculum organisation, the breadth, balance and consistency of the curriculum experienced by pupils must be of central concern' (DES 1992 p. 23). The Three Wise Men Report was written by Robin Alexander, Jim Rose and Chris Woodhead, all of whom had a further impact on primary education beyond this document.

Assessment

Before the Education Reform Act, pupil progress was tracked by teacher assessments. The Act introduced compulsory national standard attainment tests (SATs) at 7, 11 and 14. The tests were based on the 1988 Black Report produced by the National Curriculum Task Group on Assessment and Testing (TGAT). The results had to be published annually in league tables. This allowed the government to compare schools directly in terms of this data.

Local Management of Schools

Local Management of Schools (LMS), flagged in the Education Act, was not introduced until 1991. It allowed the delegation of financial and managerial responsibilities to schools. Management for the budget was the responsibility of the school and budgets were taken away from LEAs. There were some centrally held resources in the LEAs, such as curriculum advisory and support services and school library services, although these increasingly diminished during the 1990s. There were mixed views amongst head teachers as to whether LMS gave schools greater flexibility but they certainly had greater responsibility.

Grant Maintained schools

Although grammar schools were not reintroduced, Grant Maintained (GM) schools were introduced. Schools were able to opt out of LEA control and be funded directly by central government. It was seen as a bribe to schools to encourage them to opt out, especially as they were offered additional funding. Grant Maintained schools also had more control over admissions and were allowed to select up to 10 per cent of their pupils on ability.

The Office for Standards in Education

The creation of the Office for Standards in Education (Ofsted) also resulted from the 1988 Education Act, although it wasn't actually set up until 1992, when it replaced visits to schools by Her Majesty's Inspectors with a more rigorous inspection system. When Ofsted inspected schools, a report was to be published, and the emphasis was on inspection and not support. It came across as an antagonising system and stressful for teachers as there was naming and shaming of failing schools when they were put into 'special measures'. Chris Woodhead, one of the authors of the Three Wise Men Report, was appointed Her Majesty's Chief Inspector of Schools and Head of Ofsted in September 1994.

The National Curriculum Revised: The Dearing Report 1993

The Dearing Report made several key proposals about the National Curriculum and the changes cost an estimated £744 million. He advised that the curriculum should be slimmed down, the time given to testing should be reduced and around 20 per cent of teaching time should be freed up for use at the discretion of schools. However, the proposals were difficult to implement as government wanted literacy and numeracy to take up 50 per cent of the timetable, leaving the other eight subjects to be squashed into the remaining 50 per cent.

'Education, Education, Education' 1997

'Ask me my three main priorities for government and I tell you education, education, and education' (Blair 1996). Blair put education right at the top of the political agenda during the election of 1997. Speaking to the Labour Party conference after becoming Prime Minister in 1997, he stated: 'Our goal: to make Britain the best educated and skilled country in the world; a nation, not of a few talents, but of all the talents. And every single part of our schools system must be modernised to achieve it' (Blair 1997).

Excellence in Schools 1997

This White Paper (DfEE 1997) pointed towards the importance of the basics and set a target of 80 per cent of all 11-year-olds to reach the 'required standard' of literacy and 75 per cent to reach the 'required standard' of numeracy by 2002.

It was proposed that class sizes should be less than 30 for 5–7-year-olds and this was adopted in the School Standards and Framework Act 1998. There was to be at least an hour a day spent on English and mathematics in primary schools and this set the scene for the literacy and numeracy strategies.

LEAs set targets for raising standards in individual schools. Governors had to publish school performance tables which showed the rate of progress pupils made against the targets set. Schools deemed 'failing' by Ofsted could not hide. LEAs could intervene in the schools, which were given two years to improve or they would be closed or have management changes imposed on them.

Back to basics 1998

Yet again the 'back to basics' theme returned, and schools no longer had to teach National Curriculum programmes of study in all subjects, just in the three core subjects. This set up the background for introducing the literacy and numeracy strategies.

Literacy and numeracy strategies 1998 and 1999

Both these strategies were very prescriptive, giving both the content of what had to be taught and the delivery method. These were daily lessons which, although not statutory, were often seen as mandatory. Schools had to be very brave to break the mould and deliver their own ideas of lessons and schemes for literacy and numeracy. The National Literacy Strategy (DfEE 1998), the National Numeracy Strategy (DfEE 1999b) and National Learning Targets were introduced (DfEE 1999a). The Labour government was now seen to be telling teachers how to teach, in addition to teaching the National Curriculum, which had been seen as telling them what to teach.

National Curriculum 2000

The launch of a National Curriculum review took place in 1997. However, it was 2000 before all the changes took place. To the huge relief of teaching staff, the curriculum was slimmed down, but not without the addition of Citizenship. However, whilst testing was happening at the age of 11, creativity was not top of the list in the classrooms of Years 5 and 6. The paper, *Schools – Achieving Success* (DfES 2001), proposed allowing successful primary schools to opt out of the National Curriculum and seek to develop innovation. The Foundation Stage for children aged 3–5 years was introduced and had six Areas of Learning. This may have influenced the thinking for the development of the curriculum in the Rose Review (DCSF 2009).

Every Child Matters 2003

In 2003, the government published its Green Paper *Every Child Matters* (ECM) (DfES 2003a) following the death of Victoria Climbié. The ECM agenda had five clear outcomes which schools needed to consider in the development of their curriculum. These were: to be healthy; stay safe; enjoy and achieve; make a positive contribution; and achieve economic well-being.

Excellence and Enjoyment 2003

Excellence and Enjoyment (DfES 2003b) claims to promote excellence in teaching 'the basics' and enjoyment through the broader curriculum. The existing National Numeracy Strategy (1999) and National Literacy Strategy (1998) conflated into one document, the Primary National Strategy (PNS) (DfES 2006). The PNS again aimed to promote high standards which should be achieved through a rich, varied and exciting curriculum. It aimed to build on the literacy and numeracy strategies but to give teachers more chance to take control of their teaching. There was more flexibility for schools to adopt ways of working that suited them. Testing and target setting were all part of the PNS and assessment for learning developed out of this report.

Towards a new curriculum

The Children's Plan (DCSF 2007) announced a root and branch review of the curriculum and this was to be headed by Sir Jim Rose, another author of the so-called

Three Wise Men Report (DES 1992). Running concurrently with this was a review by Robin Alexander and a team of researchers, The Cambridge Review. This is a more philosophical and research-based report, published as *Children, their World, their Education* (Alexander 2010). Neither review became policy.

Where to next?

The Cambridge Primary Review (Alexander 2010) provides firm research evidence that, despite these intense pressures, primary schools are highly valued by children and parents. Primary schools were seen as largely happy places which consistently celebrate the positive, while not, as some claim, neglecting the '3 Rs', and 'those who regularly make this claim are either careless of the facts or are knowingly fostering calumny'.

Beyond 2010

The Conservative/Liberal Democrat Coalition government, elected in 2010, immediately planned changes in education: in the curriculum, in teacher education, in management of schools, in examinations at secondary level and in policies on, for example, behaviour management and Special Educational Needs. The new Teachers' Standards (DfE 2013a) are discussed in the introduction (pp. 11–12). Behaviour management and Special Educational Needs policies are discussed in Chapters 8 and 9.

National Curriculum 2014

Draft versions of the new National Curriculum were published for consultation in February and July 2013, accompanied by much media discussion, before the new curriculum was agreed by parliament, prior to the implementation of the final version from 2014. This requires state-funded schools and maintained schools, community special schools, voluntary aided and voluntary controlled schools to follow the statutory curriculum. This new curriculum retained the four Key Stages (5–7, 7–11, 11–14, 14–16) with English, Mathematics and Science as core subjects and Art and Design, Citizenship, Computing, Design and Technology, Geography, History, Music and Physical Education compulsory throughout the primary phase, with a foreign language at Key Stage 2. The Curriculum also requires that all state schools make provision for a daily act of collective worship, teach Religious Education and provide good practice in Personal, Social and Health Education. These schools, and also academies, must 'provide a balanced and broadly-based curriculum which, similar to the previous National Curriculum, promotes spiritual, moral and physical development … prepares pupils for opportunities, responsibilities in later life and makes provision for personal, social, health and economic education'. State-funded, voluntary aided, voluntary controlled and maintained schools may, in addition to the National Curriculum, include 'other subjects or topics of their choice in planning their own programmes of education' (DfE 2013b p. 4). However, academies and free schools are only required to offer a 'broad and balanced curriculum' (Academies Act 2010, www.legislation.gov.uk/ukpga/2010/32/section/1). All schools must publish their curriculum, by subject and academic year, online (DfE 2013b p. 4).

The purposes, aims and content for each subject are set out, with greater detail for the core subjects, and each subject is supported by non-statutory notes and guidance. This subsumes the necessity for supplementary strategies for English, Mathematics, and, for example, for Citizenship. A significant difference from the previous National Curriculum is that the progression in skills and processes involved in each subject are embedded in the Purposes and Aims of Study for each subject and the Attainment Targets require pupils to know, apply and understand these skills and processes at the end of each Key Stage. This seems to make it easier for teachers to continuously plan for and monitor differentiated progress. Unlike the previous curriculum, it does not make detailed claims for an artificial notion of what progress in some subjects may consist of.

Schools

Teaching Schools

Teaching Schools were planned to lead the training and professional development of teachers and head teachers and performance-related pay was proposed. It became government policy that, by the end of the Parliament, 10,000 students a year could be trained by schools which are full providers of teacher training or offer 'School Direct Places'. The School Direct strategy allows primary and secondary schools to train top graduates as teachers in the subjects they need. Placements usually last one year and students are eligible for a bursary of up to £20,000 a year while they train. For the School Direct salaried programme, trainees need three years' previous work experience and earn a salary while they train.

Teach First

Teach First is a charity, founded in 2002, which aims to train outstanding graduates to address the problems of low educational achievement in challenging circumstances. An increasing number of graduates have trained through Teach First since 2010.

Free schools

Soon after the election, groups of parents, teachers and charities were invited to submit proposals for free schools. These are all-ability state-funded schools set up in response to what local people say they want and need, in order to improve the education of their children. They are run by teachers, not local authorities. They have the ability to choose the length of the school day and terms, the curriculum, teachers' salaries and how they spend their money. By May 2013 there were 81 free schools, with 109 aiming to open in September and permission given to open 102 more, many in areas of deprivation. When full this will create 50,000 extra school places.

Academies

The Academies Act 2010 allowed existing schools to convert to academies, with the approval of the Education Secretary. Academies are publicly funded independent schools. They have freedom from local authority control to set the pay and conditions of staff, to create and deliver the curriculum and to set the length of days and terms. They receive the same funding from the Education Funding Agency as they would from a local authority but have greater freedom on how they use their budgets. 'Failing schools' were turned into academies. Some academies, often those which were failing schools, have a sponsor from, for example, a business, university, charity or faith group background. The sponsor is responsible for improving school performance by challenging traditional thinking on how schools are run and what they should be like for students. By July 2013 2,000 new academies had been created, an increase from 203 under the previous Labour government, and it was the government aim for academy status to become the norm.

University Technical Colleges

UTCs were introduced to provide technical education for 14–19-year-olds. Sponsored by a local university and employers, they are intended to meet the needs of modern business.

Studio Schools

These were introduced to teach 14–19-year-olds an academic and vocational curriculum in a practical way which includes experience in the workplace.

Local Education Authorities

The 2010 White Paper stated that local authorities would continue to have an important role in education, but recognised that the increasing number of academies raises questions about what their role would be.

Reflective task: Perspectives on the curriculum

In groups discuss the advantages and disadvantages of a National Curriculum. Collate the ideas of the whole group as a basis for whole-group discussion.

Summary

This chapter has outlined changes in the philosophy, curriculum, organisation and accountability in primary schools, moving from the 1800s to the ideas espoused in the Plowden Report, then to more centralisation, beginning with the Education Reform Act of 1988 and the creation of education fashioned by the concept of market forces and economic growth and measured attainment. In the final section it outlined changes, since 2010, in the curriculum, teacher education and the funding of new types of schools. Against this constantly changing background, the chapter aimed to encourage readers to understand the need to develop, defend and implement robust personal and professional philosophies which will enable them to respond to changes with professional integrity.

Supplementary information on legislation, Alexander (2010), The Final Report of the Rose Review (DCSF 2009), an overview of the implications for classroom practice of legislation described in this chapter and an additional reflective task and bibliography can be found on the website related to this book, pp. 4–6.

Questions for discussion

- Do we need Ofsted or is there an alternative? Consider: teacher stress, cost, standards, accountability, closure of schools, improvement.
- Consider the areas of reform in the 1988 Education Act: the National Curriculum, national testing at 7 and 11, league tables, religious education and collective worship, local management of school budgets (LMS), governing bodies, Ofsted and Grant Maintained (GM) status. How have these had an impact on our schools over the last 20 years?
- Discuss your ideas about what you want your classroom environment to look like, types of grouping you would try and the balance of time you would place on each subject.

Further reading

Clark, A. (2010) '"In-between" Spaces in Postwar Primary Schools: A Micro-study of a "Welfare Room" (1977–1993)', *History of Education* 39 (November: 767–778).

This very interesting article explores the ways in which, after the Second World War, architects and educationalists in the UK began to explore how learning environments could be redesigned, replacing rows of chairs and 'a yard' with spaces and objects which reflect and enhance the learning and teaching needs of children and adults. This paper focuses on how 'in-between spaces' can be used in different ways.

McCulloch, G. (2011) *The Struggle for the History of Education*. London: Routledge.

This exciting book broadens our understanding of the significance of the history of education by exploring the reasons why different groups have struggled to improve education and society at large; for example struggling for social change, social equality and new methodologies. It argues that an education system which ignores its past is unlikely to achieve its own best future. It seeks to understand the nature of issues and trends and to assess the prospects of addressing them effectively.

Nutbrown, C. and Clough, P. (2008) *Early Childhood Education: History, Philosophy and Experience*. London: Sage.

This accessible book recognises that, with persistent policy changes, early education practitioners might have few opportunities to ask where ideas began, how practice developed and what roots and philosophical ideas lie behind them. It gives an historical overview of the development of key ideas, biographical accounts of contributors in the fields, a comparison of their ideas and an analysis of their links with current practices.

References

Alexander, R. (ed.) (2010) *Children, their World, their Education: Final Report and Recommendations of the Cambridge Primary Review*. London: Routledge.

Blair, T. (1996) Speech to the Labour Party Annual Conference, 1 October, Brighton.

Blair, T. (1997) Speech to the Labour Party Annual Conference, 30 September, Brighton. Available at: http://www.prnewswire.co.uk/cgi/news/release?id=47983 (accessed 29 September 2010).

DCSF (2007) *The Children's Plan*. London: DCSF.

DCSF (2009) *The Independent Review of the Primary Curriculum: Final Report*. (The Rose Review). London: DCSF.

DES (1978) *Primary Education in England: A Survey by Her Majesty's Inspectors of Schools*. London: HMSO.
DES (1980) *A Framework for the School Curriculum*. London: DES.
DES (1981a) *The School Curriculum*. London: DES/HMSO.
DES (1981b) Circular 6/81. London: DES/HMSO.
DES (1985) *Better Schools: A Summary*. London: DES.
DES (1988) *The National Curriculum*. London: HMSO.
DES (1992) *Curriculum Organisation and Classroom Practice in Primary Schools* (The Three Wise Men Report). London: DES.
DfE (2013a) *Teachers' Standards*, Ref. DFE-00066-2011 (www. education. gov.uk)
DfE (2013b) *National Curriculum: A Framework* (www.gov.uk)
DfEE (1997) *Excellence in Schools*, White Paper. London: DfEE.
DfEE (1998) *The National Literacy Strategy*. London: DfEE.
DfEE (1999a) *The National Curriculum for England*. London: DfEE.
DfEE (1999b) *The National Numeracy Strategy*. London: DfEE.
DfES (2001) *Schools – Achieving Success*. London: DfES.
DfES (2003a) *Every Child Matters*. London: DfES.
DfES (2003b) *Excellence and Enjoyment: A Strategy for Primary Schools*. London: DfES.
DfES (2006) Primary National Strategy: Primary Framework for Literacy and Mathematics, www.webarchives.gov.uk
Galton, M., Simon, B. and Croll, P. (1980) *Inside the Primary Classroom* (The ORACLE Report). London: Routledge and Kegan Paul.
HMI (1978) *Primary Education in England: A Survey by HM Inspectors of Schools*. London: Her Majesty's Stationery Office.
HMI (1980a) *Framework for the School Curriculum*. London: HMSO.
HMI (1980b) *A View of the Curriculum*. London: HMSO.
HMI (1984) *Parental Influence at School: A New Framework for School Government in England and Wales*. London: HMSO.
HMI (1985) *The Curriculum from 5–16: HMI Series Curriculum Matters No. 2*. London: Her Majesty's Stationery Office.
Morris, M. (ed.) (1988) *Education, the Wasted Years? 1973–1986*. Lewes: Falmer.
Plowden Report (1967) *Children and their Primary Schools*. Report of the Central Advisory Council for Education (England). London: HMSO.
QCA (1999) *The National Curriculum: Handbook for Primary Teachers in England, Key Stages 1 and 2*. London: QCA.
TGAT Report (1988) *Report of the Task Group on Assessment and Testing*. Chaired by Professor Paul Black.
Warnock Report (1978) *Report of the Committee of Enquiry into the Education of Handicapped Children and Young People*. London: HMSO.

CHAPTER 2

PHILOSOPHY OF EDUCATION AND THEORIES OF LEARNING

Hilary Cooper

By the end of this chapter, you should:

- understand the kinds of questions educational philosophers ask, how they discuss them and why it is important for you to practise engaging in the kinds of enquiries which underpin this book
- understand the relationship between educational philosophy and theories of how children learn
- have a basic understanding of key learning theories and of their implications for teaching and learning
- be aware of the contribution neuroscience is making to our understanding of learning.

Introduction

This chapter is relevant for educators in early years settings, in primary schools and beyond. You will see from Chapter 1 that, for a variety of reasons, the aims of education and the degree of political influence and central control over all dimensions of education are dynamic; they change as society changes. Teachers have had little encouragement recently to question what or how to teach. And 'primary education suffers more than its share of scare-mongering and hyperbole, not to mention deliberate myth-making' (Hofkins and Northen 2009 p. 5). The report continues: 'Isn't it time to move on from the populism, polarisation and name-calling which for too long have supplanted real educational debate and progress? Children deserve better from the nation's leaders and shapers of opinion'. The Teachers' Standards (DfE 2013) which apply to teachers, regardless of their career stage, do not expect you to explore questions about the aims, purposes and value of education. However, they do require teachers to, 'act with honesty and integrity … and to be self-critical' (p. 7). If children's lives are not to be at the mercy of political whim, it is essential that teachers learn the skills of robust, critical evaluation, based on their reading, experience and reflection, in order to develop strong personal philosophies about what, how and why we teach children, and to interpret changes in ways which are professionally valid and have integrity. It is important to learn scepticism, and have a concern about the larger questions and a deep understanding of what we teach, to have time to reflect, research and study. This chapter aims to help you do this. First, it gives an overview of the questions philosophers have asked about education in the past, and ask currently, and shows you how to engage with them. Then it links these to theories about how children learn.

What is primary education for?

This is a fundamental philosophical question. Discussing a broad set of aims will prevent you from narrow thinking about what children can and should do. And it is essential that, having begun to discuss educational aims, through reading this chapter, you use these to shape what you do as a teacher and what the children you teach experience in the curriculum, teaching and assessment. Since the beginning of state education until the Rose Review (DCSF 2009), the 'basics' have generally been seen as central to primary education. But what is basic in the twenty-first century? How can we empower children to find meaning in their lives? Independence and empowerment are achieved through exploring, knowing, understanding and making sense, through imagination and dialogue, through constructivist approaches. And before you can educate your pupils, based on these aims, you must learn to empower yourself (see also Chapter 3 p. 62).

The long tradition of educational philosophy

Plato to Rousseau

Since Plato in the fifth century BCE and Aristotle in the following century, philosophers have considered the aims, processes and content of education and the relationship between education and society; and their ideas remain relevant today. Plato and Aristotle saw education as holistic, balancing the practical and theoretical. Avicenna (980–1037 CE) (in Goodman 2005) said that children should discuss, debate and learn from each other. John Stuart Mill (1859) also wrote of the importance of contesting and defending ideas. Jean Jacques Rousseau (1762) saw education as developmental, changing in response to pupils' needs and based on learning from the environment.

Spencer to Steiner

Spencer (1851) advocated moving from concrete to abstract. Heywood Cooper (1892) championed the rights to education of women and ethnic minorities. Froebel (1895) emphasised learning through play and seeing children as the centre of their own worlds, and Montessori (1914) was confident that young children could make decisions for themselves, and that they should learn from their environments. Dewey (1916) wrote about the social and moral nature of schooling, and Steiner (1919) believed in the freedom of teachers to shape their own curriculum.

Educational philosophy over the last 50 years

As philosophies proliferated and since everyone was now entitled to education, it became necessary to examine more critically what was meant by education and what it should aim to achieve. R.S. Peters (1966, 1967) and Hirst (1965, 1974) made a major contribution to showing how this might be done, through analysing concepts related to education which are often 'fuzzy' and which people may understand differently and by critically analysing and arguing about claims made for education. Peters asked, as Socrates had, questions such as: What is worth knowing? What do we mean by an educated person? Is the education system fair? Who knows best what children should learn? Is education different from training, teaching different from learning? How? These are questions which are complex and have no single answer and in an open society they must be argued over. Peters explored such questions by asking: What do you mean by this question? How do you know? To explore these questions, we need to collect a range of different examples, drawing on our experiences and reading. Can we find some key principles, which will allow us to interpret the constantly changing demands made of us?

Using this process, Peters' conclusion to the question, 'What is an educated person?' was essentially: someone who has been changed, by their knowledge and understanding, in the way they look at the world around them; has a body of principles for organising knowledge (subjects or areas of learning); can make connections between areas of knowledge, and cares about what they know and understand. But this concept of an educated person raises questions. Peters claimed that this process of conceptual analysis was free from politics and had universal significance, identifying certain values and ideals, irrespective of culture and society. Matthew Arnold had said that education should convey the best that has been thought and said. But is that still appropriate? Educational aims must be relevant to the culture, society and world in which children live, and knowing only 'the best' may not reflect their own worlds. Yet should they have access to it?

By 1973 Peters accepted the criticisms of Dearden et al. (1972) and McIntyre (1998) that this was not the case, and that educational aims, values and methods are inevitably embedded in society and change with society. Hirst (1998) and Hirst and White (1998) agreed that Peters' analytical approach could not produce universal answers but was part of an evolving tradition and that the process of analysis must be closely linked to practical problems. Subsequent educational philosophers, for example Rorty (1979), took a more Aristotelian approach to addressing philosophical questions, based on a conversational style and pragmatic, practical discussion of current issues.

Contemporary educational philosophers take a rich variety of approaches to examine current educational policies and questions. Self-determination or autonomy is still seen as an important educational aim, but in the context of maximising opportunities to choose, while recognising social responsibilities (Hogan 1997; Walker 1999; Winch 1999). There is a growing interest in the links between political philosophy and the notion that before we ask, 'What is education?' we need to say 'What are the values of this society?' For what our society values underpins discussion of educational issues such as: multiculturalism, identity, and religion, inclusion, education for citizenship and for democracy, the curriculum, educational methods, organisation and assessment, the role of adults in the classroom, governance and who controls schools, education and moral practice, behaviour and personal and social development. For example, Hirst (1974) considered what the curriculum should consist of, a continuing contentious issue. Pring (2001) explored educational issues through the lens of moral questions. Crick (2000) discussed the nature of citizenship education. Pendlebury (2005) explored feminism and education. You will learn how to engage with such questions in the following chapters of this book.

How does philosophical questioning enable us to achieve our vision within changing political constraints?

Education embodies values and ideals. Most student teachers I have known have been highly motivated by a vision of the kind of teachers they want to be.

They have ideas about what they think is valuable and how it might be achieved. But visions vary. For example, interviewees often talk of their aim to help children 'to be creative', 'to love art or books', 'to be independent'. But when such aims are analysed in a group they become controversial. They are all based on value judgements about what the student thinks is important, which not everyone agrees with. They involve concepts which are abstract and are understood in different ways. What exactly is meant by 'creative', 'loving books', 'independent'?

When philosophical discussion becomes a habit, it enables us to take responsibility for developing our own practice with integrity. It allows us to react against outside mandates. We stop accepting simple solutions to what we know are complex problems. It stops us being knee-jerk in reaction to change by enabling us to define and work towards what we value. It allows us to ask what values and beliefs underpin our work and to use these as the basis for interpreting our responses to change and refining our practice. We can set our personal goals rather than simply responding to those we are given. This constitutes professionalism. Philosophical analysis allows us to dissect slogans such as 'education for democracy', or for 'citizenship', 'equal opportunities', 'learning to learn', 'collaboration'. Once we do this, we realise that such slogans are by no means self-evident or beyond criticism. A useful, recent book on educational philosophy is Bailey, Barrow, Carr and McCarthy (2010).

Reflective task

Begin to tease out your own philosophy by asking, 'What should be the aims of education in the UK today?' Then answer Peters' question: what do you mean by this? Then give any evidence from your reading and experience to support your claims. Share your list, directly or through a discussion board, with a partner or group of colleagues.

Do people disagree about any of the aims? If so, why?
Identify any aims shared by several people.
Is it possible to create a list of key principles, which underpin some of the aims?

Draft the first statement of your personal philosophy of education. As you read through this book, you will add to this, modify it and add your responses to the many other philosophical discussions you will have.

Philosophy of education and educational theory

Another response to the need to provide mass education explored what is involved in the process of learning, by seeking to define systematic rules, based on the evidence of observed behaviour. In psychology, hypotheses are tested in experiments and, if confirmed to a reliable degree, suggest theories. These theories inform practice and through practice the theory is refined. There is an expectation, today, that teaching should be a research-based profession. All teachers can, and should, reflect on how learning theories impact on their teaching in different contexts, consider in what ways they might develop, evaluate or modify theory–practice links and share their reflections through professional discussion and professional publications (DfE 2013 Standards 4.4, 4.5).

Theory in education cannot be as reliable as scientific theory but is nevertheless genuine theory. An enormous amount of data has been accumulated about, for example, how children learn; although there is no single theory but several overlapping theories. The dominant theories over the last century were: Behaviourism, in which the teacher controls the learning; Constructivism, in which the teacher supports the child in constructing their own learning; and Hierarchies of Needs, which identify conditions necessary for learning to take place.

Behaviourist theories

During the first half of the twentieth century, the dominant theory about how children learn was behaviourism. The central idea is that most of human behaviour, like that of animals, is susceptible to simple, mechanistic explanation. It ignores the fact that language significantly distinguishes us from animals.

Classical conditioning

Behaviourism begins with classical conditioning. Pavlov's finding that dogs which salivate at the sight of food (an unconditioned stimulus), when presented with food accompanied by an aural signal, learned to salivate in response to the signal when no food was present (a conditioned stimulus). This is classical conditioning. Don't we still train young children to stop talking when they hear the wind chimes, a special tune, a hand clap? But the uses for this classical conditioning are limited.

Operant conditioning

Thorndike (1903) put a rat in a cage with a lever which it pressed to release food. However, when the food was replaced by shocks the rat stopped pressing the lever – hence, there are responses to reward and punishment. This is known as operant conditioning because the animal (or person) has to do something, which has an associated consequence. And don't we give stars or points or 'golden time' and praise to encourage good work or behaviour and 'traffic lights' to warn against, then punish, undesired work or behaviour? Don't we apply Ferster and Skinner's (1957) 'different intermittent schedules of reinforcement': fixed intervals for some rewards (marbles in a jar at the end of the week), fixed ratio schedules (names on the board, four times and you stay in), varied ratio schedules which reward only after a number of positive responses, and variable interval schedules (rewards given irregularly to keep the children on their toes)?

Implications of behaviourism for teaching and learning

Behaviourist theory was largely unquestioned during the first half of the last century. Teaching was seen as instructing and training, transmitting information, without understanding the connecting principles and rationale behind the information, which was often piecemeal and not necessarily considered of immediate use or intrinsic interest, but necessary to know later in life. This attitude to education was instrumental and materialistic. Since behaviourism aims to mould behaviour and depends only on observed behaviour, it is not concerned with the inner life: emotions, the child's world, relationships between pupils or teacher and pupils, ideas and concepts. It is hardly likely to change children's views, knowledge or understanding of the world or their relationships or teach them to make decisions or take responsibility. The teacher's function is to manipulate and it is difficult to see this as moral. It leads to the teacher deciding on the curriculum irrespective of children's interests and setting the pace, which aims at the middle, involves much rote learning and makes no differentiation for individual needs.

Constructivist theories

Constructivist theories explore the mental processes involved in learning. They see learning as an active process in which the learner is motivated to ask questions, based on experience, and tries to investigate the questions and find answers. Piaget was the first to explore the processes of learning, generally focusing on individual children. Vygotsky and Bruner saw learning as a predominantly social activity. Although a great deal of subsequent research has explored and criticised aspects of their work in different contexts and in some cases modified it, their approach to learning underpins the thinking of educationalists today and, it can be argued, reflects a society which values the individual and is essentially democratic.

Jean Piaget (1896–1980)

Stage theory Piaget's wide-ranging empirical studies make three major contributions to the enquiry into how learning takes place (Piaget and Inhelder 1969). First, he saw learning as occurring in four main successive stages, characterised by qualitatively different thinking processes:

> The *sensori-motor stage* is dominated by exploring through the senses: children like to feel things, to draw in their own dribble(!) and shake a rattle to make a noise.

The *pre-operational stage*, Piaget says, is dominated by perception and egocentricity: children are happy to talk to themselves without needing to convince others. Their thinking is dominated by what they perceive. A smaller person (or tree) is younger than a taller one. I've certainly seen children convinced that a short, middle-aged student is much younger than a taller 20-year-old. It is fascinating to try out Piaget's claims in the classroom with children of different ages. At the pre-operational stage, dominated by what children see, they think that a large empty box must be heavier than a small box containing heavy weights or that a litre of water changes in quantity when poured into a differently shaped container. But they begin to reason at the pre-operational stage, for example to classify objects according to one characteristic, as in putting all the blue bricks together.

At the *operational stage*, learning is defined by reasoned thinking. A child can take in information from the outside world, retain it and supply it to new situations, as well as applying rules. Children can 'conserve' information, understanding that objects or sets of objects stay the same even when moved around or changing shape. A line of six counters remains six counters, when scattered; when matched one to one (correlation) they form two equal sets of three, the basis of multiplication and division, or divided into unequal sets (four and two), of addition and subtraction. They can use equal units to calculate mass, weight, volume, and classify sets into subsets, for example sort a set of blue bricks into subsets of shape and size (class inclusion) or sort 'yellow flowers' into daffodils, dandelions, primroses. Children learn to use the word 'because' to make causal statements.

At the *formal reasoning stage*, Piaget concluded that it is possible to bear in mind and compare a number of variables, to systematically test hypotheses and to discuss ideological and abstract ideas.

Piaget: progressing through the stages A child takes in information from experience of the environment to build schema – these are mental maps to make sense of the world (assimilation). New information is added to this map, which continues to make sense until this schema is challenged by information which does not fit into it. The child has to adjust the schema to encompass the contradictory information (accommodation). Everything in the water tray floats – but now put in the toy car. The previous rule no longer makes sense. Put some more things into the water tray to try to find a new rule – 'heavy things' sink? Children, Piaget says, try to balance the processes of applying previous knowledge and changing schema to account for new knowledge (equilibrium).

Piaget evaluated Recent neuroscience has contested Piaget's stage theory, challenging a sequence of qualitively different kinds of thinking, which ignores the possibility of intervention and social interaction to accelerate learning. Neuroscience suggests that children learn to think in much the same way as adults but lack the experience to make sense of what they find. This involves networks of neurons concerned with seeing, remembering, deducing and with the social and emotional aspects of learning. And yet there is a basic logic to the progression Piaget outlined, and if you try out some of his ideas, about conservation for example, his basic findings are reinforced. The important thing about Piaget is that he was the first person to explore the process of learning.

Lev Vygotsky (1896–1934)

Concept development and the Zone of Proximal Development Vygotsky's empirical research (1962) emphasised the importance of social interaction and language in learning. He also explored the way in which concepts are learned through trial and error. We saw from Piaget's work that concepts are categories of words/ideas which have something in common. There are hierarchies of concepts: concrete concepts such as chairs or tables, and higher-order concepts into which they fit as sub-sets, such as furniture. Sometimes there are three levels with an abstract concept which cannot be visualised (e.g. gun, weapon, power or family, village, community). All language is an organisation of concepts, identifying shared properties through the use of language and trial and error. All small furry animals are dogs – until you encounter a cat. Concepts form the building blocks of thinking and are learned through communication. This reflects the emphasis we now put on discussion in classrooms. Children support or contest each other's ideas, give examples and reasons. In this way they take each other's thinking forward and can reach levels of thinking none of them could on their own. In the early years, this process of forming categories of things which have common properties is evidenced in tiles of different colours, sizes and shapes and hence concepts, which children can group in different ways. This activity stems directly from Vygotsky's research into concept development. He passed around tiles which differed in shape, colour and thickness and asked participants to identify a nonsense word/a new concept which had two criteria in common, so creating, through trial and error, a new concept (e.g. thick and yellow, it is 'guk').

Vygotsky (1978) suggested that progress in thinking and in doing takes place through the 'Zone of Proximal Development' (ZPD), when a learner is supported by a 'slightly more able other' until he can complete the task independently; this underlines the current emphasis on pairs and partners in classrooms. Support might also be through differentiation in resources provided for different pupils, whether a teaching assistant, books at different levels of difficulty or mathematics apparatus.

Differentiation, another strategy to promote learning by providing tasks at levels individual children can engage with, is reflected in this way. Vygotsky thought that children are not naturally motivated to learn academic subjects and that the motivation to do so comes from the environment for learning provided by the teacher and the satisfaction experienced in having learned something in response to this.

J.S. Bruner (1915–)

The first of Bruner's three interacting contributions to explaining the learning process is emphasis on the importance of providing materials in a form which enables pupils to engage with what is being taught – differentiation again. Although he does not see these 'modes of representation' (1966) as entirely successive, he suggests that resources and experiences may be kinaesthetic, explored through physical engagement, iconic, presented as visual images or symbolic, diagrams, maps, mathematics and language.

Second, Bruner (1963) pointed out the need to identify the key concepts, questions and methods of answering them which are at the heart of each discipline or subject. And, third, Bruner said that, having identified the concepts and questions at the heart of each discipline, we need to structure progression in learning the key concepts, questions and ways of answering them (the spiral curriculum, 1966), so that a child, from the very beginning, can engage with the essential questions and processes of every subject. The English National Curriculum (QCA 1999) made a good attempt to do this.

More recently, Bruner (1986) has written about the importance of culture – beliefs, values, symbols, shared meanings and cultural narratives – in determining how individuals make sense of the world, and hence the importance of educators being aware of the thinking and diverse experiences pupils bring to bear on their learning.

Play

Piaget, Vygotsky and Bruner all extended their theories to consider the learning processes involved in play. Piaget (1951) suggested that play helps to overcome egocentrism since children may encounter conflicts of interest and so realise that others have goals and ideas too. It is a means of accommodating and assimilating reality. A child may imagine that a wooden brick is an aeroplane, 'assimilate' the brick into his existing schema of aeroplanes, seeing no problem in that its shape has no resemblance to an aeroplane, but may also role play the experience of seeing a street fire, in a serious attempt to 'accommodate' the reality of what he saw.

Vygotsky (1978) saw the Zone of Proximal Development as relevant to play, in that through play a child can achieve a level of thinking far higher than she can outside play. The child may, for example, wish to ride a horse. There is no horse so he might use a stick as a symbol for a horse and hence be able to ride. In order to separate the idea of a horse from a real horse, the child uses the stick as a 'pivot' for moving towards thought which is not constrained by situations. This releases the child from the constraints of the objective world to enter the world of ideas, imagination, interpretation and will.

Social Constructivism

Social Constructivism developed from the work of Vygotsky (1962, 1978) and Bruner (1986). It argues that an individual's learning takes place as a result of interactions and talk with others, in the family, school and wider society. We construct our knowledge and understanding of the world, both in everyday life and in school, through talk. Therefore, language plays a central role in mental development. The process is illustrated in Figure 2.1, which shows how, in talking to others, our thought and our speech overlap and so become 'verbal thought' (Figure 2.1).

Vygotsky and Bruner also focus on the cultural and historical aspects of social interactions. Children acquire a rich body of knowledge through their culture, which influences their knowledge and thinking.

Implications for practice

Learning through social interaction is motivating. Teachers create learning situations in which children can talk together. They share their expertise and understanding to construct learning together. They explain, question, interpret and play an active social role in the group. Children see themselves as sense making, problem solving, assuming a part of the knowledge construction and playing an active social role in the group. Contributions which draw on their personal perspectives and experiences value cultural and other differences. Learning can be assessed by observing the part each child plays in the enquiry, their explanation of their reasoning and the competence of their participation. Studying how children create meaning gives

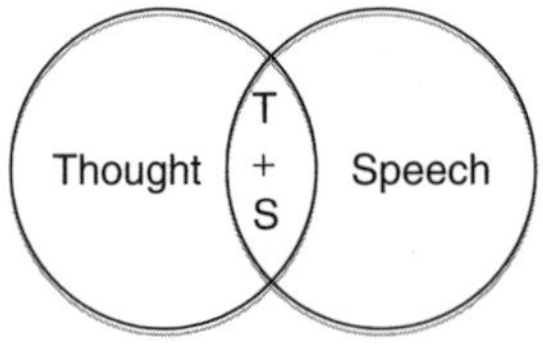

Figure 2.1 The central role of language and social contexts in developing new thinking

insights into children's thinking. Siraj-Blatchford et al. (2002) in the REPEY Project (Researching Effective Pedagogy in the Early Years) analysed effective talk. They found that good curriculum knowledge as well as an understanding of child development were as vital in the early years as in later education. Recent, useful books on Social Constructivism applied to practice include Doherty and Hughes (2009), Pritchard and Woollard (2010), Pelech and Pieper (2010) and Lindon (2012).

Work in school

Student: I don't see how philosophy of education is relevant on school placement. I'm a student – just trying to meet the Standards.

Mentor: Well, education reflects society and its aims change with society. So while you are in school, talk to some experienced teachers about ways in which, in their professional experience, society, families and children have changed. Ask, how have schools responded to these changes?

Ask about changes in the statutory curriculum within their professional experience; were there any with which they disagreed? If so, were they able to adapt them in line with their personal philosophy?

Student: I'm placed in a reception class. How can I relate the theories in this chapter more closely to my early years placement?

Mentor: Too much has been written about early years education to outline in this short chapter, but all the theorists mentioned have been very influential in developing early years practice. I suggest you look at the Reggio Emilia Approach to Education, which they use in Scotland (www.education/Scotland.gov.uk), and identify the number of theorists in this chapter who are seen as central in early years education. Then try to add some more!

Student: When I read about learning theories, I thought, surely they have been absorbed into everything we do now, so why do I need to know about these people?

Mentor: Remember that Standard 2.3 (DfE 2013) requires you to, 'Demonstrate knowledge and understanding of how pupils learn'. This is because you need to identify the theory that underpins your practice. Otherwise you can't develop your own professional practice; you become a

(Continued)

(Continued)

clone of the practice around you and of the statutory requirements, rather than interpreting theory in new contexts. Standard 2.5 says that you should encourage children to take a responsible and conscientious attitude to their work and study. Re-read the second part of the chapter. How does a Social Constructivist approach help you to do this? And how does Social Constructivism and the theory of self-efficacy help you to meet Standards 1.1 and 1.2, which refer to mutual respect and to challenging pupils of all backgrounds, abilities and dispositions? I think it would be useful to annotate your planning, showing how it relates to learning theories.

Bronfenbrenner (1917–2005)

Vygotsky and Bruner focus on the social and cultural aspects of social interactions. Bronfenbrenner (1979) developed further the importance of a child's environment in learning. He proposed an 'ecological model' of child development, in which the child is at the centre. The child affects and is affected by the settings in which s/he spends time: extended family, early care and education settings and health care and community learning sites – libraries, neighbourhoods and playgrounds. A child's development is determined by what is experienced in these settings. There needs to be communication between the settings and they need to have similar expectations. This model was very influential in the development of the Sure Start programmes introduced between 1999 and 2003, which aimed to combine family health, early years care, education and improved well-being programmes for children under 4 and their families, through integrated services, where possible in children's centres.

Bandura's theory of self-efficacy (1925–)

Bandura (1997) published his theory of 'self-efficacy', which lies at the heart of social cognitive theory. A person's attitudes, abilities and cognitive skills comprise their 'self-system' and determine the extent to which people believe that they can succeed in different situations, by planning and carrying out a course of action required to manage a situation. A person with a strong sense of self-efficacy sees challenging tasks as problems to be mastered. People with weak self-efficacy overestimate the difficulty of achieving a good result and so avoid challenging tasks, believing that they are beyond their capabilities. Teachers therefore should support those with low self-efficacy by providing tasks they can achieve, giving verbal encouragement and minimising negative stress and emotional responses.

Maslow (1908–1970)

The emphasis placed on the environment in terms of family, school and community by Vygotsky, Bruner and Bronfenbrenner and Bandura's recognition of the significance of self-esteem are relevant to the work of Maslow, although his work stems from a behaviourist approach. His theory of a Hierarchy of Needs (1943) (see www.google.co.uk/images) raised awareness that learning is impossible until a hierarchy of basic needs is met. First, basic physiological needs such as the need for air, food, drink, shelter, warmth and sleep must be met before we can learn effectively. At the next level, security, stability, safety and order are necessary. Then come affection and relationships with family and others. If these needs are met, we can achieve, take responsibility and develop self-esteem. And when this has been achieved, we reach a level which Maslow calls 'self-actualisation'. Essentially this is self-fulfilment, the ability to be autonomous, to accept one's self and others, to be spontaneous and creative. Later, Maslow added three more categories of need: esteem needs; cognitive needs (the need for knowledge and meaning); and aesthetic needs (appreciation of beauty). Maslow's sequence of needs and his methodology and the claim that only a few people ever reach self-actualisation have been criticised. Some children certainly succeed in spite of economic, social, environmental or emotional disadvantages – but many do not. Educators have responded by providing 'nurture groups', and breakfast clubs, raising awareness of children who may lack adequate sleep or may show signs of abuse at one end of the scale, and at the other, providing opportunities for children to be independent, to treat each other with respect and to be creative.

Gardner (1943–)

Following the 1944 Education Act, selection examinations for Grammar Schools consisted mainly of Intelligence Tests – tests of reasoning, which claimed to establish each person's fixed Intelligent Quotient 'IQ'. As an alternative to this, Gardner (1983) developed a theory of multiple intelligences, which identified seven separate intelligences: linguistic, musical, logical/mathematical, visual/spatial, kinaesthetic, intrapersonal (our ability to understand ourselves) and interpersonal (our ability to understand others). Later (1999) he added 'naturalistic' intelligence, which combines a core ability with the way it is represented in different cultures. This theory has been seen as encouraging children's self-esteem by discovering their strengths, and also as helpful in encouraging a cross-cultural perspective of intelligence in a society with many different cultures. It is now generally accepted that intelligence is not 'fixed'. The importance of intra-and interpersonal skills and creativity are now seen as significant in learning and development. Gardner's theory led to, for example, the concept of extra support for the 'Gifted and

Talented' in whichever area they excelled. Although there is some basis for the theory of multiple intelligences in neurology, it has been said that there is no evidence to prove that these different intelligences exist or that they undermine the theory of general intelligence. Later, Gardner (2006) argued that we do not need to focus on subjects but on thinking skills which will help pupils to deal with the future: a disciplined mind, a synthesizing mind a creating mind and a 'respectful mind'.

Reflective task

In groups, if possible, research the work of one of the theorists outlined above. One person can find out the biography, another more about the theory, a third the empirical research on which the theory is based. Next, through group discussion, critically analyse the theory – what are its strengths and weaknesses? Evaluate the implications for classroom practice. As a group, present your findings and views to your colleagues and invite questions and discussion.

Summary

This chapter began by considering the kinds of questions educational philosophers ask and why it is important for you to engage in this process, followed by a look at developments in the methods and scope of philosophical enquiry about education over the past 50 years. The second part of the chapter focused on empirical research into the *processes* of learning and the implications for classroom practice. During the last 10–20 years, neuroscience has begun to shed new light on the processes of learning. Website material discusses the potential of neuroscience to develop our understanding of the aims and processes of teaching and learning.

Questions for discussion

- Think of an area of expertise you have which is not directly related to school (e.g. playing an instrument, performing a magic trick, cooking a particular dish, dancing). Write a lesson plan to show how you could teach this skill to a group of peers, using as many aspects of learning theories as possible. List the learning theories you apply and say why you used them. Present the lesson and invite your peers to identify the theories you applied.

- What are your most enjoyable experiences of learning something, in or out of school? What did they have in common? How can this inform your philosophy of teaching and learning?

Further reading

Bailey, R. (ed.) (2010) *The Philosophy of Education*. London: Continuum.

After initial chapters on the nature of educational philosophy, authors engage in philosophical discussion of such current issues as citizenship, educational opportunities and who should control education.

Kirk, J. and Wall, C. (2010) 'Resilience and Loss in Work Identities: A Narrative Analysis of Some Retired Teachers' Work–Life Histories', *British Educational Research Journal* 36(4): 627–41.

This explores ways in which teachers have negotiated the radical changes in the profession in recent years through the notion of 'teacher resilience' to attempt to retain the characteristics of caring, vocation and 'child-centredness' developed by academics and practitioners as the most effective way to educate children and gradually eroded since the 1980s by political policy initiatives from central government.

Matheson, C. and Matheson, D. (eds) (2000) *Educational Issues in the Learning Age*. London: Continuum.

This is a series of essays on current debates on, for example, education and cultural identity, education and professionalism, education and effectiveness.

Swann, M., McIntyre, D., Pell, T., Hargreaves, L. and Cunningham, M. (2010) 'Teachers' Conceptions of Teacher Professionalism in England in 2003 and 2006', *British Educational Research Journal* 36(4): 549–71.

This investigates what teachers understand by their professionalism and their philosophy of education. It finds that reforms have shut down the spaces in which teachers can think for themselves, theorise and generate their own practice.

The Royal Society (2011) *Brain Waves 2: Neuro Science – Implications for Education and Lifelong Learning*. London: The Royal Society (www.royalsociety.org/policy/projects/brainwaves/education-lifelong-learning/).

An interesting report that highlights advances in neuroscience with potential implications for education and lifelong learning.

References

Bailey, R., Barrow, R. Carr, D. and McCarthy, C. (2010) *The Sage Handbook of Philosophy of Education*. London: Sage.

Bandura, A. (1997) *Self-Efficacy: The Exercise of Control*. New York: Freeman.

Bronfenbrenner, U. (1979) *The Ecology of Human Development: Experiments by Nature and Design*. Cambridge, MA: Harvard University Press.

Bruner, J.S. (1963) *The Process of Education: A Landmark in Educational Theory*. Cambridge, MA: Harvard University Press.

Bruner, J.S. (1966) *Towards a Theory of Instruction*. Cambridge, MA: Harvard University Press.

Bruner, J.S. (1986) *Actual Minds, Possible Worlds*. Cambridge, MA: Harvard University Press.

Cooper, A.J.H. (1892) *A Voice from the South*. Available at: www.docsouth.unc.edu

Crick, B. (2000) *Essays on Citizenship*. London: Continuum.

Dearden, R.F., Hirst, P.H. and Peters, R.S. (eds) (1972) *Education and the Development of Reason*. London: Routledge and Kegan Paul.

Department for Children, Schools and Families (DCSF) (2009) *The Independent Review of the Primary Curriculum: Final Report*. London: DCSF.

Department for Education (DfE) (2013) *Teachers' Standards*. Available at: www.education.gov.uk

Dewey, J. (1916) *Democracy and Education: An Introduction to the Philosophy of Education*. Available at: www.ilt.columbia.edu

Doherty, J. and Hughes, M. (2009) *Child Development: Theory and Practice 0–11*. New York: Pearson Longman.

Ferster, C.B. and Skinner, B.F. (1957) *Schedules of Reinforcement*. New York: Appleton-Century-Crofts.

Froebel, F. (1895) *The Pedagogies of the Kindergarten*. New York: D. Appleton and Company.

Gardner, H. (1983) *Frames of Mind: The Theory of Multiple Intelligences*. New York: Basic Books.

Gardner, H. (1999) *Intelligence Reframed: Multiple Intelligences for the 21st Century*. New York: Basic Books.

Gardner, H. (2006) *5 Minds for the Future*. Boston, MA: Harvard Business School Press.

Goodman, L.E. (2005) *Avicenna: Arabic Thought and Culture*. London: Routledge.

Gray, C. and MacBain, S. (2012) *Learning Theories in Childhood*. London: Sage.

Hirst, P.H. (1965) 'Liberal Education and the Nature of Knowledge', in R.D. Archambault (ed.) *Philosophical Analysis and Education*. London: Routledge and Kegan Paul.

Hirst, P.H. (1974) *Knowledge and the Curriculum: A Collection of Philosophical Essays*. London: Routledge and Kegan Paul.

Hirst, P.H. (1998) 'Philosophy of Education: The Evolution of a Discipline', in G. Haydn (ed.) *50 Years of Philosophy of Education*. London: London University, Institute of Education.

Hirst, P.H. and White, P. (eds) (1998) *Philosophy of Education: Major Themes in the Analytical Tradition*. London: Routledge.

Hofkins, D. and Northen, S. (eds) (2009) *Introducing the Cambridge Primary Review*. Cambridge: University of Cambridge, Faculty of Education. Available at: www.primaryreview.org.uk

Hogan, P.J. (1997) 'The Politics of Identity and the Epiphanies of Learning', in W. Carr (ed.) *The Routledge Falmer Reader in Philosophy of Education*. London: Routledge, pp. 83–96.

Lindon, J. (2012) *Understanding Child Development 0–8 years: Linking Theory and Practice*. London: Hodder Education.

Maslow, A. (1943) 'A Theory of Human Motivation', *Psychological Review* 50(4): 370–96.

McIntyre, A. (1998) 'An Interview with Giovanna Borradori', in K. Knight (ed.) *The McIntyre Reader*. Cambridge: Polity Press, pp. 255–66.

Mill, J.S. (1859) *On Liberty*. Charleston, SC: Forgotten Books (republished 2008).

Montessori, M. (1914) *Dr. Montessori's Own Handbook*. Mineola, NY: Dover Publications (republished 2005).

Pelech, J. and Pieper, G.W. (2010) *The Comprehensive Handbook of Constructivist Teaching: From Theory to Practice*. Greenwich, CT: Information Age Publishing.

Pendlebury, S. (2005) 'Feminism, Epistemology and Education', in W. Carr (ed.) *The Routledge Falmer Reader in Philosophy of Education*. London: Routledge.

Peters, R.S. (1966) *Ethics and Education*. London: Allen and Unwin.

Peters, R.S. (1967) *The Concept of Education*. London: Routledge and Kegan Paul.

Piaget, J. (1951) *Play, Dreams and Imitation in Early Childhood*. London: Routledge.

Piaget, J. and Inhelder, B. (1969) *The Psychology of the Child*. London: Perseus Books.

Pring, R. (2001) 'Education as a Moral Practice', *Journal of Moral Education* 30(2): 101–12.

Pritchard, A. and Woollard, J. (2010) *Psychology for the Classroom: Constructivism and Social Learning*. London: Routledge.

QCA (1999) *The National Curriculum: Handbook for Primary Teachers in England*. Available at: www.webarchive. Available at: nationalarchives.gov.uk

Rorty, R. (1979) *Philosophy and the Mirror of Nature*. Princeton, NJ: Princeton University Press.

Rousseau, J.J. (1762) *Emile*. Available at: www.gutenberg.org/ebooks/5427

Siraj-Blatchford, I., Sylva, K., Muttock, S., Gilden, R. and Bell, D. (2002) *Researching Effective Pedagogy in the Early Years* (Research Report 356). Annesley: Department for Education and Skills. Available at: www.ioe.ac.uk/_research_report.pdf

Spencer, H. (1851) *Essays on Education and Kindred Subjects*. Available at: www.gutenberg.org/files/16510/16510-h/16510-h.htm

Steiner, R. (1919) *The Renewal of Education*. Available at: www.ebook3000.com

Thorndike, E.L. (1903) *Educational Psychology*. New York: The Science Press.

Vygotsky, L.S. (1962) *Thought and Language*. Trans. E. Hanfmann and G. Vakar. Cambridge, MA: MIT Press.

Vygotsky, L.S. (1978) *Mind in Society: The Development of Higher Psychological Processes*. Cambridge, MA: Harvard University Press.

Walker, J.C. (1999) 'Self-determination as an Educational Aim', in R. Marples (ed.) *The Aims of Education*. London: Routledge, pp. 112–23.

Waller, T., Whitmarsh, J. and Clarke, K. (2011) *Making Sense of Theory and Practice in Early Childhood: The Power of Ideas*. Maidenhead: McGraw-Hill International.

Winch, C. (1999) 'Autonomy as an Educational Aim', in R. Marples (ed.) *The Aims of Education*. London: Routledge, pp. 74–84.

CHAPTER 3

SHORT, MEDIUM AND LONG-TERM PLANNING

Suzanne Lowe and Kim Harris

By the end of this chapter, you should be able to:

- identify the teaching and learning priorities for your school context and make an informed, positive contribution to curriculum development
- confidently plan to provide learners with engaging and meaningful learning experiences which motivate and promote understanding and development of skills
- use a wide range of assessment strategies to inform future planning and develop learning and independence.

Introduction

This chapter addresses the following Teachers' Standards (DfE 2013a) which apply to trainees and teachers across all Key Stages:

Standard 1 Set high expectations which inspire, motivate and challenge pupils
Standard 2 Promote good progress and outcomes by pupils
Standard 3 Demonstrate good subject and curriculum knowledge
Standard 4 Plan and teach well-structured lessons

Statutory curricula are dynamic and change to meet new needs and with new governments. This chapter introduces you to ways in which schools and teachers translate national requirements (DfE 2013a) into long-term plans for their school, develop medium-term plans from the whole school plans and use these to plan lessons on a weekly and daily basis. It is integrally related to assessment so that sequences of work continuously build on pupils' previous knowledge. Chapter 4 further develops issues related to assessment. This chapter examines the decisions involved in planning and some of the controversial aspects of the process, thus illustrating an aspect of how teaching is 'a complex engagement with children' (John 2006). Constructivist theory, put very simply, indicates that children build their knowledge through challenging prior understanding with new experiences. Early years education, particularly, is based around providing stimulating opportunities for children to construct their own learning through a range of experiences, many of which are 'play' based. Children are given the opportunity to choose from the range of experiences available and to repeat an experience while it has interest for them. Planning for the teacher is therefore concerned with listening to the interests of the children, assessment of their prior learning, and then providing opportunities for the children to challenge and develop their understanding.

This chapter will help you to adapt to changing curricula. It will not address in detail all of the professional standards to which it relates.

There is a range of approaches to planning. This chapter aims to meet students' beginning needs and give a firm foundation for further development, whilst being mindful that 'for some, the encounter holds creative possibilities; for others, it is a brick wall of bewilderment and anxiety' (John 2006 p. 483).

Different approaches to the primary curriculum

The National Curriculum

The National Curriculum (NC) was introduced following the Education Reform Act of 1988. It comprised a subject-focused approach which outlined the knowledge, skills and understanding that children should be taught within a particular subject and Key Stage. It included attainment targets against which children are 'measured'.

A new National Curriculum in England was introduced by the Conservative and Liberal Democrat Coalition Government, for implementation from September 2014 (DfE 2013b). Stating the government rationale for a new National Curriculum, the Prime Minister (David Cameron) said that:

> We are determined to give all children in this country the very best education – for their future, and for our country's future. The new national curriculum is a vital part of that.
>
> This curriculum marks a new chapter in British education. From advanced fractions to computer coding to some of the greatest works of literature in the English language, this is a curriculum that is rigorous, engaging and tough. . . .
>
> This is a curriculum to inspire a generation – and it will educate the great British engineers, scientists, writers and thinkers of our future. (https://www.gov.uk/government/news/education-reform-a-world-class-curriculum-to-drive-up-standards-and-fuel-aspiration [accessed 08.07.13])

This National Curriculum specifies the aims, purposes and content for English, Mathematics, Science, Art and Design, Citizenship, Computing, Design and Technology, Geography, History, Music and Physical Education for each Key Stage, with the introduction of a foreign language at Key Stage 2. Attainment targets state that, by the end of each Key Stage, 'pupils are expected to know, apply and understand the matters, skills and processes specified in the relevant programme of study'. The programmes for English, Mathematics and Science are set out in detail and replace the Primary Framework for Literacy and Numeracy (see Chapter 1 p. 28).

A cross-curricular approach to the National Curriculum

However, to teach all subjects in a discrete (subject-specific) way can sometimes introduce seemingly rigid boundaries between subjects which some children may not recognise as artificial and so may not transfer their learning between subject areas.

Some schools attempted to redress the balance by using a cross-curricular approach rather than always teaching through discrete subjects. In using a cross-curricular approach it is important to ensure that there is breadth across the curriculum and that *all* the necessary curriculum objectives are taught. In an effective cross-curricular lesson there will be shared emphasis on the learning outcomes from different subject areas. Barnes (2011 p. 259) explains how effective units of work may also include opportunities for children to use creative approaches to applying the learning to new situations, thus allowing the teacher (and child) to assess how well the learning has been understood.

A thematic approach to the National Curriculum

Many schools use 'themes' to link subjects under an umbrella context. Lessons can be taught using either a subject-discrete or a cross-curricular approach. The choice depends on what knowledge, skills or understanding is intended to be developed, and teacher judgement about how the children will best be able to learn this. The chosen theme may be taught in a variety of ways, for example one day per week for several weeks or it may be fully timetabled with all lessons linked to the theme.

One of the key advantages of a thematic approach is that, as for cross-curricular lessons, it is thought to be a more contextually based approach to learning, by encouraging children to make connections between different areas of learning. In addition, many believe that this promotes deep learning and supports transference of skills, knowledge and understanding between the areas of learning.

A concern in some schools is that children may not transfer the skills learned in one subject, say literacy, into other subject areas. Conversely, some teachers believe that depth of subject knowledge can only be taught through discrete subject teaching and are concerned that a surface approach to the curriculum may be the result of a thematic approach.

Combining subjects as areas of learning

One approach to making cross-curricular links which is still relevant was proposed in the Independent Review of the Primary Curriculum (IRPC) (DCSF 2009). The Rose proposal outlined 'a design for the curriculum which promotes challenging subject teaching alongside equally challenging cross-curricular studies' (p. 4) but 'insists that literacy, numeracy and ICT must be prioritised' (p. 6). An additional emphasis is placed on the importance of talk, as Rose considered the 'prime skills of speaking and listening to be essential in their own right and crucial for learning to read, write, to be numerate and, indeed, to be successful in virtually all of the learning children undertake at school and elsewhere' (p. 6). A further recommendation from the IRPC is a restructuring of the curriculum into six 'areas of learning':

- Understanding the arts
- Understanding English, communication and languages
- Historical, geographical and social understanding
- Mathematical understanding
- Understanding physical development, health and well-being
- Scientific and technological understanding.

'The areas of learning capture the essential knowledge, key skills and understanding that children need to develop as they progress through their primary years' (QCDA 2010 p. 16). These 'areas of learning' may be a useful place to start when considering combining subjects in your lesson planning.

Starting with the locality

A large-scale piece of research which made suggestions about the interpretation of the primary curriculum which remain relevant is the Cambridge Primary Review (Alexander 2010). This is based on extensive research undertaken between 2006 and 2009, which comprised an investigation into the views of the general public on primary education including suggested changes, as well as 31 research reports investigating 10 key themes. Chapter 14 focuses on the curriculum and Chapter 16 on assessment. This report makes the interesting suggestion that, where possible, 30 per cent of the overall framework and programmes of study should be based on the locality.

Reflective task

Consider your personal views on this issue of subject-based teaching versus theme-based and cross-curricular teaching. Are these *values*-based judgements? Are they linked to how much worth we apportion to each subject? Do you believe it is necessary to prioritise basic skills over the arts and humanities? In your experience so far what do you believe to be the 'best' approach? Why? What strategies do you have to address the potential issues? What do you consider may be the benefits of using 'the locality' to promote and inspire learning? What potential difficulties may arise?

It is possible and important to interpret changes in statutory requirements mediated by your own professional philosophy; this chapter will give you strategies for doing this, in terms of planning and assessing what is taught and learned, with confidence.

Some international comparisons

The examples below illustrate the impact government agendas can have on teaching and learning in the classroom, particularly on the curriculum content and how it is organised. A focus on wider curricular agendas can help us to understand a global perspective on education priorities, although the examples given present a narrow view in terms of global priorities as they are all from more economically developed countries.

The USA

US educational priorities, outlined by President Obama in his State of the Union address 2013, are:

- to have the most dynamic, educated workforce in the world
- to support all 50 states to provide access to pre-school for all low- and moderate-income families
- to focus on developing the high school curriculum to prepare students for a real-world high-tech economy
- to make higher education more affordable. (Obama 2013)

Scotland: 'Curriculum for Excellence'

The Scottish Curriculum for Excellence:

> aims to ensure that all children and young people in Scotland develop the attributes, knowledge and skills they will need to flourish in life, learning and work.
>
> The knowledge, skills and attributes learners will develop will allow them to demonstrate four key capacities – to be successful learners, confident individuals, responsible citizens and effective contributors.' (http://www.educationscotland.gov.uk/thecurriculum/whatiscurriculumforexcellence/understandingthecurriculumasawhole/index.asp [(accessed 08.07.13])

Sweden

Swedish schooling has the following key elements:

- 'free schools' system began in the 1990s
- pre-school is available from age 1
- 'formal' timetabled schooling starts age 7
- national curriculum with local elements devised by municipalities
- teacher and school autonomy for teaching strategies
- improved initial teacher education
- a nationally valid timetable stating the number of hours per subject over all nine years of compulsory education – 6665 hours – but each municipality/school decides on the distribution of hours and in what year a subject is introduced. (https://webgate.ec.europa.eu/fpfis/mwikis/eurydice/index.php/Sweden:Overview [(accessed 08.07.13])

The National Curriculum in England, statutory from 2014

The 2014 National Curriculum is the result of the Coalition Government's consultation on how best to meet the educational needs of children. It states that:

> Every state-funded school must offer a curriculum which is balanced and broadly based and which:
>
> - promotes the spiritual, moral, cultural, mental and physical development of pupils at the school and of society, and
> - prepares pupils at the school for the opportunities, responsibilities and experiences of later life. (DfE 2013b)

It is worth noting that free schools and academies do not have to follow the National Curriculum.

The National Curriculum in Wales

The Welsh curriculum 3–13 (www.wales.gov.uk) identifies skills for each subject and the range of contexts, opportunities and activities through which these should be assessed. Making the Most of Assessment (2010) (www.gov.wales/docs) offers detailed guidance on the different methods and purposes of assessment. The Welsh Government has a vision of schools for the future which:

- provides high quality and inspirational teaching and learning
- provides a broad and stimulating curriculum offering choice
- allows learners to develop at their own pace with attainment targets and methods of assessment designed to recognize a wider range of achievement
- incorporates social inclusion, sustainable development, equal opportunities and bilingualism into all aspects of school life. (The School Curriculum for Wales, revised 2008)

The way forward?

It is worth considering that the Rose Review and the Cambridge Primary Review proposed a reorganisation of the curriculum into areas or domains rather than maintaining a separate subject-specific focus. Whatever the curriculum, and acknowledging that change is likely to occur throughout a teacher's career, it is likely that schools and teachers will increasingly need to make decisions about how different curricular areas can be linked in meaningful ways.

There are many opinions on, and rationales for, this (Barnes 2011; Rowley and Cooper 2009). One suggestion might be some units of work 'blocked' and taught intensively over a short period of time, for example. Would there be an advantage in this? Another consideration could be the extent to which the local community and expert visitors could be utilised to enhance children's learning within a thematic curriculum. Some schools have worked with local archaeologists, for example, or with a local firm of architects, builders, the National Trust, a theatre – even fashion designers – or with a children's writer, ballet dancer, artist, musician. What contribution can parents or grandparents make to a wider and more diverse curriculum? Even within the constraints of recent years, many schools have developed exciting curricular opportunities, so be brave and 'think outside the box'.

Applying your philosophy to mediate statutory requirements

Epistemology is the branch of philosophy concerned with different ways of knowing and considering what are the most valid ways of knowing. How can we get beyond our personal opinions to something we can feel has validity? Some things we know because they are based on reason. Other things we know from experience. We think we know how children learn based firstly on reason, on what we have learned from research and from the authoritative experience of others about learning. In addition, we have our empirical knowledge, what we observe about the children in our classrooms. We develop our personal educational philosophy based on a combination of what we learn from scholarly authorities and our personal experience. We may therefore find ourselves in agreement with the current prevailing ideology of education or at times find ourselves teaching in ways which we fundamentally believe to be misinformed. It is vital that we adopt the view presented by Pollard:

> Professional ideologies are always likely to remain strong among teachers – they represent commitments, ideals *and* interests. Reflective teachers should be open-minded enough to constructively critique their own beliefs, as well as those of others. (Pollard 2008 p. 94)

As government education policy changes in response to what is believed to be necessary for future generations' learning needs and workforce requirements, so curricular change is necessary and ITE (Initial Teacher Education) changes to reflect this. A current emphasis on school-based training and the School Direct training programme (www.education.gov.uk) is an example of the need for student teachers to be confident in being able to contribute to teams and to take responsibility for making their own decisions about planning and assessment (see also Introduction, pp. 3–4).

There is an ongoing tension related to the prioritisation of literacy and numeracy above other areas of the curriculum, with some teachers believing it is important for children's education to focus on core subjects and others believing that core skills can be taught contextually through other subjects.

Work in school

The following discussion takes places during a staff meeting:

Amy: I prefer to teach my literacy skills when the children are learning other subjects so they have a context. So this week we are looking at the structure of newspaper reports and writing up our activities in groups to make a report for Year 2, to let them know about what happens in Y3, when they come to visit.

Andrew: No, I prefer to teach the skills separately. How can you tell how much each child understands about the newspaper features? Once we have learned the skills in literacy then we use them in history to write about the Ancient Egyptians.

Amy: If I do it that way I don't feel I have enough time to give quality teaching to all the subjects. I find a more thematic approach works better for me.

Barbara: But how do you make sure you plan for all the individual needs? In my class some children prefer the 'joined-up' thematic approach but others really seem to thrive when they can focus on one subject at a time. So I plan from knowing my children, their prior knowledge, and then what I am to teach is tailored to that. So sometimes I plan to teach in a theme, sometimes not.

This discussion explores some of the issues facing teachers today. How to teach areas of the curriculum can be dependent on teachers' own philosophical beliefs concerning how children learn or on school approaches to learning and ethos. Changes to the curriculum at national level will resonate with some teachers and not with others.

Planning a successful learning experience then depends on the children, the teacher, the school, and its community, all within the context of a wider curriculum.

Reflective task

Consider your initial observations of planning and assessment practices. How did the school organise the curriculum?

How did this fit with your own emerging professional philosophy of education?

As you progress through your training, revisit these questions in light of your developing knowledge and understanding.

We now look at some key questions that you may have as a student teacher:

1. 'What MUST I get right when I'm writing a lesson plan?'

Five key things are:

- Know what children have previously done, and whether they remember and understand this.
- Know exactly what you want children to achieve and have a target that reflects this.
- Plan for differentiation.
- Know what resources are available.
- Plan and manage the length of each stage of a lesson and what you and any other adults in the classroom will be doing at each stage.

2. 'How can I plan for differentiation?'

This is an essential question to ask in order to have both a child-centred and a focused approach to learning and teaching. It indicates that you recognise that personalisation and differentiation are necessary in each effective lesson. You need to learn how to set the correct level of challenge for individual children. The Teachers' Standards (DfE 2013a) require you to 'set goals that stretch and challenge pupils of all backgrounds, abilities and dispositions' (Standard 1.2). There are lots of ways you can begin to do this. For example:

- Ask the class questions at the beginning of, during, and at the end of a lesson to gauge different levels of understanding.
- Ensure that children are comfortable about asking questions.
- Observe children working and listen to them talking to each other. Talk to them about their work.

Then you can plan different levels of work within the same topic. This might work well in mathematics.

Always plan extensions for those who may not be sufficiently challenged.

Get to know and take into account children's different personalities, interests and backgrounds, including cultural backgrounds, their language levels and any special educational needs, and consider what will motivate and interest different children (Standard 5.2, 3, 4; DfE 2013a).

In many subjects, for example in art or history, design open activities which children can respond to at their own levels. You can give children the choice of working at the level of challenge they want to try … using labels such as hot/spicy, medium or mild (or curry types vindaloo, dhansak, korma).

For some activities ask children to work in pairs or groups of mixed abilities so that they can support and extend each other.

3. 'I don't know much about this so I'm having trouble finding ideas for activities which will fit the learning objective. Where can I find ideas? I don't have enough time to research this thoroughly.'

Standards 3.1 and 3.2 (DfE 2013a) expect you to 'have a secure knowledge of the relevant subjects of the curriculum'. But this isn't acquired overnight! You increasingly consolidate your subject knowledge (Standard 8.4; DfE 2013a). It can be fun to research a topic at a level which will benefit you and the children.

The internet can be a useful resource, both websites for teachers and those which are not specifically educational. Websites for art galleries or museums, for example, can stimulate informed creative thinking – see, for instance, the National Gallery's Take One Picture at http://www.takeonepicture.org – or books of course, including those for children. And don't be afraid to ask other students – and experienced teachers; they will appreciate your request for ideas. Are there visitors with expertise in this subject who might be invited to work with you: archaeologists, musicians, artists, parents, local businesses? Are there resources in the local history or archive library, or a local museum with an education department?

There are often many opportunities for collaborative planning practice in schools and students have said that they have learned many good strategies in this way: children devising the lesson focus, cross-curricular teaching, interactive lessons, learn-apply-experiment, and learning outside.

4. 'I have learned, at university, that I should take initiatives in my planning, but when I have been in school the teachers expect me to rely on their planning methods, which I don't really agree with. In one school differentiation was frowned upon and in another I was criticised for responding to a surprise opportunity that arose during a lesson rather than sticking to my lesson plan. Yet we are assessed on our ability to do these things. This has caused tensions with my mentor and not done my self-esteem much good!'

The research of Hattie (2012) shows that the greatest benefits to all involved come from:

- increased experience in schools observing a range of teachers
- planning for a wider range of children
- being part of the community of teachers
- having dialogue related to planning.

As John has said: (2006):

> It seems that greater exposure to teaching challenges the novices to see planning and preparation less as an unalterable event and more as a concept associated with unpredictability, flexibility, and creativity. It was as if the student teachers were seeing planning as the glue that held the various pieces of learning and teaching together and the linear format, despite being a course requirement, was largely superfluous to their needs as teachers. (p. 489)

What are the children going to learn or what am I going to teach?

Planning and assessment or assessment and planning, which comes first? There is no definitive answer. It is like the proverbial 'chicken and egg'. Many beginning teachers become involved in what they need to teach rather than focusing on what the children will learn. If governments continue to define prescriptive and crowded curricula, teachers may be led to 'covering' the objectives, for example 'delivering the literacy objectives' rather than fostering a love of literature or focusing on 'facts' to be learned rather than the excitement of enquiry-based learning.

This leads us to consider, *what is* knowledge?

Kinds of knowledge

Biggs (2003 pp. 41–43) gives a theoretical analysis of the kinds of knowing which can result from the need to 'get through the prescribed curriculum' and the kind of knowing which changes the way we tackle problems and look at life, leading to learning which is deep and transformative:

- demonstrating what you know, without necessarily understanding it (declarative or propositional knowledge) – for example, rote learning, repeating times tables, delivering the curriculum, learning that 'area' is length times breadth
- using such knowledge to solve problems ('functioning knowledge') – for example, planning a class party, solving problems in maths or science, applying your formula for area in a context
- knowing what comes next in a sequence without understanding why (procedural knowledge) – for example, following through a series of lessons as outlined in a 'scheme' or unit as written, or knowing that after area comes teaching of volume
- using what you know in order to make informed judgements, which is by far the most important kind ('conditional knowledge') – for example, you know the area of carpet needed for your classroom, but now you consider the use of the room, the children and alternative solutions.

Reflective task

You may wish to refer to Chapter 2, if you have not already looked at it, to link this discussion with the aims of education and the political dimensions, and consider 'just what are society's aims and values?'

Planning for learning

Levels of planning

The statutory curriculum is mediated and interpreted at different levels through a statutory curriculum and policies which are then translated into a whole-school curriculum plan and then further broken down into policies.

In addition, all schools have an individual ethos which is comprised of their philosophy and values and this is what makes every school different. When you walk in you get the 'feel' of the school from the environment (displays, welcome, orderliness, the learning conversations around you), and as a student you need to adapt to this as quickly as possible, although when you are a member of the teaching team you contribute to the ethos and to the development of the whole-school curriculum plan and policies.

Whole-school plan

Whatever the statutory content, schools must translate it into whole-school plans for their school. For example, looking at the National Curriculum 2014 requirement to teach 'significant people in British history' at Key Stage 1 teachers may decide to teach about Queen Victoria, Christopher Columbus, Rosa Parkes or Mary Seacole. These may be selected for good reasons. But have they thought about the locality of the school, available resources and the personal skills, interest areas and knowledge of the teaching team? It is also possible to respond to the enthusiasms and interests of the children in your class, although this is more normally at lesson level than for longer-term planning.

Reflective task

Now consider your own knowledge – which famous British people do you feel you would like to teach the children in your class about? What else do you need

(Continued)

(Continued)

to know other than the chosen person's story? Use relevant statutory requirements to devise a medium-term plan. You should include assessment opportunities and identify some strategies. Also consider how you may use this to teach thematically. How might a school come up with a long-term plan? What would it be based upon other than statutory requirements? Your answer should include contextual links, e.g. local geography, history.

The whole-school curriculum plan is developed from national requirements and the school ethos and priorities. This is usually organised in Key Stages/age phases and is often referred to as the 'long-term plan'. In this you can observe the cyclical 'spiral' nature of the curriculum, with subject areas being revisited throughout a child's time in school. Also, cross-curricular links or themes can be identified and the long-term plan ensures all areas of the curriculum are taught at appropriate times and in relevant detail across the age phases.

Long-term plan

Table 3.1 shows how a long-term plan for a Y4 class based on the new National Curriculum (DfE 2013b) might look.

Reflective task

Some of the areas lend themselves to a cross-curricular approach and would be taught in this way. Examine the long-term plan in Table 3.1 to see which lessons you would teach using this approach. For example, explain how you might combine sound in science and music, art with history, design and technology with geography or dance and music.

The 2014 curriculum requires children to learn about electricity in Y1 (electric lights), Y4 (circuits) and Y6 (circuits, voltage and symbols). This illustrates the spiral nature of the curriculum, with subjects being revisited to 'build' on prior knowledge and allow for consolidation of learning through experience. After each unit of work has been taught, teachers would make a 'summative' assessment to ascertain the level of individual understanding. Formative assessment is used regularly to inform planning and support learning. We will return to this later.

Table 3.1 Example of a Year 4 long-term plan

Year 4/ Curriculum Area	Autumn 1	Autumn 2	Spring 1	Spring 2	Summer 1	Summer 2
Science	Living things	Animals, including humans	States of matter	Sound	Electricity	Choice
History	Britain's settlement by Anglo-Saxons and Scots	Depth study of Anglo-Saxon art and culture			Earliest civilisations: Mayan	Ancient Greece
Geography					Similarities and differences between own region of United Kingdom and a region in Europe	
Citizenship	Understand political system of the UK and how citizens participate in democratic government					
Art		Great artists	Sketch book recording of observations		Drawing and painting	
Computing/ Design and Technology	Design and write programmes			D/T design/ make/ evaluate a game		D/T cooking and nutrition: cook a series of healthy savoury dishes
Music	Compose music for play related to Christmas concert	Play composition Prepare for performance	Choice		Choice	
PE	Dance Basic skills	Gym		Swimming	Games; adventure camp	Athletics
Foreign language (French)	Portraits		Les Quatre Amis		Ça pousse! On y va	

Medium-term plan

To help deliver specific areas of the curriculum, the whole-school long-term plan is organised into medium-term plans which are targeted at specific year groups and often for specific half term, theme or 'unit' periods. The long-term plan can be delivered in cross-curricular themes or subject-specific chunks or a mixture of the two, as decided by the school management team to best meet the learning needs of the children. Barnes (2007 p. 184) states that 'a medium term plan should show the proposed relationship between key questions and attention to specific subject-based skills and knowledge. It must show progression towards a questioning stance and the development of ever-deeper understanding'.

The medium-term plan (unit of work) should also show when assessment is to take place and begin to make clear the differentiation strategies to be used across the 'unit of work'. These should include a range of approaches to assessment to enable all learners to demonstrate their successful learning. We will discuss differentiation and assessment later in the chapter and in Chapter 4.

Weekly plans

Short-term plans are often called 'weekly plans'. From these an individual lesson plan can be constructed. These are necessary to ensure that all areas of the curriculum are taught effectively and in adequate depth to enable children to learn. Although weekly plans are meant to outline specific activities and sessions throughout the week, they need to be flexible, so that you can respond to changes, in order to extend children's learning. The different levels of mediation/interpretation at each level are shown in Figure 3.1.

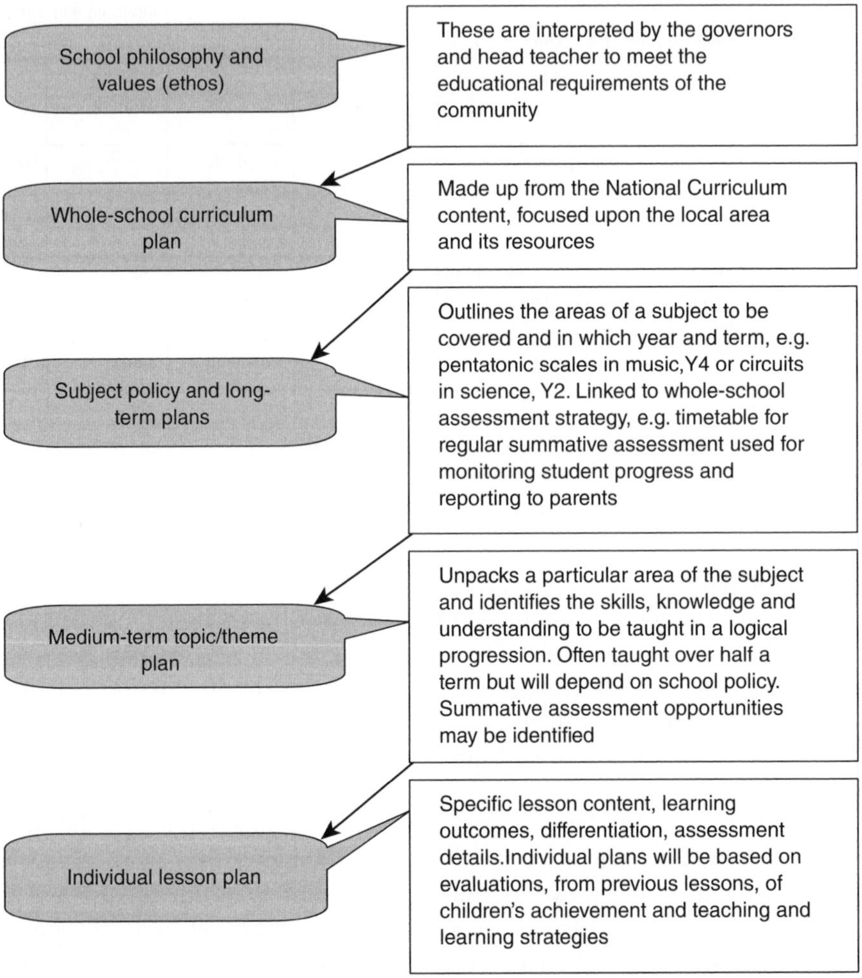

Figure 3.1 Showing the different levels of planning and the stages at which teachers can interpret the statutory curriculum and policies to reflect the philosophy of the school and teachers

Individual lesson plans

Each school will have a particular approach to the individual lesson plan with a preferred proforma. Your Initial Teacher Education provider may also have a recommended format. So rather than confuse you with a table to be completed, we thought it more important to identify the key elements which should be included in an individual lesson plan.

General information

- Year (e.g. 4)
- Class – no. of students, may be wanted in gender numbers, i.e. male and female
- Teacher
- Time of lesson and duration.

Lesson-specific information

- Title of lesson (usually taken from medium-term plan)
- Intended Learning Outcomes
- Previous assessment information (if any is available)
- Current assessment opportunities and strategies
- Activities (these should be linked to the learning outcomes and the assessment – the more aligned with each other these are, the better the learning opportunities, will be)
- Differentiation – this is generally divided into at least three attainment/ability levels and should include reference to any IEP (Individual Education Plan) strategies for specified children, though some activities may be better differentiated by outcome
- Groupings – these may be based on partners, mixed ability or friendship or ability. There are good reasons for any of these groupings but it is essential to be clear about why you have chosen a particular grouping for a particular activity and do not keep the same groups all the time. Why?
- Key vocabulary
- Key questions
- Possible misconceptions (particularly important in science)
- Resources, including staff (other adults)
- Plenary – or a series of mini-plenaries, to correct misunderstandings, consolidate learning or introduce next learning steps.

Once you are familiar with the needs and abilities of your class and the intricacies of planning for learning, then it is possible, and enjoyable, to move to less structured/linear approaches. It is important to note that experienced teachers may seem to have minimal planning but this is usually because a large amount of the information has been 'internalised', much akin to the skills needed in driving a car.

Consider adopting inquiry-based learning approaches such as is exemplified in the 'Mantle of the Expert' approach of Dorothy Heathcote (further information is available at http://www.mantleoftheexpert.com/category/planning/). James Nottingham (2013) discusses promoting the ASK approach (attitudes, skills and knowledge) along with a strong focus on Philosophy for Children (P4C). This has a key focus on inquiry and questioning as the basis of lessons.

Teachers use the statutory curriculum and national strategies to devise ILOs (Intended Learning Outcomes) for each lesson. These are then shared with the class, sometimes in the form of 'We Are Learning To…' (WALT) or child-friendly notices. From these and the discussion that follows, 'Success Criteria', which may be called 'What I'm Looking For' (WILF), can be constructed. As each child is an individual, then how they will learn and be able to demonstrate this learning may be evidenced differently. The ILOs may be differentiated for differing groups of ability within the class, and consequently there will be a similar number of differentiated success criteria. Personalisation of approach to enable individualised learning is perhaps too idealistic a goal for every teacher in every lesson if it is the teacher who has the 'control' and determines what is learned. However, through self-determination and personalisation of the success criteria, children can be encouraged to be involved in the lesson outcomes. This does come with a caveat though. Whilst children perceived to be 'gifted and talented' and those confident in the curriculum area in question may relish this 'challenge', there may be some children whose self-esteem is too poor for them to believe they can achieve in any way. Giving this group of children the opportunity to set realistic, attainable yet high standards may take some encouragement and support until they become comfortable and confident in this area. Good planning based on prior knowledge (from assessment) will ensure allocation of the correct resources (including staff) to support the children in their early steps until they become more confident in this approach. A useful approach may be through adding a context to the lesson by presenting a 'This Is Because…' (TIBS) aspect to help children understand how the knowledge and/or skills they have learned in the lesson may be of wider use. This could also be linked with an aspect of children's prior experience and learning.

Homework

The Teachers' Standards (Standard 4.3) requires teachers to 'set homework and plan out of class activities to extend the knowledge and understanding pupils have acquired'. Careful consideration needs to be given to what kind of homework is set and why. Bearing in mind that Standard 4.2 also requires teachers to 'promote a love of learning and children's intellectual curiosity', many primary schools expect children to at least undertake reading, literacy and/or mathematics tasks at home. The amount increases with age, and the frequency is variable, although weekly spelling homework and daily reading are still fairly common. Some teachers and many parents believe that homework is a useful extension to the school day and if parents are supportive then this may well be the case. However, limited space at home, insufficient backup from adults, and limited access to computers must be taken into consideration (Alexander 2010 pp. 83–4).

Thought needs to be given to the content of the homework. Is it to be carried out independently by the child, or with the support of their parents or carers? Do they have the support of parents and carers and the necessary equipment at home to be able to complete the homework successfully?

When work is returned judgements need to be made about how much the child has understood independently and how much they may have been supported. For this reason it is important to have additional evidence of learning by the child before conclusions are reached about their understanding and achievement.

Differentiation

Planning should include 'differentiation'. This is the term used to explain when the teaching and learning are specifically targeted and made different, to meet the needs of all children within the class. This will include varied aspects of education: learning, social, emotional, and any physical needs. In any classroom of children there will be a range of abilities; whether this is linked with understanding of concepts, skill levels or factual knowledge, for example for children for whom English is an Additional Language (EAL), or who have physical, social or emotional barriers to learning. Because of this expected range of abilities (for want of better terminology), which may well alter for individual children across the curriculum, teachers should aim to plan specifically to support children to succeed at the differentiated levels.

In addition to this there are children who require a more individualised approach to their learning, which may involve an Individual Education Plan to meet their specific needs. Children who need help in addition to classroom differentiation are identified as needing support at School Action (SA) level. The school will allocate staffing and resources to support the child in their development and learning.

Teachers will need to use their thorough understanding of whichever statutory curriculum requirements apply and its underlying principles with regard to inclusion and their knowledge of the strengths and needs of the individual child to plan with a flexible approach. This approach will in no way involve reduced expectations of achievement, rather a personalised approach with each child achieving appropriately.

Reflective task

Consider a class of children you have worked with at some point of your Initial Teacher Education so far. Can you identify a spread of abilities? What strategies did you and the class teacher use to remove any barriers to learning and help all children to achieve? How were these identified in your planning?

Strategies you may have noticed could include grouping (classroom organisation), support, outcome, task or resource. If so, make notes about how well you feel these worked for the child, the teacher, other children.

Logically, as planning involves many aspects to ensure inclusion and achievement by all, then assessment must also be varied and differentiated in approach to allow all children to demonstrate their strengths. As Wearmouth (2009) puts it, 'Students' sense of themselves as having the potential to be effective in the community of practice of learners may be constructed and/or constrained by the forms of assessment that are used with them' (p. 93).

Remember, you cannot plan effectively without reference to previous assessment and you must include opportunities for assessment throughout the lessons you plan.

The National Centre for Excellence in the Teaching of Mathematics (NCETM) illustrates the development of planning for maths into the useful structure outlined below, which can be applied in any subject area, and the principles can also be applied in thematic approaches to planning.

Features of effective practice

An effective structure for curriculum planning shows how mathematics is planned for at the long-, medium- and short-term level. Effective planning:

Has a long-term plan (planning for progression) which:

- clearly states an expected pathway of progression across the Key Stage
- breaks down the Key Stage progression into a yearly plan
- reflects the school's vision and national priorities.

Has a medium-term plan (structuring the planning of units) which:

- links clearly to the long-term- plan
- makes clear what is to be taught and when

- is based on prior attainment, not what year group the pupils are in
- contains differentiated teaching objectives addressing process as well as content
- gives clear links to rich and interesting activities and resources
- indicates teaching approaches which will engage and interest the pupils
- contains a schedule for various assessment items in line with school policy
- reflects the school's vision and national priorities.

Has a short-term plan (lesson planning) which:

- links clearly to the medium-term plan
- makes clear what is to be taught
- encourages the teacher to plan a sequence of lessons rather than 'standalones'
- gives guidance for a range of teaching approaches to be used within the sequence of lessons
- indicates key vocabulary that might be barriers to learning
- gives guidance to support teachers plan in more detail the approaches and resources which will engage and interest the students
- gives guidance for assessment activities and strategies, for example probing questions, self- and peer-assessment opportunities
- gives examples of ways in which learning can be taken beyond the classroom, for example consolidation, extension, application, historical links
- offers prompts for reflecting on and evaluating the lesson in order to inform/review the planned next steps for this unit
- reflects the school's vision. (https://www.ncetm.org.uk/resources/21510)

Lesson evaluations

These should focus first on the learning and then on the teaching, leading to an end product which informs the next planned teaching (Standard 4.4; DfE 2013a). A further area to consider is children's attitudes to, and enjoyment of, the learning. These are professional judgements which will both support teacher knowledge of an individual child and inform future planning decisions.

Case study

Sometimes a surprise event can help you rethink your teaching strategy, such as in the following example.

(Continued)

(Continued)

In a music lesson with a Year 4 class of 20 boys and 9 girls, the children were listening to Saint-Saëns' *The Carnival of the Animals,* identifying how the musical elements combined to create the effect and help us relate this to particular animals. The children used language to describe how the music represented the animals, and described the mental images the music evoked. Part way through the lesson the 'surprise' happened; a group of boys asked if they could dance to illustrate the movement of the animals, in addition to describing the musical elements which contributed to the effect of the music. The assumptions this teacher made when planning had not included the boys wishing to dance. The children's desire to respond this way impacted on future planning to include more opportunities for dance.

An evaluation of each lesson taught will support the teacher's knowledge through identifying children who have achieved the Learning Objectives, those children who have achieved more than expected and those who have yet to fully achieve the ILOs, as well as any children who have misconceptions which will need to be addressed. Teachers will also evaluate how children responded to the teaching strategies used and which learning strategies children relied upon.

Resources, learning environment and classroom management are also areas for consideration due to the impact they have on a lesson. It is important also to obtain feedback on your teaching from the children, for example with young children through drawing or role play, by consulting a focus group of children you perceive to be having problems, or by pupils commenting on an aspect of their learning through analysing a video of a lesson.

Purposeful lesson evaluations and record keeping are useful tools to aid memory and impact upon future planning, therefore they need to be 'user-friendly'. In most situations, making annotations on the planning sheet is an acceptable form of record keeping for day-to-day evaluation. This should be clear and specific to aid planning for the next appropriate lesson.

Teachers and schools have differing methods for recording children's achievement through records of progress and attainment; it is usually the medium-term end of unit summative assessments which go to build up this record.

Reflective task

When next on placement ask your school for a copy of the long-term plan and a subject-specific or themed medium-term plan and then try to see how an individual lesson you have observed (or taught) fits into the big picture. Evaluate the lesson to identify the strategies needed to teach the next lesson to the same class. Which misconceptions need to be corrected? What will the gifted and talented children learn? How will you differentiate appropriately?

Summary

This chapter began with an overview of the statutory curriculum, then discussed different ways in which it may be structured, as single subjects or through cross-curricular approaches, the value judgements involved and the impact of changing government priorities on these decisions. The English National Curriculum (DfE 2013b) and its rationale was compared with the curricula for Scotland, Wales and Sweden, with US educational priorities as outlined in the presidential address (Obama 2013), and with previous recommendations (DCSF 2008) and the Cambridge Primary Review (Alexander 2010).

A consideration followed of the many decisions which teachers must make in order to mediate national requirements at the levels of long-term, whole-school planning, medium-term planning, daily planning and lesson planning. The importance of integrating planning and assessment in a cyclical way, at all levels, was emphasised and is developed in Chapter 4. Finally, the process of needing to reflect on teachers'planning and on children's learning was explained in order that both may be taken forward.

Questions for discussion

Refer to *The National Curriculum: A Framework* (DfE 2013b)

- It was said (p. 64) that teachers' planning involves 'listening to the children'. Discuss ways in which this can be done, based on the planning guidance above, within the statutory curriculum.
- David Cameron said that the new curriculum is a curriculum to 'inspire a generation'. Discuss ways in which you aim to make it inspiring.

(Continued)

(Continued)

- Discuss ways in which planning for different subjects in the new curriculum can begin with the locality, as advised in the Cambridge Primary Review (Alexander 2010) and how this would link with the National Curriculum subject content.
- Differentiation: reflect on how you have differentiated for a particular child; how might you have done this better?

Further reading

Barnes, J. (2011) *Cross-Curricular Learning 3–14*, 2nd edn. London: Sage Publications.

Clear discussion related to planning and teaching through a cross-curricular and thematic approach. There are strong links to creativity and research-based pedagogy throughout. Chapter 11 is focused on planning for cross-curricular activity.

Goodhew, G. (2005) *Meeting the Needs of Gifted and Talented Students*. London: Network Continuum.

For ITE generalist students and educators this is a useful resource to focus on an aspect of inclusive practice termed 'a bit of a Cinderella' by Goodhew in the introduction. From the necessary discussion relating to the difficulty in coming to a definitive definition of the terms 'gifted', 'talented' and 'exceptionally able', Goodhew uses a variety of sources to develop a shared understanding for the purpose of the book, examining a variety of perspectives. Perhaps the most relevant chapter in relation to planning and assessment is Chapter 4, which discusses classroom practices.

Hattie, J. (2012) *Visible Learning for Teachers*. Abingdon: Routledge.

Pages 39–76 focus on preparing the lesson. Key points focus on the importance of planning with other teachers and the necessity of knowing the children in a holistic way.

John, P.D. (2006) 'Lesson Planning and the Student Teacher: Re-thinking the Dominant Model', *Journal of Curriculum Studies* 384: 483–98.

John considers the role of lesson planning in Initial Teacher Education. He raises interesting points related to a range of models of lesson planning and focuses on the importance of dialogue in planning for student teacher development.

Newton, D.P. and Newton, L.D. (2009) 'Knowledge Development at the Time of Use: A Problem-based Approach to Lesson Planning in Primary Teacher Training in a Low Knowledge, Low Skill Context', *Educational Studies* 353: 311–21.

Nottingham, J. (2013) *Encouraging Learning*. Abingdon: Routledge.
This book is a key text for supporting the development of your personal philosophy of planning. It is research based and begins from the focus of what is important … the learning and the individual child.

Terhart, E. (2011) 'Has John Hattie Really Found the Holy Grail of Research on Teaching? An Extended Review of Visible Learning', *Journal of Curriculum Studies* 433: 425–38.
A review of the research of John Hattie, this article is both interesting and provides a challenge to consider multiple perspectives on any one area of research.

References

Alexander, R. (2010) *Children, their World, their Education: Final Report and Recommendations of the Cambridge Primary Review*. London: Routledge.

Barnes, J. (2007) *Cross-Curricular Learning 3–14*. London: Sage Publications.

Barnes, J. (2011) *Cross-Curricular Learning 3–14,* 2nd edn. London: Sage Publications.

Biggs, J.B.(2003) *Teaching for Quality Learning at University: What the Student Does*. Society for Research into Higher Education, Buckingham: HRE and Open University Press.

Department for Children, Schools and Families (DCSF) (2009) *Independent Review of the Primary Curriculum,* available at: www. webarchive national archives. gov.uk

Department for Education (DfE) (2013a) *Teachers' Standards*, available at: http://www.education.gov.uk/

DfE (2013b) *National Curriculum*, available at: www.education.gov.uk

Hattie, J. (2012) *Visible Learning for Teachers*. Abingdon: Routledge.

John, P.D. (2006) 'Lesson Planning and the Student Teacher: Re-thinking the Dominant Model, *Journal of Curriculum Studies* 384: 483–98.

Mantle of the expert, available at: http://www.mantleoftheexpert.com

National Centre for Excellence in the Teaching of Mathematics: https://www.ncetm.org.uk/resources/21510

National Curriculum Framework document, available at: https://www.education.gov.uk/consultations/downloadableDocs/NC%20framework%20document.pdf (accessed 10.07.13).

Nottingham, J. (2013) *Encouraging Learning*. Abingdon: Routledge.

Obama, B. (2013) 'State of the Union Address', available at: http://www.whitehouse.gov/sites/default/files/uploads/sotu_2013_blueprint.pdf (accessed 03.07.13).

Pollard, A. (2008) *Reflective Teaching*, 3rd edn. London: Continuum.

QCDA (2010) *The National Primary Curriculum Handbook*. London: QCDA.

Rowley, C. and Cooper, H. (eds) (2009) *Cross-Curricular Approaches to Teaching and Learning*. London: Sage Publications.

Wearmouth, J. (2009) *A Beginning Teacher's Guide to Special Educational Needs*. Maidenhead: Open University Press.

CHAPTER 4

MONITORING, ASSESSMENT AND RECORD KEEPING

Kim Harris and Suzanne Lowe

By the end of this chapter, you should be able to:

- make assessment choices and decisions with confidence
- use a wide range of assessment strategies to inform future planning, develop learning and independence
- understand the wider implications of assessment within primary education contexts.

Introduction

In the new National Curriculum (DfE 2013b), set levels of attainment are removed to allow schools to develop their own curriculum assessment strategy. The government plan is to allow schools more flexibility to meet the needs of their pupils and to discourage teachers from focusing on narrow attainment bands rather than children's broader educational progress. In future, schools will continue to benchmark their performance through statutory end of Key Stage assessments, including

National Curriculum tests, but will not continue to use the attainment levels from the previous National Curriculum document. Schools will also be able to develop their own approaches to formative assessment. There are challenges and opportunities related to this development but certainly school teams will need to engage in curriculum and assessment development in a way that they have not previously needed to (http://www.education.gov.uk/a00225864/assessing-without-levels).

The previous chapter on planning outlined the importance of using assessment to inform future planning. This chapter explores ways in which this may be done in the more flexible context of the 2014 National Curriculum assessment strategy.

Why assess?

Skilful assessment linked to learning is essential to effective teaching throughout Foundation Stage and the Key Stages. The central purpose of assessment is 'to promote good progress and outcomes for pupils' and, as a teacher, it is you who is accountable for 'their attainment, progress and outcomes' (Standard 2, DfE 2013a). Assessment is an integral part of teaching and learning but tends to be one of the most difficult areas for student teachers to master. By assessing children we aim to construct a bridge between teaching and learning in order to enable children to progress. When we assess children we need to use professional judgement, but this must be informed by evidence.

Selecting types of assessment for different audiences and purposes

There are several different types of assessment which are used for different purposes and for different audiences and it is the teacher's job to decide which assessment tool to use in any given context. Standard 6 (DfE 2013a) refers to 'making accurate and productive use of assessment'.

Assessment contributes to and derives from effective planning. Any activities planned for children should be assessed either formally or informally in order to support and extend children's learning. Different types of assessment each have different advantages and disadvantages. It is important to consider who the assessment is for and this will inform the type of assessment chosen.

Is the assessment for:

- the children, to inform their future learning? Comments need to be age-appropriate and shared in a format that the children can understand, such as annotating their work or giving verbal feedback.
- parents, to let them know how their children are doing? This will probably be in the form of a written report but could also be verbal when appropriate. There is a legal requirement for an annual written report for parents but many schools supply more. Parents' evenings or open days are a good opportunity for verbal

reporting. There is often informal feedback given to parents at the end of the school day, particularly for younger children.

- yourself, the class teacher, to inform your future planning, to inform reporting to parents, to identify specific difficulties in individual children, to support SEN provision? This could take a variety of formats although most schools have an assessment policy that will stipulate the minimum requirements expected and also outline strategies for best practice. You may want to support this by developing your own individual records in an indexed file of some description.
- the school – to meet the requirements of the School Improvement Plan (SIP) and School Development Plan.
- government agencies, for statistical information, for example Statutory Assessment Tasks.

The planning, teaching and assessment cycle

Regardless of the assessment strategy adopted by schools, a clear connection between planning, teaching, assessment and recording is essential in order to effectively manage and extend children's learning. Figure 4.1 outlines the planning,

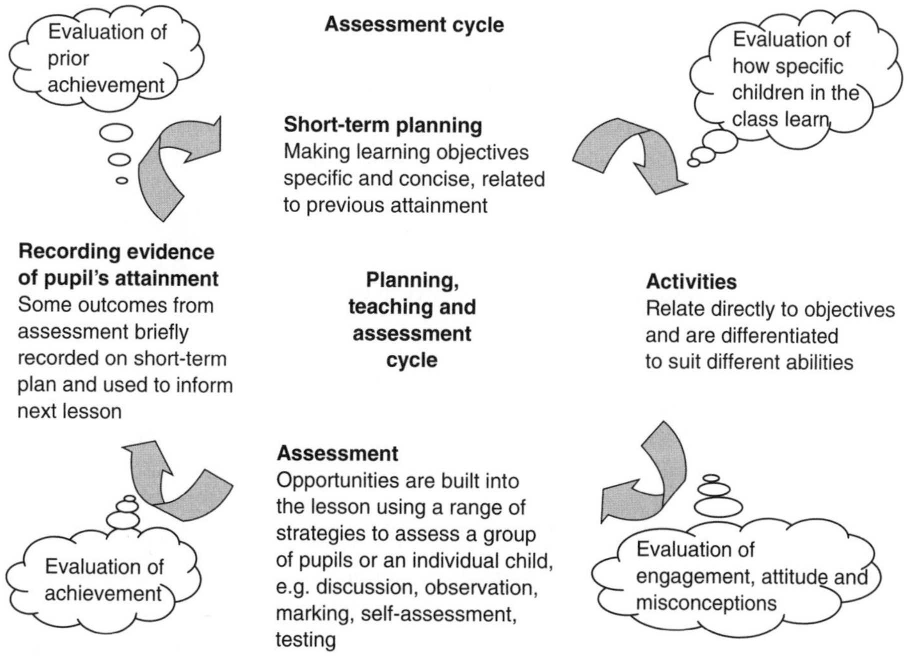

Figure 4.1 The assessment cycle, with an explanation of how the key parts of the planned lesson fit together

teaching and assessment cycle at the heart of effective teaching. Good planning for children's individual needs is dependent on knowing 'where they are' so that challenge can be incorporated into activities alongside appropriate scaffolding. Therefore, accurate and detailed assessment and recording is a key element of good teaching in order to identify next steps in learning, misconceptions to be addressed and effective differentiation. Linking teaching to an on-going cycle of learning and assessment is an effective way of implementing Standard 6 (DfE 2013a), which states that teachers must 'use relevant data to monitor progress, set targets and plan subsequent lessons'.

Summative assessment

Standard 6 (DfE 2013a) requires teachers to make 'summative assessments to secure pupils' progress'. Assessment at the end of a theme, topic or unit of work is generally summative, giving an indication of how much the child has learned through studying that area. This form of quantitative data can be used to produce evidence that children have been working at a particular level or can help to identify individual or group difficulties within the class. Records could include tick sheets linked to learning objectives, multiple-choice tests or grouping children according to guiding statements, for example: 'Some children/most children/a few children will...' and highlighting children's names.

For children in the Early Years Foundation Stage summative assessment is in the form of Early Learning Goals, which is a set of criteria to be reached by the end of the Foundation Stage of schooling. The record for each child is kept in the Foundation Stage Profile.

Summative assessment through standard assessment tasks

The Teachers' Standard 6 (DfE 2013a) requires teachers 'to know and understand how to assess using statutory assessments requirements'. Since 1991 national summative assessments (Standard Assessment Tasks) have taken place at the end of Key Stages 1 and 2 in England and Wales. They have been adapted and updated over time. Currently at KS1 these tests are not formal and are assessed by class teachers. The KS2 SATs, however, are still formal written tests and are externally marked, although this continues to be a subject of contention for many educationalists. The results (products) reported to schools, Local Authorities and parents form league tables which are published by the government every year and are used as part of the Ofsted process to measure the efficacy of teaching and learning in schools. As there is a level of accountability through this process, many children, parents and teachers can feel an unnecessary degree of 'stress'. A search of the internet will quickly show that there are numerous websites aimed at parents and devoted to strategies for relieving SATs stress for children in Year 6.

The SATs in England are currently limited to the curricular areas of Literacy and Numeracy. Alexander (2010 p. 498) believes that:

> While the assessment of literacy and numeracy is essential, a broader, more innovative approach to summative assessment is needed if children's achievements and attainments across the curriculum are to be properly recognised and parents, teachers and children themselves are to have the vital information they need to guide subsequent decisions and choices.

Arguments against national standardised assessments include the view that they can be interpreted as identifying weak or ineffective teaching rather than supporting children's learning. There is a further limitation associated with externally marked summative assessments in that they are dependent upon pencil and paper methods of assessing which therefore focus on a child's literacy ability rather than being a true reflection of the child's ability in the subject under test. The questions that can be asked in this form of testing and external marking may lead to narrow answers limited to factual knowledge or short answers which need good examination technique to complete well.

Other criticisms suggest that testing on a particular day can disadvantage children who are ill or have had some sort of upset that affected their performance at a specific time. In this case formative assessment is essential in order to develop an overview of each child over a longer period of time. Many secondary schools throughout England carry out further testing for Year 7 children, which they claim gives a more accurate understanding of the children's ability than the SATs. Perhaps one solution is to make several wider-stroke summative assessments across the broad curriculum, at the end of a topic or unit of study, either as a result of cumulative formative assessments or by assessing a product resulting from the topic or unit – for example, by making a summative statement about a book or file of work on the topic, a piece of drama which has drawn on what is learned in a history topic, a series of art works using different techniques, or a musical composition resulting from a sequence of lessons. A further consideration when assessing is how a teacher can assess a child's enjoyment of or attitude to a piece of art or music, dance or drama. It is possible through observation and discussion to understand how much a child is enjoying what they are learning and their attitude to it; self- or peer-evaluations of work by children can also give an insight. This is an area where formative assessment is a valuable source of information.

Statutory assessment arrangements in Scotland and Wales

It is important to mention here that since devolution there are differences in the statutory assessment arrangements in England, Scotland and Wales. Schools in Scotland follow the 'Curriculum for Excellence' which 'aims to achieve a transformation in education in Scotland by providing a coherent, more flexible and enriched curriculum from 3 to 18' (http://www.educationscotland.gov.uk/thecurriculum/whatiscurriculumforexcellence/index.asp).

Assessment in Scottish primary schools is carried out continuously throughout a child's schooling at appropriate times, which are identified and managed by the teacher, according to individual needs. Scottish teachers are supported by a new national resource – the National Assessment Resource (NAR) – which provides examples to ensure consistent standards and illustrations of children's work to clarify expectations at each level (http://www.educationscotland.gov.uk/Images/AssessmentforCfE_tcm4-565505.pdf).

In Wales the curriculum is organised into Foundation Phase 3 – 7, Key Stage 2 and Key Stage 3/4. Statutory assessment is carried out in Key Stage 2 but it is in the form of Teacher Assessment and there are resources available to support teachers in their judgements (http://wales.gov.uk/docs/dcells/publications/100511assessment714en.pdf).

In England Assessing Pupil's Progress (APP) is a similar initiative to that used in Scotland, and in some instances can be used to bridge the gap between summative and formative assessment, but it has never been introduced as a statutory requirement. Schools can choose to use APP to support their assessment and moderation, however this may be more difficult to do in future with the abolition of Attainment Levels and the expectation of increased autonomy in schools regarding assessment processes and procedures.

Diagnostic assessment

Diagnostic assessment is a useful tool when it is necessary to find out what children already know before starting a new topic, for example: 'What do you know about forces?' This could be done through a spider diagram, either individually or in small groups. Children can then develop their diagram and this can be assessed to enable the teacher to know at what point in the topic to begin teaching and in order to support appropriate progression for different abilities. This form of assessment can also help to identify children who have particular strengths due to external influences. Many children have extensive knowledge of a variety of different subjects such as science, music, art, geography or history because of the interests or occupations of their parents. Alternatively, this form of assessment could be used to identify specific difficulties that individual children are experiencing in order to develop a teaching strategy to ensure appropriate progress is made. Diagnostic assessment can also be used to identify individual Special Educational Needs, but in this case the focus is on identifying strengths and weaknesses rather than previous knowledge.

Formative assessment

Standard 6 (DfE 2013a) also states that teachers must make 'formative assessments to secure pupils' progress'. Formative assessment has been shown to be most valuable for children's learning because of its potential to empower each learner to recognise where they are in their learning, where they need to go next and how they are going to get there. This type of on-going and in the moment assessment provides a broad overview of a child's achievement over a period of time. It generally focuses on the whole child and includes both academic and pastoral aspects, enabling teachers to identify children's personal interests and ways of learning. Formative assessment 'is not a test or a tool but a process with the potential to support learning beyond school years by developing learning strategies which individuals may rely on across their entire life-span' (Clark 2012 p. 217). Recording methods include observation, questioning, pieces of work, self-assessment, peer-assessment or a combination of these.

Standard 6 (DfE 2013a) states that teachers must 'give pupils regular feedback, both orally and through accurate marking and encourage pupils to respond to the feedback'. However, effective formative assessment is very much dependent on the interactions and emotional connections between the teacher and the children and the children and their peers. Hargreaves (2013) discusses the importance of relationships between teachers and pupils concluding that if children are to be encouraged towards autonomous learning both they and their teachers must learn to spend much time reflecting and talking together. The crucial message here is that teachers need to have an excellent understanding of their pupils, both personally and academically, to ensure that they are motivated and appropriately challenged in order to progress in their learning. Black and Wiliam (1998) state that 'the dialogue between pupils and a teacher should be thoughtful, reflective, focused to evoke and explore understanding, and conducted so that all pupils have an opportunity to think and express their ideas' (Black and Wiliam 1998 p. 144). A key difference from other forms of assessment is the engagement of the children with the assessment process. Harrison and Howard (2009) emphasise this point by saying that 'What is paramount in this process is the children realising that their thinking is valued by their teacher, so that they are encouraged to discuss their understanding and misunderstandings openly' (Harrison and Howard 2009 p. 9). Learning is an emotive business, which concerns the whole child and centres around self-esteem and the ability to take risks. Assessment is about teachers noticing minute shifts in children's conceptual understanding by listening carefully to their responses, using their observations to inform and enhance planned learning opportunities and ensuring that the impact of this process is the children's ability to recognise their development within a nurturing environment, celebrate their individual achievements, and identify next goals for themselves as they become self-regulatory.

Reflective task

Consider the relationships and ethos of your classroom:

- How does the teacher encourage the children to take risks and learn from their mistakes?
- What assessment strategies support this?
- How can you incorporate these ideas into your planning?

Collecting evidence for assessments

A further consideration is the need for 'evidence' in assessment to support the teacher's judgements and to show any interested parties how these were reached. Being able to balance this with fair and varied assessment methods which promote learning is a significant skill. Assessment methods for formative assessment use can include: observations, questioning, peer- or self-assessment against known criteria, discussion, poster creation and concept maps (some are more appropriate at different ages).

But significantly, it is the feedback that is received that helps children know what they need to do next, this requires active engagement by the child in their own learning.

Feedback and assessment for learning

Black and Wiliam's (1998) research into assessment led to the development of 'Assessment for Learning' (AfL). Figure 4.2 shows the key principles of assessment for learning.

Black and Wiliam found that the use of strategies including sustained and relevant feedback, and peer- and self-assessment improved the learning of the pupils involved. Feedback should be kept separate from grades or levels because most children will simply take note of their level but not necessarily read the accompanying feedback to improve their work further. In order to develop children's independent learning strategies, teachers must share specific information about their work in such a way

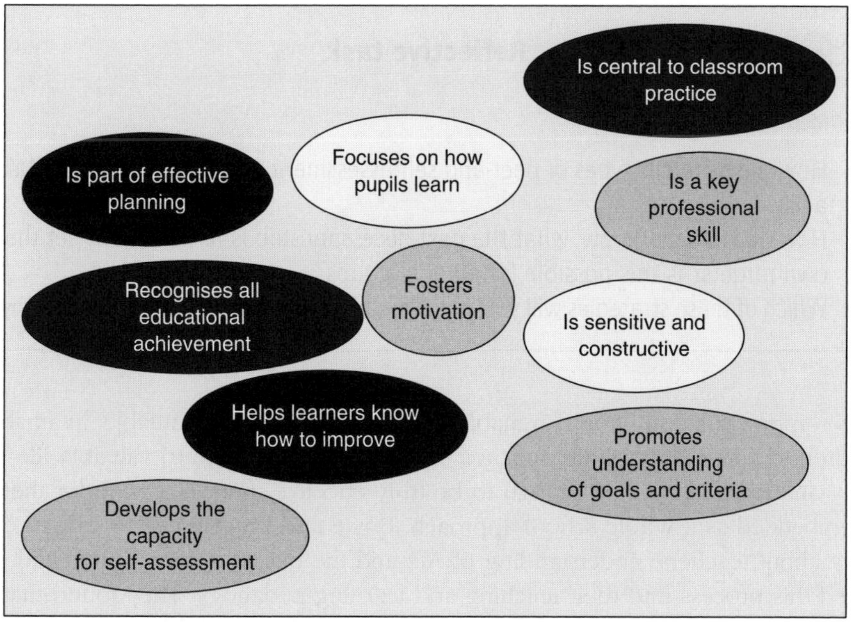

Figure 4.2 Assessment for learning principles

that they know what they need to do to improve. By implementing developmental marking strategies, teachers can change the ethos of their classrooms into communities of learning where everyone feels valued and able to learn at their own pace. Marking is not done so that teachers can tell children what they have done right or wrong, it should be for their benefit so that they understand how they can improve.

The Department for Children, Schools and Families National Strategies documentation (2008) promotes the use of AfL in schools but also includes grades. This is an example of a focus on the product of learning (summative) rather than the process of learning (formative), and as such gave a confused message to teachers about what was expected of formative assessment.

Platforms for children to use self-assessment could include:

- whole-class discussions
- one-to-one reviews
- paired comments
- choosing a question to respond to
- writing/responding at the end of a piece of work
- pupils doing the first marking – either peer or self
- writing self-evaluative logs and journals.

Reflective task

Consider in the classroom:

- How the different types of peer-and self-assessment strategies are used. Make a list.
- How do children 'know' what the next necessary step is to accurately set their own targets? Is this possible for all age groups?
- Which of these strategies will you use when planning your own lessons and why?

These approaches, although arguably time-consuming, are valuable in enabling children to take responsibility for their own learning and lead to valuable life-long study and learning skills, although to be truly effective there is a need for them to be embedded as a whole-school approach. Boyle and Charles (2010) carried out a study about teachers' understanding of AfL and the extent to which they had integrated this process into their teaching and learning pedagogy. They found that the majority of teachers stated that they used AfL to enhance children's learning, but actually there was no shared vision of AfL practice and no shared definition for its use in the classroom. A key motivator for the lack of precision in implementing AfL was found to be the frameworks that teachers used to support planning, for example the National Curriculum and SATs, which had the effect of reducing the teachers' role to that of technicians following pre-set teaching and learning patterns rather than starting from a child-centred position.

AfL and differentiation

Using AfL to support differentiation and personalised learning was found to have the greatest impact on children's learning and effective planning and teaching. Therefore, to effectively implement AfL schools would need to develop a shared understanding of AfL processes and procedures in their particular context, moderate frequently across ages and phases to make sure that professional judgements and attainment were shared, and use appropriate whole-school record keeping systems to enable progression to be monitored throughout the year.

As we improve our understanding of how learning happens through research, literature and professional dialogues, for example, how we teach to facilitate that learning also changes. Standard 8 (DfE 2013a) recognises the importance of developing 'effective relationships with colleagues, knowing how and when to draw on advice and support'. Black and Wiliam's work shows that AfL works best when children begin to self-assess efficiently and engagement with learning increases. This could be considered to be as a result of a deconstruction of the 'mystique' surrounding teaching and a more transparent consideration of teaching and learning skills. Children no longer simply 'receive knowledge' in the form of facts to be memorised, as in Victorian schooling and rote methods. Skills are not taught only as though one method is correct, for example in handwriting or in strategies in mathematics.

Questioning

Questioning should not be used only as a pedagogical tool but also as a deliberate way for the teacher to find out what students know, understand and are able to do. Good questioning should cause children to think but is also a valuable method to find out what children know in order to inform your planning.

Questioning from the teacher can be 'open', where the pupil can give explanation and detail in the answer, or 'closed', when the expected response is generally limited to factual knowledge and is correct or incorrect. Questions can be targeted towards specific children or groups during a lesson for the teacher to assess ongoing understanding and engagement or can be used at the start or end of a lesson to review learning and check for misconceptions. There is a further level of questioning which needs flexibility in planning and this involves 'enquiry-based learning', with questions generated by children. Often these questions will suggest areas for research or discovery, or children asking questions for clarification indicates when they are motivated and engaged in the tasks at hand. This may originate with something they have learned during the lesson or outside school. It can be difficult to assess imagination and enquiry, yet these are key skills within society and should be encouraged. Good subject knowledge is essential to support learning, however children often do not need to be told the answer to their questions, they need to be taught how to find the answer and how to weigh the validity of the answers they have found. In order to extend children's ability to debate and discuss, it is sometimes good to use a statement to engage their interest rather than a question, for example 'Woodlice only eat wood'. Children then would need to find a way to prove or disprove the statement. It is important to be specific when replying to children's answers to your questions; don't just move on, but probe for a deeper engagement with the misconception. Why did they think that? Good questioning means there is less opportunity for children to get it right by accident. Teachers need to plan questions in advance and give children time to answer before intervening. Children do not need to be right all of the time to learn but they do need to have opportunities to learn from their mistakes and this should ideally be through discussion and collaboration with their teacher.

New Bloom's Taxonomy (Figure 4.3) clearly shows the hierarchy of questioning language from remembering to creating. The original Bloom's Taxonomy (1956) was

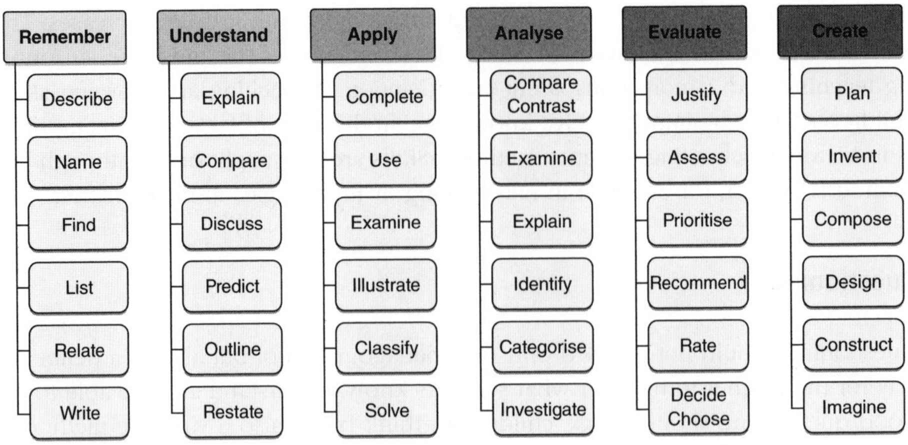

Figure 4.3 New Bloom's Taxonomy (http://maasd.edublogs.org/files/2012/04/BloomsVerbs-24dwzts.png)

devised to be a tool to support the development of exam questions but has changed over time to become a much more useful instrument because of the use of verbs. Try to devise questions that enable children to be challenged and engaged rather than simply remembering facts. Use the table below to devise learning outcomes, success criteria and questions for children of different abilities around the same theme or topic.

Reflective task

- Choose a subject or topic you will be teaching. Use Figure 4.3 to design learning objectives and set related success criteria at different levels.
- Compose some questions that you could ask to assess what children know, can do and understand related to the topic.

Transference of skills, knowledge, understanding and personal development

Teachers need to engage in ongoing formative assessment to allow and encourage transference of knowledge and skills across subjects and topic areas to enhance children's development of skills, knowledge and understanding. For example, children collaborating in a music activity not only learn about music but they are also learning to collaborate and are developing social skills. These skills are generic and transferable into other areas of the curriculum and crucial to their future success as adults. So teachers need to be aware of the attainment of each child not only in skills, knowledge and understanding across the curriculum domains but also in relation to their personal development. This will enable best practice when planning is employed as a holistic approach to each child's strengths and areas for development; it will help promote a more cohesive classroom environment, thus further promoting learning and enabling children to reach their potential. Consider being more creative with assessment tasks, especially when teaching cross-curricular topics. Transferring knowledge into different contexts consolidates learning and enables children to apply what they already know. Sometimes, rather than starting the lesson with a learning objective, teach the lesson and then ask the children to tell you what the objective was. This will allow you to see if the children have learned what you intended and how effective the lesson was.

Differentiation

Effective differentiation is a key outcome of formative assessment whereby the teacher can create appropriate activities for all groups of learners at their own level and stage of ability. This is related to Standard 5 (DfE 2013a) which focuses on the need to 'adapt teaching to the strengths and needs of pupils, knowing when and how to differentiate properly, using approaches which enable children to learn effectively'. Differentiation is often planned as an extension task, an open-ended activity where children are assessed by outcome, or more of the same activity, which some children can feel is a punishment rather than an acknowledgement that they have achieved what was required of them. Good differentiation is derived from effective formative assessment so that tasks can be set for children that challenge and extend their learning, creating a motivated and inspired classroom environment. If teachers do not have an in-depth understanding of the abilities of the children in their class, they cannot plan appropriate activities to enable appropriate progression.

Vygotsky (1978) developed the idea of a 'Zone of Proximal Development' which identifies the gap between what children can do alone and what they are able to do with support from an adult or peer. By differentiating appropriately, teachers can access this learning opportunity by grouping children or deploying teaching assistants effectively to provide the optimum environment for learning.

Another challenge when considering differentiation is that many teachers ability-group their children for Literacy and Numeracy but keep the same groups for other subjects. This means that children who may have particular strengths in art but have difficulty in literacy, for example, may be working within art at a level where they are not challenged or motivated because of this mismatch of activity. Gardner's

(1993, 1999) work on multiple intelligences suggests that there are nine different types of intelligence; it is the job of the teacher to notice what children are enthused by so that they can plan lessons to develop those interests.

Personalised learning/autonomous learning/active learning/ self-regulated learning

All of the above terms relate to an aspiration for children to be able to take ownership of their learning by developing a deep understanding of their strengths and areas for development through shared learning objectives and target setting in collaboration with their teacher.

To what extent can children's learning be personalised when you have a class of 30? Ideally this can be achieved through assessment by developing autonomous learning strategies whereby children actively participate in their learning. Is it possible for children to be part of the decision-making process about what they will learn and how they will do it? It is possible to begin a new topic, for example 'the Egyptians', by asking the children what they would like to know, drawing up a list and allocating roles and responsibilities, but would this work for all subjects and topics? Clark (2012) argues that 'In the formative classroom, tacit knowledge is made explicit and accessible through active participation and mutual discourse' (p. 209). In some classrooms there is an expectation that children will learn simply by 'doing' without having the opportunity to unpack what that learning means or where it links to existing knowledge and understanding. To develop effective learning approaches, children need to know where they are going (this is usually through specific learning outcomes), how they are doing, which links specifically to monitoring and assessment criteria, and lastly what the next steps would be. Using success criteria is an important way to help children to know what you are looking for and what they are working towards. Children learn best when they are intrinsically motivated because they have an interest in the topic being studied. In early years classrooms there is a free-flow ethos whereby children move from activity to activity both inside and outside the classroom, seemingly as they wish, but is this type of classroom organisation appropriate for all age groups? Early years assessments are often made on Post-it notes using observations from teachers and teaching assistants of individual children. To what extent could this method of assessment be applied to KS1 and KS2 classrooms? These are questions which perplex and intrigue all teachers and certainly with the introduction of the new National Curriculum in England and the changes in assessment strategy it would seem that schools and teachers will be able to devise curricula and assessment strategies suitable for the needs of their pupils. Schools will be able to experiment and employ new methods, especially if they have Academy or Free School status as they do not need to adhere to the National Curriculum at all.

Reflective task

- To what extent do you believe that the notion of personalised or autonomous learning fits into your personal philosophy of teaching and learning?
- How will this manifest itself in your work in the classroom?
- To what extent do you believe personalised learning can be applied to the primary classroom?

Formative assessment throughout each lesson

Ongoing evaluation of the learning *throughout a lesson* is vital. The use of questioning and observation to collate an accurate picture of children's (or a child's) depth of understanding related to the learning outcomes will be needed to inform your teaching. This could be through adding a mini-plenary to redirect or extend the class's learning, through specific questioning or teaching to correct a misconception, or through adding a resource to support learning, to name a few actions you may need to take.

Good lesson planning based on accurate assessment and evaluations, coupled with secure subject knowledge, is necessary to facilitate effective learning. These foundations allow the teacher to be flexible in response to the needs of the children and to have confidence in a range of teaching strategies that are best suited to the group of children being taught. Teaching a well-structured lesson and reflecting systematically on how effective the lesson and approaches to teaching it were is an essential aspect of effective formative assessment, as stated in Standard 4 (DfE 2013a).

Work in school

Student 1: How do I know what is appropriate for children of different ages?

Mentor: The National Curriculum in England Framework Document (DfE 2013b) outlines, in the statutory guidance for the programmes of study, the areas children will be learning about in each year, in English, mathematics and science. In other subjects there is subject content, knowledge and skills and Attainment Targets for each Key Stage. This will be the starting point for schools to devise an assessment grid (rubric) for staff to use. The planning ILOs will be aligned with the assessment and so should all be age-appropriate.

(Continued)

(Continued)

One thing to consider though is that some children may be working above, or below, the nominal age for the subject you are assessing. These children should have the work appropriately differentiated and be assessed against the ILOs set for this work.

This comes through practice by assessing more and more work, and also by speaking to experienced teachers about it, as well as attending assessment tutorials on placements, or moderation meetings with other staff.

Student 2: When using APP how do I decide whether children meet the criteria sufficiently or not?

Mentor: Assessing Pupils' Progress (APP) is becoming less common. However, the key component of the question is about children meeting the criteria of whatever assessment system is used. Again, this comes with practice and is actually linked with devising accurate success criteria with the children and ensuring alignment of the assessment with the ILOs for the lesson.

Many schools choose to design and use assessment grids or rubrics specific to the needs of classes or individuals in their school as identified through analysis of past assessment. The most effective assessment grids will be designed through teacher collaboration and will involve the concept of a continuum which will show progression for the individual and allow for monitoring of this. Effective assessment grids will address the breadth of learning and account for different foci, in a similar way to APP. The continuous sampling of work showing a child's meeting of the range of skills, knowledge and their understanding will develop an extensive evidenced picture of the child's progression. This can then be used to show parents, or other stakeholders, perhaps governors, or Ofsted.

Assessment grids which are created through collaboration promote the sharing of expertise and experience across the school staff team. In line with the research of Hattie (2012) for promoting effective learning, it allows for moderation and a shared understanding of expectations, and standards and has a quality assurance base. Assessment grids based on success criteria and the input of the children also promote high expectations, as all staff and children know the incremental steps for improvement, and thus can be used for self-, peer- and teacher-assessment.

Sometimes illustrated rubrics, particularly in cross-curricular work, are very useful in allowing children to see what the next increment 'looks like' and can therefore promote self-regulation and challenge setting for children.

Student 3: How do I find time and maintain consistency?
Mentor: Useful strategies include:

- using Post-it notes, or a small notebook, to jot down your observations through the day's lessons
- using photographs to supply evidence – especially for P-level students
- using teaching assistants' notes alongside your own notes to gather evidence
- moderating regularly until you are confident you are in line with the other staff when you make a judgement. Then have regular moderation meetings to ensure parity and maintain quality assurance
- making effective use of self- and peer-assessment, based on children understanding the success criteria
- remembering that assessment is a dialogue between child and teacher. It is not simply a question of identifying what is correct or incorrect, but rather identifying next steps.

There is no need for the teacher to assess every child in every lesson, however you should ensure you make brief notes related to which children have exceeded, or not met, the ILOs to inform your planning for any following lessons so you can plan for the appropriate level of challenge.

Student 4: What kind of records should I keep?
Mentor: This is very much related to the record keeping and tracking systems that your school uses, although many teachers also keep their own records for their personal use.

The simplest form of recording is a tick sheet with children's names down one side and the learning objectives or success criteria across the top. This is a quick way to assess the whole class but doesn't always give you much information about what the children were thinking or their learning processes. Using a triangle icon – one line shows they were there, the second shows they completed the task, the third shows they understood it – or using a red/amber/green coding system is a more sophisticated way of tracking achievement because it can be updated over time.

(Continued)

(Continued)

Many teachers add an extra box at the end or down the side of their lesson plans so that they can record particular children's responses throughout the lesson and use this to adapt future planning. An additional way to record children's achievement throughout the lesson is to ask the teaching assistant to make records about the children that they work with. If this strategy is to work effectively, it is important that you spend time with the teaching assistant before the lesson, explaining what the learning outcomes are and what kind of comments you would like – 'good work!' will not tell you anything about the child's achievement.

You could stick a grid to the inside front cover of each child's exercise book, allowing spaces for the date, activity, learning objective or success criteria and a section for formative comments and next steps/targets to be addressed next time.

An index box or an Excel file on the computer would enable you to make informal notes relating to pastoral matters, such as personal issues, particular interests or additional information about the children which could have a bearing on their learning. Make sure that this is confidential and kept securely if it contains sensitive information. When you are writing reports, this type of information is invaluable to demonstrate to parents that you know their children well because you know what interests them and what their particular passions are.

These are just a few ideas; there are many more but the important point is that assessment should be informative, manageable, ongoing and specific in order to be effective.

Assessing the concepts, methods of enquiry, knowledge and understanding of each subject

We said in our introduction that there are challenges and opportunities related to assessment in the 2014 National Curriculum and that schools will need to engage in curriculum and assessment development in ways they have not previously needed to. For the core subjects – English, mathematics and science – there is non-statutory guidance on what a pattern of progression in learning might be, but in other subjects assessment is based on 'knowing, applying and understanding the matters, skills and processes specified in the programme of study'. In some ways this is liberating; it has been argued that progression in the skills of historical enquiry or in art, for example, are too complex, dependent on variables and lacking in research-based evidence to define. However, given the limited subject knowledge, due to time constraints, that it has been possible to acquire through teacher training in recent years, and with no likely improvement in this situation, it is arguable whether teachers will feel confident to plan for progression in thinking across the curriculum.

Summary

One of the challenges in writing this and the previous chapter is the integrated nature of planning and assessment. We have tried to show how good planning is based on meaningful assessment and that accurate assessment comes through good planning. To avoid confusion, we have perhaps reinforced the separation of the two areas in your mind, although we believe assessment and planning to be intricately linked. Certainly, if you look at the Teachers' Standards that assessment is related to at the beginning of the chapter, you will begin to realise how it permeates through all teaching and learning activities.

The complexity of planning and assessment practice is linked to the discussion we had earlier on kinds of knowledge. You can know the facts of what and how to do it, you can know the sequence, but effective planning and assessment will only come when you have reached the point of 'conditional knowledge', allowing you to make informed judgements. What is important is that you become an expert on the children that you teach so that you can make a real difference to their education, aspirations and ultimately their future careers.

The following chapter will show the importance of classroom organisation and the learning environment in promoting children's learning.

Questions for discussion

- In Chapter 3 we asked you to consider your own philosophy of learning and teaching and how this may impact upon your planning. Now consider how this will impact on your assessment methods. Discuss with your colleagues.
- How does the creativity agenda fit with planning and assessment? How can you be creative in a subject-based curriculum? Is teaching in this way more or less 'creative' than teaching through themes?

Further reading

Alexander, R. (2010) *Children, their World, their Education*. London: Routledge.
Chapter 16 gives a thorough overview of assessment practices in primary schools. Pages 83–84 highlight some of the complexities involved in the homework debate.

Goodhew, G. (2005) *Meeting the Needs of Gifted and Talented Students*. London: Network Continuum.
For ITE generalist students and educators this is a useful resource focusing on an aspect of inclusive practice termed 'a bit of a Cinderella' by Goodhew in the introduction. From the necessary discussion relating to the difficulty in coming to a definitive definition of the terms 'gifted', 'talented' and 'exceptionally able', Goodhew uses a variety of sources to develop shared understanding for the purpose of the book, examining a variety of perspectives. Perhaps the most relevant chapter in relation to planning and assessment is Chapter 4 which discusses classroom practices.

Jacques, K. and Hyland, R. (2007) *Professional Studies: Primary and Early Years*, 3rd edn. Exeter: Learning Matters.
Many chapters of this accessible book will support and extend your developing understanding of planning and assessment practices, especially Chapters 2–4 and 14.

Johnson, S. (2012) *Assessing Learning in the Primary Classroom*. Abingdon: Routledge.
This book gives a very good overview of assessment including statutory assessment, recording and reporting and how this links to international perspectives.

Martin, D. (2012) 'Rich Assessment in a First-Year Teacher Education (Primary) Mathematics Education Subject', *International Journal of Pedagogies and Learning* 7(1): 62–72.
This paper demonstrates rich and cohesive learning and teaching, linking practical and theoretical work to build a strong base of understanding. Student teachers are introduced to a range of assessment activities and to their role in implementing them.

Murphy, C., Lundy, L., Emerson, L. and Kert, K. (2013) 'Children's Perceptions of Primary Science Assessment in England and Wales', *British Educational Research Journal* 39(3): 585–606.
This study is based on a survey of 1000 children as co-researchers. Most appreciated the usefulness of frequent monitoring and non-testing in science assessment. It demonstrates that including children's views can improve policy making.

References

Alexander, R. (2010) *Children, their World, their Education: Final Report and Recommendations of the Cambridge Primary Review.* London: Routledge.

Black, P.J. and Wiliam, D. (1998) *Inside the Black Box.* London: King's College London, School of Education.

Bloom, B.S. (ed.) with Englehart, M.D., Furst, E.J., Hill, W.H. and Krathwhol, D.R. (1956) *Taxonomy of Educational Objectives: The Classification of Educational Goals. Handbook 1: Cognitive Domain.* New York: David McKay.

Boyle, W.F. and Charles, M. (2010) 'Leading Learning through Assessment for Learning?', *School Leadership and Management: Formerly School Organisation* 30(3): 285–300.

Clark, I. (2012) 'Formative Assessment: Assessment is for Self-Regulated Learning', *Educational Psychology Review* 24: 205–49.

DfE (2013a) *Teachers' Standards* (DFE-00066-2011), available at: https://www.gov.uk

DfE (2013b) *The National Curriculum: A Framework*, available at: https://www.gov.uk

DfES (2004) *Primary National Strategy Part 4: Day to Day Assessment Strategies,* available at: http: www. lancsngfl.ac.uk/curriculum/assessment/getfile.php?stc=700/

Gardner, H. (1993) *Frames of Mind: The Theory of Multiple Intelligences*, 2nd edn. London: Fontana Press.

Gardner, H. (1999) *Intelligences Reframed: Multiple Intelligences for the 21st Century.* New York: Basic Books.

Hargreaves, E. (2013) 'Inquiring into Children's Experiences of Teacher Feedback: Reconceptualising Assessment for Learning', *Oxford Review of Education* 39(2): 229–46.

Harrison, C. and Howard, S. (2009) *Inside the Primary Black Box.* London: GL Assessment.

Hattie, J. (2012) *Visible Learning for Teachers.* Abingdon: Routledge.

Vygotsky, L. (1978) *Mind in Society: The Development of Higher Psychological Processes.* Cambridge, MA: Harvard University Press.

Websites

England

National Centre for Excellence in the Teaching of Mathematics: https://www.ncetm.org.uk/search?q=assessment

New Bloom's Taxonomy: http://maasd.edublogs.org/files/2012/04/BloomsVerbs-24dwzts.png

Assessing without Levels – DfE: http://www.education.gov.uk/a00225864/assessing-without-levels

Scotland

Assessment for Curriculum for Excellence: Strategic Vision, Key Principles: http://www.educationscotland.gov.uk/Images/AssessmentforCfE_tcm4-565505.pdf
Curriculum for Excellence: http://www.educationscotland.gov.uk/thecurriculum/whatiscurriculumforexcellence/index.asp

Wales

Making the Most of Assessment 7–14: http://wales.gov.uk/docs/dcells/publications/100511assessment714en.pdf

CHAPTER 5

CLASSROOM ORGANISATION AND THE LEARNING ENVIRONMENT

Jan Ashbridge and Jo Josephidou

By the end of this chapter, you should be able to:

- discuss the key factors to consider when providing for an appropriate learning environment
- consider how theory and research impact on how the learning environment is designed
- reflect critically on learning environments you have observed on placement and question assumed practice
- examine how your own values and attitudes as a teacher can impact on the learning environment and the children's learning.

Introduction

Teachers Standard 1 (DfE 2013) requires that teachers set up learning environments for their pupils which are safe, stimulating and rooted in mutual respect, where positive attitudes, values and behaviour are promoted. But learning environments are complex and creating them involves making many sensitive decisions. In the early years, practitioners will use the terminology 'Enabling Environment' to describe a learning environment where children feel safe, supported and able to work and play independently; an environment which Malaguzzi (1920–1994) would describe as 'a third teacher'. Malaguzzi took it for granted that 'the environment is the third educator, the other two being the teachers assigned to each group of children' (Smidt 2013 p. 100).

In some schools you have visited you may feel that children no longer have these learning needs once they enter Key Stage 1 and 2. This chapter will explore why the learning environment is so important, regardless of the age of the child. It begins by discussing a common classroom scenario in order to explore the reasons why learning environments are complex, significant and shaped by a teacher's personal educational philosophy. Constructivist learning theories are drawn on to suggest starting points for creating effective learning environments which promote independence, social skills, self-esteem, positive attitudes to learning and give children a sense of ownership of their environment.

Different perceptions of the learning environment

The child's voice

'It's in-time!'

Whistle goes and it's time to go into school but first I need to line up. If I'm really quick then I can get to the front. I make it in time but then Sally pushes ahead of me and stands on my toe. I dig her in the ribs with my elbow just as Mrs Jones is coming around the corner to collect us. Oh no, trouble again before I've even got into the classroom. I hate hanging my coat up because everyone pushes and the coat pegs are too near together. I get trampled on so I try to hang back until everyone else comes back. Trouble again, I'm late.

'It's register time!'

I sit on the carpet quickly but then I realise that my name has been put on the amber traffic light and I'm really worried. Am I going to miss playtime? If I sit really still and listen, Mrs Jones will put my name back on green but then I feel the cold, hard floor digging into my bottom and I realise that the Velcro on my left shoe has stuck to the carpet. I'm concentrating so hard on sitting still so the Velcro doesn't make a noise that I miss my name being called and I'm in trouble again.

'It's handwriting time'

Once register is finished it's handwriting time. I'm on the Yellow table. Books are ready in the middle of the table and the pencils are sharpened in the yellow pot. I try to get comfortable on my chair because I know I am not allowed to get up until the big hand is on the 6. Oh no, I should have gone for a wee when I was hanging my coat up. I know I have to look at the handwriting display and practise the letters on the yellow balloon. My teacher calls it being in-de-pen-dent. Red group have to practise the letters on the red balloon. Mrs Smith always comes to help Yellow table but she calls the letters different names to Mrs Jones and I get a bit confused. Rosemary gets a sticker because she is holding her pencil beautifully. Sometimes, near the holidays, we are allowed to play in the role-play area and with the sand and water. The holidays seem a long way off.

The teacher's voice

'Going into class'

The bell is about to go. Time to go and get the children in from the playground. You'd think by Year 2 they could make a straight line. Look at Sally, she's always at the front standing so smartly, having the maturity to ignore the little boy behind her who's trying to push in front. I'm so glad we line them up, it makes it so much easier. I have worked very hard on training the children to make them independent and most of them manage to sort themselves out quickly and come back to the classroom to sit quietly on the carpet. They know my expectations.

'Taking the register'

Simon is back 3 minutes after everyone else. I won't tell him off because I don't want to lower his self-esteem but I quietly get up and move his name from the green traffic light to the amber. The children sit beautifully for register and show really good listening. Everyone sitting still, all eyes towards me. I don't have to remind them, I just have to point to the good listening checklist on the wall.

'Handwriting practice'

It's good to start the morning off with handwriting because they can all get on with it quietly whilst I hear readers. To make sure they can be independent I have prepared all the resources and put them out ready on the table for the children. The activity is carefully differentiated and all children know what level they are working at. My colour-coding system works a treat. I have directed Mrs Smith to Yellow table today as they need an extra bit of input. Those who finish quickly will get 15 minutes to choose a free activity.

Reflective task

Read the above scenarios and note down the key themes and issues where mismatches in perceptions are apparent:

- What has the environment taught the child?
- What does the teacher believe the environment is teaching the child?
- How does the environment do this?

Use the grid below to observe and reflect on the way that children respond to the environment and routine in the classroom.

Aspect of the environment or routine	Possible teacher's intention	Impact on the child	Possible reason for response	Reflection

The importance of the learning environment

The learning environment is a complex and ever-changing place. It is a physical area with resources and furniture and has to fit in children and adults comfortably. It is an emotional environment too, where people form relationships, learn rules and develop attitudes, beliefs and values relating to themselves, each other and the world they live in. It is a place where children learn not only the curriculum but begin to understand their strengths, weaknesses and how they measure up to the others around them. Boundaries are set and particular behaviours are expected. It is not only where children learn but where children learn to learn. It is vital then to give much consideration to the way that it looks, feels and operates from a range of perspectives.

Organising the learning environment

The learning environment of the classroom is first and foremost a place where effective learning needs to take place. A key characteristic of this is where clear aims are agreed and teaching is purposeful. Theories of cognitive development tell us that for children to learn effectively they need to be actively involved in their learning: creating and constructing new knowledge in ways that are meaningful to them. It stands to reason, therefore, that the environment in which they are to do this must reflect their ways of learning and their individual needs. It must allow them to develop the skills they need to become independent learners and also to interact with the environment and resources, as well as with each other, in ways that make constructing knowledge purposeful and motivating. In order for this to happen, children need to be seen as central to the learning process, not only in planning but also in the creation, organisation and management of the learning environment.

The scenario

Let us take the scenario above and consider what the teacher was trying to achieve. She is aiming to make the children in her class as independent as possible. She has done this through ensuring that the children know what is expected of them, ensuring that all necessary resources are easily accessible and that carefully differentiated work is provided along with additional adult support for those who may need it. The children are able to complete the activity with the minimum of fuss and noise. She aims to make them aware that their behaviour affects others and that they should respect the right of those others to be able to get on quietly. The clear ability grouping and the associated classroom display support this. She has set the environment up to enable the children to be able to learn by themselves.

Constructivist theories, classroom organisation and the learning environment

Exploration and stimulating experiences

What do theories of cognitive development have to tell us about the learning environment and how can they shed light on what happens in the scenario above? If we take the work of Piaget, we can see that his influential ideas about children needing developmentally appropriate activities are reflected in many classrooms, especially in Foundation Stage and Key Stage 1, although the same principles, differently interpreted, apply in any primary classroom. Piaget believed that the environment and children's interactions with it and within it are the key to children's learning and it is through engagement and exploration of real, concrete experiences that they are able to learn and develop. Piaget felt it was important for children to have stimulating activities, opportunities for symbolic play and an environment to actively explore

(Daly et al. 2006). We can see that despite the teacher's good intentions, these opportunities are not offered and perhaps the learning needs of the children are not being met.

Social interaction and talk

Vygotsky focused more on the role of the adult in guiding children's learning. He also saw how important social interactions and language were to children's intellectual development. His work has influenced teachers and encouraged them to provide children with a challenging environment and activities. Such activities provide opportunities to work alongside adults and more knowledgeable others, including peers, to extend their understanding within the 'zone of proximal development'. More recent research has also stressed the importance of children developing effective communication skills with a broad cross-curricular vocabulary. This ability to articulate their thoughts helps them to make links in their learning and therefore their thinking (Daly et al. 2006).

Planning for exploration and talk

In the situation described above, although the children are grouped together, social interaction between the group or between groups is not encouraged; nor does the task given to the children encourage constructive talk. The way that teachers organise the physical environment (tables, chairs, etc.) sends out messages to the children about what kind of activities they are likely to be engaged in. Where children are all sitting looking at the front, they expect that the teacher will be talking to them and that they will be expected to focus their attention there and that any activity will probably be of an individual nature. When children are sitting around a table together, it appears that a more social and collaborative way of learning is expected and children will interact. It appears in the example above that there is a mismatch between the organisation of the classroom and the task given to the children. Social grouping is a valuable tool for teachers in supporting learning but it is very often used simply for convenience as a seating arrangement (Moyles 1992 p. 18). Conflicting messages such as this can be avoided by keeping the environment flexible and making the organisation match the task.

Effective adult interventions

In our scenario, the children on the Yellow table have access to a teaching assistant. She is available to scaffold the children's learning, helping them to achieve with support what they could not do unaided. This idea, first introduced by Wood et al. (1976), requires the adult to match their interventions to the needs of the individual child and decide what sort of support is necessary (Doherty and Hughes 2009 p. 270).

Effective groupings

Vygotsky's model of social constructivism may best be played out when children are seated in mixed ability groups. This provides opportunities for 'less academically confident' children to work within their zone of proximal development, having input from a more knowledgeable other. More confident learners who take on this role of more knowledgeable other can, therefore, both consolidate and articulate their learning. Gnadinger (2008) demonstrates in her research that peer collaboration is an effective learning strategy for children. In addition, other research has shown that higher achieving children who work in ability groups actually have their potential limited rather than enhanced, as they 'develop a crystallized view of their ability which may lead them to avoid challenges which are necessary for effective learning' (Dweck and Legget 1988, cited in MacIntyre and Ireson 2002 p. 250). Dweck (2008) distinguishes between two types of pupils: those with a 'growth mindset' and those with a 'fixed mindset':

> In the fixed-mindset world, students worry about making mistakes. They see making mistakes as a sign of low ability. They also worry about effort and view it in the same way – as a sign of low ability. They believe that if they have high ability they shouldn't need any effort. These are both terrible beliefs because mistakes and effort are integral parts of learning. Because students with fixed mindsets make them into things to be avoided, they actually stand in the way of learning. In fact, research in psychology indicates that the main thing that distinguishes people who go to the top of their fields and make great creative contribution from their equally able peers is the effort they put in. The fixed mindset cannot take people to that level. (p. 56)

Elsewhere she highlights learning environments where 'teachers praise the learning process rather than the students' ability, convey the joy of tackling challenging learning tasks, and highlight progress and effort' (Dweck 2010 p. 20), saying that 'Students who are nurtured in such classrooms will have the values and tools that breed lifelong success' (2010 p. 20).

Moving around

All that we know about children's cognitive development tells us that active learning and problem-solving approaches can be beneficial. They enable children to engage with their learning in individual ways depending on their preferred way of learning and thinking. Active learning involves problem solving and this requires children to move around, talk, collaborate and gather resources. Any environment for learning needs to facilitate these approaches and teachers need to be sure they know the children well enough to be able to anticipate these needs and reflect them in the organisation of the classroom.

Reflective task

Consider the information above and your own experiences of classroom environments. What do you think a classroom for children of a given age needs to look like, in order to support children's learning as described? How might your use of the learning environment be reflected in your planning?

Encouraging independence and autonomy in the learning environment

Return to the scenario

Classroom layout and organisation

Let us return to the scenario. Consider for a moment what messages the classroom layout and organisation is giving to the child:

- How does he think that the class teacher wants him to use the environment?
- How does he think that the teacher views learning?
- How independently is he able to think and learn in this environment?
- What skills is he learning?
- What do you think the teacher's priority was for his learning?

Classroom organisation reflects your educational philosophy

Waterson (2003) claims that the classroom needs to reflect the way in which an individual teacher intends to organise and teach the children. It sends messages to the children about how they are going to learn and what their part in that learning is likely to be.

Much of what happens in primary classrooms is directed through print in the form of worksheets, over-reliance on schemes and lots of written recording. These are quite individual acts which do not necessarily develop children's critical thinking skills or their creativity – skills that are required if children are going to become independent and autonomous learners (Bowles and Gintis 1976). If we as teachers have abandoned the notion of the child as a 'tabula rasa' or 'empty vessel' (Kehily 2010 p. 5) onto which we transmit relevant knowledge, then surely as class teachers we should be encouraging those skills which enable the children to think for themselves and therefore to take some control over their own learning.

How much better it is not only to teach children, but also to ensure that our learning environment encourages the consolidation of skills such as 'information processing, reasoning, enquiry, creative thinking, [and] evaluation' (DfEE 2000 p. 22)? We want to plan for and provide as many opportunities as possible for children to develop skills of metacognition, the ability to think about thinking (Goswami 2008 p. 295). If the children's learning is determined by how much we as teachers allow them to learn, then how limited will their learning be?

Encouraging independence

What do children actually need in order for them to become independent learners? A good place for teachers to start is by overtly giving children the permission to learn in this way. Even so, the skills required for independent learning do not develop by themselves and need the teacher to provide structure and support.

Children need to be clear about what they are learning and how they are able to engage with this learning. If aims and objectives are shared clearly and reinforced through displays and resources, ambiguity is avoided and children are then able to focus on the task in hand. Teachers' own beliefs and attitudes about learning are thrown into stark relief at this point. As Alexander (1992) points out, 'notwithstanding the classroom layout and organisation, they are but the framework within which the acts and interactions central to teaching and learning take place' (Moyles 1992 p. 11). The objectives that teachers choose, the way they are shared and the ways that teachers expect that learning to be carried out, will influence the ability of the children to work in independent and autonomous ways just as much as the physical environment.

Teachers who believe that knowledge is a 'public discipline' (Kendall-Seatter 2005 p. 97) will create a classroom where the interactions and the environment focus on transmission of knowledge, whereas if knowledge is seen as being 'a fluid act of interpretation' (Kendall-Seatter 2005 p. 97) then a very different ethos pervades. Autonomous and independent learners have control and ownership over their learning. This needs to be supported by and negotiated with the teacher, who will use classroom interactions and the environment to encourage collaborative working and more meaningful contexts for learning.

Organisation of resources and classroom layout

If this is to succeed, the emotional and physical environment must be equally supportive. Resources must be easily identifiable, relevant and available, as well as flexible enough for the children to use them in the way that they need to. The physical layout of the room also needs to be flexible enough for children to work in ways that are appropriate for the task in hand. Planned opportunities for paired and group work, along with careful differentiation of tasks, are required in order to build up the skills to enable children to learn with and from each other and their environment.

The scenario again

In our scenario, the teacher believes that she is enabling independence, and within the context and purpose of this particular task, it could be argued that she is. The learning for the session is explicit to the children but it is tightly controlled by the teacher, illustrating nicely Fang's point (1996) that there is often a lack of consistency between what teachers think they are doing and what is actually happening. If this is representative of other teaching and learning interactions within this classroom, then children become at risk of 'learned helplessness'. Children become accustomed to accepting extrinsic motivation and organisation and are not able to succeed without it. They do not have the necessary strategies. The teacher in our situation has created an environment where children have little need to be independent: they are lined up, sat down, moved to tables and given a specific task with specific resources. It is all organised and done for them. This teacher believes it is for the benefit of the children but in reality it could have more to do with convenience for herself. Children do not have to consider others or the effect of their behaviour as they are closely monitored. It is perhaps for this reason that in the only part of the scenario where the children are not under the direct supervision of the teacher, in the cloakroom, there is a breakdown of order. Children have not been helped to think independently and behave autonomously. These skills enable children to be resilient, to tolerate and adapt to new and different ideas and experiences, and to stay engaged with things that are outside their comfort zone.

Reflective task

Think about a classroom that you have spent time in. Make notes on:

- the routines
- the types of tasks
- the resources used and the ways they were organised
- the physical layout used in the classroom.

Put these into two columns – those that supported independence and autonomy and those that hindered it. How can you ensure that your learning environment encourages those skills that support independence and autonomy?

Supporting positive behaviour through the learning environment

Disruptive behaviour, whether low level or with greater impact, will of course always hinder effective learning, so it is important to consider how our learning environment may help the children to choose appropriate behaviours which enable all to make good academic progress. Ecological psychologists note that the learning environment is important for children and that it can affect their behaviour (Bronfenbrenner 1979; Gump 1987; Pointon and Kersher 2000, cited in Pollard 2008). Learning dispositions can be influenced by the environment: 'creating a positive climate' has been highlighted as a 'prime characteristic of quality teachers' (Muijs and Reynolds 2011 p. 128). An environment that is scruffy and untidy will not be respected by the children. If it is dull or cold, then they will not be happy about being there. If it is cluttered, it can make children feel stressed and overwhelmed, whereas a tidy, organised environment can help children to feel calm and positive, ready to learn in a place where there is a perception of order and structure (Cowley 2006). This can be achieved through carefully organised stations or areas of provision so children know how, and where, to access equipment. Signs, labels and displays will help to clarify these areas. Interactive displays are an effective learning tool, which, alongside the use of music, sound and light, can encourage interest and focus engagement with the environment.

A sense of ownership

Learning environments are places where a complicated mix of factors come together – local community values, parental expectations, religious values, children and their attitudes, and so on. McNamara and Moreton (1997) cited in Kendall-Seatter (2005) showed that where children were actively engaged in their classroom, a higher level of involvement was ensured and shared ownership, shared values and mutual respect were fostered.

Looking at the scenario, the child did not seem to feel any sense of ownership over the environment he was in. He was not involved in setting it up nor does it appear to consider the ways in which he needs to behave in order to learn effectively. Too many classrooms are sterile laboratories where the children are fenced in by table arrangements and not allowed to move from their places unless it is a key transition time. Everything is put in front of them – paper, pencil and books – so that they have to make few decisions or interactions with peers and adults.

The classroom should be more like a workshop, a bustling busy place with children moving between different areas, collecting resources independently, sometimes standing, sometimes sitting, sometimes even working on the floor. Sometimes it may look messy – workshops are full of very busy, productive people. This positive engagement appears to be the key to encouraging appropriate behaviours. It has been suggested that children should not only be involved in designing their classroom environment but also in working with teachers and architects in redesigning old buildings and in creating new ones (Alexander 2010 p. 355).

Evaluating engagement with the environment

As teachers, how can we tell if children are able to engage with an environment? Do the children sit still for too long? Are they uncomfortable? Do children know what is expected of them? Are instructions clear? Can they get the resources they need? What should they do if they finish the set task? What strategies can they use if they get stuck? Are they bored? Is the work too easy or too hard? Can they make decisions about their learning? Are they able to choose how to approach a task? Can they talk to their peers about their learning?

The scenario

Let us consider the scenario again. The child knows that he is expected to sit still for quite some time. He is also aware that he finds this difficult. Ouvry (2000 p. 23) asserts that 'the most advanced level of movement is the ability to stay totally still, which requires entire muscle groups to work in cooperation with balance and posture'. The struggle to do as he knows he should requires him to concentrate on the issue of staying still and as a result he misses other information. What is he engaged with? At all points, he is trying very hard to behave and this has a detrimental impact on his ability to engage with the learning he is being presented with. The teacher's perception of his behaviour is very different to his own desire to behave appropriately within the constraints of the environment she has created. How could the teacher have set the environment up differently to enable a more positive experience for this child? Muijs and Reynolds (2011) highlight how 'teaching and learning in school need to be adapted to the needs and developmental levels of pupils' (p. 115). They stress boys' preferences for 'active learning styles' and how they 'may not react well to prolonged periods of having to sit still and listen' (p. 115), suggesting that the teacher introduces short periods of physical activity within the teaching and learning sequence.

Creating a work-centred atmosphere

Where the teacher creates a work-centred atmosphere, classes tend to behave better (Docking 2002). There is, however, a wide range of advice and research about how this is best achieved. Plowden (1967) advised teachers to put children in mixed-ability groups in order to promote active, problem-solving discussion. Later studies showed that although teachers grouped children, they were usually directed to work individually. The group situation but individualised nature of the task meant that children were often found to be off task and talking inappropriately (Whedall and Glynn 1989). In 1995, a study by Hastings and Schwieso found that primary children concentrated better in rows, where disruptive children were less distracted. There was no eye contact to disturb them and the better they behaved, the more positive reinforcement came from the teacher. So are rows the answer? Probably as primary teachers, something inside us recoils at the idea! Why is this? Could it be that we really do believe that children learn better in a social environment and that our training tells us that it cannot be right that teachers' requirements for conformity and rules should override the child's need for 'understanding and engagement in high quality learning tasks' (Holt 1982, cited in Pollard 2008 p. 309). We need, therefore, to be challenged to provide a flexible environment where the needs of the children, the classroom, the tasks and experiences, groupings, levels of challenge, boundaries and routines, and expectations all come together to support children's positive behaviour. A challenge indeed!

Encouraging self-esteem and emotional development through the learning environment

Few would disagree that the learning environment may also have a powerful impact on the child's self-esteem and emotional development. Without a doubt, the class teacher in the above scenario will have spent many long hours planning and resourcing her delivery of the curriculum, but one wonders how much time was spent planning the hidden curriculum and how to 'manipulate the environment' (Child 1997 p. 265) to offer opportunities to make the children feel valued, safe and that they have a contribution to make.

Case study

Simon's low self-esteem was reinforced by the seating arrangements, the use of wall displays and his observation of rewarded behaviours. Teachers are fond of using and applying the label of low self-esteem and may take up a one-woman/man crusade to help re-educate parents or offer strategies to develop self-esteem in the home, but how do we know that Simon did not arrive at school aged 4 ready to conquer the world and it is actually school that has taught him he is failing?

Our understanding of brain development informs us that a child under stress is unable to learn effectively. If you re-read his perception of the scenario, you will note that there were many issues for Simon in his environment which were sources of stress for him and which could have prevented him from learning. Sometimes empathetic teachers or teaching assistants will recognise stress issues for children but may inadvertently impact on their achievement and therefore self-esteem even more by removing challenge from tasks they are required to do and encouraging the 'learned helplessness' we have already made reference to. Kendall-Seatter (2005) speaks of the necessity to provide environments which are 'low-stress–high-challenge' (p. 59) to ensure achievement for all children regardless of ability.

Simon's concerns will not just be with how his teacher perceives and values him, but the opinions of his peers will also be of great importance to his positive self-esteem. The 'ripple' action (Jacques and Hyland 2003 p. 161) set into motion by the classroom teacher as she sets up the learning environment to reflect her own values and beliefs about learning and children will continue until all children included in that environment cannot help but be influenced by them. There will be a shared, if unspoken, understanding that some children are failing, therefore 'lesser', whilst others are successful and 'apart' and will always continue to be so. The failing children, the 'Simons' of this world, may feel they are powerless to move from the level in the hierarchy they have been assigned by the learning environment, the teacher and their peers, and it is then, once they have decided there is no point any longer in trying, that disaffection may set in. If, on the other hand, the ripple that the teacher, through the environment, sets in motion is an inclusive one that demonstrates that all children are valued for the unique and individual talents and attributes they bring, all children will see themselves as learners regardless of their ability. Muijs and Reynolds (2011) remind us that 'teachers should emphasize pupils' successes rather than their failures' and that 'Pupils should be encouraged to strive for their own personal best, rather than ... constantly comparing their results with those of their classmates' (p.187).

Children's perceptions of their place in society

The environment will dominate children's understanding of their own role and place in society regardless of the teacher's discourse. This is why, as classroom teachers, it is so important to get it right and leave nothing to chance. We may feel we have a group of learners, but in reality we have a group of individuals (Kendall-Seatter 2005 p. 62).

Work in school

'It's hard when you're a student teacher because you have to follow the class teacher's ways of doing things even if you don't agree...'

'When you're busy in the classroom doing all the practical stuff with the children you haven't got time to think about all the theories we've looked at during uni sessions – it can leave you thinking "What's the point?!"'

How will you apply your learning from this chapter to your school placement when you may feel as a student teacher you can have limited impact on how the learning environment is set up. Look back at the bullet points on p. 103 and then reflect on the last time you were in a school setting:

- What small changes could you have made to the learning environment which would have impacted on the children's learning and well-being? Make sure you can provide an appropriate rationale for your decisions.
- Consider Piaget and Vygotsky's work, highlighted on pp. 107–9. What opportunites were there to (i) 'actively explore', (ii) 'socially interact', (iii) work with or be 'a more knowledgeable other'. How could you extend these opportunities?

Summary

For effective learning to take place, the environment needs to be flexible enough to be created around the needs of children. However loud the teacher's voice may be, the environment will always be able to shout louder, declaring to every child in the class the values and attitudes of that teacher. Children pick up these subliminal signals, adapting their behaviour accordingly where possible to fit into the requirements of their environment. Our challenge to you, whatever your level of experience, is to think hard about your underpinning values and attitudes towards teaching and learning and to create, within the limitations in which you find yourself working, an environment that will demonstrate to the children what you truly believe learning is.

Questions for discussion

- Children's voices: how might teachers find out how children feel about and respond to the learning environments they provide?
- How might children at each Key Stage be involved in creating their own learning environment?
- How might learning in the classroom be linked to learning outside the classroom at Key Stage 1? At Key Stage 2?
- What might your ideal learning environment at either Key Stage be like? What might be the constraints in creating this environment?

Further reading

Hewitt, D. (2008) *Understanding Effective Learning: Strategies for the Classroom*. Maidenhead: Open University Press.

This book explores these important concepts by examining learning in a range of classroom settings and drawing on evidence from teachers and pupils, through interviews and observations. The focus is two-fold: to understand learning in the classroom, and to develop practices which will support learning.

Roffey, S. (2010) *Changing Behaviour in Schools*. London: Sage.

Taking an holistic approach to working with students, the author provides examples of effective strategies for encouraging pro-social and collaborative behaviour in the classroom, the school and the wider community. Chapters look at the importance of the social and emotional aspects of learning, and ways to facilitate change.

Skinner, D. (2010) *Effective Teaching and Learning in Practice*. London: Continuum.

Based on excellent summaries of recent research on teaching and learning, this book presents a clear framework around which teachers can build their classroom practice. It provides an excellent starting point for new entrants to the profession as well as a source of reflection for their more experienced colleagues.

References

Alexander, R. (1992) *Policy and Practice in Primary Education*. London: Routledge.

Alexander, R. (ed.) (2010) *Children, Their World, their Education: Final Report of the Cambridge Primary Review*. London: Routledge.

Bowles, S. and Gintis, H. (1976) *Schooling in Capitalist America*. London: Routledge and Kegan Paul.

Bronfenbrenner, U. (1979) *The Ecology of Human Development*. Cambridge, MA: Harvard University Press.

Child, D. (ed.) (1997) *Psychology and the Teacher*, 6th edn. London: Continuum.

Cowley, S. (2006) *Getting the Buggers to Behave*, 3rd edn. London: Continuum.

Daly, M., Byers, E. and Taylor, W. (2006) *Understanding Early Years Theory in Practice*. Oxford: Heinemann.

Department for Children, Schools and Families (DCSF) (2008) *Assessment for Learning Strategy,* available at: www.webarchive.nationalarchives.gov.uk

Department for Education (DfE) (2013) *Teachers' Standards* (DFE-00066-2011), available at: (http://www.gov.uk)

DfEE (2000) *The National Curriculum Key Stages 1 and 2* (revised edition). London: HMSO.

Docking, J. (2002) *Managing Behaviour in the Primary School*, 3rd edn. London: David Fulton.

Doherty, J. and Hughes, M. (2009) *Child Development: Theory and Practice 0–11*. Harlow: Pearson.

Dweck, C. (2008) 'Mindsets: How Praise is Harming Youth and What Can Be Done about It', *School Library Media Activities Monthly* 24(5): 55–8.

Dweck, C. (2010) 'Even Geniuses Work Hard', *Educational Leadership* 68(1): 16–20.

Fang, Z. (1996) 'A Review of Research on Teachers' Beliefs and Practices', *Educational Research* 38(1): 47–65.

Gnadinger, C. (2008) 'Peer-mediated Instruction: Assisted Performance in the Primary Classroom', *Teachers and Teaching* 14(2): 129–42.

Goswami, U. (2008) *Cognitive Development: The Learning Brain*. Hove: Psychology Press.

Gump, P. (1987) 'School and Classroom Environments', in I. Altman and J.F. Wohlwill, *Handbook of Environmental Psychology*. New York: Plenum Press, pp. 131–74.

Hastings, N. and Schwieso, J. (1995) 'Tasks and Tables: The Effects of Seating Arrangements on Task Engagement in Primary Classrooms', *Educational Research* 37(3): 279–91.

Jacques, K. and Hyland, R. (2003) *Professional Studies: Primary Phase*. Exeter: Learning Matters.

Kehily, M. (ed.) (2010) *An Introduction to Childhood Studies*, 2nd edn. Maidenhead: McGraw-Hill.

Kendall-Seatter, S. (2005) *Primary Professional Studies: Reflective Reader*. Exeter: Learning Matters.

MacIntyre, H. and Ireson, J. (2002) 'Within-class Ability Grouping: Placement of Pupils in Groups and Self-concept', *British Educational Research Journal* 28(2): 249–63.

McNamara, S. and Moreton, G. (1997) *Understanding Differentiation*. London: Taylor and Francis.

Moyles, J. (1992) *Organising for Learning in the Primary Classroom*. Buckingham: Open University Press.

Muijs, R.D. and Reynolds, D. (2011) *Effective Teaching: Evidence and Practice*. London: Sage.

Ouvry, M. (2000) *Exercising Muscles and Minds*. London: The Early Years Network.

Plowden Report (1967) *Children and their Primary Schools: A Report of the Central Advisory Council for Education (England)*. London: HMSO.

Pollard, A. (2008) *Reflective Teaching: Evidence-informed Professional Practice*, 3rd edn. London: Continuum.

Smidt, S. (2013) *Introducing Malaguzzi: Exploring the Life and Work of Reggio Emilia's Founding Father*. London: Routledge.

Waterson, A. (2003) 'Managing the Classroom for Learning', in K. Jacques and R. Hyland (eds) *Professional Studies: Primary Phase*. Exeter: Learning Matters, pp. 74–85.

Whedall, K. and Glynn, T. (1989) *Effective Classroom Learning: A Behavioural Interactionist Approach to Teaching*. Oxford: Basil Blackwell.

Wood, D., Bruner, J. and Ross, G. (1976) 'The Role of Tutoring in Problem Solving', *Journal of Child Psychology and Psychiatry* 17: 89–100.

CHAPTER 6

THE ROLE OF THE ADULT

Jan Ashbridge and Jo Josephidou

By the end of this chapter, you should be able to:

- discuss the many roles of the teacher in the education and care of children
- examine how teachers work with other adults within and beyond the classroom to develop effective practice which will impact on children's achievement
- consider how positive relationships between adults and children can impact on their learning
- reflect critically on the values and philosophies you hold regarding the education of children.

Introduction

The best early years practice focuses on the importance of 'positive relationships' to lay the foundations of successful learning for young children. Once these children make the transition to Key Stage 1 and then later Key Stage 2, it is vital that these 'positive relationships' are maintained to ensure that these transitions are smooth and supportive for each child. But what is your role in the establishing and maintaining of these 'positive relationships' as a classroom teacher? The first part of this chapter will ask you to consider some of the people you will need to develop positive relationships with and how this might be achieved. Then the second part of the chapter will use metaphors to consider the many other dimensions of the teacher's role: supporting the development of the whole child, facilitating and scaffolding learning, pastoral care, inspiring learners, and coordinating all these roles. This chapter reflects Standard 8 (DfE 2013) which refers to the importance of making a positive contribution to the life of the school, developing effective professional relationships with colleagues, deploying staff effectively and communicating well with parents with regard to their children's achievements and well-being.

Reflective task

Imagine yourself in your first classroom with your first class of children. Take a mental photograph of the picture this creates in your head. Now describe this image to a peer.

Describe the following:

- What you are doing?
- What are the children doing?
- Is there anyone else in the classroom?
- What are they doing?

It will be interesting to see whether the image you have described has changed by the end of this chapter.

Teachers are a cog in a much bigger mechanism. It is easy to focus only on the cogs immediately around us, where it is obvious how they affect our work and how we affect them. Understanding the bigger picture is a key way of beginning to grasp the main issues in partnership working and avoiding the appearance of a 'muddled system of education and care' (Penn 2008 p. 193).

Reflective task

Who are we in partnership with?

In small groups, write down on separate sticky notes all the different professionals who might be working alongside a teacher in their work and who may influence their practice. What different ways can you find in which to group them? By role? By sphere of influence? By the immediacy of their impact on the teacher's work?

On a large sheet of paper, draw the teacher in the middle – can you organise your sticky notes around them? Who seems nearest, who seems less important?

This activity should have illustrated the number of people that teachers work with. A study of roles and responsibilities (adapted from Siraj-Blatchford et al. 2002 p. 7) found the following roles and responsibilities in today's primary schools:

- teaching assistant (and equivalent learning support assistant, nursery nurse, therapist)
- pupil welfare workers (education welfare officer, home–school liaison officer, learning mentor, nurse and welfare assistant)
- technical and specialist staff (ICT network manager, ICT technician, librarian, science technician, technology technician)
- other pupil support staff (bilingual support officer, cover supervisor, escort, language assistant, midday assistant, midday supervisor)
- facilities staff (cleaner, cook, other catering staff)
- administrative staff (administrator, finance officer, office manager, secretary, personal assistant to the head teacher)
- site staff (caretaker and premises manager).

This list is considerably extended when we add colleagues within the school and the community and multi-agency working.

Let us now examine some of these key partnerships for the classroom teacher.

Working with others: the teacher as partner

Partnership with parents and carers

Perhaps the key partnership teachers must engage in is with parents and carers. Parents are statutorily responsible for their child's education, are legally entitled to

Perceived power balance	Openness and honesty	Poor communication	Judgemental attitudes	
Lack of understanding	Poor listening	Lack of trust	?	?

Figure 6.1 Stumbling blocks

state a preference for a particular school and have a legal right to parental representation on the governing body. As a result of this, they are major stakeholders in children's education and are able to influence school policy. This responsibility is shared, as when a child is at school teachers are *in loco parentis* and have a common-law duty to promote children's safety and well-being as well as their education (Children Act 1989).

What might be some of the stumbling blocks to effective partnership with parents? Figure 6.1 suggests possible barriers to successful school/parent relationships. Parents know their children better than the teacher ever can. They are the children's first educators and have vital information on what the children enjoy, how they learn, etc. Most learning happens outside school (Dean 2000 p. 140), and this needs to be recognised and valued by those within the school too.

Opportunities to share information with parents

Teachers can usually think of many ways to share information with parents. Before the first, nervously anticipated 'parents' evening', you may have met many of the parents informally at the beginning or end of the school day. You may have written notes to them about school events or out-of-school visits. You may have been encouraged to invite them to a meeting at the beginning of term to introduce yourself, explain what the children are going to be learning about and why, and to discuss how they may like to be involved. If you have managed initial encounters with parents in a friendly and professional way, this will be a good basis for meeting them on more formal occasions to discuss their children's progress. Some schools invite parents to meetings to learn more about how the school teaches, for example, reading or mathematics, so that they can be more involved in their children's learning. But this is not a partnership if you do not also learn from the parents: 'For partnerships to be truly collaborative … learning must be part of the experience for all involved' (Loughrey and Woods 2010 p. 85).

Opportunities for parents to share information with teachers

Even confident parents may feel threatened by meeting a teacher to discuss their child's progress, attitudes, social skills and behaviour. Less confident parents may have had poor experiences of school themselves and feel insecure or alternatively confrontational. How might parents feel about sharing family information with a teacher? How can you help parents to feel confident in telling you about their children? What might you want to know, and why?

Parents' contributions to school life

There may be many reasons why parents seem reluctant to get involved with school life and it is not necessarily because 'they can't be bothered' or that they don't care about their child's progress: Desforges and Abouchaar (2003, p. 6) suggest that 'the extent and form of parental involvement is strongly influenced by factors such as family social class, maternal level of education, material deprivation, maternal psycho-social health and single parent status'.

A key aspect of your role as classroom teacher is to build strong professional relationships with parents so that you can encourage them to contribute to the life of the school, because there is a wealth of research to indicate that parental involvement will impact on the achievement of their child. How can parents contribute to the life of the school? Through your formal and informal communications with parents, you may find that they have special expertise, through their work or their interests, which would enrich an aspect of your teaching. Some parents are eager to 'help in class'. Can there be difficulties in welcoming this and, if so, how could they be resolved? Some parents may have little English. How might you involve them in helping in school? How might you make parents from different cultural backgrounds feel included in school life?

Reflective task

In pairs: one person thinks of a child they have taught who was finding school difficult in some ways. The partner, in role as the class teacher, needs to find out why. Role play a meeting between parent and teacher. Share what you both know and feel about the child and agree how you can work together to support her. Then share your thoughts about the difficulties encountered and how well both partners negotiated them. Share the role play with others. Compile a list of ways in which you might work in partnership with parents to support a child.

This relationship has considerable influence over the way parents feel able to support their children's learning, resulting in a shared purpose, understanding and belonging for all (Dean 2000 p. 151).

Social events with teachers and parents

Partnerships can be strengthened by situations in which parents and teachers work together on a more equal footing to support the school. One head teacher set up a number of projects more enterprising than the 'school fete', themed dance evenings and fancy dress parties, although these were greatly enjoyed. The projects included a school garden, the construction of an 'adventure fort' and a pet shed. Children, teachers and parents worked together on these projects. The fort project was particularly successful in involving dads, some of whom did not live at home. Loughrey and Woods (2010) describe a creative project involving children, parents, teachers and artists which impacted positively on all those involved in an area of great poverty where previous attempts at engaging parents had been unsuccessful.

True partnerships with parents cannot flourish where respect and power are not equal. Home–school communication is a complex process in which 'issues of control and power are present and shape the forms of communication'. However, when effective communication with parents is achieved, 'the contribution that parents make to their child's learning is often rich and varied' (Alexander 2010 p. 81).

Partnership with teaching assistants

The same skills are required to work alongside the other adults in the classroom. Teaching assistants (TAs) and other support staff often have a slightly different relationship with children and families and can, therefore, add another perspective to planning and to supporting children's needs, although it is fair to say that the TA's role has changed considerably over the past few years and is shifting to include work that would previously only have been carried out by teachers, such as teaching, planning and assessment (Mackenzie 2011). Involving them and using their knowledge and experience can ensure more effective learning outcomes for the children and can create a more responsive and motivated team approach in the classroom.

It was the intention that the considerable increase in teaching assistants and other support staff between 2003 and 2006, as a result of 'workforce reform', should strengthen teaching and learning, by using the full potential of teaching assistants, allowing them to take on wider and deeper roles, and allowing schools to focus on the individual needs of every child. However, TAs can feel that their role in the classroom is ambiguous and at times not clearly defined. In Mackenzie's research (2011) TAs voice their confusion over the 'lack of clarity' about their role and she signposts other research which shows that teachers and TAs often have very different perspectives on their role in the classroom.

How to work with teaching assistants in ways that will realise these opportunities involves decisions about how best to use their expertise in ways that meet the needs of the children in your class, and the ability to forge mutually supportive relationships. Don't forget that the research shows that 'TAs very often have a strong commitment to their work' (Mackenzie 2011 p. 65). It is essential that teachers include teaching assistants in planning, monitoring and assessment, medium term, weekly and daily, and this requires time. They also need to be clear about what their role is within what the teacher is planning, with an individual, a group or the whole class and how they are going to monitor and assess this. Reflect on how one of Mackenzie's TA interviewees discusses the tension of working with a class teacher:

> I never get lesson plans. You've got to think on your feet, you've got to adapt material when you don't even know what they're doing. You have to listen to what the teacher is teaching the class so that you understand everything. But at the same time you are meant to be out of the class changing all the materials. You don't get any time to change or adapt things. (2011 p. 67)

They may have particular areas of curriculum expertise to contribute, in art, or music or dance, for example. But the most important aspect of working effectively with your teaching assistant is to develop a mutually supportive relationship so that you enjoy working together. Bear in mind that working collaboratively with your TA is not a simple matter but when you persevere and have the determination to make it work, both you, as class teacher, your TA and the children will benefit greatly. Another of Mackenzie's interviewees noted how she enjoyed working with teachers who were: 'fair, firm, adapting the curriculum, understanding the needs of the classroom, making sure that the kids love you and empowering them so that they become active learners' (2011 p. 67).

Partnership with other teachers

A school is a community, a collaborative, inclusive community for learning. This community creates and conveys values, attitudes and purposes. Relationships between teachers and the ways in which they behave have an important impact on the ethos of that community. They are models which children notice. A positive and mutually agreed and shared whole-school philosophy, shared values, mutual respect and support are a powerful, formative influence on children and on the community. Whole-school policies and planning contribute to the school ethos.

Within schools, there are teams which must work effectively with each other and the school community: management teams, curriculum leaders, Special Educational Needs coordinators, year group teams, Key Stage teams. And there is evidence that if all these groups work effectively, this has an impact on all aspects of children's learning.

Partner with local schools

In rural areas particularly, schools work in local clusters to share resources and expertise and to support each other. It is important that they work together cooperatively rather than submit to government encouragement of competition.

Partner with global colleagues

Many teachers also think that it is important to develop the global dimension of education and liaise with teachers and schools in other countries and continents. This demands sensitivity, for example when resources and opportunities are unequal.

Working in partnership with professionals in other agencies

Primary Health Care Trusts

In 2000 Primary Care Trusts (PCTs) replaced the former Health Authorities. The PCTs work with families, children and schools. Teachers therefore may work with the PCT services such as: disabled children's teams, child development teams, health visitors, health education programmes, occupational therapists, speech therapists, physiotherapists, community parent schemes, children's mental health teams.

Behaviour and Education Support Teams

These multi-agency teams were set up in partnership with schools in 2002 to promote well-being, positive behaviour and attendance and to raise attainment through early intervention.

The 2004 Children Act

In 2003 the Every Child Matters initiative was introduced. This became part of the Children Act 2004. It was intended to secure the well-being of all children and in particular those in danger of abuse. Local authorities were to provide 'joined up' education and care services with multi-agency cooperation. Schools were to work with health care agencies, social services, family law and criminal justice agencies and services concerned with the arts, recreation and sports. These include public, private and voluntary agencies.

Children's trust boards

In 2007 the government announced that children's trust boards would be set up. These were to consist of representatives from schools and the other integrated services and would be held responsible for child protection measures.

Implications for teacher as partner

It has been complex to manage multi-agency work and some schools have been criticised for lack of involvement, but where it has been successful children and parents have benefitted. It has been suggested that agencies should liaise with clusters of schools. However multi-agency work develops in the future, its success will depend on teachers being prepared to work with other professionals and to share information and expertise.

Extended schools

Extended schools were created to provide all children with access to a variety of clubs and sports and adults with access to education classes and parenting support. The aim was that by 2010 all children would have access to an extended school. Teachers are not required to contribute to extended schools, but may choose to.

Partnership and the community

'To establish itself as a thriving cultural and communal site should be the principal aim of every school' (Alexander 2010 p. 500). The community of the school – its pupils and their families, and often the school staff – is part of the wider community. So the wider curriculum needs to gain meaning by starting with that community, its geography, its history, its opportunities for creating art, music, drama and all kinds of writing related to the community and the people who lived and live there.

Children need to learn about citizenship through taking an interest in and contributing to their community. This might involve discussing a proposed development, making suggestions to the town council about changes they would like to see, attending council meetings, becoming aware of sustainability and environmental issues, contributing to a display in the local library (if there still is one) or presenting a performance at an old people's home.

Parents can contribute in all sorts of ways. One Year 1 class had a 'teddy museum'. Children brought in their teddy bears and wrote brief information labels. Parents did the same with their teddies. In another school, in groups, children from each KS2 class were helped by parents to prepare a lunch related to a theme they were learning about, then invited a member of the community, perhaps a librarian or nurse or policeman, to share their lunch. Parents may demonstrate skills or hobbies or talk about their interests or working day.

People from local businesses can enrich the curriculum in all sorts of ways, perhaps inviting children to make a positive contribution: making designs for a new flower bed in the park, or a new building in town, or a new recipe for the sandwich bar. Alexander (2010 p. 276) suggests that community–curriculum partnerships should be convened by the local authority, including representatives from schools and the community and experts in contributory disciplines, and involving consultation with children. This community curriculum would include elements agreed collectively by the schools, with each school responding in ways which build on and respect the lives of their children.

Having discussed the role of the teacher as partner, let us now consider the multi-faceted role of the teacher through the use of metaphors. Hattingh and de Kock (2008) cite Inbar's research (1996) which highlighted that student teachers naturally used metaphors when discussing their role. His research pinpointed 7042 such metaphors in use. In this part of the chapter we will ask you to consider only five:

- teacher as signpost
- teacher as magician
- teacher as gardener
- teacher as bridge
- teacher as superhero.

By considering the role of the teacher in this way, we are hopeful you will reflect on your present perceptions of how you see yourself as a teacher and how you can impact on the achievement and well-being of those children you teach.

The developing child: teacher as signpost

Children's learning is often seen as a journey. Children move along a path from the early years, through the primary school and on to high school and beyond. Along the way they develop, they grow, they learn. Careful planning ensures that the children's itinerary takes them to visit a variety of different places and experience a range of situations.

The teacher's role here is perceived to be to lead and manage the curriculum at a number of different levels and in a variety of ways. As seen in the previous chapter, the environment and its careful management and use is key to effective learning and teaching. Children need to be kept safe, resources organised and accessible, and social interactions, groups and tasks carefully considered and appropriately employed.

It is interesting here to note who is making the decisions about these issues. Many of these management decisions are taken for the benefit of the adult. The image of a signpost offers us a slightly different perception of the role of the teacher. It is one where some of the control over decisions about learning is given to the children. They are able to indicate a choice of where they want their learning to go, how they want to engage with it, and how much time they need to master it. It is still very much about moving children on and supporting their progress, but with a key difference: the children are more involved in the direction their learning may take them.

In order to be able to respond appropriately to children in this situation, teachers need to understand that 'teaching and learning [are] a continuous unfolding of related knowledge, skills and understanding' (Hayes 2004 p. 151). We cannot simply give children complete free choice over what and how they learn. We need to have an overview. Continuity of learning is 'achieved when there is a discernable thread of knowledge, skills and understanding' which runs through different learning experiences (Hayes 2004 p. 151). Aiming for this will enable us to be effective signposts, allowing children to progress smoothly along their learning journey.

Facilitating learning: teacher as magician

Magic moments

Sometimes the classroom teacher glimpses small nuggets of gold when a child grasps and articulates a concept in a way the teacher had not considered before. Or a group of children display a skill or ability beyond that same teacher's expectation. Or the wisdom of children as opposed to the knowledge of adults is allowed to take centre stage so that the classroom becomes a real learning community. By being the catalyst, the facilitator of all these events, the teacher could be forgiven at times for feeling as if they were a magician, an alchemist, a producer of gold.

Catering for individual differences

The teacher as magician is there to do the seemingly impossible – to facilitate learning for all. The successful teacher will do this by being very clear about the individual learning needs of the children. Some children learn more effectively by having their learning introduced in small steps, while others like to view the bigger picture and proceed from there. The wise teacher will not seek to impose strategies that may not work for all children and will not succumb to the flawed opinion that because they themselves learnt successfully in one way then so will all children. Some children will disengage much more quickly than others so the teacher as magician will seek to captivate their attention for as long as possible by creating an exciting learning environment, rich with stimulating and purposeful activities and opportunities to succeed.

A learning community

The teacher as magician will be clear about learning outcomes, will know that at the end of the show the white rabbit has to come out of the hat, but at the same time will read her audience and be flexible about how this outcome is achieved. Audience participation is encouraged because by fostering interaction between teacher and children, and children and children, the effective teacher is aware that a learning community is being constructed which everyone can both contribute to and learn from. Talk and questioning are used to extend learning rather than as a focus for 'guess what is in the teacher's head' type activities.

Transformative learning

It could be argued that indeed the analogy of the magician does stand up as a description of the teacher. Just as the magician can change the silk handkerchief into the white rabbit, so can the class teacher bring about real transformation and change. On the other hand, just as the magician's feat is an illusion of change, so too can the education system support the illusion of change by the introduction of strategies and the massaging and analysis of statistics and data, teaching to tests which inflate key assessment results rather than deliver any lasting change, growth in knowledge and skills or transformation. Just as the magician puts on a show to bring a real sense of wonder and excitement to his audience, so too does the classroom teacher, at times, draw her audience in, sometimes to entertain, sometimes to enthral, at other times to turn the mundane and simple into spectacles worthy of the children's attention.

Pastoral care: teacher as gardener

We cannot afford to ignore the social and emotional development of children. Children who are happy at school, who share good relationships with both adults and peers in that environment, are children who will make good progress academically. So this is why we turn now to the analogy of the teacher as gardener, carefully considering and providing the best possible environment and conditions for the children to thrive and grow in all areas of their development.

Praise

Teacher praise has always been an effective motivator for children, though Child (1997 p. 119) reminds us that it must be used carefully if it is to have any impact, otherwise it can become meaningless and limiting. Moyles too warns us to be careful about how we offer it: 'praise may appear to make children work harder, but what was the cause of any reluctance to do so in the first place?' (2001 p. 69). Instead, many would argue that appropriate behaviours should be considered the norm, not something to be rewarded, and that the present fashion for acknowledging teacher pleasure through the constant bestowing of certificates and stickers actually decreases children's intrinsic motivations and undermines them as learners.

Lifelong learners

Teachers who are aware that their role is much more than a transmission of knowledge will work hard to plan for resilient lifelong learners who are enthusiastic about learning because they know they have the freedom to make mistakes, seeing mistakes as necessary stepping stones on the way to academic success. They will look to provide opportunities for children to build on and demonstrate their strengths rather than focusing on the child's weaknesses within the rigid framework of assessment 'where the threat to self-esteem is ever present' (Cockburn and Handscomb 2006 p. 45).

Fostering independence

The teacher is an expert at asking questions of the children but it may be pertinent for her to ask herself about how it feels to be a learner in the classroom environment she has created. Do the children feel quite dependent on the teacher for their learning or are they confident enough and skilled enough to see and use their peers 'as a resource' (Moyles 2001 p. 13)? Children who are strong and healthy, not just physically and cognitively but also emotionally resilient, need the correct conditions or learning environment to grow and thrive.

Scaffolding learning: teacher as bridge

Teachers are curriculum makers. They take their detailed knowledge of the frameworks and statutory expectations of children, combine this with an understanding of children's needs, their development and their current skills and understandings and create an environment with meaningful and challenging learning experiences for all. This professional responsibility means that we are ultimately accountable for the learning situations that we create for the children in our class and for the children's responses to these in terms of learning and progress. Teachers are constantly using their professional judgement but must be able to justify their decisions.

Progressing learning

A bridge is something that gets you from one side of a gap of some kind to the other. As classroom teachers, we aim to support children as they travel from their current knowledge to concepts and skills as yet unknown and unexplored but perhaps anticipated and eagerly awaited. In supporting children from one side of this gap to the other, we need to have our eyes fixed firmly on the connection, the learning itself and on the process of connecting. To get this right, we must return again to theories of cognitive development. These can give us an insight into the way that children make connections and what we can do to make these as strong as possible. In this way, we can interpret the curriculum in appropriate ways for specific groups of children.

Siraj-Blatchford et al. (2002) argue that it is this bringing together of children and adult in a learning situation that enables co-construction of knowledge where both are engaged and involved. Their research showed that where adults and children were engaged together in these 'sustained shared thinking interactions' (Siraj-Blatchford et al. 2002 p. 10), a high level of intellectual challenge enabled children to make good progress in their learning.

Interventions

It would seem, therefore, that we support children's learning and their interpretation of what they are experiencing through careful scaffolding and sensitive yet challenging adult interventions. These interventions, which are designed to make connections between existing understanding and new knowledge, form part of a complicated process. On their own, children may not be able to make these connections or could make inaccurate ones. Enabling children to bridge this gap will lead to 'principled understanding' (Edwards and Mercer 1987 p. 95, cited in Myhill et al. 2006 p. 87), where children make deep, meaningful, conceptual connections in their learning.

Listening to children's voices

The challenge for the teacher is to enable and support all children to make these connections when each child has a 'uniqueness and individuality of … prior knowledge … that has to be incorporated into a classroom setting' (Myhill et al. 2006 p. 85). The answer seems to lie in listening to children and their thoughts and ideas rather than more formal recapping of previous curriculum coverage and relating this to a current learning focus which narrows children's thinking rather than provoking 'speculation and extend[ing] imagination' (Siraj-Blatchford et al. 2002 p. 47). The types of questions used by teachers are instrumental in helping children to truly explore their prior knowledge and also to share their understanding and begin to construct an extended understanding together.

The inspiring teacher: teacher as superhero

Modelling

Children's media are full of superheroes. They are enthralled by characters with super powers and look up to champions of good over evil. For many primary school children, their teacher can be a superhero figure. When trainee teachers are asked to consider how they perceive the role of the teacher, they will often use the term 'role model' but what exactly are they implying by their use of this phrase? Certainly, the idea of modelling is a key theme that runs through issues surrounding effective teaching and learning at primary level. The effective teacher models a range of skills, from how to solve mathematical problems to how to deal with conflict in the playground, and then supports the child in their own interpretation of this modelling until finally the child has the confidence and is ready to use these skills independently. This view of children and their 'guided participation' (Rogoff, cited in Penn 2008 p. 49) mirrors practices in cultures across the world where the child is viewed as competent and ready to learn skilled adult activity, and also links with the work of Bruner and Vygotsky already discussed in Chapter 2. The effective teacher may also feel that not only is their role one of modelling for children but also for other adults working in the classroom and, at times, parents and other teaching colleagues. We can disseminate excellent practice by allowing others to observe us at work, by the way the learning environment we have created speaks of our values and expectations and by articulating clearly and explicitly why we have chosen to adopt certain strategies and philosophies.

The metaphor of the superhero was chosen because this is a powerful, inspirational figure, a defender of children who will ensure that their learning needs are at the forefront of everything the teacher does. However, it is important to recognise that these same children are strong, competent individuals who need an advocate to fight their corner rather than a rescuer to come and save them.

Work in school

'I'm there to teach lessons – surely it is up to the teaching assistants to do all the caring stuff!'

As their teacher you are an important person in a child's life; it is important that they know you care about them as 'a whole child' for them to succeed as learners. Think about the teachers you responded best to when you were at school. Did you matter to them? How do you know? How did that impact on you as a learner? Think back to what you have learnt in Chapter 5 on the importance of providing a safe and secure environment.

'I find it really hard when I have to tell people who are older and more experienced than me what to do – you know like teaching assitants, I feel like I'm being rude.'

A common target given at the end of placement is to be able to plan effectively for other adults in the classroom and often students respond, as in the comment above, that as young adults, with limited experience in the classroom, they feel uncomfortable directing those not only older but much more competent in working with the children. Remember though what Mackenzie (2011) found out in her research; these are highly committed professionals who have an expectation that you will share your planning and direct them so that they can do their jobs properly. If you do not do this effectively you are impacting on their job satisfaction.

'I try very hard to engage with parents but they don't seem to want to know.'

As a young professional you need to consider objectively why they might not seem bothered. We explored some of the reasons above but other things you may want to reflect on are your body language and your 'teacher presence'. If you are in the class as a student teacher, it is normal that parents will prefer to engage with the class teacher; after all they will be the ones picking up the pieces when you have left! However, this should not prevent you from seeking them out at home time or in the morning to share news about a good piece of work their child has completed. At the beginning and end of the day, be a visible presence in the playground, this will help you build up your confidence in relating to parents and let both them and their children know that you care.

Summary: Teacher as conductor

As we have explored, the role of the teacher is complex and multifaceted. It requires partnership with a wide variety of others. We need to have excellent knowledge of child development and subject knowledge. We must understand how to facilitate learning, how to scaffold learning, how to nurture the whole child, how to inspire. At some points, we can feel like a conductor, orchestrating children's learning experiences, their responses, the curriculum, resources, routines and other adults. This wider view is important as it ensures that we can pull all this together into a holistic, coherent experience, with each child expressing themselves and performing positively.

Questions for discussion

- For many children, their socio-economic circumstances are a barrier to learning. In what ways can a school 'make a difference' in spite of this?
- It has been suggested that children should have specialist subject teachers rather than generalist class teachers in the primary school. Do you agree?
- In most European countries, subject knowledge is included in the field of Professional Studies but there is less emphasis on pedagogy. What are the advantages and disadvantages of this?
- It has been said that multi-agency working and classroom assistants are a threat to teachers' professionalism. Do you agree?

Further reading

Eaude, T. (2011) *Thinking Through Pedagogy for Primary and Early Years*. Exeter: Learning Matters.

This user-friendly text encourages readers to consider how children learn, and how teachers can best support their learning. It begins by asking 'what is pedagogy?' and goes on to examine the wider context, including how language and education impact on pedagogy.

Loughrey, D. and Woods, C. (2010) 'Sparking the Imagination: Creative Experts Working Collaboratively with Children, Teachers and Parents to Enhance Educational Opportunities', *Support for Learning* 25(2): 81–90.

A case study which describes effective and powerful collobarative working between children, teachers, parents and artists.

Mackenzie, S. (2011) '"Yes, But...": Rhetoric, Reality and Resistance in Teaching Assistants' Experiences of Inclusive Education', *Support for Learning* 26(2): 64–71.
This interesting piece of research will give you a real insight into teaching assistants' perspectives.

Muijs, D. and Reynolds, D. (2010) *Effective Teaching*, 3rd edn. London: Sage.
This book encompasses the latest research on effective teaching and learning. Appropriate for all age groups, it provides a comprehensive overview of what is now a large body of knowledge on effective teaching.

Pritchard, A. and Woollard, J. (2010) *Psychology for the Classroom: Constructivism and Social Learning*. London: Routledge.
A discussion of interactive approaches to teaching, this book provides a background to research in constructivist and social learning theory, offering a broad and practical analysis which focuses on contemporary issues and strategies, including the use of e-learning and multimedia.

References

Alexander, R. (ed.) (2010) *Children, their World, their Education: Final Report and Recommendations of the Cambridge Primary Review*. London: Routledge.

Child, D. (1997) *Psychology and the Teacher*, 6th edn. London: Continuum.

Cockburn, A. and Handscomb, G. (2006) *Teaching Children 3 to 11*, 2nd edn. London: Paul Chapman Publishing.

Dean, J. (2000) *Improving Children's Learning*. London: Routledge.

Department for Education (DfE) (2013) *Teachers' Standards*, (https://www.gov.uk).

Desforges, C. and Abouchaar, A. (2003) *The Impact of Parental Support and Family Education on Pupil Achievements and Adjustment: A Literature Review*. Research Report No. 433. Nottingham: DfES.

Hattingh, A. and de Kock, D.M. (2008) 'Perceptions of Teacher Roles in an Experience-rich Teacher Education Programme', *Innovations in Education and Teaching International*, 45(4): 321–32.

Hayes, D. (2004) *Foundations of Primary Teaching*, 3rd edn. London: David Fulton.

Loughrey, D. and Woods, C. (2010) 'Sparking the Imagination: Creative Experts Working Collaboratively with Children, Teachers and Parents to Enhance Educational Opportunities', *Support for Learning* 25(2): 81–90.

Mackenzie, S. (2011) '"Yes, But ...": Rhetoric, Reality and Resistance in Teaching Assistants' Experiences of Inclusive Education', *Support for Learning* 26(2): 64–71.

Moyles, J. (2001) *Organising for Learning in the Primary Classroom*. Buckingham: OUP.

Myhill, D., Jones, S. and Hopper, R. (2006) *Talking, Listening, Learning: Effective Talk in the Primary Classroom*. Maidenhead: OUP.

Penn, H. (2008) *Understanding Early Childhood: Issues and Controversies*, 2nd edn. Maidenhead: McGraw-Hill.

Siraj-Blatchford, I., Sylva, K., Muttock, S., Gilden, R. and Bell, D. (2002) *Researching Effective Pedagogy in the Early Years*. Nottingham: DfES.

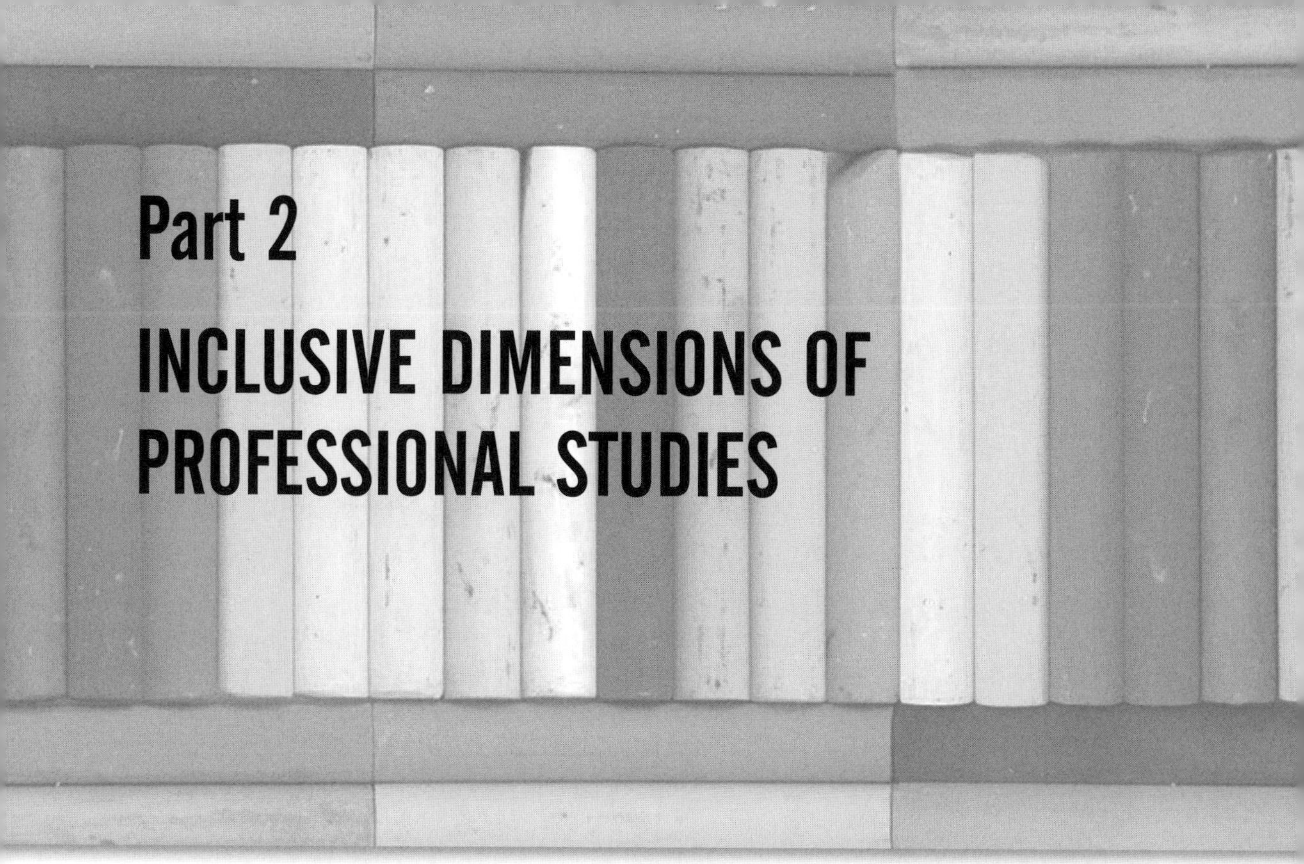

Part 2

INCLUSIVE DIMENSIONS OF PROFESSIONAL STUDIES

In Part 1 you were introduced to the philosophy underpinning this book and to the broad foundations of Professional Studies: planning and assessment, classroom organisation and ethos and the significance of relationships with children and adults. Part 2 builds on these foundations by focusing on a range of themes which have in common the concept of inclusion – the need to take into account children's individual needs. These depend on children's levels of ability and maturation, social, cultural and ethnic backgrounds, and personal and social development. You will consider inclusive teaching and learning strategies which will enable you to provide children with equal opportunities to learn and to meet their potential. And you will realise that each of these themes involves informed value judgements about how best to proceed.

CHAPTER 7

REFLECTIVE PRACTICE IN THE EARLY YEARS: A FOCUS ON ISSUES RELATED TO TEACHING RECEPTION-AGE CHILDREN

Lin Savage and Anne Renwick

By the end of this chapter, you should:

- have an informed understanding of controversial issues related to teaching 4–5-year-olds in reception classes
- have some understanding of the importance of the play-based curriculum and how to protect it in mixed-age classes, the importance of creative and innovative practice and how to develop this
- have some understanding of the importance of developmentally appropriate approaches to teaching 3–5-year-olds and of how to do this
- have some understanding of theories underpinning the teaching of 3–5-year-olds
- understand some international perspectives on early years education.

Introduction

This chapter will focus on issues related to teaching reception-age children. It will address several controversial issues such as school starting age, the entitlement to a play-based curriculum and different pedagogical approaches to early reading. The chapter will focus on the need for reception teachers to develop an evidence-based personal philosophy and to use this to develop innovative and creative teaching practice, which extends young children's learning in a manner appropriate to their age and stage of development.

Through reflective, enquiry-based activities, readers will be encouraged to consider issues particular to teaching reception class children, including how to protect the entitlement to a play-based curriculum for reception-age children in mixed-age classes. Some consideration of the Teachers' Standards and their interpretation and application for teachers of children aged 3–5 will be included. Theoretical models and international perspectives will be drawn upon to encourage a consideration of education in the wider context.

Some challenges and issues

Adapting to a new environment

As the leader of the first class in a child's statutory education, the reception teacher has particular challenges and issues to consider. Children arrive in the reception class having had a variety of diverse experiences prior to beginning statutory school. While a reception class is likely to include many children who have had some nursery or pre-school experiences, it is possible that some children will be leaving their home and family for their first experience of the wider world. Settling children successfully at the beginning of their school life is a skill many student teachers do not get an opportunity to practise in training, but is a crucial aspect of the reception teacher's role, and can heavily influence a child's attitude to school and disposition for learning.

The chances of a child's successful adjustment to school can be increased by the adoption of certain transition strategies, such as home visits, familiarisation with the buildings and close communication with parents throughout the process (Fabian and Dunlop 2002). Margetts (2002) has noted that children who have difficulties adjusting to school in the early days are more likely to experience difficulties in adjustment throughout their schooling; this reinforces the responsibilities of the teacher in this crucial period.

Dealing with differences in maturation

Additionally, in this age range the 11-month gap between a September and August born child can amount to approximately a quarter of the child's life span and developmental stages of individual children can be extremely varied. The only way to deal with this wide range of experience and development is to start where the children are. The reception teacher will need to be skilled in observation and child development in order to begin to make sense of the range of experiences of each specific group of children, and to learn about their abilities, needs and motivations in order to plan appropriate learning experiences.

Good practice includes:

- practitioners with a sound knowledge of child development
- regular use of a variety of observation approaches, used to build individual profiles of children
- observation used to inform planning of appropriately matched learning experiences.

The importance of relating to parents and carers

Relationships with parents and carers are an important aspect of the reception teacher's work. There is a rare opportunity, while the children are young and brought to school, to have daily contact with parents and carers. This can create the climate for forming the all-important relationship between home and school which will hopefully last throughout the child's primary education. Research (Desforges 2003; Sammons et al. 2007) indicates that parents and home learning have the most significant impact on children's attainment, and understanding and working with parents is, therefore, a central concern for reception class teachers and one that was emphasised in the 2012 Review of the Early Years Foundation Stage (Tickell 2011).

In addition to the possible anxieties of children adapting to new surroundings, the reception teacher has also to be mindful of the feelings and views of the child's parents. There are occasions when difficult separations are not only about the child's needs; some parents can require significant support during the early days and weeks of leaving their children at school. Parents' preoccupations and anxieties in these early days are often focused on school dinners, toileting behaviours and social aspects of transition, and reception teachers need to recognise the significance of the child's holistic experience of the school environment and be versed in communicating sensitively with parents about children's learning in its widest sense.

Good practice includes:

- offering home visits to meet families in their own environment
- clear and user-friendly information packs
- planning for parents to stay and settle children
- use of a noticeboard for informing parents
- allocating time to listen to parents.

A meeting of cultures

In trying to analyse the specific issues inherent in the challenges and issues for reception-age children and teachers, it can be useful to analyse the various cultural perspectives impacting on the reception-class experience. The child's first encounter with school life involves the meeting of a number of cultures which may be typified by different values and beliefs, different traditions, behaviours and rules.

At least three specific cultures meet and impact on the reception-age child: the culture of the home, what we will refer to as the culture of 'early years provision', and the culture of the primary school. Of course, there are also additional cultures impacting on the child's situation such as the community and national cultural influences, but in this chapter, the three cultures outlined above will provide the focus for reflection and analysis.

The culture of the home

Children's home lives will, of course, vary considerably, but some significant generic aspects of home life might be:

- family traditions and routines
- cultural and religious identity
- the amount and quality of attention from key adults
- relationships with older or younger siblings
- the home environment – the amount and quality of space, familiarity and ownership of space and key objects (such as children having their own room, toys, cup, plate, and so on)
- freedoms (for example to sleep, eat, drink when they need to).

It can be too easy to underestimate the impact of arriving in a building which is completely unfamiliar and unlike 'home'. This has been brought to the attention of the authors on many occasions, for example when children look around the room wide-eyed and ask, 'Where's your bed?' or emerge from the school toilets having washed their hair.

Fabian (2002) refers to this experience for the child in terms of a 'physical discontinuity', which in transition is accompanied by 'social discontinuity' as the child adjusts to different key adults and larger social groups of children.

The culture informing early years provision

In this section, we refer to the culture informing early years provision which has developed in England over the last two centuries, stemming from the work of early pioneers such as Susan Isaacs and Margaret McMillan and informed by more recent research such as *Researching Effective Pedagogy in the Early Years* (Siraj-Blatchford et al. 2002) and *Effective Provision of Pre-School Education* (Sylva et al. 2003). The early years community has a strong body of researchers, writers and practitioners with a well-researched and deep-seated set of principles. This was endorsed in the

2012 Tickell review of the Early Years Foundation Stage and continues to inform the revised statutory Early Years Foundation Stage curriculum (DfE 2012), as it has influenced the ethos and documents of the last decade and includes:

- commitment to a curriculum, which starts from observations of the child rather than specific curriculum content to be taught
- providing a curriculum which uses play as a vehicle for planning meaningful learning experiences
- planning a curriculum appropriate for the child's developmental stage
- a focus on active learning, which deepens conceptual understanding
- the equal importance of all areas of learning when planning learning experiences
- the centrality of partnership with parents and families
- an emphasis on using the environment to facilitate learning, including the outdoors
- a balance between adult-led and child-initiated activity
- the interlinked nature of education and care
- routines such as small group times with key workers, snack time, singing and story sessions.

Children's experiences of early years provision before entering reception will reflect the principles outlined above in varying degrees as quality varies. The Early Years Foundation Stage (DCSF 2008) and its revised 2012 curriculum (DfE 2012) apply to children until the end of their reception year and should be the guiding ethos for the reception teacher. In some reception classes this is not evident in practice.

A report published in 2004 by the Association of Teachers and Lecturers, entitled *Inside the Foundation Stage: Recreating the Reception Year*, concluded:

> There is a demonstrable gap between the quality of children's experiences in the reception classes in our sample, the *second year* of the Foundation Stage, and the quality of their experiences in the *first year* of the Foundation Stage in our best nurseries and family centres as highlighted in other research, e.g. Bertram and Pascal, 2002; Whalley 1994. (Adams et al. 2004 p. 19)

Reflective task

Summarise the main findings of the EPPE (Sylva et al. 2003) and REPEY (Siraj-Blatchford et al. 2002) reports as though you were explaining them to:

- a Key Stage 2 colleague
- a parent
- a health or other integrated services practitioner.

(Continued)

(Continued)

What would be the key points you would want to communicate to each of these people? Role play a conversation in order to extract key points.

What are the main recommendations of the 2012 Tickell Report and the subsequent review of qualifications by Cathy Nutbrown (2012)? To what extent do you agree/disagree with these recommendations? What evidence can you cite to back up your position?

The culture of the primary school

Here we consider the culture of the wider primary school and some of its principles, traditions and routines in order to raise awareness of some of the tensions which can have an impact on reception-age children and their teachers.

The statutory documentation for the primary curriculum in England is the National Curriculum. As in early years provision, the ethos of different primary schools can differ considerably, but external factors have impacted on the culture of the English primary school with certain generic consequences.

Some features of the primary school culture include:

- a curriculum presented in 11 discrete subjects
- a curriculum focus on subject knowledge and content
- priority given to core subjects (English, mathematics, science and, initially, ICT)
- the current and historical impact of the primary strategies
- standard assessment tasks which inform school league tables
- routines such as assembly, undressing and dressing for PE, playtimes, school dinners.

Practice in reception classes can vary a great deal and we have found it useful in explaining and analysing this with regard to the cultural perspectives model outlined above. In different schools, the meeting of the cultures outlined above will favour some cultural perspectives and associated values more than others and practice will reflect the dominant ethos.

The Early Years Curriculum Group, a nationally recognised group of early years specialists, identified a number of factors that have placed constraints upon the adoption of the early years ethos in reception classes (EYCG 2002).

These factors include:

- the false assumption that the earlier children learn something, the more high achieving they will later become
- fear of the inspection process, which has resulted in a strong emphasis on literacy and numeracy targets

- the top-down pressure of Year 2 SATs, which has created inappropriate expectations about early success in particular aspects of literacy and numeracy
- confusion about the principles of early years pedagogy, and an erosion of the practitioner's commitment to the importance of play as a vehicle for learning. (Adams et al. 2004 p. 12)

Reflective task

Consider a reception class in a school you are familiar with – to what extent do the three cultures outlined above impact on practice? Draw a diagram representing the interplay of the three cultures outlined in this chapter and the dominant influences in a reception class you have experienced.

In mixed-age classes, the pressure to pursue the primary school values and routines is even stronger than with a straight reception class. This has been resisted by some teachers who have planned for Key Stage 1 children using some of the principles of early years provision. Attempts to bring the primary provision closer to the early years culture have been made with the introduction of the Continuing Learning Journey (QCA 2005) training and, to some extent, the Primary Curriculum (2009), which reconfigured discrete subjects into areas of learning. England has not been as successful in this as Wales, where the Foundation Phase refers to the 3–7 age phase. The imposition of daily phonics sessions suggested in the *Letters and Sounds* (DCSF 2007) document, discussed below, and the failure of the 2010 Coalition Government to adopt the primary curriculum, have been precursors of a shift to a more formal and traditional approach for primary school teaching, as can be seen in the draft proposals for the new national curriculum (DfE 2013) – available for consultation at the time of writing. This shift will increase the challenge of synthesising the child-centred early years ethos with the increasing subject knowledge content requirements of the current Education Minister's (Michael Gove) vision for the future of the primary curriculum.

Good practice for children in mixed-age classes includes:

- using active learning and play-based activities inside and outside to deliver the 5–7 curriculum, including tasks differentiated to provide the full range of challenge
- expecting older children to work independently at times and interact with younger children in child-initiated play situations
- planning mixed-age group work for some curriculum delivery.

Reflective task

Consider the Teachers' Standards, available at: https://www.gov.uk/government/publications/teachers-standards and the current standards for EYPS available at: http://media.education.gov.uk/assets/files/pdf/r/eyps%20standards%20from%20september%202012.pdf.

Analyse the extent to which both sets of standards, including the language adopted, reflect the early years ethos and training needs of an early years teacher, and particularly a reception teacher.

Compare the Teachers' Standards with those for Early Years Professional Status. Would you like to amend the standards for the early years workforce in any way in the light of this comparison?

School starting age: international comparisons

The statutory age at which a child begins formal schooling varies across the world and has become an area of controversy within the UK. Even within the UK, there are differences, with children in Northern Ireland beginning at 4, while England, Scotland and Wales have an official statutory starting age of 5, though many begin reception at 4. In most other European countries, age 6 or 7 is the norm (Sharp 2002). Debate and discussion centres around the quality of the provision accessed by these young children and its appropriateness for their age and stage of development. In those countries with a later school starting date, most children will have access to some form of pre-school provision in a nursery or kindergarten.

The formality, structure, expectations and demands on the children of each country's curricula, whether prescribed or not, vary considerably. When comparing England with the rest of Europe, and indeed other countries around the world, it becomes apparent that as a society we impose a statutory curriculum and assessment process on our children at a younger age than most (Bertram and Pascal 2002). However, in international comparisons of later achievement, UK children do not perform significantly better than those starting school at 6 or 7 (OECD; PISA).

The recent reviews of the primary curriculum (Alexander 2010; Rose 2009) have only served to fuel the debate. While Rose suggests an earlier school starting age of 4, Alexander proposes 6 as a more appropriate starting age, saying that anxiety focuses on the fact that, at the age of 5 – against the grain of evidence, expert opinion and international practice – children in England leave behind their active, play-based learning and embark on a formal, subject-based curriculum. For many, this process begins at 4. The report continues to say that there is overwhelming evidence that children of this age need structured play, talk and interaction with others and that this is particularly true for children from disadvantaged homes. (For the key recommendations of the Cambridge Primary Review, see Alexander [2010 p. 491].) Yet the Labour Government's commendable investment in the early years collided with its 'standards agenda' and downward pressure from KS1 and 2. Formal schooling at too early an age has been counter-productive, resulting in England's appallingly large attainment gap.

In England, one of the key findings from a review of recent international research and policy on the issue of relative age highlights the fact that pupils who are younger in the year group (known as 'summer borns' in the UK) do less well in attainment tests, are more frequently identified as having special educational needs and are more frequently referred to psychiatric services (Sharp et al. 2009).

Sue Palmer has been drawing our attention to wider issues related to childhood in the twenty-first century and the 'dangers' children face in the modern world. Poor diet, lack of exercise and the dangers of television and computers, to name a few of her concerns, are all impacting on the quality of childhood (Palmer 2006).

A UNICEF report published in 2007 assessed the well-being of children and young people in 21 industrialised countries and gave the UK the lowest ranking (UNICEF 2007). This shocking result provided the impetus for improvements to be the focus for those in both education and government. The latest UNICEF report of 2013 places the UK at 16 out of 29 countries in the new league table and indicates that 'the UK has moved up the league table, but there is still a way to go to be near where we should be' (UNICEF 2013).

A Good Childhood was a landmark report for the Children's Society, looking at the condition of childhood in the UK, drawing our attention to the higher levels of child poverty and lower levels of well-being experienced by children in the UK compared with their counterparts in Europe (Layard and Dunn 2009). Subsequent reports from the Children's Society continue to document the issues and offer suggestions for improvement for policy makers (Rees et al. 2013).

With children in the UK attending school from the age of 4 and amongst the youngest in Europe, there are significant implications and responsibilities for the reception teacher to ensure that the children's needs are appropriately met and that they are prepared for the pressures of the modern world. While protecting children from real risks, we must be careful to ensure that we do not produce children who are 'wrapped in cotton wool', with little resilience or ability to cope in the modern world (Gill 2009).

Creative and innovative practice, based on first-hand experience, which enables children's self-esteem as well as social and emotional learning to develop and thrive, must be key.

International inspiration from the world-renowned pre-schools of Reggio Emilia in Northern Europe, the Forest Schools of Scandinavian countries and Te Whāriki, the curriculum of New Zealand, with their emphasis on the social and creative needs of young children, have all influenced the development of recent practice within the UK.

Good practice includes:

- planning for children's developmental needs, abilities and interests, whatever the setting
- using the curriculum in a flexible way to ensure that children's needs and interests are met
- practitioners who use their developing knowledge of the experiences from other countries, to extend their own thinking and allow this to impact on the experiences they plan for children
- challenging our own thinking about the needs and interests of children
- allowing children to take the lead – this requires a confidence and underpinning understanding of child development
- listening to children – verbally and through observation – in order to create an environment that allows for creativity.

The importance of a play-based curriculum

The importance of play, indoors and outside, is generally recognised by early years practitioners as of crucial importance. It is well researched, documented and part of early years pedagogy. High involvement levels and the maximising of learning through child-initiated experiences are supported though the work of Ferre Laevers (2005). The recent statutory curricula have placed high importance on using play as the means through which children learn. The EYFS (DCSF 2008) included 'Play and Exploration' as one of the key commitments within the learning and development theme and recognised its importance: 'Children's play reflects their wide ranging and varied interests and preoccupations. In their play children learn at their highest level. Play with peers is important for children's development' (DCSF 2008 pp. 10–14). The Revised EYFS (DfE 2012) describes 'playing and exploring' as one of the three 'characteristics of effective teaching and learning' for children of this age. Alongside 'active learning' and 'creating and thinking critically', play is recognised as an important way in which children learn. In planning for children's learning and development, reception teachers are required to ensure that this is translated into practice. Further guidance is available in *Development Matters in the Early Years Foundation Stage (EYFS)*, non-statutory guidance material supporting practitioners in implementing the statutory requirements of the Revised EYFS (Early Education, 2012).

International influences, referred to above, reinforce the role of play and follow the interests of children in order to maximise learning.

The well-trained early years teacher will recognise play's importance in delivering all areas of the curriculum and resist those top-down pressures associated with a concentration on literacy and numeracy. At the beginning of their school career, before they have acquired the formal skills of reading and writing drawn upon by so many primary lessons, the reception year requires a pedagogy of its own which builds on what children can do and develops fundamental skills in a meaningful context. The process of planning meaningful learning experiences that cannot, by their nature, rely on the skills of reading and writing, which have not as yet been fully mastered, presents a challenge to many trainee and experienced teachers.

It must also be recognised that children require a balance of child- and adult-initiated experiences in order for their learning to be maximised (Siraj-Blatchford et al. 2002; Sylva et al. 2003). There are skills and concepts which need to be directly taught to children through the support of a knowledgeable adult who has provided a suitable environment to support learning through play, while at the same time scaffolding children's learning in an appropriate way. Interactions in a well-organised and planned learning environment are essential. '"Sustained shared thinking" occurs when two or more individuals "work together" in an intellectual way to solve a problem, clarify a concept, evaluate an activity, or extend a narrative. Both parties must contribute to the thinking and it must develop and extend the understanding' (Sylva et al. 2003 p. 5). This concept requires highly skilled adults to support children in an appropriate way. The challenge for reception teachers, and perhaps particularly when working in a mixed-age class, is to enable staff to contribute to these interactions within the areas of continuous provision. An emphasis only on direct teaching to small groups, or the whole class, will miss the opportunities for spontaneous interactions at the most relevant time for the child. In mixed-age classes, it can be all too tempting to allocate support for the reception children to those least qualified, or in some cases to volunteers. Challenges to providing an appropriate play-based curriculum, indoors and outside, may also include the lack of resources and the size of the space available to many reception classes. Where there is no access to an outdoor area enabling continuous free-flow of movement in both environments, teachers must think creatively in order to meet the need for daily access to an outdoor environment.

Good practice includes:

- a well-planned, organised and resourced environment – indoors and outside – appropriate to the developmental needs of children
- practitioners who plan to extend and widen children's experiences, while enabling children to follow their own interests

- practitioners who engage, extend and develop creativity and critical thinking across the curriculum, allowing children to be independent in a safe, yet challenging environment.

Early reading

Children bring a variety of early reading experiences to the reception class in school. Some children may have few books in the home, while others have a whole 'library' of books in their bedrooms. Whatever their home circumstances, most children will have some experience of print in the environment, on television or a computer screen, and those attending nursery or pre-school will have accessed books in these settings. Learning to read is a complex process and can be challenging for those with little prior experience of books or a secure language base on which to build.

The most appropriate age and method through which to teach children to read has long been a subject for heated debate. To date, there is no significant research that suggests that starting reading earlier produces long-term benefits (Suggate 2009) and, as suggested above, those countries who have later school starting ages do not suffer significantly in terms of reading competence – quite the opposite (OECD; PISA). Following the *Independent Review of the Teaching of Early Reading* (Rose 2006), teachers are currently strongly encouraged to adopt a 'synthetic phonics' approach and use the 'simple view of reading'.

Reception staff with weighty responsibility for the introduction of children to statutory education and in particular for the teaching of early reading, must be mindful that this experience can significantly impact on children's lifelong attitude to school.

Introducing children to fundamental skills is a complex process and it can be too easy for young children to feel like a failure before they even begin Key Stage 1. Pace and appropriateness of delivery are crucial and differentiation for different stages of child development is imperative.

As Rose (2006) suggests: 'The introduction of phonic work should always be a matter for principled, professional judgment based on structured observations and assessments of children's capabilities' (p. 3). Parents want their children to succeed in school and can unwittingly communicate unrealistic expectations to young children of their potential achievements 'now they are at big school'.

Reception staff should provide beginner readers with a rich curriculum that fosters language: speaking, listening, reading and writing (Rose 2006).

Good practice includes:

- teachers who protect children from the pressures of 'learning to read' before they are developmentally ready to do so
- a stimulating environment with an attractive reading area, containing a wide variety of reading materials, as well as books, story sacks and materials for storytelling
- adults who model the reading process and engage children in enjoyable reading experiences, including 'talk' about books and stories.

Different curricula will come and go but good practice will continue to require a focus on child development and provision, which is appropriate for individual children.

Work in school

Early years students and practitioners are often in the minority in school situations and find it difficult to access information and reassurance on aspects of good quality early years provision.

The following are some of the questions we are frequently asked.

Play

Question: 'If I have 30 children in my reception class, how do I support them all to follow their own interests?'

Answer: If the classroom is organised into areas of well-resourced continuous provision, then children can follow their own interests on a daily basis, accessing the areas and resources they need. The child or group of children who are interested in a birthday or wedding experienced by one of the group, for example, can be given access to the resources to support their role play.

Children can be grouped for larger projects according to their interest in a particular idea, event or theme, that may need to involve adults planning with the children, on an outing or visit for example.

Reading

Question: 'How can children be encouraged to independently practise their developing reading and writing skills?'

(Continued)

(Continued)

Answer: Children do need to be directly taught certain knowledge and skills, which the teacher plans for according to the ability and needs of individuals and groups of children. However, children then need to be able to practise independently, in an interactive way that allows children to follow their own interests and needs. Reading and writing resources available to children in areas of provision around the classroom enable children to then use the skills they have been taught in play scenarios, thus reinforcing and developing them. Children's involvement in their self-chosen activities is generally at a much higher level than during teacher-initiated activities, allowing deeper level learning.

Formative assessment

Question: 'How can I manage the formative assessment process?'

Answer: Formative assessment should be an integral part of everyday planning, as unless you know what the children can do, you will be unable to plan their next steps. In adult-led learning experiences you should decide how you are going to assess learning. Sometimes this may be possible by annotating a piece of writing, a drawing or model after the session. Ephemeral objects can be photographed and the photos annotated. Often you will need to make observation notes during an activity, as it will be the children's comments that reveal what they know and any misconceptions they may have. It is also important to record observation notes in children's free-flow play, as it is in this context that they will demonstrate the conceptual knowledge, skills and information that they have assimilated. A notebook or Post-its are suitable methods of recording; they are working documents so you can develop your own abbreviations for speed. It is important to train all adults working in the classroom to undertake formative assessment; they will need some training from you on what to look for and how to record it, but the pay-off will be worth the time spent.

Balance of adult- and child-led activities

Question: How can I convince my primary colleagues of the importance of child-initiated learning?

Answer: Research on effective pedagogy (REPEY. 2003) has underlined the importance of both learning activities involving direct teaching and free-flow play situations in a well-designed learning environment. Planned learning experiences give children the opportunity to learn specific skills, concepts and knowledge planned by the teacher to ensure curriculum coverage and must be differentiated to meet children's specific needs informed by formative assessment. This is complemented by children's free-flow play. Children's motivation in this context will be high and they will rehearse skills and knowledge recently gained, as well as exploring concepts and following their own lines of thought and creativity. In both contexts the important consideration is the quality of the learning experiences provided and the skill of the adult in developing critical thinking skills by sensitive and challenging adult interventions.

We argue that effective pedagogy in the early years involves a balance of the first two approaches, both the kind of interaction traditionally associated with the term 'teaching', and also the provision of instructive learning environments and routines. We argue that where young children have freely chosen to play within an instructive learning environment, adult interventions may be especially effective.
(Siraj-Blatchford et al. 2002 p. 12)

For more information on all the issues above, refer to the REPEY 2003 report on Organisation (Siraj-Blatchford et al. 2002 p. 12)

Developing an evidence-based philosophy

Earlier in this chapter, we used a cultural perspectives approach to consider the differences in ethos that underpin practice variations in reception classes. Reception teachers can approach their role with more confidence and clarity if they have considered their own values and beliefs and how these will influence the ethos, guiding principles, behaviours and rules they wish to adopt with reception-age children.

It is important to inform a personal philosophy with evidence in order to support practice with rigour. There is a wealth of existing research on matters related to aspects of provision for children of 4 and 5 years of age in England. Additionally, a range of research from other countries can provide an interesting comparative view (Bertram and Pascal 2002). Some starting points to engage with this research can be found in the reference list below.

Classroom teachers are increasingly completing their own classroom research, in order to inform their philosophy and improve the quality of experience for young children. Taking the 'teacher as researcher' approach in your reception class will enhance your own understanding of the issues particular to your context. The Centre for the Use of Research and Evidence in Education (CUREE) produces materials to support practitioners in developing evidence-based practice.

Reflective task

List some of the important values and beliefs that will guide your personal philosophy when working with reception-aged children.

Summary

In this chapter, we have introduced the reader to some of the controversial issues related to teaching 4–5-year-olds in reception classes. This included the tensions between formal and play-based learning and the importance of protecting an active approach to learning for children in mixed-age classes.

For young children to develop a positive disposition to school, their experience in the classroom needs to be exciting and inspiring. The reception teacher requires creative and innovative approaches to retain children's motivation and interest. Well-matched learning events, tailored to children's developmental achievements, are essential, and this requires a sound knowledge of child development. The wealth of existing research can be drawn upon to develop an evidence base to underpin practice. Inspiration can be gained from the study of international perspectives on early years education.

The website related to this book gives further suggestions for web-based activities and reading.

Questions for discussion

- What training do you think would support potential reception teachers to induct new children into school?
- Considering the relevant research referred to above regarding school starting ages, what age do you believe is most appropriate for children to start formal schooling?

- How can we promote a lifelong love of reading? What strategies should teachers deploy in order to develop enjoyment as well as skills in early reading?
- How would you organise the environment in a mixed-age class to support active and play-based learning?
- It has been identified that the development of thinking skills is an area that needs further development in early years provision (Siraj-Blatchford et al. 2002). What would you do in your own classroom to ensure the engagement of children in experiences that promote critical thinking?

Further reading

Van Oers, B. and Duljkers, D. (2013) 'Teaching in a Play-Based Curriculum: Theory, Practice and Evidence of Development', *Journal of Curriculum Studies* 41(4): 511–34.
This study of 4–8-year-old children describes the theoretical basis of a play-based curriculum and the teachers' strategies for promoting development, as well as reporting on research into children's vocabulary acquisition.

Linked to topics of interest, the following readings have been chosen because the authors are among the leading experts in the field.

Generic issues affecting early years provision

Brooker, L., Rogers, S., Ellis, D., Hallet, E. and Robert-Holmes, G. (2010) *Practitioners' Experiences of the EYFS*. London: DfE.

Duffy, B. and Pugh, G. (2009) *Contemporary Issues in the Early Years*. London: Sage.
This book includes chapters written by several leading authors on current issues related to policy and research, practice and the workforce, and provides a sound insight into important influences on the current field of early years work.

Garrick, R., Bath, C., Dunn, K., Maconochie, H., Willis, B. and Wolstenholme, C. (2010) *Children's Experiences of the Early Years Foundation Stage*. London: DfE.

Moylett, H. and Stewart, N. (2012) *Understanding the Revised Early Years Foundation Stage*. London: Early Education.

Ofsted (2011) *The Impact of the Early Years Foundation Stage (EYFS)*. London: Ofsted.

Sylva, K., Melhuish, E., Sammons, P., Siraj-Blatchford, I. and Taggart, B. (2008) *Final Report from the Primary Phase: Pre-school, School, and Family Influences on Children's Development during Key Stage 2 (Age 7–11), Effective Pre-School and Primary Education 3–11 Project (EPPE 3–11).* Research Report DCSF RR061. London: DCSF.

Parents and home influences

DCSF (2008) *Parents as Partners in Early Learning Project (PPEL).* London: DCSF.

Melhuish, E. (2010) 'Why Children, Parents and Home Learning are Important', in K. Sylva, E. Melhuish, P. Sammons, I. Siraj-Blatchford and B. Taggart (eds) *Early Childhood Matters: Evidence from the Effective Pre-school and Primary Education Project.* London: Routledge, pp. 95–114.

This research emphasises the impact of home and parental interest in supporting children's achievements at school and will support early years practitioners in understanding the importance of their work with parents.

Whalley, M. (2007) *Involving Parents in their Children's Learning.* London: Sage.

Pen Green Children's Centre has completed some seminal work in teaching parents about child development and developing parents as partners in their children's learning. This book explains the work with parents in detail.

A play-based curriculum

Bilton, H. (2010) *Outdoor Learning in the Early Years.* Oxford: Routledge.

A useful book to support setting up and extending outside provision and developing outdoor learning.

Brooker, L. and Edwards, S. (eds) (2010) *Engaging Play.* Maidenhead: McGraw-Hill.

Bruce, T. (2004) *Developing Learning in Early Childhood (0–8).* London: Sage.

This book includes practical ideas for supporting early active learning experiences.

Lindon, J. (1999) *Too Safe for their Own Good.* London: NCB.

Reading this book will help you to consider your own position with regard to balancing risk and challenge in children's lives.

Moyles, J. (1989) *Just Playing?* Maidenhead: Open University Press.

This book will help you to pursue ideas introduced above about the value of play. It includes sections on play and progress to aid record keeping and the tracking of children's learning.

Early literacy

Bayley, R. and Palmer, S. (2008) *Foundations of Literacy*, 3rd edn. London: Continuum Books.

A practical book full of inspired ideas for planning literacy in the early years.

Whitehead, M. (2010) *Language and Literacy in the Early Years 0–7*. London: Sage.

This book gives both a theoretical and practical perspective on teaching literacy for enjoyment, across the full early years age range.

Additional websites

DfE EYFS website: http://www.education.gov.uk/schools/teachingandlearning/curriculum/a0068102/early-years-foundation-stage-eyfs

Foundation Years website: http://www.foundationyears.org.uk

References

Adams, S., Alexander, E., Drummond, M.J. and Moyles, J. (2004) *Inside the Foundation Stage: Recreating the Reception Year*. London: Association of Teachers and Lecturers. Available at: http://www.atl.org.uk/Images/Inside%20the%20foundation%20stage.pdf

Alexander, R. (ed.) (2010) *Children, their World, their Education: Final Report and Recommendations of the Cambridge Primary Review*. Oxford: Routledge.

Bertram, T. and Pascal, C. (2002) *Early Years Education: An International Perspective*. Birmingham: Centre for Research in Early Childhood.

DCSF (2007) *Letters and Sounds*. London: DCSF.

DCSF (2008) *Early Years Foundation Stage*. London: DCSF.

DfE (2012) *Revised Statutory Framework for the Early Years Foundation Stage*. London: DfE

DfE (2013) *The National Curriculum in England: Framework Document*. London: DfE.

Desforges, C. (2003) *The Impact of Parental Involvement, Parental Support and Family Education on Pupil Achievements and Adjustment: A Literature Review*. Research Report RR433. London: DfES.

Early Education (2012) *Development Matters in the Early Years Foundation Stage (EYFS)*. London: Early Education.

Early Years Curriculum Group (EYCG) (2002) *Onwards and Upwards: Building on the Foundation Stage*. Oxford: Early Years Curriculum Group.

Fabian, H. (2002) *Children Starting School*. London: David Fulton.

Fabian, H. and Dunlop, A.W. (2002) *Transitions in the Early Years: Debating Continuity and Progression for Children in Early Education*. London: Routledge Falmer.

Gill, T. (2009) *No Fear: Growing Up in a Risk Averse Society*. London: Calouste Gulbenkian Foundation.

Laevers, F. (ed.) (2005) *Well-being and Involvement in Care Settings: A Process-oriented Self-evaluation Instrument*. Leuven: Research Centre for Experiential Education, Leuven University.

Layard, R. and Dunn, J. (2009) *A Good Childhood*. London: Penguin Books.

Margetts, K. (2002). 'Early Transition and Adjustment and Children's Adjustment After Six Years of Schooling', *European Early Childhood Education Research Journal* 17(3): 309–24.

Nutbrown, C. (2012) *Foundations for Quality: The Independent Review of Early Education and Childcare Qualifications*. London: DfE.

Palmer, S. (2006) *Toxic Childhood: How the Modern World is Damaging Our Children and What We Can Do About It*. London: Orion.

QCA (2005) *Continuing the Learning Journey*. London: QCA.

Rees, G., Goswami, H., Pople, L., Bradshaw, J., Keung, A. and Main, G. (2013) The Good Childhood Report, The Children's Society and the University of York. Available at: http://www.childrenssociety.org.uk/sites/default/files/tcs/good_childhood_report_2013_final.pdf

Rose, J. (2006) *Independent Review of the Teaching of Early Reading*. London: DfES.

Rose, J. (2009) *Independent Review of the Primary Curriculum: Final Report*. London: DCSF.

Sammons, P. et al. (2007) *Summary Report: Influences on Children's Attainment and Progress in Key Stage 2: Cognitive Outcomes in Year 5: Effective Pre-school and Primary Education 3–11 Project (EPPE 3–11)*. Research Report RR828. London: DfES.

Sharp, C. (2002) *School Starting Age: European Policy and Recent Research*. Slough: NFER.

Sharp, C., George, N., Sargent, C., O'Donnell, S. and Heron, M. (2009) *International Thematic Probe: The Influence of Relative Age on Learner Attainment and Development*. Slough: NFER. Available at: http://www.nfer.ac.uk/what-we-do/information-and-reviews/inca/RelativeAge ReviewRevised2012.pdf

Siraj- Blatchford, I., Sylva, K., Muttock, S. , Gilden, R. and Bell, D. (2002,) *Researching Effective Pedagogy in the Early Years*, DES Research Report RR 356. Available at: http://www.ioe.ac.uk/REPEY_research_report.pdf

Suggate, S.P. (2009) 'School Entry Age and Reading Achievement', *International Journal of Educational Research* 48(3): 151–61.

Sylva, K., Melhuish, E., Sammons, P., Siraj-Blatchford, I. and Taggart, B. (2003) *Effective Provision of Pre-School Education (EPPE)*. Nottingham: DfES.

Tickell, C. (2011) The Early Years Foundations for Life, Health and Learning: An Independent Report on the Early Years Foundation Stage to Her Majesty's Government. Available at: http://www.education.gov.uk

UNICEF (2007) *Child Poverty in Perspective: An Overview of Child Well-being in Rich Countries*. Innocenti Report Card 7. Florence: UNICEF Innocenti Research Centre.

UNICEF (2013) *Child Well-being in Rich Countries: A Comparative Overview*, Innocenti Report Card 11 Florence: UNICEF. Available at: http://www.unicef.org.uk/Latest/Publications/Report-Card-11-Child-well-being-in-rich-countries/

Whalley, M. (1994) *Learning to Be Strong*. London: Hodder and Stoughton.

Websites

Centre for the Use of Research and Evidence in Education (CUREE): http://www.curee.co.uk/

Forest Schools: http://www.forestschools.com/

OECD: http://www.oecd.org/

PISA: http://oecd.org/pisa/

Reggio Emilia: http://zerosei.comune.re.it/inter/reggiochildren.htm

Te Whāriki: http://www.educate.ece.govt.nz/learning/curriculumAndLearning/TeWhariki.aspx

The Children's Society: http://www.childrenssociety.org.uk/sites/default/files/tcs/good_childhood_report_2013_final.pdf

UNICEF UK: http://www.unicef.org.uk/Images/Campaigns/Report%20card%20briefing2b.pdf

CHAPTER 8

INCLUSION AND SPECIAL EDUCATIONAL NEEDS

Verna Kilburn and Kären Mills

By the end of this chapter, you should be able to:

- engage with fundamental questions concerning special educational needs as a contested concept
- develop your own values and demonstrate a commitment to social justice and inclusion
- construct and sustain a reasoned argument about some issues of inclusion, in a lucid and coherent manner
- demonstrate a clear understanding of the implications of whole-school issues relating to inclusion and special educational needs.

Introduction

Special Educational Needs (SEN) is an area that is simultaneously fascinating and complex. Although in historical terms it is a relatively recent expression, being brought to prominence through the Warnock Report (1978), in many ways it involves questions that are central to concepts of our humanity. What is the duty of the State to the individual? What compromises must the individual make to be part of a group? What is it to be different and who decides what the parameters of difference are? SEN has grown out of the fertile soil of politics, philosophy, medicine, ethics and pedagogy and all are set in a linguistic minefield.

This chapter considers interpretation of the terminology associated with inclusion and SEN. It considers changes in attitudes to children with SEN over the last century and the reasons for this, as well as recent legislation on provision for children with SEN and the implications for teachers in primary schools. Throughout, there is a discussion of inclusion as a contested concept, the efficacy of the legislation, the disparity between ideology and practice and the complex and difficult decisions which teachers are involved in making. Case studies and activities involve readers in developing their own understanding of their roles in decision making and their views about problematic issues.

Why is discussion of inclusion issues complex and emotive?

It is not uncommon for students to be apprehensive before a school placement, and this anxiety may be increased by uncertainty about how to deal with children in the class who have SEN. This may be because of problems encountered on a previous placement, perhaps having a sibling with SEN, students themselves having experienced a barrier to learning in their own schooling or a student's own philosophy of education. The implications are that SEN is an area fraught with emotional and academic tensions. This is because responding to SEN involves not just academic and pedagogical skills but is also concerned with moral issues. By reflecting on the terminology you use and that others use, you can begin to participate in informed discussions of these issues.

Reflective task

In small groups, select a word from the following list:

Equality	*Inclusion*	*Disabled*	*Democracy*	*Management*
Special	*Diversity*	*Education*	*Labelling*	*Community*

(Continued)

(Continued)

- Write down the connotations of the term (words or ideas suggested by the word). (This should only take a few minutes and should reflect a quick, emotional reaction to the word.)
- Underline which connotations are positive and which are negative.
- Write a *short* definition of the term.
- Share all of this with a larger group and ask them to critique the definition.
- Which was the most difficult part of the activity?
- Are the definitions representative of the connotations?
- Which may have the most power?

According to Graber (2002), the use of some high-value words can distort an argument as their accompanying emotive power can hide the fact that there is little agreement over their definitions. This can not only obscure the argument, but lead to a manipulation of the feelings and thoughts of the reader/listener. This may be something in which politicians demonstrate a high level of skill (listen to a party political broadcast and notice the 'high-value words').

It is possible that the same difficulty is also encountered in the area of inclusion and education in general. We perhaps need more respect for the approach of the young child who asks 'What does it really mean?'

Words and meanings

The world of SEN contains sufficient of these emotive idioms to ensure a high level of anxiety in any student. Consider the following: handicap, disabled, impairment, barrier to learning, normal, segregation, integration … and this is not including the terms that are *definitely* not used in academic circles. The question arises as to why this is more prevalent in the area of inclusion than in other subjects. If I use the wrong term in mathematics or science, it may indicate a factual mistake or misunderstanding but may tell the other speaker little about my belief system or ethics. This is not true in SEN, which is value-laden. There are, however, dangers in this because:

- the study of inclusion/SEN can be *ideologically* driven
- there is little agreement over the *definition* and use of the key terms.

Ideologies

The Teachers' Standards give prominence to the values and attitudes expected of teachers and it has long been acknowledged that teaching should have a strong ethical and belief-based foundation. This may not be synonymous, however, with an ideological stance. According to Haralambos and Holborn:

> The term ideology refers to a set of ideas which present only a partial view of reality … it involves not only a judgement about the ways things are, but also about the way things ought to be. (2000 p. 19)

An ideology may be a partial, one-sided view, but one that is in harmony with the speaker's world view. Any cognitive dissonance is 'brushed under the carpet' in the mind. This may make life exceptionally difficult for the student as they need to constantly examine what evidence the author supplies (and what is omitted) and to be critical of the terminology used.

Definitions

The term inclusion has long been associated with children with SEN but it could be argued that it is relevant to all groups that are marginalised in and by our education system. There may be a strong case that educational failure is a form of exclusion as much as separate schooling. This could include, for example, children with English as an Additional Language (EAL), children in care, refugee children, traveller children and the division by ethnicity, gender, faith and social class into separate institutions. The UK has a growing number of different types of schools and the number seems set to increase in the near future. This expands the argument concerning special versus mainstream schooling into a debate on whether we can have inclusive education while maintaining the myriad form of faith schools, private schools, academies, grammar schools, and so on.

Ainscow et al. (2006) clarify the difficulty of defining inclusion by distinguishing between narrow and broad definitions; narrow referring to aspects of SEN, and broad to all aspects of marginalisation and diversity, but Armstrong et al. (2010) also point out the key dangers by stating:

> the meaning of 'inclusion' is by no means clear and perhaps conveniently blurs the edges of social policy with 'feel-good' rhetoric that no one could be opposed to. (p. 4)

Indeed, bearing in mind the statement in the 1999 National Curriculum that 'Education influences and reflects the values of society, and the kind of society we want to be' (QCA 1999 p. 10), then what possibility is there for inclusive education if the society it reflects is non-inclusive? Definitions of inclusion vary from the absolute, to be found in the statement by the Centre for Studies on Inclusive Education (CSIE):

> We fully support an end to all segregated education on the grounds of disability or learning difficulty, as a policy commitment and goal for this country … the existence of special schools represents a serious violation of students' human rights … (2002)

to the more hesitant one in the Fundamental Aims of the previous SEN Code of Practice (DfES 2001): 'the special educational needs of children will normally be met in mainstream schools or settings' (1.5).

It may not surprise you at this point, but there is also disagreement over the use and definition of the term SEN. According to the draft SEN Code of Practice (COP) (DfE 2013), children are deemed to have a SEN if they:

> …have a learning difficulty or disability which calls for special educational provision to be made for them. A child of compulsory school age or a young person has a learning difficulty or disability if they:
>
> (a) have a significantly greater difficulty in learning than the majority of others of the same age; or
>
> (b) have a disability which prevents or hinders them from making use of educational facilities of a kind generally provided for others of the same age in mainstream schools or mainstream post-16 institutions.
>
> (c) a child under compulsory school age has special educational needs if they fall within the definition at (a) or (b) above or would so do if special educational provision was not made for them. [Clause 20 Children and Families Bill]. (section 1.3)

At a NASEN (formerly the National Association for Special Educational Needs) debate (2009), however, some of the leading thinkers in the area held the view that the use of the term SEN was not only outmoded, but damaging (although in true academic style, there was little agreement). Norwich (2008) argued that the use of the term was problematic as it:

- led to negative labelling
- was poorly defined
- led to the expansion of SEN as a 'separatist industry'.

It is worth reading the debate in full as it gives a good picture of the complexity in the area.

The most common focus in SEN, however, is centred around the contentious issue of placement, usually concerning the argument of special versus mainstream provision. However, there is no clear division between those who may benefit from a full-time special school and those who may not, or in the levels of support pupils may need in a mainstream school. Norwich (2008 p. 136) outlines the full range of possibilities, which are shown in Figure 8.1.

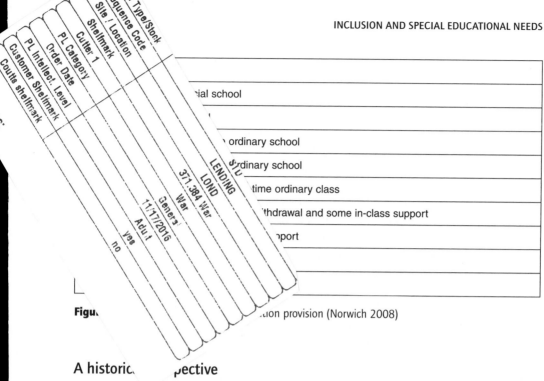

…ial school
… ordinary school
…rdinary school
…time ordinary class
…thdrawal and some in-class support
…pport

Figu… …tion provision (Norwich 2008)

A historic… …pective

The nineteenth century was essentially one of educational and social hierarchies. Children who were considered 'handicapped' were to some extent treated as the 'deserving poor' in that a charitable response was advocated to 'help the helpless', which was largely done by an act of separation. While it cannot be argued that this was not a vast improvement on the reaction of previous centuries, it was nevertheless set heavily in the deficit model; the fault lay in the child for not being 'normal' and not in the education being offered. In 1870 elementary education became compulsory, but only for children that could be thought to benefit from it. This excluded all those who were deemed to be imbeciles, idiots, and other groups who were either educated at a separate institution, or not at all.

Although segregated education has been widely rejected as discriminatory and unjust, it would be wrong to view the introduction of special schools as being motivated by any deliberate intent to exclude people with disabilities from the mainstream of society. Humanitarian motives were equally if not more important.

Medical/social models

The medical model is often known as the child-deficit or within-child model. This has its origins in medical or psychological approaches where the *pathology* of differences was advocated (Clough and Corbett 2000). For example, assessment of an individual child would be carried out by a doctor or psychologist to determine the child's capabilities, 'but at the heart of these approaches was a view of the individual child as somehow deficient' (2000, p. 12).

The inclusion movement had its roots in the social model of disability, which holds that it is 'society's failure to adapt the environment to accommodate an individual's condition that is the disabling factor' (Kellett 2008 p. 163). The implication is that the problem is not the child's 'deficiency' but schools' failure to adapt teaching approaches, to sufficiently differentiate and to accept the culture of differences. These two approaches were supported with an almost religious fervour by what was becoming a simplistic split in philosophy, with each side becoming increasingly entrenched in a claim to the moral high ground and thus decreasing the possibility of acknowledging the more complex dilemmas and contradictions that may have existed. It is now being proposed that the area may not be so 'black and white'. The term 'child deficit' influences the debate simply by its emotive connotations and may be rejected in favour of the previously mentioned 'feel good rhetoric of inclusion' (Armstrong et al. 2010 p. 4). This is not a plea to return to the era of labelling children as either deficient or uneducable, merely one to acknowledge the possible complexities. As McKay states, 'our job is not to make disability go away, not to pretend that it is not there. Instead, it is to respect its complexity, and to respond to it with honesty, vision and intelligence' (2002 p. 162). Many, including Lindsay (2003), now advocate an 'interactive model'.

It was only in 1970 that all children came under the aegis of education as, before that, any child who was deemed to be 'uneducable' was under the control of health authorities (Florian 2008 p. 202). There was growing dissatisfaction with the medical model, and, echoing a growth of various national and international movements for social justice generally, in 1974 the Government ordered an enquiry into the education of 'Handicapped Children and Young People'. While it could be argued that the resulting Warnock Report (1978) was in some ways an epistemological break from previous thinking, Wedell (2008) is of the opinion that it merely 'caught up with recent thinking' (p. 127).

The Warnock Report

The main tenets of the Warnock Report (1978) were:

- One in five children would at some time require special educational provision.
- Eighteen per cent of these would be in mainstream schools (with the remaining 2 per cent being in special schools).
- Use of the term SEN (although this was not new: it was first used by Gulliford in 1971).
- Recognition that 'special educational needs arose from the context of the child's experience which includes family life and the quality of schooling' (Armstrong et al. 2010 p. 19).

Although this was a move away from the purely medical model, taking into account contexts, it still acknowledged the concepts of individual and institutional 'failure' and this reflected tensions in the dichotomy of the social/medical model.

Special Educational Needs and Disability legislation

Until recently, SEN in England and Wales was largely based upon the Education Act (1996) which was amended in the Special Educational Needs and Disability Act (SENDA) (2001). This led to the revision of the 1994 Special Educational Needs Code of Practice (SEN COP). The fundamental principles of the Code of Practice (DfES 2001, Section 7.5, p. 7) are shown below.

The 2001 Code of Practice stated that:

- Children with SEN should have their needs met.
- The SEN of children will normally be met in mainstream schools or early education settings.
- The views of the child should be sought and taken into account.
- Parents have a vital role to play in supporting their child's education.
- Children with SEN should be offered full access to a broad, balanced and relevant education, including an appropriate curriculum for the Foundation Stage and the National Curriculum.

This was applied in schools through the graduated approach of School Action and School Action Plus. The draft COP has modified and expanded the fundamental principles as being intrinsic to the proposed legislation:

- **Early identification of needs** so that professionals can intervene early with the most appropriate support for a child and their family
- **High expectations and aspirations for what children and young people with SEN and disabilities can achieve**, including paid employment, being supported to live independently with choice and control over their lives, and participating in society
- **Focus on the outcomes that children and young people and their families want to achieve**, so that all decisions are informed by these aspirations
- **The views and participation of children and their parent/carer and young people are central** and supported throughout the system, and person-centered planning is used to place children and young people at the heart of the system
- **Choice and control for young people and parents over the support they/their children receive**, including greater choice of schools and colleges and personal budgets to tailor services

- **Education, health and social care partners collaborate** so that a coordinated and tailored support can be provided to children, young people and families
- **Clarity of roles and responsibilities** to ensure that collaboration goes hand in hand with accountability
- **High quality provision to meet the needs of most children and young people**, alongside rights for those with EHC plans to say where they wish to be educated
- **The skills, knowledge and attitude of those working with children and young people are central to achieving excellent outcomes.**

The Children and Families Bill

At the time of writing, there are major legislative changes proposed for the education and provision for children, families and people with special educational needs. These changes involve discarding the previous structures of the graduated approach of School Action and School Action Plus, and replacing the Statement with an Education, Health and Care Plan applicable from birth to 25. The new Code of Practice for Special Education (2013) is currently in the draft stages and will reflect these changes.

Children and Families Bill summary

The Bill seeks to reform legislation relating to the following areas:

- adoption and children in care
- aspects of the family justice system
- children and young people with special educational needs
- the Office of the Children's Commissioner for England
- statutory rights to leave and pay for parents and adopters
- time off work for ante-natal care
- the right to request flexible working.

  - replacing statements and learning difficulty assessments with a new birth to 25 **Education, Health and Care Plan**, extending rights and protections to young people in further education and training and offering families personal budgets so that they have more control over the support they need;
  - improving **cooperation between all the services that support children and their families** and particularly requiring local authorities and health authorities to work together;
  - requiring local authorities to **involve children, young people and parents** in reviewing and developing provision for those with special educational needs and to publish a **'local offer' of support**. (https://www.gov.uk/government/uploads/system/uploads/attachment_data/file/170551/Children_20and_20Families_20Bill_20Factsheet_20-_20Introduction.pdf.pdf)

The proposed changes came about in reaction to a series of criticisms of SEN provision.

1. Over identification

The Green Paper: *Support and Aspiration: A New Approach to Special Educational Needs and Disability. A Consultation* (DfE 2011) claimed that too high a proportion of pupils were being identified as have a Special Educational Need, stating that:

> Previous measures of school performance created perverse incentives to over identify children as having SEN. There is compelling evidence that these labels of SEN have perpetuated a culture of low expectations and have not led to the right support being put in place. (DfE 2011 p. 57)

This is a concept that was discussed in the NASEN debate (2009), as mentioned earlier in the chapter, where there was a proposal that SEN had developed into a 'separatist industry'.

2. Statements

Statements came into force following the 1981 Education Act which stemmed from the Warnock Report (1978). The problematic nature of Statements was raised as long ago as 1998 when Williams and Maloney claimed that the result was that 'many people became increasingly invested in a highly adversarial approach to special educational needs ... which reflects the traditions of British legal practice rather than those of British education' (p. 19). They also commented that the most common request for additional resources came in the form of the use of a teaching assistant and on the possible irony of the child who may have the most complex needs being assisted by the person with the fewest qualifications in the area. At present, it is difficult to see how the proposed legislation will counter these points.

3. Individual Education Plans (IEPs)

There is a long history of contention over the use of IEPs. Whilst it could be argued that they highlighted both the needs and provision of children with SEN, some thought them to be time-consuming and bureaucratic. A more complex argument is that they represented a particular philosophy of education that is more closely linked to the business model, with SMART targets and constant assessment (Frankl 2005). Hrekow (2004) raised a point that will be central to discussion later in the chapter, that the use of IEPs merely supported the existence of a curriculum which was not inclusive by nature as it provided support for pupils that were not the 'norm'. The use of IEPs will no longer be obligatory in the proposed legislation.

The Special Educational Needs Code of Practice (draft)

The new legislation will retain the use of SENCOS in schools and a Code of Practice for SEN, which is currently in the draft stage. It is probable that it will continue to use the four areas of need.

Areas of need

There is an acknowledgement that these are not 'hard and fast' categories and that it 'is recognised that many children and young people experience difficulties that do not fit easily into one area, and may have needs which span two or more areas' (DfE 2013, Section 5.5) but the Code of Practice identifies four areas of need:

- communication and interaction
- cognition and learning
- behaviour and emotional and social development
- sensory and/or physical needs.

It could certainly be argued that some formal system is needed to acknowledge that some pupils need more support than others, but it remains problematic. In many ways, these four areas of function reflect the contradiction that Dyson pointed out (2001) between an 'intention to treat all learners as essentially the same and an equal and opposite intention to treat them as different' (pp. 24–9).

The success of the proposed legislative changes appears to be predicated upon two key themes:

1 Inclusive pedagogy
2 Working in partnership.

1. Inclusive pedagogy

It may be unwise to consider recent thinking on Inclusive Pedagogy without taking into account the current educational climate in which the debate on SEN is placed, as the two may be in conflict. For several decades, education has been set in an approach adapted from practices in business. Somekh (1996) points out that what is applicable in manufacturing may not be relevant to the world of education and goes on to comment:

> It is a simplification to view the outcomes of schooling merely as attainment of targets, or to believe that the curriculum is a package that can be delivered following closely defined targets. (p. 135)

Armstrong (2012) argues that 'the current market-based ideology in UK education is a major barrier to transforming and modernizing our current system' (p. 114).

The adoption of the market forces paradigm has not only affected the language used in education, with the adoption of terms such as 'stakeholders' and 'delivering the curriculum', but has distorted the basic assumptions on the nature of teaching and learning. Knowledge is seen as a commodity to be delivered and assessed, with Ofsted acting as 'quality control', as in the process of manufacturing (with the corollary that what cannot be measured does not exist). Nearly 20 years ago, Apple (1995) pointed out the dangers inherent here, claiming that this marketisation has resulted in a reductionist curriculum based on 'atomised bits of knowledge and skills measured on pre-tests and post-tests' (p. 139). To a certain extent this is reflected in the recent government dictacts regarding the teaching of reading, where the proposed SEN Code of Practice now contains the requirement to employ structured synthetic phonics as the route to literacy. There is the strong implication that this is the panacea for all children, which is not only problematic for inclusive teaching, but tends to ignore any evidence that queries this approach. Uribe (2009) wrote a short article regarding this in America, and outlines the key arguments in the area, but there seems to be little credence given to alternative methods. Synthetic phonics, as opposed to a more holistic method of teaching reading, are an example of Apple's statement (1995) on atomised knowledge that is measurable by testing and therefore deeply set in the market forces approach. There seems to be a certain incongruity in the current claim to strive for inclusion while accompanied by the statement that all children will learn by the same method.

The Children and Families Bill (2013) presages major changes, but if these are merely structural and not pedagogical then they are illusionary. They will be new icing on an old cake.

How is this relevant to inclusion and SEN? How is criticism of a curriculum based on a uniform pedagogy relevant to Inclusion and SEN? If a one-dimensional view of knowledge and pedagogy is adopted then a proportion of children are seen as 'the other' who do not fit into the 'norm'. When I first started class teaching, my class had children who between them spoke 24 languages, and many children who would now be considered to have some form of SEN. There was minimal whole-class teaching and ability grouping (and not a SMART target to be seen). The result was that there was simply not a norm that the children could 'deviate' from. This was not the inclusion of uniformity, but of diversity.

Inclusive Pedagogy, although not a new idea, gained impetus from work carried out at Aberdeen University on the Inclusive Practice Project funded by the Scottish Government. Florian and Linklater (2010) define the term as 'what is ordinarily available as part of the routine of classroom life as a way of responding to differences between learners rather than specifically individualizing for some' (p. 370).

This approach does not accept the categorization of some children as being 'the other' but it also accepts that there may be barriers as it is founded upon the teachers' ability and freedom to 'respond to the demands of their professional responsibilities to act to enhance all children's learning, rather than focusing on learners' capacity to conform to predetermined standards for attainment, more traditionally reflected by the learning outcomes of the curriculum' (Florian and Linklater 2010 p. 385).

This may have some key implications for the culture and organisation of a primary classroom. Prunty et al. (2012) carried out a small research project, as part of a larger study, into the views of children and young people with SEN on their schooling in both special and mainstream schools in England and Ireland. They found that in their sample, the children viewed class size as one of the key factors of success. (This is a view that may resonate with many teachers.) Another key feature was the use of peer support and collaborative learning as opposed to the whole-class 'delivery' approach. Interestingly, the definition of 'peer support' can also be a key factor, and Frederickson (2010) raised the concern that if the peer support is not reciprocal, then it may only serve to widen the gulf between children and place the child with a disability or SEN in the role of passive recipient of help. Many of the pupils held quite clear views concerning the amount of help required from a teaching assistant, as the majority expressed the wish to work independently and to then negotiate the support needed. This, in addition to the acknowledgment of the importance of friendships with peers and good relationships with the teachers, seems to support a more Vygotskian approach to pedagogy in contrast to that found in the market forces paradigm of curriculum delivery and the hierarchical structures of ability grouping. If the intention is to highlight pupil voice in the Children and Families Bill and the SEN COP, one could hope that these voices will not be ignored. They go some way to advocating Inclusive Pedagogy and the benefits for all children.

To return to the more specific area of the Children and Families Bill, if the graduated response is discontinued in schools, and not replaced by Inclusive Pedagogy, then the result may be a further isolation of children whose needs may never be sufficiently severe or complex to warrant an Education, Health and Care Plan.

2. Working in partnership

The success of the implantation of the Children and Families Bill is intrinsically based on the ability of a range of individuals and agencies to work together. As can be implied from the draft Code of Practice (DfE 2013), the voice of the child must be taken into consideration, as must the views of the parents. The role of the parent has been given even more importance where the possibility of an Education, Health and Care Plan is being considered. Obviously, the teachers, SENCOs, teaching assistants (TAs) and, potentially, external services will also be required to not only give some input, but to work collaboratively. The Every Child Matters (ECM) agenda (DfES 2005) crystallised and formalised the need for multi-agency working, but it had existed in one form or another long before that, with varying degrees of success. It is likely that each person will come to this process with differing and perhaps conflicting perspectives, depending on which 'discipline' they belong to (Education, Health, Psychology, etc.), their personalities, stress levels, loyalties and knowledge. Porter and Lacey (2005) state that to understand any phenomenon 'we need to see it through the varied perspectives of those who are part of it' (p. 86). Although they are referring to the inclusion of the views of the child, the point regarding the empathy for varying perspectives could be applied to any collaborative process.

At best, this diversity of approach and knowledge could lead to a problem-solving, holistic approach, where all knowledge is shared and respected. Conversely, it could also result in a hierarchical culture, where some points of view are held to be of a higher status and thus may have more power. There are some excellent journal articles discussing this point and addressing the roles of the parent, child, SENCO and teaching assistant, some with potential solutions (see list of further reading).

The dangers of labelling and reductionist categorisation have been thoroughly discussed in SEN, but usually in reference to the child. It could be argued that a similar argument could be made for the category of parents. It is self-evident that they are not a monolithic, homogenous group, but with the current culture of tension and accountability in education, the danger exists that any partnership between schools and parents may become adversarial. Laluvein (2010) points out that anxiety may decrease amongst parents as their knowledge grows, but the same cannot always be said about teachers as they may fear that their professional status is being eroded. This can result in a 'culture of professional exclusivity' (p. 198), thus reducing the probability of a true partnership. This is not an accurate picture of all interaction, as Laluvein (2010) also cites examples of what she terms 'networking' partnerships where a consensus evolves for all parties and differing knowledge is not set in a hierarchical structure.

In a small-scale research project carried out in 2008, Barnes found a wide range of rationales for undertaking multi-agency working from parents' points of view, but the main conclusion was that it was perceived to be 'the means whereby many frustrations and anxieties, encountered within a fragmented system of time-consuming multiple appointments, assessments and poor information sharing, would be alleviated' (p. 239).

Summary of legislation

There is much to be praised in the proposal for the Children and Families Bill (2013) and the new SEN COP (2013). Potentially they could alter the dynamics of provision for children with SEN and result in a more holistic and 'user friendly' approach. It would, however, be optimistic to the point of inanity not to acknowledge any barriers that may result in their becoming merely a structural reform. There is a certain irony in discussing inclusion in the UK without also recognising the ever-increasing divisions in our educational system. We have, I suspect, more different types of schools than any other country, with a government which is pressing for the creation of more faith schools and free schools. We are still set in the market forces approach to schooling and are facing the tensions between the need for Inclusive Pedagogy and the constraints imposed by the new National Curriculum, which seems to advocate the delivery of knowledge in what could be considered to be, at best, a reductionist approach to teaching and learning. As Wedell (2012) points out, while the proposals are aspirational, 'The pilot programmes will reveal how realistic and relevant they are, particularly at a time of constrained resources' (p. 49).

The following describes a series of tutorial sessions between student teachers and their university tutor.

Work in school

Study one

Student teacher: I made my first visit to the school yesterday and the teacher told me that quite a few children had SEN. One has Down syndrome. What if I don't know how to teach them? I don't know enough about it.

Tutor: First of all, stop panicking. I would be more worried if you were filled with confidence about teaching a child you hadn't met yet. A certain level of nervousness may be healthy. You are not doing this in total isolation. You will be able to observe the class teacher and talk to her and the child's previous teachers. Don't assume that you don't already have the knowledge. If you want to know what specific help or approaches the child needs, take the obvious route and ask the child. If the school allows it, ask the parents, as they may not only be a font of knowledge about their own child, but also the specific barrier.

Analysis

There is a long history of students and Newly Qualified Teachers feeling a lack of confidence in their ability to teach children with SEN (Richards 2010). This was possibly linked to the Inspection reports of ITE programmes (Ofsted 2008) which reported a wide range of practices in HEI provision. Richards (2010) reported an equally wide range of philosophies amongst students, with some regarding 'anything to do with special educational needs as superfluous to their role as teacher, or [they] had an anxiety level about this area of work that resulted in avoidance of any related situation' (p. 114). A similar reaction was to be found in Northern Ireland (Winter 2006), where there were also calls to increase the amount of SEN covered in Initial Teacher Education (ITE). Standalone SEN modules were considered to be an essential recommendation, but combined with a model of permeation into other subjects.

Small-scale research into children with Down syndrome (Johnson 2006) reported that while some teachers were initially apprehensive about teaching a child with Down syndrome, experience of this in the classroom tended to alter their attitude to one which was more supportive of inclusive practice. The fear was founded upon uncertainty and a perceived lack of knowledge.

With particular reference to childen with Down syndrome, obvious physical differences can lead to the mistake of assuming the existence of a homogenic group rather than one which explemifies a wide range of intelligences, personality types and individual differences.

Study two

Student teacher: I have a TA in the class with me but she only works with one child (he has dyslexia). She withdraws him in every English session to work in the corridor with him doing work on phonics and handwriting. Can I tell her to do it another way? I think he could work with the rest of the children but the TA has been at the school for years and I am only a second-year student. I don't feel like ordering her about and it is the school policy to withdraw children.

Tutor: This is an awkward one but not uncommon. I know it can be hard for you when the TA is 20 years older than you and with years of experience in the school.

Firstly, even when you qualify there will be a balancing act between the fact that you have responsibility for every child in the class, and that includes the child who may be working with a TA, and the recommendation that you will work in *collaboration* with the TA. It will be your job to know what and how that child is learning, but this may be achieved by establishing a mutual respect between yourself and the TA.

(Continued)

(Continued)

Your first task is to ask the child for his preference. Some children actually *prefer* withdrawal, but not all. Ask, if for a few lessons, you can try to include the child in the class and share your plans with the TA. She may have some relevant advice. If the child cannot complete the work without full-time support, then consider the probability that the work is too difficult or the wrong approach is being taken. Much of the advice on teaching children with dyslexia merely reflects good teaching.

Analysis

Inclusive classroom practice has been claimed to be more effective if the teacher and the TA work together in collaboration (Wedell 2012), but it is equally important that the child is involved in the process and planning of support. In a study by Woolfson et al. (2007) it was found that pupils expressed the wish to negotiate the amount and type of support they were given and, wherever possible, preferred to work independently. As mentioned previously, it was also pointed out by Prunty (2012) that the presence of peer support was valued, which became a recurring theme in the research. Long et al. (2007) point out the importance of the teacher, bearing in mind the personal, social and emotional needs of the child, in addition to the academic needs, which returns to the question of the balance between social and academic inclusion and the possible tensions between them.

As regards the question of withdrawal of pupils with dyslexia in order to provide more relevant, interactive teaching, Casserley (2011) found that many pupils preferred this approach, but concluded that this was an indictment of the general approach to literacy teaching in the classroom in that a quick pace of delivery resulted from a pressure to cover the curriculum. This in turn resulted in the creation of a barrier to learning for some children with dyslexia, but was also highly questionable for many pupils. Although this research was carried out in Ireland, it may have a certain resonance in England with what could be considered to be the constraints of the National Curriculum.

Questions for discussion

- Does a child either 'have SEN' or not?
- What should you take into account?
- Can SEN provision ensure a broad, balanced, relevant curriculum?
- What classroom problems, and solutions, have you seen in schools so far?

Reflective task: Barriers to learning

- In small groups, select a barrier to learning. This may be one of the more common ones such as dyslexia, dyspraxia, autistic spectrum disorder, visual impairment, hearing impairment, or a behaviour difficulty. (You need to treat ADHD as being contentious.) You may, however, wish to select one that you have already had some experience of in schools.
- Research this area (see further reading).
- Consider how you would use the following strategies to support a child in your class who has this barrier to learning. (You need to specify a particular age.)

differentiation	use of resources	assessment
classroom grouping	use of other adults	provision on an educational visit
the creation of an inclusive culture in the class	communication with parents	involving the views of the child

- Feed back to the whole group. (A poster presentation may be an effective way of doing this.)

In completing this task, you may have found that the necessary range of knowledge, skills and roles was intimidating, yet class teachers do this on a daily basis. It may help to bear in mind that your aim is competence and care, not divinity, and that no one gets it right all of the time. You should also not expect to be alone in this process. The teaching assistants, parents and the child can all help you come to a solution that benefits the whole child. This can also increase your expertise in reacting to all the children.

Case study

Read the following critical incident and, individually or with others, discuss the questions it raises.

Ben

Ben is 6 years old, from a traveller family and has been admitted to your school recently. He is the middle of five children. His academic attainment is below

(Continued)

(Continued)

that of most of the other children in the class, especially in written work. He rarely completes these written tasks and his work is generally untidy, his writing being typical of a younger child, with letter reversals and immature spelling. He enjoys activities that are based on talking and giving verbal feedback to the group, teacher or class. Art and science lessons are a particular strength for him and he appears to have a good understanding of geography. In class, he is slow to settle into tasks and can be disruptive. Socially, his peer group describe him as a loner who prefers to seek out the company of his siblings during playtimes; the class teacher commented to other staff members that he had few friends. The class has a full-time TA, but Ben does not like working with her in withdrawal situations. His parents did not attend the open evening, but the mother brings Ben to school. She does not come into the classroom but will talk amicably to the teacher in the playground before and after school. What questions does this raise?

Critical incident

Ben is working with a group of another five children. He has just started to write and is getting restless. His writing is very slow and he repeatedly stops and wanders round the room. He then breaks his pencil and throws it on the floor. The TA approaches him, tells him to behave and to work at a small table with her. Ben swears at her and refuses. He is becoming increasingly upset and disruptive. When he is reseated at the table, the other children complain that they don't want him, stating that 'he can't do any work' and 'I don't want to sit next to *him*'.

Analysing the incident

There are many possible conclusions that can arise from analysis of this critical incident, but they tend to fall into four possible categories:

1. Ben has a form of Specific Learning Difficulty (SpLD). The observations that Ben has disproportionate difficulties with his written work compared to verbal tasks, has immature spelling and letter reversals and has devised task-avoidance strategies (breaking the point of the pencil, 'wandering off') could lead us to think that Ben has dyslexia.
2. Ben does not have SpLD. His difficulties can be explained by his educational history and background. It is possible that an interrupted schooling has had

an effect on his academic progress. If he is operating at an earlier stage of literacy, then letter reversals and immature spelling are representative of this and not dyslexia. If he is aware of this, then the ensuing tensions may explain his behaviour. If he also feels excluded because of his ethnicity, and so chooses not to interact with his peers at playtime, this will give him the reputation of a 'loner' with other children.

3 Ben may come from a traveller culture, have had interrupted schooling *and* have dyslexia.
4 It may be explained by something totally different that only future information may shed light on.

You may want to explore the following questions:

- How could the incident have been avoided?
- What do you need to do next?
- What could explain the incident?
- What information do you now need?
- Does Ben have a special educational need?
- Does the problem lie solely inside Ben?
- What extra knowledge do you need?
- How will you involve the parents?
- How will you find out what Ben thinks?
- What will the role of the SENCO be now?
- How will you deploy the TA?

Summary of case study

In considering the case study, it should be becoming clear that not only are there many factors that can affect a child's progress, but that inclusion may be reliant on more than the interaction between the teacher and the child. What of the general culture of the classroom? Does Ben *feel* included by the other children? If not, what should the teacher do? How many of Ben's difficulties are 'within child' and does it make a difference at this stage? Much of the advice by the British Dyslexia Association (BDA) merely reflects good literacy teaching. The major focus may have to be on inclusion and not solely a 'medical approach' to SEN.

International perspectives

One way of appreciating that inclusion has social, political and cultural roots is to examine international perspectives.

The Cambridge Primary Review (Alexander 2010) states that many of England's 800,000 pupils with special educational needs are still offered patchy and inadequate services, according to parents, teachers and local authorities, and that, while the principle of inclusion has been accepted, the 'concerted effort the United Nations warned would be needed to make it successful has not been achieved' (p. 126). The Review expressed concerns that pupils are being labelled and segregated unnecessarily by the type of school they attend and the experiences they receive when there, and that they are therefore vulnerable to stereotyping and discrimination. The Review recommends a thorough overhaul of the system.

The findings of the Cambridge Primary Review are endorsed by a report, *How Fair is Britain?* (Equality and Human Rights Commission 2010), which found that children with a disability face shocking levels of bullying and that there are significant inequalities based on gender, poverty and race.

Summary

This chapter has discussed the controversial aspects of what might at first appear a fairly simple question: how can we have inclusive classrooms, which allow equal educational opportunities for all children? The reasons why there are tensions between the ideal and its implementation were discussed. The chapter considered definitions of and provision for children with special educational needs and for inclusion. It set out the relevant legislation and the implications of this for teachers. It concluded with a consideration of how other countries address special educational needs.

Participation in the suggested reflective activities aimed to actively involve readers in developing their own philosophies and in making the judgements and decisions they will be required to make as teachers in implementing the legislation which aims to promote equal opportunities.

The website related to this book gives additional references to books on English as an Additional Language, on Gifted and Talented Children, Travellers and Children with Special Educational Needs. It also gives the addresses of useful websites.

Questions for discussion

- What is the relevance for us of the report, *How Fair is Britain?* (EHRC 2010)?
- Are there tensions between economic development and equality?
- Is it ever possible to justify utilitarianism? (That good is whatever brings the greatest happiness to the greatest number of people.)
- If so, what are the implications for inclusion/SEN in the UK?

Further reading

The following suggestions are only an indication of the wealth of information in the area.

Baron-Cohen, S. (2008) *Autism and Asperger Syndrome (The Facts)*. Oxford: Oxford University Press.

This is an excellent introduction to autism and Asperger's syndrome from one of the great names in the field. The author covers the key issues in the area, including genetic influences, intervention, education and treatment. Complex information is presented in a clear, coherent style which nevertheless portrays aspects which are as yet uncertain and worthy of future research.

Cigman, R. (ed.) (2007) *Included or Excluded: The Challenge of the Mainstream for Some SEN Children*. London: Routledge.

An excellent book in which key authors in the field of Inclusion address many of the most important debates and information in the area. It includes chapters on autism, children with emotional difficulties, the inclusion debate and the views of parents, written by some of the best-known authors in the field of Inclusion/SEN.

Dillinberger, K., Keenan, M., Doherty, A., Byrne, T. and Gallagher, S. (2010) 'Living with Children Diagnosed with Autistic Spectrum Disorder: Parental and Professional Views', *British Journal of Special Education* 37(1): 13–23.

This research examines the tensions between the differing perspectives of parents and professionals in the support of children with autism.

Florian, L. and Black-Hawkins, K. (2011) 'Exploring Inclusive Pedagogy', *British Educational Research Journal* 37(5): 813–28.

A research paper that examines teachers' craft knowledge of their practice of 'inclusion' in Scotland. It focuses on the role of inclusive pedagogy in inclusion in distinction to that of categorising 'differences'. It discusses the relevance and importance of the views of teachers who are committed to inclusion but work in an education system that is dominated by the categorisation of pupils by ability levels.

Gross, J. (2013) *Time to Talk: Implementing Outstanding Practice in Speech, Language and Communication*. London: Routledge.

This text addresses communication difficulties, which are often considered to be the most common and growing barriers in schools. It covers key theories in language development, whole-class approaches to speaking and listening, strategies for children with limited communication, and how to develop effective partnerships with parents, speech therapists and others involved in the child's life.

Higashida, N. (2013) *The Reason I Jump: One Boy's Voice from the Silence of Autism*. London: Hodder and Stoughton.

Written by Naoki Higashida when he was 13, this books gives an excellent explanation of the sometimes baffling behaviours of many autistic children. The young author has autism and and this beautifully written account of his life and and perceptions gives a deep insight into the autistic mind.

Hodkinson, A. (2010) 'Illusionary Inclusion – What Went Wrong with New Labour's Landmark Educational Policy?', *British Journal of Special Education* 39(1): 4–11.

A journal article which analyses the definitions of Inclusion in great depth.

Hodkinson, A. and Vickerman, P. (2009) *Key Issues in Special Educational Needs and Inclusion*. London: Sage.

This book gives a good overview of the major themes in Inclusion, both internationally and historically. It includes many relevant and interesting case studies for discussion in an accessible way.

Paige-Smith, A. and Rix, J. (2011) 'Researching Early Interventions and Young Children's Perspectives: Developing and Using a "Listening to Children Approach"', *British Journal of Special Education* 38(1): 28–36.

An interesting journal article on the research carried out to investigate the views of parents and children on an early intervention programme for two young children with Down syndrome and the importance of the role of the child in the process.

Pavey, B. (2007) *The Dyslexia-Friendly Primary School*. London: Paul Chapman Publishing.

This book is an accessible and reader-friendly introduction to dyslexia. It includes clear definitions of dyslexia, without distorting the complexities of the subject. It includes practical activities and approaches, many of which could not only benefit a child with dyslexia, but all children in a primary classroom.

Ricci, L. and Osipova, A. (2013) 'Visions for Literacy: Parents' Aspirations for Reading in Children with Down Syndrome', *British Journal of Special Education* 39(3): 125–9.

An account of research in the US on the perspectives of 50 parents of Down syndrome children on reading development. The parents had high expectations of their children and reported an enjoyment of reading. The research highlighted the need to support and empower parents and to create a collaborative partnership with the schools in building these skills.

Rosen-Webb, S. (2011) 'Nobody Tells You How to be a SENCo', *British Journal of Special Education* 38(4): 159–68.

A research article addressing the question of how SENCOs identify themselves and the dynamics of maintaining a balance between management training and specialist teacher training.

References

Ainscow, M., Booth, T. and Dyson, A. (2006) *Improving Schools, Developing Inclusion*. London: Routledge.

Alexander, R. (ed.) (2010) *Children, their World, their Education: Final Report and Recommendations of the Cambridge Primary Review*. London: Routledge.

Apple, M. (1995) *Education and Power*, 2nd edn. London: Routledge.

Armstrong, A., Armstrong, D. and Spandagou, I. (2010) *Inclusive Education: International Policy and Practice*. London: Sage.

Armstrong, D. (2012) 'The Ideal School', in D. Armstrong and G. Squires (eds) *Contemporary Issues in Special Educational Needs: Considering the Whole Child*. Maidenhead: McGraw University Press.

Barnes, P. (2008) 'Multi-agency Working: What are the Perspectives of SENCos and Parents Regarding its Development and Implementation?', *British Educational Research Journal* 35(4): 230–40.

Casserley, A.M. (2011) 'Children's Experiences of Reading Classes and Reading Schools in Ireland', *Support for Learning* 26(1): 17–24.

Centre for Studies in Inclusion in Education (CSIE) (2002) *The Inclusion Charter*. Bristol: CSIE.

Clough, P. and Corbett, J. (2000) *Theories of Inclusive Education*. London: Sage.

Department for Education (DfE) (2011) *Support and Aspiration: A New Approach to Special Educational Needs and Disability. A Consultation*. London: HMSO.

DfE (2013) *Indicative Draft: The (0–25) Special Educational Needs Code of Practice*. London: DfE.

Department for Education and Skills (DfES) (2001) *Special Educational Needs: Code of Practice*. London: DfES.

DfES (2005) *Every Child Matters: Change for Children*. London: HMSO.

Department of Education and Science (DES) (1981) *Education Act*. London: HMSO.

Dyson, A. (2001) 'Special Needs in the Twenty-first Century: Where We've Been and Where We're Going', *British Journal of Special Education* 28(1): 24–9.

Equality and Human Rights Commission (EHRC) (2010) *How Fair is Britain? Equality, Human Rights and Good Relations in 2010. The First Triennial Review*. Scotland: HMSO.

Florian, L. (2008) 'Special or Inclusive Education: Future Trends', *British Journal of Special Education* 35(4): 202–8.

Florian, L. and Linklater, H. (2010) 'Preparing Teachers for Inclusive Education: Using Inclusive Pedagogy to Enhance Teaching and Learning for All', *Cambridge Journal of Education* (40)4: 369–86.

Frankl, C. (2005) 'Managing Individual Education Plans: Reducing the Load of the Special Educational Needs Coordinator', *Support for Learning* 20(2): 77–82.

Frederickson, N. (2010) 'Bullying or Befriending? Children's Responses to Classmates with Special Needs', *British Journal of Special Education* 37(1): 4–12.

Graber, D. (2002) *The Power of Communication: Managing Information in Public Organizations*. Washington, DC: CQ Press.

Gulliford, R. (1971) *Special Educational Needs*. London: Routledge and Kegan Paul.

Haralambos, M. and Holborn, M. (2000) *Sociology Themes and Perspectives*, 5th edn. London: Collins.

Hrekow, M. (2004) Talk at SENJIT on provision mapping, with LEA Officers, 5 November.

Johnson, D. (2006) 'Listening to the Views of Those Involved in the Inclusion of Pupils with Down's Syndrome into Mainstream Schools', *Support for Learning* 21(1): 24–9.

Kellett, M. (2008) 'Special Educational Needs and Inclusion in Education', in D. Matheson (ed.) *An Introduction to the Study on Education*, 3rd edn. London: Routledge.

Laluvein, K. (2010) 'Variations on a Theme: Parents and Teachers Talking', *Support for Learning* 25(4): 194–9.

Lindsay, G. (2003) 'Inclusive Education: A Critical Perspective', *British Journal of Special Education* 30(1): 3–12.

Long, L., Macblain, S. and Macblain, M. (2007) 'Bridging the Holistic and Academic Divide: Beyond the Mechanics of Learning to Read', *Journal of Adolescent and Adult Literacy* 51(2): 124–34.

McKay, G. (2002) 'The Disappearance of Disability? Thoughts on a Changing Culture', *British Journal of Special Education* 29(4): 159–63.

NASEN (2009) *Special Educational Needs has Outlived its Usefulness: A Debate*. Series 6, Policy Paper 4, March.

Norwich, B. (2008) 'What Future for Special Schools and Inclusion? Conceptual and Professional Perspectives', *British Journal of Special Education* 35(3): 136–43.

Ofsted (2008) *How Well New Teachers are Prepared to Teach Pupils with Learning Difficulties*. London: HMSO.

Porter, J. and Lacey, P. (2005) *Researching Learning Difficulties*. London: Paul Chapman.

Prunty, A., Dupont, M. and McDaid, R. (2012) 'Voices of Students with Special Educational Needs (SEN): Views on Schooling', *Support for Learning* 27(1): 29–36.

QCA (1999) *The National Curriculum: Handbook for Primary Teachers in England*. London: QCA.

Richards, G. (2010) '"I Was Confident about Teaching but SEN Scared Me": Preparing New Teachers for Including Pupils with Special Educational Needs', *Support for Learning* 25(3): 108–15.

Somekh, B. (1996) 'Collaboration through Networking: The Collaborative Action Research Network', in D. Bridges and C. Husband (eds) *Consorting and Collaboration in the Education Marketplace*. London: Falmer Press.

Uribe, D. (2009) 'Rejecting the Indiscriminate Use of Phonics', *Literacy Today*, March.

Warnock, M. (1978) *Special Educational Needs: Report of the Committee of Enquiry into the Education of Handicapped Children and Young People*. London: HMSO.

Wedell, K. (2008) 'Confusion about Inclusion: Patching up or System Change?', *Journal of Special Education* 35(3): 127–36.

Wedell, K. (2012) 'Points from the SENCo-Forum', *British Journal of Special Education* 39(3): 49.

Williams, H. and Maloney, S. (1998) 'Well-meant, but Failing on Almost All Counts: The Case against Statementing', *British Journal of Special Education* 25(1): 16–21.

Winter, E. (2006) 'Preparing New Teachers for Inclusive Schools and Classrooms', *Support for Learning* 24(2): 85–91.

Woolfson, R., Harker, M., Lowe, D., Shield, M. and Mackintosh, H. (2007) 'Consulting with Children and Young People Who Have Disabilities: Views of Accessibility to Education', *British Journal of Special Education* 34 (1): 40–9.

CHAPTER 9

BEHAVIOUR MANAGEMENT

Deborah Seward

By the end of this chapter, you will:

- understand your rights and responsibilities as set out in school behaviour policies
- understand how the learning environment you create impacts on pupils' behaviour
- have considered a range of behaviour management strategies.

Introduction

The purpose of this chapter is to provide an introduction to some of the issues surrounding behaviour management in the primary classroom. It will consider why behaviour management is important, statutory requirements concerning school behaviour policies, and the importance of the learning environment you create, in influencing self-esteem, motivation and so, good behaviour. The chapter refers to the Early Years Foundation Stage and Key Stages 1 and 2.

Planning dynamic, stimulating lessons, based on sound assessment and evaluation and excellent subject knowledge is the most effective way to good behaviour. *Improving Teacher Training for Behaviour* (DfE, 2012a) also makes the point that, while it is essential to know about generic behaviour management systems and techniques (such as use of voice, body language, eye contact and an authoritative presence), the way these are used depends on the teacher's personal style and the context in which they are teaching. Teachers need to reflect on their style and strategies and be prepared to change them when necessary. You will continually have to make rapid decisions about how you interpret the school policy, because individual children and situations are never quite the same. This chapter recognises that inappropriate behaviour can arise for a variety of reasons, and considers legislation relating to how it must be dealt with as well as strategies for addressing it decisively and with authority. However, the underlying theme of the chapter is that behaviour is most effectively managed if a good, safe learning environment is created, in which boundaries are recognised and good relationships are developed between teacher and pupils (and parents), which promote courtesy, and if children are involved and motivated by differentiated and stimulating activities and valued and praised when appropriate (Standard 7; DfE 2013a).

Reflective task

- Make a list of the rights and powers you believe teachers have to discipline pupils.
- Note down your experiences of behaviour management, as a pupil and/or as an adult in a primary classroom.

Is behaviour management important?

To answer the question above, we need to consider the rights we have as teachers as well as the rights pupils have. Teachers have a right to teach, indeed as Steer (2009 p. 18) notes: 'Teachers have a right to work in an environment that allows them to use their skills to the full for the benefit of all their pupils'. All children have a right to learn. 'Children have a right to attend school in safety and to learn without disruption from others' (Steer 2009 p. 18). This clearly identifies the necessity for a safe, calm learning environment where teachers can make decisions about pedagogy based on the context and the needs of their pupils, in order to ensure that effective learning occurs. So, behaviour affects the pupil's learning experience, in terms of cognitive, social and emotional development, as well as the teacher's teaching experience and personal well-being.

Establishing a clear framework for classroom management

What do I, the teacher, need to know?

In order to establish a clear framework for discipline in your classroom, you first need to accept that there is no one way of managing behaviour; you need to recognise that what works in one context with one group of children will not necessarily work in the same context with a different group. Challenging behaviours may be a result of a range of contextual issues related to the community, family, school, classroom, peer group and teacher, as well as the individual pupils themselves. This is what makes behaviour management so complex. The challenge is to find something which works for you and your children.

Policies, rights and responsibilities

You need to be familiar with your school's behaviour policy and consider the ways in which you will be expected to implement it. *Teachers' Standards* (DfE 2013a) states that trainees and teachers are responsible for achieving the highest possible standards in work and conduct, working with parents in the best interests of their pupils, establishing a safe environment for pupils, rooted in mutual respect, and consistently demonstrating the positive attitudes, values and behaviour which are expected of pupils. They should employ a range of strategies, using rewards and sanctions consistently to manage classes, taking into account pupils' different needs and taking responsibility for implementing clear rules of behaviour, in accordance with the school's behaviour policy. This policy is a legal requirement.

The *Statutory Framework for the Early Years Foundation Stage* (DfE 2012b, 3.50–3.52) requires all providers to have a behaviour management policy and procedures, with a named and suitably qualified practitioner responsible for implementing it and for ensuring that no child is given corporal punishment. This is an offence. A child must not be threatened with corporal punishment or any other punishment which could affect the child's well-being. However, physical intervention is allowed if absolutely necessary to prevent injury to the child or anyone else, although a record must be kept and parents informed.

In primary schools the behaviour management policy is based on general principles agreed by the school governors, in consultation with the head teacher, staff, parents and pupils. Head teachers are responsible for developing the policy for their school. This must reflect expectations set out in *Ensuring Good Behaviour in Schools: A Summary for Headteachers, Governing Bodies, Teachers, Parents and Pupils* (DfE 2012c). Pupils should show respect and courtesy towards staff; parents should encourage them to do so and support the school policy. All teachers should be good at managing and improving children's behaviour. A school policy states what behaviour is expected of the pupils, how it will be achieved, rules and penalties for breaking these and rewards for good behaviour. When in schools you need to be clear how you are expected to discipline pupils who fail to follow a reasonable instruction or break the rules in school, and, in certain circumstances, how you should deal with behaviour outside school. Teachers are allowed to use 'reasonable force' to prevent children harming themselves or others or damaging property; you should discuss with your mentor what is expected of you in this respect. You may also be expected to liaise with parents over a child's behaviour, as set out in a home/school agreement (DfE 2013b), which schools are required to have, and to ask parents to sign. This explains the school's aims and values, its responsibilities towards its pupils, the responsibility of each pupil's parents and what the school expects of its pupils. It is important to discuss with your mentor in school how you, as a trainee teacher, are expected to implement the behaviour policy, and where you should ask for guidance and support.

Bullying

The school behaviour policy must include the measures taken to prevent bullying. This too is an area to reflect on and discuss with your mentor. Teachers and schools have to make their own judgements about each case. It is recognised (DfE 2012d) that there is no single solution, which will suit all schools, but it is stated that bullying is best prevented where schools have created an ethos of good behaviour and of respect between pupils and between pupils and staff.

Bullying is defined as behaviour by an individual or group, repeated over time, that intentionally hurts another individual or group, either physically or emotionally (DfE 2012d). It can take many forms and is often motivated by prejudice against particular groups, for example on grounds of race, religion, gender, sexual orientation, or because a child is adopted or has caring responsibilities. It might be motivated by actual differences between children, or perceived differences. Ideally teachers develop sophisticated systems to address issues such as difference and other issues which might cause conflict between pupils, in class discussions, dedicated events or projects.

Some of the ways of preventing bullying suggested in *Preventing and Tackling Bullying* (DfE 2012d) are general, good practice. For example, create an inclusive environment where pupils can openly discuss differences between people that could motivate bullying, such as religion, ethnicity, disability, gender or sexuality.

A fascinating in-depth research study involving nearly a thousand primary schools investigates strategies used to prevent bullying and their effectiveness (DfE 2010). Again, the successful strategies identified reflect good practice generally. The findings include school, classroom and playground strategies and peer support strategies used to promote good behaviour. Successful classroom strategies involved curriculum work, including examining issues through drama and literature, cooperative group work and circle time. Playground strategies included improving school grounds, training lunchtime supervisors and playground policies. Peer support included buddy schemes, circles of friends and peer mentoring to support younger pupils.

The new Ofsted *Common Inspection Framework* (2012) includes behaviour and safety as one of the key criteria for inspections. It states that in inspection, 'it is important to test the school's response to individual needs by observing how well it helps those whose needs, dispositions, aptitudes or circumstances require a particular perspective and expert teaching and/or additional support'.

Reflective task: Reflections on beliefs and values

How did your initial reflections at the beginning of the chapter match up with the points above? Is there anything which surprised you?

It is extremely important that as a professional you have a clear set of beliefs and values which underpin your teaching, as these will drive how you operate in the classroom and will be reflected in your interactions with pupils and those around you. Consider your own beliefs and values about education, for example do you value pupils' opinions and ideas? Do you aim to empower pupils? Do you value authority? Consider how these values and beliefs may translate into ways of managing behaviour.

Beliefs and values

As behaviour is learnt, whether this is in school, home or the wider community, it is an area we, as teachers, need to teach and it is our beliefs about learning theory which will affect how we go about teaching this. If, for example, you believe in behaviourist theory, then you will adopt a 'rewards and sanctions' approach to managing behaviour, rewarding appropriate behaviour and punishing inappropriate behaviour – for example using charts, stickers, house points, certificates, or excluding a child from playtime for inappropriate behaviour. If, however, you value social constructivism as an approach to learning, then you are more likely to adopt a culture in which children are encouraged to discuss and identify classroom rules, which are then used and talked about when dealing with behaviour issues.

However, this is not a question of 'either, or'. Often, when students first work with a class, they need to use 'behaviourist' strategies, because these are clear to understand and implement, and perhaps because this is an approach used by the class teacher. It takes time to get to know children well and establish mutual respect. But a research study investigating what 130 children from Years 1–6 in 30 schools thought about working with trainees on a final 10-week placement showed that gradually trainees moved away from the charts and stickers, as the children perceptively evaluated their learning with the trainees (Cooper and Hyland 2000 pp. 7–18). Transcripts of interviews showed that the children enjoyed activities the trainees planned, inside and outside the classroom, liked the way they supportd their learning, often on an individual basis, felt valued by them and observed their strategies for creating a purposeful learning environment. Children enjoyed students' sense of humour:

> 'We did jokes with her. We all had our own joke to tell.' Grant, aged 5.
>
> 'She's funny; she's generous. She has a giggle with us and the work is always more fun – but she sorts things out.' Lucy, aged 10.

And the children appreciated ways in which trainees made the classroom a safe, productive place:

> 'She's kind but not soft. She's strict enough. She treats everyone with respect. She's always fair. She stops us going over the top.' Sam, aged 11.

Work in school

Student 1: James, in my Y2 class, is polite, anxious to please, and gets on well with everyone. But he often ignores my instructions to the whole class, fiddles in story time and only listens when I talk to him individually. I can't understand this.

Mentor: From what you say he wants to conform. I suggest you discuss with his parent whether he might have an undiagnosed hearing problem.

(Continued)

(Continued)

Student 2: Edward is driving me mad. I know that his mother is erratic – she has mental health problems – and I try to treat him consistently in school, but he comes in, in the mornings, in a dreadful state – throws things – yesterday he pulled out a handful of a girl's hair...

Mentor: Does he ever settle down?

Student 2: He LOVES art – drawing and painting – he gets really immersed in art – and he's brilliant at it.

Mentor: Then I suggest you let him do this when he first comes in – and praise his work and calm behaviour. Explain to the rest of the class that, 'we are helping Edward to settle down; he will do his work later in the day'. They will accept this.

Student 3: In my class the rules the teacher agreed with the children are on the wall, but everyone ignores them.

Mentor: I suggest you ask the class to explain the rules to you and discuss why they help to make the classroom a place where everyone can learn. Ask if they still agree with them. Do they think any changes are necessary? Then remind them about *their* rules whenever necessary, and apply sanctions rigorously if they are ignored.

Student 4: When I'm in class and someone misbehaves I try to remember the advice we've been given, but my mind goes blank and I tend to panic.

Mentor: Read through the advice about strategies at the end of this chapter. Note and evaluate any you have used. Find one that you think might be useful for a particular situation that occurs in your class, try it and evaluate whether/how it worked.

Student 5: Jack, in my Y5 class, was diagnosed with Attention Deficit Hyperactivity Disorder. He doesn't get on with the other children, can't concentrate and is generally disruptive. How can I handle this?

Mentor: Jack should have been given a care plan, which his teacher and parents understand. Talk to them about this and how they implement it. His care plan may include helping him to develop social skills with peers and self-control, help with expressing and dealing with his feelings, active learning activities and rewards for success. Make sure that you plan opportunities to work with Jack towards these targets and praise him when he meets them.

A negotiated classroom

Mutual respect between pupils and adults involves children as active partners in and taking responsibility for their learning. This involves key ideas in the concept of creative learning and teaching (Cooper 2013 pp. 3–8). There is consensus that these include recognising problems and asking questions which will help to address them. Doing so requires possibility thinking and imagination. Thinking in this way requires taking risks and accepting uncertainties. This needs confidence. It may benefit from collaborative enquiries. The importance of the organisation of the learning environment, of differentiated work, enquiry and critical thinking in promoting children's self-esteem, self-efficacy, well-being and motivation is discussed in Chapters 4, 7 and 13. Current philosophy of behaviour management sees it as involving, for example, values education, inclusivity, diversity education and pupil support plans. A nurturing learning environment, good relationships and a dynamic curriculum, which is relevant and interesting to the children, minimises poor behaviour.

Talking about behaviour is part of this philosophy. The notion that children should be encouraged to talk about potentially contentious issues reflects Cooper's views (1993 p. 129) as he argues that teachers have a 'moral obligation to enable pupils to articulate their views as effectively as possible'. It can be argued that a key aspect of education is the moral development of the child and, as Piaget argued, morality is actively constructed through 'peer interaction'. This allows children to develop ideas around the notion of fairness, allowing them to actively develop their own moral reasoning and appreciation of others' views. Kohlberg further developed Piaget's ideas (Gross 2004; Moshman 2005; Sheehy 2004), outlining three levels and six stages of moral maturity (Kohlberg et al. 1983). If children learn to think and talk about issues of behaviour and their ideas are challenged, they begin to operate at the level of 'conventional morality' – making choices about behaviour, based on the will of the whole school community.

If behaviour management has been openly negotiated with pupils in a 'partnership' approach (Ingram and Worral 1993), in which both adults and pupils are working together to influence an important aspect of school culture and staff strongly believe in the importance of involving the pupils and listening to pupils' views and involve pupils in the creation and management of behaviour, pupils are seen as partners in the education enterprise. They have a right for their voice to be recognised and respected, just as much as the adults in this context do. The importance of a whole-school approach cannot be underestimated in successful behaviour management, and, as we said earlier, one of the first policies you need to familiarise yourself with is the behaviour management policy.

Reflective task

Find a copy of your school's behaviour management policy. How does it help you, the class teacher, to manage behaviour?

What are the underpinning values or beliefs about children and behaviour?

On placement, observe how the class teacher manages behaviour – what works successfully? Consider how you can implement the strategies he/she employs.

As part of this relational aspect of the learning environment and in order to manage behaviour successfully, you need to be aware of your own feelings and emotions and how and why you react in different ways. This level of personal emotional intelligence is critical if we are to teach children how to handle their emotions and subsequently manage their own behaviour. There are times when we all, no matter how experienced, feel angry and frustrated when dealing with a difficult class or individual. This is normal. The challenge is to learn how to deal with these emotional responses in a way that provides self-control and results in you establishing and remaining in control. Basic advice would be to take a deep breath, count to 10 and consider your options before reacting. Offer the child a choice – for example, you can choose to finish this now or at playtime. Avoid direct confrontation and remain calm, as how you behave will affect the child's reaction.

What do pupils need to know in order to successfully manage their own behaviour?

From day one pupils need to be aware of your expectations of them and the consequences of pushing the boundaries and how this dovetails with whole-school policies and expectations.

Sharing expectations can be done through dialogue and discussion and frequently classroom rules are established and displayed during the first days of teaching. However, what is crucial is how these classroom rules are subsequently used. Pupils quickly learn whether you have valued their ideas and input into the rules through how you use them in the everyday context. If you are serious about listening to pupils' opinions, then you will use the classroom rules, collaboratively created, in your discussions and dealings with behaviour, constantly referring to them. This will contribute positively to the developing relationship you establish with your class. If, however, you allow children to create and then display classroom rules and never use them, then children will learn that you do not value their input, and, because they will be unsure of expectations and boundaries, there will be a temptation, on their part, to constantly test and judge you, especially in terms of what is acceptable behaviour, fairness and equality.

If you are not going to consult pupils about behaviour, then you need to clearly set out what you expect and what the rewards and sanctions will be and how this fits in with whole-school expectations. They will test you out – you can be assured of that – so it is important to remember to be consistent.

Pupils need to know you value good behaviour and what it is like, so praise it! This helps illustrate what you expect of them and provides concrete role models for those children who may not see much good behaviour in other aspects of their life.

You, yourself, are a powerful role model and as such the children will watch and observe how you behave in and around school and this will affect how they behave. You set the standards of politeness, punctuality, dress and way of being. If they see you speak to the teaching assistant or midday supervisor politely, then they are more likely to do so. The choices adults make in terms of their own behaviour are crucial in influencing children's choices as to how they will behave. In Part 2 of the *Teachers' Standards* (DfE 2013a) it is made clear that pupils must be treated with dignity, built on relationships of mutual respect, and that teachers are tolerant and respect the rights, and the faiths and beliefs of others. Additionally, pupils need to know how to manage their own behaviour and feelings; this needs to be taught and developed. Ultimately, you are aiming for them to have self-control over and regulation of their own behaviour. They need to know you value them as individuals and that you are interested in their well-being and see them managing their own behaviour as an integral aspect of personal well-being.

Reflective task

Identify how you would plan to engage children in a circle-time discussion around creating a set of classroom rules. Consider how you would manage this session. What teacher skills are necessary to enable this to happen?

What do parents need to know?

The support from parents in dealing with behaviour is crucial – if there are issues, they need to be aware of them and what you are doing to overcome them so that they can further support your work at home if necessary. Initially, parents need to be aware of school expectations, the behaviour policy and how the school goes about managing behaviour on a daily basis. The home/school agreement will include details of expectations. Parents will also be aware of how you manage behaviour from observing staff at school events, for example at assemblies and performances. However, you may need to be more explicit and talk them through what you do to manage specific behaviours.

Daily contact with parents provides a good opportunity to mention good behaviour, as well as any concerns you may have, and parents' evenings also present an opportunity for a more in-depth discussion about specific individual issues. By discussing issues with parents, you often find they are having similar problems at home, so approaches and ideas can be shared. This process illustrates to parents that you value their input and helps build relationships around the child, ensuring consistency. Very often, once you have established good relationships with parents/carers, they will ask you for advice and this may be an opportunity for you all to source additional support as necessary.

How do I do it? How do I manage behaviour?

Ultimately, in your classroom, it is your responsibility to provide a safe, secure environment where successful learning can take place. Your classroom needs to be well organised and presented, with materials for the lessons accessible, resources ready and stimulating, interesting, engaging lessons well planned. Clear routines and good organisation reduce opportunities for children to disrupt lessons by implying they cannot find materials or because you have to leave to photocopy a worksheet. In order to do this, you need to establish yourself and have presence. Be proactive – don't wait for unacceptable behaviour to occur – set out and establish expectations early on and be consistent with these.

Setting expectations

The pupils will test you out but as long as you are clear and consistent then in the longer term they will respect you. As Sammons et al. (2008 p. 16) note, in relation to both pre-school and primary education, 'a proactive approach to classroom management may help promote better learning and assist children to become better at managing their own learning behaviour'.

Having a presence means being in the classroom at the start of the lesson, welcoming children and establishing a purposeful start – show you are ready to teach and they should be ready to learn. Have strategies which indicate that the lesson is about to start, counting down from 10, with a timer displayed on the interactive whiteboard, a clapping rhyme or whatever suits you and your children, but ensure everyone is ready to listen, wait and be patient. Be omnipresent – have that ability to know what is happening around you – as all teachers have eyes in the back of their heads! Be aware of what all pupils are doing – position yourself so you can see and observe everyone. Sometimes a look, a tap on the desk, a hand on the shoulder is enough to signal you know what is happening. These quiet approaches do not break the flow of learning but are enough to signal to individuals and groups that you are tuned into their engagement with learning. Often a quiet word also helps to stop behaviour escalating into something more disruptive. Being proactive and dealing with little incidents means you don't allow things to escalate to the point of having to shout or apply more intrusive methods which disrupt the whole group. Consider your organisation and grouping of pupils – who will work well together? Seating plans mean you control the interaction taking place and this can limit opportunities for inappropriate behaviour.

While these less intrusive methods may help with low-level behaviour, there are frequently times when more needs to be done. These steps should always be taken in the light of school and classroom rules, so expectations are consistent.

In many cases, behaviour can be a reaction to something in school and, for some children, if there is a pattern of inappropriate behaviour, it is well worth analysing any antecedents to the behaviour exhibited. For example, if a child regularly has issues in the playground at lunchtimes, they may exhibit inappropriate behaviour during the afternoon session or there may be a particular grouping of pupils which causes problems. These issues may only come to light in discussions with pupils about why they behaved inappropriately, which is why opportunities for dialogue with individuals are important. If you can work out triggers for inappropriate behaviour, you can avoid the situation occurring or at least support the child in making suitable choices for their actions.

For some children, the exhibition of inappropriate behaviour can be a signal that their learning needs are not being met; perhaps work is too easy or too challenging, or they may need instructions or to have explanations given in a different way. This is why it is important to establish meaningful relationships so you know each individual and can match the learning to their needs. There may be a case for seeking additional support both for the child and for you as the teacher in meeting their individual learning needs.

It should be noted that behaviour can be a reaction to something you, as the teacher, have little control over, for example a family breakdown or bereavement. This is why it is important to have good relationships with both parents and pupils so that these (often short-term issues) can be addressed and the child supported through a difficult situation.

Strategies

The *Teachers' Standards* (DfE, 2013a, 8) require teachers to manage behaviour effectively to ensure a good and safe learning environment. This includes having rules and routines for behaviour, promoting courteous behaviour, in accordance with the school's behaviour policy, establishing a framework for discipline, and using a range of strategies, praise, sanctions and rewards consistently and fairly. Again, it is recognised that using approaches appropriate to pupils' needs in order to interest and motivate them and maintaining good relationships with pupils is essential to good classroom management.

A simple checklist

Getting the Simple Things Right: Charlie Taylor's Behaviour Checklists (DfE 2012e) is the result of a meeting of outstanding head teachers, who identified a checklist of key principles, to get the basics right, with links to examples of how schools adapted it to their own practice and to a series of short films about classroom behaviour (http://www.education.gov.uk.). This is a menu of ideas, which does not claim to be exhaustive, from which schools can develop their own checklists. The emphasis is on consistency. It recognises that classroom management is complex but, as you see (below), the underlying principles are simple, so simple they may seem obvious, but, for this reason, may be overlooked.

Classroom

Know the names and roles of any adults in class. Meet and greet pupils when they come into the classroom. Display rules in the class – and ensure that the pupils and staff know what they are. Display the tariff of sanctions in class. Have a system in place to follow through with all sanctions. Display the tariff of rewards in class. Have a system in place to follow through with all rewards. Have a visual timetable on the wall. Follow the school behaviour policy. Know the names of children. Have a plan for children who are likely to misbehave. Ensure other adults in the class know the plan. Understand pupils' special needs.

Teaching

Ensure that all resources are prepared in advance. Praise the behaviour you want to see more of. Praise children doing the right thing more than criticising those who are doing the wrong thing (parallel praise). Differentiate. Stay calm. Have clear routines for transitions and for stopping the class. Teach children the class routines.

Practical examples of strategies discussed

Relationships

Know your own tolerance thresholds, what is likely to make you 'fly off the handle' and pre-empt this! Model good behaviours: calmness, predictability, fairness, being a good listener, giving a child the right to reply. If you do slip up, acknowledge it and apologise. Children respect this. If you have difficult personal circumstances, put on a professional act in order to behave as you would wish to.

Building good relationships

It is important to know and value children individually; know something about their lives and interests. Don't forget a sense of humour. Be prepared to repair relationships. You are an adult and a child may feel hurt after being reprimanded. Try to catch the child doing something good and praise this.

Interactions

Don't focus on one or two children you think might be misbehaving and ignore the rest of the class. See behaviour as unacceptable but not the pupil, because this links poor behaviour with the pupil's identity and does not allow room for change. Use the language of choice ('you can choose to do X or Y'). This removes a power struggle, places responsibility with the pupil and treats misbehaviour as a learning experience. It also emphasises choice and responsibility. A child may deflect attention from initial misbehaviour by shrugging or muttering. This could lead to a debate about the muttering. So stay focused on the initial misbehaviour and deal with that.

Triggers

Always have your resources prepared. Differentiate work so that everyone can achieve. Make sure everyone understands the rules for transitions from one activity to the next. Be flexible; if a test is immanent, or if it starts to snow, or has been a wet lunchtime, be prepared to change the planned activity. If a child's behaviour is being affected by personal circumstances, be prepared to treat the child differently. You can find an opportunity to explain this to other children with sensitivity and they will accept it and be supportive.

Rewards and sanctions

Give more rewards than sanctions. Reward children close to the learner who is not doing what is expected. Decide when it is best to ignore behaviour, especially secondary behaviour; your consistent follow-up will ensure that everyone understands that the behaviour will be dealt with eventually. Respond to a piece of minor misbehaviour with a response low in the behaviour hierarchy and move to a higher one if compliance is not forthcoming.

Language

Give conditional directions.'When you have done X, then you can do Y'. Use language of 'choice'. 'By doing X you have chosen Y ... it is your choice', or 'I would like you to sit here, or here (where both choices are acceptable to you) ... it is your choice'. Use positive language: 'I would like you to work quietly together', rather than 'Stop calling out'. Make factual statements: 'You are chewing', rather than 'Why are you chewing?'. Assume compliance by saying 'thank you'. Give positive feedback: use frequent, genuine comments that are specific and focused on specific achievements and the process of learning – for example, effort, critical thinking, creativity, care, attention to detail and so on rather than for general talent or ability.

Appearing to be confident

Positioning: move in an unthreatening way, as if by chance, into the proximity of 'off-task' pupils. Continue to teach or support on-task pupils. Step forward, stand tall and appear to be confident, even if you are actually tired and struggling. Rather than responding immediately to 'off-task' behaviour, continue to teach or support other pupils. Then when you are seemingly looking the opposite way, make a comment to the off-task pupil(s). It will seem that you have eyes in the back of your head, as all experienced and effective teachers have of course evolved over the years.

Regaining control of the entire class

Apply selected techniques from those above to the whole class. Use body language to convey your confidence (even if you are not feeling it). For example, insist that 'We are all going to stop now while groups X and Y sit down and organise themselves'. Avoid appearing 'out of control' yourself. Do not engage in debate with any member of the misbehaving groups, nor with any other child; don't plead or enter into bargaining with groups or individuals. Don't threaten the whole class with punishment. Repeat your directive that X and Y are going to sit down and organise themselves (broken record), adding, 'when they have, we will begin again'. Commend those members of the misbehaving groups who are now complying: 'Thank you, John and Mary. Thank you, Tom, for sitting down now' (when he isn't, wait briefly while he does; be clear in your body language that you are in no doubt he will). Begin again only when all groups are ready to. Otherwise, repeat your directive and apply other techniques listed on previous pages. Reward compliance with praise. When you have re-established control, state: 'We will begin again now'. Continue the lesson, deploying, if appropriate, any classroom assistants to the groups in question.

Summary

This chapter has dealt with some of the basic areas you need to consider when dealing with behaviour management. You should have developed a greater understanding of the rights and responsibilities you have as a teacher. You should understand that managing behaviour is not a bolt-on extra to your professional portfolio but is an integral part of classroom organisation and ethos and of how and what you teach. Through reflecting on your own values and beliefs, you should have a clearer idea about how you will approach behaviour in your own classroom, as well as being in a position to consider some of the issues for parents and pupils. You should also be beginning to consider strategies you will use in the classroom to promote and teach good behaviour.

Questions for discussion

- Consider the implications for your own learning.
- What will your next steps be?
- What will you do in your own classroom to develop effective practice?
- Consider any classroom rules you are aware of.
- Are the rules clear and phrased in a positive manner?
- Are they understood by children?
- Were children involved in creating these rules?
- Do they work, do they promote learning?

Further reading

Ellis, G., Morgan, N.S. and Reid, K. (2013) *Better Behaviour Management Through Home–School Relations: Using Value-based Education to Promote Positive Learning*. London: Routledge.

The aim of the book is to improve the quality of communication, care and interaction between the home and the child's school, which is particularly important in schools in deprived catchment areas.

Kaiser, B. and Sklar Rasminsky, J. (2012) *Challenging Behaviour in Young Children: Understanding, Preventing and Responding Effectively,* 3rd edn. New York: Pearson.

This book recognises that a teacher able to cope with challenging behaviour is a better teacher for all children. Initially summarising current research into the roots of challenging behaviour, it examines how teacher–pupil relationships are built up, the role of culture in behavioural expectations, the skills of inclusion, teaching emotional literacy and social skills and dealing with controversial issues. It deals with early years and primary age groups.

Lever, C. (2011) *Understanding Challenging Behaviour in Inclusive Classrooms.* Harlow: Pearson.
This book is concerned with understanding why certain behaviours occur and how to deal with them. What other texts advise may work for the majority of children but not for children exhibiting continually challenging behaviour. This book offers strategies for how to deal with challenging behaviour on an individual level, by looking at the needs of the individual.

Reid, K. and Morgan, N.S. (2012) *Tackling Behaviour in your Primary School: A Practical Handbook for Teachers.* London: Routledge.
Ken Reid was Chair of the National Behaviour and Attendance Review in Wales (2006–08) and he and Nicola Morgan worked on a range of projects on behaviour management. This is a practical text based on modern approaches to behaviour management.

Sapouna, M., Wolke, D., Vannini, N., Watson, S., Woods, S., Schneider, W., et al. (2010) 'Virtual Learning Intervention to Reduce Bullying Victimization in Primary School: A Controlled Trial', *Journal of Child Psychology and Psychiatry* 51(1): 104–12.
This describes a successful experiment to reduce bullying.

References

Cooper, H. (2013) *Teaching History Creatively.* London: Routledge.

Cooper, H. and Hyland, R. (2000) *Children's Perceptions of Learning with Trainee Teachers.* London: Routledge.

Cooper, P. (1993) 'Learning from Pupils' Perspectives', *British Journal of Special Education* 20(4): 129–33.

DfE (2010) *The Use and Effectiveness of Anti-bullying Strategies in Schools*, Research Report DfE RB098. London: DfE.

DfE (2012a) *Improving Teacher Training for Behaviour.* London: DfE.

DfE (2012b) *Statutory Framework for the Early Years Foundation Stage: Development and Care for Children from Birth to Five.* London: DfE.

DfE (2012c) *Ensuring Good Behaviour in Schools: A Summary for Headteachers, Governing Bodies, Teachers, Parents and Pupils*. London: DfE.

DfE (2012d) *Preventing and Tackling Bullying: Advice for Headteachers, Staff and Governing Bodies*. London: DfE.

DfE (2012e) *Getting the Simple Things Right: Charlie Taylor's Behaviour Checklists*. London: DfE.

DfE (2013a) *Teachers' Standards*. London: DfE.

DfE (2013b) *Home School Agreements*. London: DfE.

Gross, M.U.M. (2004) *Exceptionally Gifted Children*. London and New York: Taylor and Francis.

Ingram, J. and Worral, N. (1993) *Teacher–Child Partnership: The Negotiating Classroom*. London: David Fulton.

Kohlberg, I., Levine, C. and Hewer, A. (eds) (1983) *Moral Stages: A Current Formulation and Response to Critics*. Basel and New York: Karger.

Moshman, D. (2005) *Adolescent Psychological Development: Rationality, Morality and Identity*, 2nd edn. Mahwah, NJ: Lawrence Erlbaum.

Office for Standards in Education (Ofsted) (2012) *Common Inspection Framework* (http://www.ofsted.gov.uk).

Sammons, P., Sylva, K., Melhuish, E., Siraj-Blatchford, I., Taggart, B., Barreau, S. and Grabbe, Y. (2008) *Effective Pre-school and Primary Education 3–11 Project (EPPE 3–11): The Influence of School and Teaching Quality on Children's Progress in Primary School*. London: Institute of Education, University of London.

Sheehy, N. (2004) *Fifty Key Thinkers in Psychology*. London: Routledge.

Steer, A. (2009) *Learning Behaviour: Lessons Learned. A Review of Behaviour Standards and Practices in our Schools*. Nottingham: DCSF.

Note: all DfE documents are available at http://www.education.gov.uk

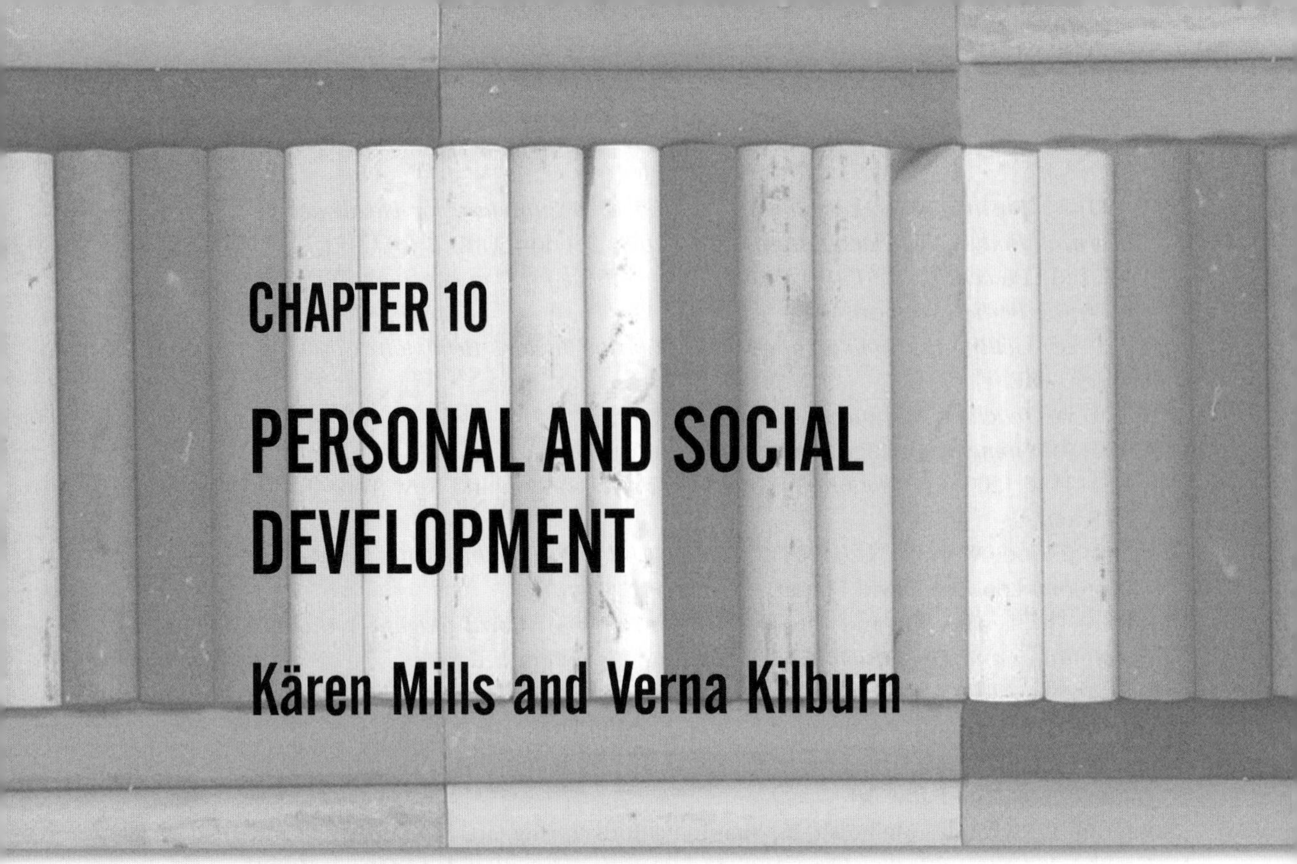

CHAPTER 10

PERSONAL AND SOCIAL DEVELOPMENT

Kären Mills and Verna Kilburn

By the end of this chapter, you should be able to:

- consider fundamental questions concerning Personal, Social and Health Education (PSHE) as a complex concept
- develop an awareness of your own values and how these can influence the teaching of PSHE
- construct and sustain a reasoned argument about the relevance of PSHE, in a lucid and coherent manner
- demonstrate a clear understanding of the importance of acknowledging PSHE in the curriculum.

Introduction

In a world where societal structures are changing on a regular basis and it could be suggested that in some cases children are 'hot housed' to look and behave like little adults, being a child may well be regarded as very complicated. For most children, growth spurts and adolescence are all part of the physical experience which requires a healthy and nutritional diet. Alongside this physical development, which includes the developing social and emotional aspects in the 'affective domain' of the brain, is the challenge to develop a moral sense of rights and responsibility (Marzano and Kendall 2007). From birth to KS1 and KS2, children experience significant periods in their life. These might include going to nursery and to school, coming to terms with family relationships and making friends. These require a sense of developing maturity and cognisance of, for example, right and wrong, what it is to share and be happy.

This chapter seeks to explore the contentious relationship between the non-statutory guidance and recent legislation, reflecting in particular the teaching of sex education in schools across the key stages and the issue of emotional health and well-being. The breadth of the current Personal, Social and Health Education and Citizenship at Key Stages 1 and 2 (PSHEC) Guidance (DfEE/QCA 1999) should prepare children for the complex issues of relationships and their own personal growth and awareness. However, it could be argued that a notional, target-driven curriculum does not fully support the principles embedded within the curriculum, most noticeably in the area of children's emotional health and well-being. The tensions between differing purposes of education, the values-based faith perspective and state-based secular education will be explored.

Rhetoric and practice

Reflective task

Individually or with others, reflect on the following questions:

1 Define and describe what you believe are the characteristics of personal and social education.
2 Can you reflect upon a lesson that you were taught at primary school which you considered to be a lesson addressing some or all of these characteristics?

This activity may well identify one significant detail, even before we consider approaches to teaching PSHE, which is the issue that defining PSHE at both a conceptual and political level can be challenging. The words 'personal' and 'social' could be considered to be value laden, 'used as a vehicle for values stemming from different ideologies' (Ryder and Campbell 1988 p. 13) and this tension is not a recent challenge. Since the 1970s, the development of PSE has attracted attention, both at a societal and at a political level, principally through public opinions concerning sex education and through a range of official government publications, most notably the HMI series *Curriculum from 5 to 16* in the mid-1980s (DES 1989) and more recent legislation related to the Every Child Matters agenda (DfES 2003a).

It is clear that in the National Curriculum (NC) (DfEE/QCA 1999) a sense of values underpins the curriculum, and this is explicitly stated in both the introduction and the non-statutory guidelines for Personal, Social and Health Education (pp. 136–41). A key consideration here is the use of the word 'values'. Rice (2005) proposes that 'values are socially constructed, adopted and adapted in the contexts in which we grow up' (p. 57). So are these values, embedded both explicitly and implicitly, open to personal interpretation?

Values in education

Values in education have historically reflected the 'perceived needs' of the society it serves. For example, in England during the 1980s, 'neo-liberalist values such as choice, competition and market-led education began to influence the aims, purposes and values of education in England' (Shuayb and O'Donnell 2008 p. 18). Across the UK through the 1980s and into the 1990s, the focus of aims and values in education continued to reflect the need for education to be a tool for initiating social change. Standardisation of the curriculum, as opposed to child-centred approaches, became the dominant ideology, and performance in the core subjects of numeracy, literacy and science became a focus of the curriculum, along with the growing awareness of the need for economic development. Additionally, the development of education for citizenship was seen as an important inclusion in the newly restructured and reorganised education system towards the late 1990s. The Education Reform Act of 1988 expressed general values and principles of education, which were then adopted but not explicitly set out in the National Curriculum (1988). However, a subsequent Act of 1996, the Schools Inspection Act, clearly stated that Her Majesty's Chief Inspectors of Schools should focus on a range of priorities which included developing children's social and personal skills. However, the emphasis on developing the core subjects and on raising pupil performance, and as a result raising standards, continued to be a priority into the New Labour Government of 1997, which seemed to adopt this neo-liberal stance on education (Shuayb and O'Donnell 2008). In 1999, when the Department for Education and Employment (DfEE) and the Qualifications and Curriculum Authority (QCA) published *The National*

Curriculum for England at Key Stages 1 and 2 (DfEE/QCA 1999), it included an explicit statement of values, aims and purposes.

Values were linked to the National Curriculum handbook (QCA 2009) and focused on four major factors: the self; relationships; society; and the environment. On reflection, the content mirrors those values which will develop, amongst other skills, self-autonomy and responsibility, respect and care for others, the skills both to contribute economically and to become aware of the need for sustainability in future global issues. It would be difficult to argue against these values, both educationally and personally, as central to being a member of society. So, these values were tacitly accepted as being those that all of us, and society in general, would want our children to aspire to. Should we leave them to chance or move towards a statutory requirement for our schools to develop and nurture these in our children?

Statutory versus non-statutory

An important issue here is the status of PSHE in schools: it is a non-statutory subject. However, the majority of schools plan to include this in their curriculum, as it makes a significant contribution to meeting schools' statutory responsibilities, which are to promote children and young people's personal and economic well-being. Here, well-being is defined in the Children Act 2004 as 'the promotion of physical and mental health; emotional well-being; social and economic well-being; education; training and recreation; recognition of the contribution made by children to society and protection from harm and neglect' (Ofsted 2013 p. 9). In addition to promoting well-being, schools offer sex and relationships education and use PSHE to prepare pupils for adult life.

Anecdotally, many schools have historically considered two levels of the National Curriculum (1999), the statutory and non-statutory guidance. In the statutory requirements, the written syllabus was clearly conveyed to teachers through detailed programmes of study. While this has, in itself, been contentious, it does give a clear indication of what must be taught. However, it could be suggested that teachers may not feel as 'secure' about the non-statutory guidance, of which PSE, sex and relationships education (SRE) and citizenship education are a significant part. The emphasis on meeting targets and delivering standards has often conflicted with the concept of inclusion, which underpins other aspects of the curriculum. In short, there is limited evidence in some schools of PSHE being taught.

This may well reflect your own experience of the inclusion, or otherwise, of PSHE in your own school and practice. This can be compounded further by considering the aims of education which were set out in statutory and non-statutory guidance. As we have just discussed, while the statutory element has Programmes of Study (PoS) the non-statutory element of the NC were not set out as a cohesive and tangible set of statements and descriptors. Although PSHE-type activities had always been implicit in primary education, the Every Child Matters agenda (DfES 2003a) became the opportunity for the Department of Education and Science to promote structure and focus in teaching PSHE. PSHE should become statutory (Macdonald 2009).

A new National Curriculum

Given these factors, a major concern among educators is that until this becomes a statutory requirement, the differing practice may well result in a tentative and unstructured approach to teaching what is considered to be a key part of children's education. In September of 2014 the new National Curriculum will be implemented (DfE 2013). However, the draft proposals do not indicate any change of status for PSHE and the opportunity to raise the status of PSHE has been lost. Section 2.3 states that 'All schools should make provision for personal, social, health and economic education (PSHE), drawing on good practice'. The difficulty here lies in the implications of 'good practice'. As already stated, the teaching of PSHE could be viewed as limited. The Ofsted website (http://www.ofsted.gov.uk) has recently developed its good practice section, reflecting observed good practice in PSHE with selected case studies. However, to further compound the difficulty of disseminating good practice, while this gives some ideas for action, the first link is to a recent document, published in 2012, which made some interesting comments about the quality of PSHE teaching in primary schools:

> Learning in PSHE education was good or better in 60% of schools and required improvement or was inadequate in 40%. The quality of PSHE education is not yet good enough in a sizeable proportion of schools in England. (Ofsted 2012 p. 4)

Standards driven?

Leaving this conflict between statutory and non-statutory teaching behind, it seems that the logical next step would be to reflect on what should be taught. The aims of education have been fiercely debated over the years and it is not the purpose of this chapter to focus on this. However, it would be unwise not to reflect briefly on some aspects of this debate in relation to the content and delivery of personal and social development education.

Historically, the standards and value for money ethos of the draft Education (Schools) Act 1992 sharply contrasted with the emerging parental opinion of the early 1990s which recognised that the ethos and values of a school and society were important. An amendment to the Bill required evidence through inspection of schools that schools were promoting 'the Spiritual, Moral, Social and Cultural (SMSC) development of pupils at schools' (Education [Schools] Act 1992, Section 2). The accountability issue now demanded that inspectors look for evidence of developing SMSC, and the challenge emerged of defining what this would look like in practice. What resulted was a reductionist approach to the processes and observable outcomes, a set of content and skills that could be measured and therefore assessed. In effect, this became a reflection on what the schools did to promote SMSC development, confusion between the moral and social, and a bias towards a religious interpretation of the spiritual (Trainor 2005).

Developments to redress the balance included guidance notes, training courses and amendments to the 'package' of SMSC to widen the brief and incorporate attitudes, behaviour and personal development. The introduction of the Primary Framework *Excellence and Enjoyment* (DfES 2003b) addressed the content further and many schools embraced the wealth of materials, using non-statutory guidance, published resources and access to training courses to enrich their understanding. In terms of delivery, some schools chose to make separate provision for personal and social development, as opposed to embedding it in a themed approach to teaching and learning.

What is important here is that the challenge of teaching and assessing values cannot be underestimated in this context. For example, what exactly is meant by 'values'? Are these the values of a homogenous society that can be identified and agreed upon or, given that the UK population is rich in diversity and culture, is there freedom for families and cultures to make choices? Can we have a shared vision of what values we want to share and teach our children? This is clearly problematic and the situation is compounded further when we consider the legislative nature of a National Curriculum. Perhaps this is why personal and social education remains outside the statutory requirement. It is evident that this is an evolving process towards a consensus about personal and social development which continues to the present day.

What do we teach and how?

Having established that the teaching and delivery of personal and social education is a complex area, it is important to make some decisions about how and what we teach.

Work in school

Student teacher: When I was in school on my last placement I did not see any PSHE being taught. I was in KS1 . . . is this because I was in KS1?

Tutor: It's not surprising that you did not formally see PSHE taught in school. Schools vary in their approach to addressing this, having been given the freedom to plan and teach this in a way that is deemed relevant and appropriate for their needs. It may be that this school's plan was not to embed PSHE discretely in the formal curriculum but to use circle time to consider a range of issues that the school or teacher has identified as a priority. In some cases PSHE may also be linked with the SEAL materials (DfE 2005), although these are now seen by many schools as in need of revision. Talk to your class teacher about her approach to planning and teaching this aspect of the curriculum.

Analysis A study by Mead (2004 p. 22) suggested that student teachers were struggling to observe lessons reflecting the characteristics of PSHE:

- 'PSHE was not explicitly taught within the school and there was no timetabled slot. Therefore I was unable to observe any teaching.'
- 'PSHE was often taken off the timetable to make room for other activities to happen. In seven weeks there was only one opportunity to observe and one opportunity to teach.'

Students in school find it difficult to establish when PSHE is being taught as often this may be 'disguised' or embedded in other areas of the curriculum. Plans may be adapted to indicate elements of PSHE being included as opposed to a plan which is solely addressing PSHE, as is the case for those subjects with Programmes of Study. More recently Formby (2011) surveyed a range of school leaders and established that in 70 per cent of KS1 classes surveyed and 73 per cent of KS2 there was a discrete focus on PSHE. This research also supported the comment that SEAL materials were outdated and needed refreshing. There was, in some cases, a reliance on these materials as opposed to using them to support elements of the PSHE requirements. Additionally, some respondents commented that this was an area that was most likely to be taken off the timetable if time was needed to address other aspects of the core curriculum.

Case study

Mrs J has been a Year 1 class teacher for three years. She has developed her practice to include aspects of PSHE in her teaching. She organises her pupils in a mixture of ability and friendship groups according to the task and pays attention to the giving of positive praise for all aspects of classroom practice. Mrs J has signs around the classroom to promote healthy well-being, for example 'Now wash your hands' and 'Let's share' over the toy area. She encourages the children to use positive language about each other and acts as a role model for this at all times. If there are specific challenges that arise from pupil conflict, she uses a mixture of positive behaviour management to deal with the incident and circle time to tease out the general issues, specifically dealing with bullying and the feelings involved. She is developing a process of evaluation and review with her class of 28 4–5-year-olds, where children begin to set their own learning goals and identify where there may be barriers to their learning.

In reflecting on this case study, it is worth considering whether Mrs J explicitly sets out a cohesive plan for her children, developing the necessary hierarchy of concepts and skills that will result in her class developing social, emotional and behavioural skills. It is clear that Mrs J *has* a plan, but given the tensions explored earlier in this chapter, it is not enough to set out a series of arbitrary 'one-off' activities, which may or may not reflect the values of the individual, school or community. Given these issues, it could be suggested that something more systematic and less susceptible to reflecting individual values is required.

Children need to develop key skills, knowledge and understanding in systematic, developmental ways. These are:

- *awareness of themselves and others*, by exploring how they think and feel and how they relate to others. This helps them to understand themselves and plan for their own successful learning
- *management of their feelings*, by recognising and accepting their feelings and seeing this as a way to manage the range of behaviours which may affect their learning, for example anger and anxiety
- *intrinsic motivation*, so that they can set their own goals, and take an active part in their learning
- *empathising with others*, by being able to view and understand things from another child's perspective, taking into account their feelings and then to modify their own responses to meet that need
- *social skills*, especially the skills to communicate with a range of audiences, to negotiate and resolve differences so that they can take part in a group.

The Social and Emotional Aspects of Learning (SEAL) resources (DfE 2005) provided an excellent example of how these skills are clearly linked to PSHE and Citizenship/NHSS and other whole-school or setting initiatives, and suggested learning opportunities and lesson plans for developing children's social, emotional and behavioural skills, with intended learning outcomes for children at each of the four colour-coded levels embedded within each theme.

There are some planned differentiated learning opportunities intended for small-group work with children who need additional help in developing their social, emotional and behavioural skills in a supplementary 'Silver' set. In addition, there is a whole-school assembly/Foundation Stage group time script and questions, with six ideas for varying it each year: these ideas are intended to launch a series of classroom-based activities on the theme. Reflecting the educational merits and requirements of extending children's achievements by the setting of homework, there are some suggested activities for families to do together at home.

While such a resource may seem prescriptive and an 'off the peg' solution to the challenges of teaching PSHE, teachers/practitioners are clearly expected to use their professional judgement to decide which activities are developmentally appropriate for their children, and how to 'mix and match' when working in mixed-age classes.

Using such a resource, the case study of Mrs J can now be cross-referenced against a generally developmental set of resources to establish if Mrs J was teaching PSHE in a systematic way, explicitly defining a progressive series of activities which contribute to her children's personal and social development. If you access the Blue set, you will see that there are key ideas which Mrs J explores. For example, her process of 'evaluation and review' is supported by the activity on page 6 ('Setting our goals') and can be cross-referenced with learning outcomes which reflect both PSHE and speaking and listening (p. 2). Her use of circle time is acknowledged good practice by another advocate of PSHE who has published extensively – Jenny Moseley (2005). She outlines the deployment of specific strategies to explore issues relating to PSHE which include 'circle time' and 'golden' rules and rewards.

What we are intending to establish here is that, despite the tensions outlined, there are opportunities to explicitly develop PSHE through the use of specific resources. What this provides is a recommended approach which supports teachers in planning and delivery of this core aspect. However, the themes do not solely represent or address all the aspects which need to be covered in the PSE curriculum.

Further research from the Good Childhood enquiry (The Children's Society 2006) called for the assessment of personal and social development. This may seem quite straightforward as there are clearly some attributes which can be identified. These may include making judgements and decisions, cooperation and independence (Lyseight-Jones 2005). However, the difficulty arises in that many of these attributes depend on our own perception of what it means to be independent. It is clearly subjective, unlike assessing tacit knowledge of, for example, combining numbers. In PSHE, there is no clear tangible outcome, whereas in other subject areas it could be argued that the child either knows the answer to, for example, 2 + 2 = 4, or not.

Work in school

Student teacher: Should I be assessing in PSHE? What is it that I am looking for? Should I be making records?

Tutor response: Assessment is an integral part of the teaching and learning process and yes, you should be assessing children's development in the four key areas of the self, relationships, society, and the environment. It is important to establish what and why you are assessing. For example, how does it benefit you to know that the child can share equipment, work alongside peers cooperatively and has a positive self-image? The benefit in knowing any or all of these links with other areas of the curriculum and activities that you plan. Think about maximising learning by working with a peer. This would be challenging if children could *not* work cooperatively and may well impact on your management of the classroom. Children need to develop as autonomous learners and this is difficult if they have limited personal and social interaction skills.

Analysis: The intangible nature of PSHE for most students leads to problems with assessment. However, this is an important part of the teaching experience and to develop as independent learners and understand about themselves, which is arguably a key component of PSHE, children need regular opportunities to consider and identify what they have learnt and their next steps. Ofsted (2012) commented in their survey that generally teachers were assessing learning regularly, although this tended to be through standardised forms of marking work and

(Continued)

(Continued)

building in assessment tasks in plans. In that sense it could be argued that, unless there is a written outcome, assessment for PSHE is limited. However, the use of teachers' questioning can be an effective assessment tool. Topics in PSE can be contentious, and challenging pupils' views by the effective use of questions at all Key Stages, deepens thinking and supports pupils of different abilities (Ofsted 2012 p. 26). What is evident is that, particularly at KS1 and KS2, lessons for PSHE seem to be more interactive, with assessment strategies being more related to monitoring and questioning as opposed to written outcomes. This style of assessment needs to be carefully planned and considered for all trainee and qualified teachers.

Sex and relationships education

One particular aspect which lends itself to exploring the tensions of values and knowledge is that of sex and relationships education (SRE).

Reflective task

With a friend ...

- What do you understand by the term SRE?
- What should schools teach?
- What do schools teach?

> SRE aims to inform children and young people about relationships, emotions, sex, sexuality and sexual health. It enables them to develop personal and social skills and a positive attitude to sexual health and well-being. (National Children's Bureau 2010)

This seems quite straightforward on the surface and there is clear guidance about what should be taught for all teachers to access. However, reflect on your own answers to the activity above. Does this take into account the age of the children and the appropriateness of the setting? Does your answer consider parental rights and wishes and possibly the conflicting cultural and religious perspectives that might well be implicit in your school?

It is clear that this is more complicated than teaching children a set of technical facts of life and answering random questions that may be asked about relationships. It is also not about parents abdicating their responsibility in favour of the schools taking the lead in teaching their child the facts of life! The roles of the parent and the school are not mutually exclusive and there needs to be a carefully structured and coordinated approach in place by the school which is transparent to the parents.

This is widely accepted and acknowledged, with both legislation and guidance which must be referred to in the teaching of sex and relationships education, and it is this which reflects the issues discussed so far about values, choices and legislation.

Legislation and guidance

The 1996 Education Act stated that the SRE elements in the National Curriculum Science Order across all key stages are mandatory for all pupils of primary and secondary age. Parents cannot withdraw their children from any science lessons which will address SRE through those elements of the PoS which teach about life processes, health and reproduction. Furthermore, all schools must have an up-to-date policy which is available for parents to refer to. This must describe the content and organisation of SRE provided beyond the statutory Science component of the National Curriculum. Schools have the right not to teach SRE beyond the Science orders in the NC and therefore their policy must include a statement which reflects what is or is not provided in SRE.

In short, the SRE Guidance (DfEE 2000 p. 7) builds on these legal requirements and states that: 'all schools must have an up-to-date policy' which:

- defines SRE
- describes how SRE is provided and who is responsible for providing it
- says how SRE is monitored and evaluated
- includes information about parents' right to withdrawal
- is reviewed regularly
- is available for inspection and to parents.

SRE is planned and delivered as part of PSHE and Citizenship. Schools are expected to have an overall policy on PSHE and Citizenship, which includes SRE. Governing bodies are expected to involve parents, children and young people, and health and other professionals, to ensure that SRE addresses the needs of the community, education and health priorities, and the needs of children and young people.

Case study

Mr S teaches a mixed Year 5 class in an urban faith school. In PSE he is teaching a cross-curricular theme of families and he has been asked by the head teacher to produce a large entrance hall display for parents' evening. To appeal to the children in his class, he has decided to ask them to bring in photographs of media personalities in family settings. One pupil brings in a picture of a civil partnership ceremony between a world-famous pop star and his male partner. As the child hands this over to Mr S she asks, 'Sir, what is a civil partnership?' She goes on to tell Mr S in great detail about how this is her mum's favourite singer but that her dad frequently ignores the conversation or says 'it's wrong'.

There are clear challenges here about the potential tensions between the school culture and the societal culture in the first instance, and school and diocese, school and parents in the second instance. In relation to the former, many religions and faiths embed rules of 'morality' as an important part of their doctrine and in many cases these can become prescriptive. However, there are also moral codes which could be seen as guides for personal conduct: in this case the individual has a point of reference for their behaviour. This could be exemplified by the following example of 'you must be married before having sex' (prescribed) or the understanding 'that it is better to be in a trusting and committed relationship'. Given the scenario above, the factor of teaching in a church-affiliated school which requires upholding the moral values inherent in that faith could create a state of unacknowledged tension where the teacher holds two contradictory opinions without feeling any discomfort, let alone dissonance. This state can be identified and is known as cognitive polyphasia. Furthermore, any delay by the teacher in addressing this moral code, either by acknowledging this issue or not taking a 'moral stance', could bring the school and the parent into conflict.

Questions for discussion

Is this only a religious conflict? Are you aware of any other cultural attitudes which may make the teaching of SRE problematic?

Proactive or reactive sex education?

Recent headlines in the tabloid press outline the government agenda for making sex education compulsory. This would appear to be a commonsense response to combat the perceived increase in teenage pregnancies and the growth of sexually transmitted diseases. Recent research by John Moores University (Downing and Bellis 2009) states that children are going through puberty earlier and that they need to understand the implications of this sooner. The research goes on to claim that unprotected sex could be avoided if this gap between children developing and adulthood, and consequently when adult information is given, is addressed. However, what is becoming clear is that education and more formal sex education in schools may now be straying into an area where many parents have clearly defined views of what should and should not be taught outside of the parental sphere of influence. The issue of age appropriateness – what should be taught to children at what age – cannot be ignored, but finding a balance between what should be taught at home and at school and at what age is demanding. Children have a voice here and research by Smith (2002) indicates strongly that some pupils see this as an important aspect of understanding the changes that happen to themselves and their bodies at critical times in their development. Feelings of isolation and misunderstandings about the process of puberty can lead to issues of low self-esteem and in some cases anxiety and depression, whereas an openness about this can enhance pupils' self-confidence.

> Learning about puberty in particular appeared to instil feelings of relief among some pupils who wanted to understand more about the changes that would happen (or were already happening) to their bodies. (Formby 2011 p. 168)

Questions for discussion

What do you feel parents *and* children want from SRE? Is there a tension?

What should you take into account when responding to contingent questions about sex-related issues from children in school?

The way forward

In April 2010, the then Labour Government accepted the recommendations of an independent review led by Sir Alasdair Macdonald into making the teaching of

PSHE statutory in both primary and secondary phases. However, this legislation has subsequently been shelved. The stance on SRE is still an interesting one and worth considering further in line with the recommendations:

> The existing right of parental withdrawal from SRE should be maintained. Where parents do choose to withdraw, schools should make it clear to them that in doing so they are taking responsibility for ensuring that their child receives their entitlement to SRE through alternative means. This right of withdrawal does not extend to the existing statutory elements of the National Curriculum requirements regarding sex education in Science at Key Stages 1 to 4 and we recommend that this should continue to be the case. (Macdonald 2009 p. 4)

Emotional health: an unnecessary extra?

The focus of this discussion has primarily been about the PSHE curriculum and the explicit nature of specific themes and topics. However, the importance of addressing issues reflecting emotional health cannot be overestimated when faced with the following statistics:

- One in 10 children between the ages of 1 and 15 has a mental health disorder. Estimates vary, but research suggests that 20 per cent of children have a mental health problem in any given year, and about 10 per cent at any one time.
- Rates of mental health problems among children increase as they reach adolescence. Disorders affect 10.4 per cent of boys aged 5–10, rising to 12.8 per cent of boys aged 11–15, and 5.9 per cent of girls aged 5–10, rising to 9.65 per cent of girls aged 11–15. (Mental Health Foundation 2010)

We live in a rapidly developing and changing society where children and young people have access to a plethora of inducements and advertisements through a range of electronic devices. They are overwhelmed with images of what can make them happy, what they should eat, wear and do. They are included or excluded from a range of social media communication sites which unchecked can result in a range of emotional responses, both positive and negative, and the rise of 'cyber bullying' is one example of a spin-off from these sites. Attention spans are challenged in this fast-paced world of technology which can lead to feelings of dissatisfaction and unhappiness, while the effects on emotional health can in some cases be damaging to say the least.

The Cambridge Primary Review (Alexander 2010) suggests that physical and emotional health should be taken together and become mandatory components of the primary curriculum. It comments that well-being is not just about physical and emotional welfare. It is also about raising aspirations through educational engagement. It recommends that this 'domain' should explore the interface between emotional and physical development and health and their contribution to well-being and attainment.

Questions for discussion

- What are your experiences of children with issues of emotional health that you have observed in schools?
- What responses to these issues have you seen from the school?

Why is attention to emotional health important?

'Health is the basis for a good quality of life and mental health is of overriding importance in this' (Article 24 of the United Nations' Convention on the Rights of the Child, cited in Smith 2002). Indeed, this notion of emotional health is embedded in the Every Child Matters agenda in its first aim of being healthy:

> Positive emotional health and well-being helps pupils understand and express their feelings, builds their confidence and emotional resilience and therefore enhances their capacity to learn. (Kent Trust 2010)

A substantial minority of children are likely to experience moderate or severe psychological problems at some point in their childhood or more commonly in early adulthood. These encompass emotional and behavioural problems and are most commonly anxiety issues and phobias. Children can be and are affected by a range of family issues, for example divorce and bereavement, and are obviously not equipped emotionally with the resources or the life experiences to deal with these in the way that most adults can do. The issue of child poverty is also heavily publicised by today's society. Statistics from the 2008/9 'Homes Below Average Income' survey show that 13.4 million people in the UK (22 per cent) are income poor. Of those 13.4 million people, 53 per cent are in households which include at least one child (Child Poverty Action Group).

Combine this with the resultant material peer pressure for children to keep up with other children who have 'sophisticated toys', mobile phones or laptops, for example, and there is an increase in some children's perception of happiness reflecting material wealth.

This subjective state of emotional well-being is present when a range of feelings are combined, feelings such as happiness, confidence and enjoyment, and results in increased learning and good school attendance. Schools undoubtedly have an impact on emotional well-being and research commissioned by Barnardo's (Smith

2002) concluded that there were some general factors which should be considered by schools to promote resilience in the middle years. These included positive school experiences, trusting relationships with teachers and good home–school liaison.

At ministerial level, the emotional health and well-being of pupils has been identified as a priority for action since 2008/9 when additional funding was made available to focus on the issue and the Department for Education began to work in partnership with all key statutory and voluntary and community sector stakeholders and interested parties to develop a 'Pupils' Emotional Health and Wellbeing (PEHAW) Programme'. The aim of the programme was to focus on positive prevention by building coping skills in children and young people. This programme was seen to enhance the personal development strand of the curriculum and to build up the resilient emotional health and well-being of pupils. This renewed and continued attention to the issue of emotional well-being reinforces that this is seen as a priority for education (Rees et al. 2013).

Summary

This chapter has discussed the controversial issues related to the teaching of PSHE. Issues of assessment, legislation and teaching approaches, which initially may seem straightforward, have been critiqued and reviewed. This has resulted in a picture that is both debatable and subjective, based on our own personal values system. By identifying more specifically the teaching of sex and relationships education (SRE), the legislative issues become even more debatable. In this area, the curriculum offered in schools has been cited as inadequate based on current headlines and societal comments. However, the overlap between school and parental responsibility is a difficult concept and getting the balance right has been discussed as challenging and controversial. In short, the legislative issues and status of PSHE to include SRE could be a paradox. By participating in the suggested reflective activities and related web material, readers will develop their own awareness of these issues and in doing so will be challenged to scrutinise their own approaches to the teaching of PSHE. These judgements and decisions will be an important aspect of their own developing knowledge and skills as a teacher.

Questions for discussion

Consider how this chapter has challenged your awareness of your own values and how these can influence the teaching of PSHE.

In your view, should PSHE be a statutory part of the National Curriculum? What are the complexities of this issue?

Further reading

Buck, M., Inman, S. and Tandy, M. (2003) *Enhancing Personal, Social and Health Education: A Framework for Learning (School Concerns)*. London: Routledge.
This text develops the teaching of personal, social, health education and citizenship (PSHEC) in primary and secondary classrooms. There is an interesting discussion about challenging policy through looking at effective practice and the purpose of schools in developing this aspect of the curriculum. Case study material presents these ideas in an accessible and meaningful way and develops class- and whole-school-based issues.

Formby, E. (2011) '"It's Better to Learn About Your Health and Things that Are Going to Happen to You than Learning Things that You Just Do at School": Findings from a Mapping Study of PSHE Education in Primary Schools in England', *Pastoral Care in Education* 29(3): 161–73.

Haralambos, M. and Holborn, M. (2000) *Sociology: Themes and Perspectives*. London: HarperCollins.
This key text sets out definitions of culture and society which are a useful basis for exploring the moral issues and societal values referred to in this chapter. Key themes including religion, sociological perspectives and education underpin the discussions of moral values and establish further evidence about the difficulty of legislating for some aspects of teaching PSE.

References

Alexander, R. (ed.) (2010) *Children, their World, their Education: Final Report and Recommendations of the Cambridge Primary Review*. London: Routledge.
DES (1989) *Personal and Social Education from 5 to 16*. London: HMSO.
DfE (2005) *Social and Emotional Aspects of Learning (SEAL)*. Nottingham: DfE.
DfE (2013) *The National Curriculum: A Framework*. London: DfE.
DfEE/QCA (1999) *The National Curriculum for England at Key Stages 1 and 2: A Handbook for Teachers*. London: HMSO.
DfEE (2000) *Sex and Relationship Education Guidance*. Nottingham: DfEE.

DfES (2003a) *Every Child Matters*. London: DfES.

DfES (2003b) *Excellence and Enjoyment: A Strategy for Primary Schools*. Nottingham: DfES.

Downing, J. and Bellis, M.A. (2009) 'Early Pubertal Onset and its Relation with Sexual Risk Taking, Substance Use and Anti-social Behaviour: A Preliminary Cross-sectional Study', *BMC Public Health* 9: 446.

Formby, E. (2011) "It's Better to Learn About Your Health and Things that are going to Happen to you than Learning Things that You Just Do at School": Findings from a Mapping Study of PSHE Education in Primary Schools in England', *Pastoral Care in Education* 29(3): 161–73.

Lyseight-Jones, P. (2005) 'Assessing Issues within Personal and Social Development', in M. Buck, H. Burke and S. Inman (eds) *Assessing Personal and Social Development: Measuring the Unmeasurable*, 2nd edn. London: Falmer Press, pp. 33–48.

Macdonald, A. (2009) *Independent Review of Making Personal, Social, Health and Economic (PSHE) Education Statutory*. Nottingham: DCSF.

Marzano, R. and Kendall, J. (eds) (2007) *The New Taxonomy of Educational Objectives*, 2nd edn. London: Sage.

Mead, N. (2004) 'The Provision for Personal, Social, Health Education (PSHE) and Citizenship in School-based Elements of Primary Initial Teacher Education', *Pastoral Care* June: 19–26.

Mental Health Foundation (2010) www.mental-health.org.uk/information/mental-health-statistics

Moseley, J. (2005) *Circle Time for Young Children*. Abingdon: Routledge.

National Children's Bureau (2010) *Sex and Relationships*, Sex Education Forum. London: National Children's Bureau.

Ofsted (2012) *Not Yet Good Enough: Personal, Social, Health and Economic Education in Schools. Personal, Social and Health Education in English Schools in 2012*. London: Ofsted.

Ofsted (2013) *The Framework for School Inspection*. Available at: http://www.ofsted.gov.uk/resources/framework-for-school-inspection

QCA (2009) 'Planning, Teaching and Assessing the Curriculum for Pupils with Learning Difficulties', *Personal, Social and Health Education and Citizenship*. London: QCA.

Rees, G., Goswami, H., People, L., Bradshaw, J., Keung, A. and Main, G. (2013) *The Good Childhood Report*, The Children's Society. Available at: http://www.childrenssociety.org.uk/sites/default/files/tcs/good_childhood_report_2013_final.pdf

Rice, L. (2005) 'Promoting Positive Values', in M. Cole (ed.) *Professional Values and Practice*. London: Fulton.

Ryder, J. and Campbell, L. (1988) *Balancing Acts in Personal, Social and Health Education*. Bristol: Routledge.

Shuayb, M. and O'Donnell, S. (2008) *Aims and Values in Primary Education: England and Other Countries*. Cambridge: Cambridge University Press.

Smith, R. (2002) *Promoting Children's Emotional Health*. Available at: http://www.barnardos.org.uk/promoting_children_s_emotional_health_a_research_review.pdf (accessed 18/10/10).

The Children's Society (2006) *Good Childhood: A Question for Our Times*. London: The Children's Society.

Trainor, D. (2005) 'Personal and Social Development Within the National Context: A Review of Recent and Current Initiatives', in M. Dowling (ed.) *Assessing Children's Personal and Social Development: Measuring the Unmeasurable?*, 2nd edn. London: Falmer Press.

Websites

Child Poverty Action Group: http://www.cpag.org.uk/child-poverty-facts-and-figures

DCSF (2004) *Every Child Matters*: http://webarchive.nationalarchives.gov.uk/20130401151715/https://www.education.gov.uk/publications/eOrderingDownload/CM5860.pdf

Education (Schools) Act 1992, Section 2: http://www.legislation.gov.uk

Kent Trust: http://www.kenttrustweb.org.uk/Children/hs_ehwb.cfm

Mental Health Foundation: http://www.mentalhealth.org.uk

Ofsted: http://www.ofsted.gov.uk/inspection-reports/our-expert-knowledge/personal-social-and-health-education-pshe

The Children's Society: http://www.childrenssociety.org.uk/good-childhood-report-2013-online/index.html

The National Children's Bureau: http://www.ncb.org.uk

CHAPTER 11

DIALOGICAL, ENQUIRY AND PARTICIPATORY APPROACHES TO LEARNING

Donna Hurford and Chris Rowley

By the end of this chapter, you should be able to:

- make connections between dialogue, enquiry and participatory approaches to learning
- discuss, in an informed way, how dialogue and participatory approaches can contribute to learning
- plan for a variety of enquiry and participatory approaches in the primary classroom.

Introduction

Dialogical enquiry and participatory approaches

This chapter is concerned with approaches to leading children into active participation and enquiry, through involvement in their own learning, both at Key

Stages 1 and 2. The terms 'enquiry', 'learning' and 'active participation' are closely related. We link these approaches to dialogue and discussion because these aspects of learning are often dealt with separately in the literature and yet clearly they are a form of enquiry and participatory learning. We draw upon a range of literature and research in order to justify these approaches and we offer some examples of how they might be put into practice in the primary curriculum. Dialogical enquiry and participatory approaches apply across educational stages and have much in common with the concept of 'sustained, shared thinking' identified in the Researching Effective Pedagogy in the Early Years (REPEY) Project (Siraj-Blatchford et al. 2002). This project found that the most effective strategies and techniques for promoting learning in the early years involved adult–child interactions in which the adult responds to the child's understanding of a subject or activity, the child responds to what is to be learnt, what is in the adult's mind, and both contribute to and are involved in the learning process, although the project also found that such exchanges do not occur frequently and that freely chosen play activities often provided the best opportunities for adults to extend children's thinking (Cooper 2004 pp. 1–2).

A rationale for dialogical, enquiry and participatory approaches

Theories

In many ways, it seems strange to need to articulate a rationale for using enquiry and participatory approaches in a primary classroom. Why would we not want children to enquire, participate, be involved with learning and to work with each other? To affirm the place of participatory approaches to learning, we can draw on a variety of literature. Dewey (1902) provides a rationale for child-centred education. Pollard gives a summary of constructivist and social constructivist models of learning in school classrooms (2008 p. 182). Freire (1970) argues for transformative and emancipatory education for communities which are otherwise unheard of and oppressed. Emergent theories of creative approaches (Craft 2000, 2005) and global education (DfID 2005; Hicks and Holden 2007; Oxfam 2006) emphasise the importance of talk and interaction. The statutory requirements in the National Curriculum at all stages (DfE 2013 p. 17) place emphasis on listening and responding to adults and peers, asking questions to extend understanding, articulating arguments and opinions, participating actively in collaborative conversations, hypothesising, imagining and exploring ideas, participating in discussions, evaluating viewpoints and building on the contributions of others.

Policies

Assessment for Learning (Assessment Reform Group 2002) focuses on learner participation. The commitment to inclusion of our current education system (QCDA 2010), and policies such as Every Child Matters (DfES 2003a), aim to ensure that no children are oppressed by their education. Furthermore, the value accorded to 'pupil voice' is evident through school councils and Personal, Social and Health Education (PSHE) and in initiatives such as Social and Emotional Aspects of Learning (SEAL 2005). However, to further develop children's participation in their learning, we should also consider the potential transferability of such methodologies as 'Participatory Learning and Action' (PLA) which seeks to enable people to fully participate in the process of learning about their needs and opportunities and in what they need to do to address them (multi-stakeholder processes). If we look to current policies on approaches to teaching and learning we can be encouraged that 'a central message of this document [*Excellence and Enjoyment*] is that teachers have the power to decide how to teach' (DfES 2003b p. 16).

Theory and policy in practice

Research also provides us with approaches to teaching and learning and by critically reviewing these from practitioner perspectives we can explore ways to enhance learning. You may wish to consider how the statements in Table 11.1 reflect your own practice. In many ways, these are challenging lists, setting high expectations of teachers and facilitators to keep learners engaged, motivated and challenged. Elements of the lists suggest that the teacher or facilitator needs to be a risk-taker and innovator. It could be argued that the very notion of learner participation requires an element in which the teacher 'lets go' of some element of control to the learners. This requires, however, a strong grasp of both the subject matter and the pedagogy on the part of the teacher, who must adopt practices which are well illustrated by the FACTS (Feedback, Application, Challenge, Thinking, Self-esteem) model from Nottingham (2010), summarised in Table 11.1.

Defining enquiry

The starting point for enquiry is curiosity, so perhaps we should really be considering first how we stimulate curiosity in the classroom. What do we understand by curiosity? To what extent can we rely on children's innate sense of curiosity and what role does the teacher have in ensuring that this can flourish? Is the curriculum

Table 11.1 Analysis of the characteristics of enquiry learning and participation

Nottingham (2010 p. 6) 'Challenging Learning' (FACTS model)	DfES (2003b p. 29) 'Excellence and Enjoyment', 'Principles of learning and teaching'	Barnes (2007 p. 134) 'Cross-curricular Learning 3–14', 'How teachers can help children learn creatively'	Chambers (2002 pp. 8–9) 'Participatory Approaches', 'Do's for facilitating participatory approaches'
Feedback			
Provide information related to the task, which helps move pupils towards their learning objectives.	Build on what learners already know. (See Table 11.2) Promote assessment for learning.	Show respect for the child's background. Identify the areas of strength in each child.	Empower and support, be confident ('they can do it'); watch, listen, learn.
Application			
Apply activity to a learning goal related to value and expectation.	Make learning vivid and real.	Give plentiful opportunities for holistic, contextualised and meaningful learning. (See Table 11.2)	Innovate and invent – try new things, be bold, take risks; be optimally unprepared and flexible.
Challenge			
Make a situation more demanding or stimulating to encourage learning.	Make learning an enjoyable and challenging experience.	Learn the arts of pedagogy. Give attention to subject knowledge.	Embrace error, learn from mistakes.
Thinking			
Develop the skills to reason and to reflect upon the ideas and concepts that you meet. (See Activity, Table 11.3)	Enrich the learning experience.		Be self-aware and self-critical; improvise; have fun, joke, enjoy.
Self-esteem	Ensure every child succeeds.	Work at engaging each child.	Establish rapport; respect and be nice to people; unlearn/abandon preconceptions.

that we have planned one which encourages curiosity? Is such a curriculum compatible with a target-driven curriculum and, if so, how? These fundamental questions have to drive our approach to enquiry for, while enquiring might be a fundamental aspect of human development, it is easily forgotten in a crowded curriculum.

The basis of curiosity is often experience, and in the primary school this can take many forms. Experience can be a visit, a visitor, an activity, a story, an image or indeed anything which has an impact and which raises possibilities for questioning. An experience is generally shared and teacher-mediated. In other words, the experience alone is not the only component of a process of developing enquiry. It must be rich, yes, but children must often be helped by the teacher, in shifting the peripheral to the meaningful. One of the great early exponents of the fundamental importance of experience in learning was Dewey, and, though some of his critics saw his proposed curriculum as one which left learning to the child with little teacher guidance or reference to well-established subject methodologies, careful reading of Dewey suggests otherwise. *The Child and the Curriculum* (Dewey 1902) shows that Dewey conceived a curriculum in which the child's experience works alongside the subject curriculum:

> Nothing can be developed from nothing, nothing but the crude can be developed out of the crude and that is surely what happens when we throw the child back upon his achieved self as finality, and invite him to spin new truths of nature or of conduct out of that. (Dewey 1956 p. 18)

In other words, Dewey recognised that the child's experiences needed mediating through the subject knowledge and expertise offered by the teacher.

Enquiry, values and dialogue

Dewey goes on to identify the importance of selecting appropriate stimuli for gaining new experience. After that, he saw what he called the 'logical' (relating to subject matter) and the 'psychological' (relating to experience *and values*) as being mutually dependent, like the dependency between 'notes an explorer makes and the finished map that is constructed' (Dewey 1956 p. 19).

Based on our understanding of this interdependence of subject matter and values, we designed the activities below which give equal importance to the values children bring to their learning and subject knowledge. Alexander (2006 p. 32) discusses the complex relationship between 'talking' and 'knowing' as a way of testing evidence, analysing ideas and exploring values. He outlines the views of cynics to these approaches but concludes that dialogue still remains a key way by which teachers can move children's understanding forwards.

Dewey did not just see education as a balance between the subject and experience either. He recognised that in a world of massive and rapid change the child's social skills were equally important. (In Dewey's time, this was the continued growth of industrial society. Today it is the shift to an information society and probably in the future there will be even more radical shifts to an ecologically sustainable society.) Dewey saw the development of values as essentially part of a process which is integral to the psychological and cognitive development of the child:

> When the school introduces and trains each child into membership of society within such a little community, saturating him with the instruments of service, and providing him with the instruments of self-direction, we shall have the deepest and best guarantee of a larger society which is worthy, lovely and harmonious. (Dewey 1956 p. 29)

Dewey, then, saw the way in which we select the material that we teach as well as how we teach as intimately connected and influential, not only on how we manage an enquiry but also on the values that are embedded in it. He saw an ability to enquire as one of the essential tasks which a school should be developing. Dewey's vision of the curriculum is different from, but not necessarily incompatible with, many aspects of the curriculum that we have today, in terms of both values and enquiry learning.

Enquiry, rigour and subjects

Participation and enquiry, then, cannot be separated from values education. What is more, these methods can all be related to subject knowledge. We would also draw attention to recent research which indicates that participation and enquiry are closely related to dialogue in learning. Alexander (2006), for example, refers to 'constructive dialogue' as more than just conversing, and this is very much the basis of the Philosophy for Children programme developed in the 1980s by Lipman (1993) and others since. Alexander (2010 p. 283) refers to the submission to the primary review by SAPERE (The Society to Advance Philosophical Enquiry and Reflection in Education), suggesting that 'teachers should be given more encouragement and preparation in stimulating and managing classroom dialogue', along with 'more opportunity in the curriculum for "open enquiry"' (see Table 11.3, for an example of this approach).

Work in school

Key Stage 2 student teacher. I am convinced that dialogical enquiry and participatory approaches are valuable but I'd like to find a way of ensuring that they are built into my planning and practice. What do you think?

Mentor: You need to be articulate about how and why you are convinced, in order to evaluate them. Let's make a list of what you think are characteristics of participatory learning, then you can see where you are using them, and perhaps where you might build in more.

Key Stage 2 student teacher (later): Here's my list of participatory learning characteristics:

- Provide information related to the task to move children towards learning objectives in ways that ensure they can reflect on their own learning

(Continued)

(Continued)

- Apply an activity to the LO related to value and expectation
- Make a situation more demanding to extend learning
- Encourage children to reflect on new ideas and concepts
- Identify children's interests and areas of strength, make learning vivid, enjoyable, real, relevant
- Ensure every child is engaged and has success and also learns from mistakes; be bold, take risks
- Ensure everyone participates in learning and has fun.

Mentor: You've listed a good number of factors which contribute to participatory learning! I noticed you have used several already – I'll give you some feedback in my written notes. But it's important that you check on the list when you're doing your planning – and also that in your evaluations you consider what worked well – or otherwise – and why. And don't forget to plan for and analyse your questions and children's discussion!!

Key Stage 1 student teacher: I have read about participatory approaches and dialogic enquiry and I try to take them on board, but in my reception class I also think play is very important. Is there a tension here?

Mentor: Of course, play is important! But think about the overlaps between the two approaches...

Key Stage 1 student teacher: I do feel that I know quite a lot about why play is important. It is a form of solving problems together, I suppose – how to use things in the environment as objects, creating imaginary situations and stories and acting them out together. I've noticed children often have different ideas – and discuss them and argue whose is best – or right ... And I've watched them engage other adults in the play sometimes, and sometimes adults may ask the children questions – or vice versa, or even help them find out more, related to the play.

Mentor: Exactly, so why don't you observe children playing when you have a chance, and jot down the ways in which participatory learning is going on?

Examples of planning a curriculum through participation, enquiry and values education

We shall now consider how we might manage this type of participation and enquiry in the classroom in ways which are both practical and yet rigorous in the contexts of today. The three short examples attempt to illustrate some of the theoretical ideas above, and in particular:

- They encourage participation where children have opportunities to make choices under guidance from the teacher.
- They encourage enquiry methods.
- They embed subject knowledge in a variety of ways, ranging from specific skills to exploring concepts.
- They make use of dialogue in the classroom and encourage the development of values.

Table 11.2 Where did my breakfast come from and how did it get here? A people map

Resources	Open space indoors or outdoors; locality map or world map; signs of local places.
Learning Outcome	To develop map skills through an experiential people map.
Success Criteria	To show awareness of relative positions of localities or countries.
Assessment	Peer review questions and group feedback. What have we learnt from this activity? What did we have to think hard about? How would we do this next time?
Organising the Activity	Depending on the children's awareness of the world map, choose either to focus on the immediate locality with the school as the central point or a world map with the country where the school is located as the central point. If the children know or are ready to learn compass points, ask them to make labels for the four main compass points and to identify where they need to go. Once the compass references are in the right places, bring all children to the map's central point, all facing in the same direction (one of the four compass points). If you are standing in a large open or outdoor space, you may need to set parameters for the 'people map' so that everyone is clear about how far they can go and begin to understand relative distances. If you are making a school locality map, you may want to provide the children with signs or symbols representing features in the local area with which they are familiar. Working either in pairs or groups, the children have to take a sign and discuss where they think the place is in relation to the school. Wait until all groups have discussed and decided where they will go and decide how they will move: all together or a group at a time. Groups will probably have to review their location once others move into their places. As children's travel experiences will vary, you may want to explore this first in class and extend it to where family members have travelled, have lived or live and then use these experiences for the map. Consider if all children need to have personal or vicarious travel experiences to be included in this activity. Alternatively, you could either give out signs for a selection of countries or ask the children to choose a country. Arrange pair or group work as explained above.

The context for the examples in Table 11.2 and 11.3 is a short topic on 'Where did my breakfast come from and how did it get here?' The context for the example in Table 11.4 is a short topic on our water supply. The plan in Table 11.2 focuses on learning-specific learning map skills through physical participation and questioning.

Reflecting on the activity

How does the approach to identifying and developing map skills, in the activities in Tables 11.2 and 11.3, differ from more traditional map work? Possibly the most striking difference is the children's physical involvement in the creation of the map. As Pollard reminds us, 'we now know that the most effective deep, long-term learning is meaningful and conceptual' (2008 p. 201). Tanner (2007), like Pollard, recognises the value of participatory approaches and notes how they can 'motivate pupils, engage their interest and provide memorable experiences which encourage deeper learning'

Table 11.3 A journey map

Resources	A class of pupils; open space indoors or outdoors; locality map or world map; signs of local places.
Learning Outcome	I will be able to work well with my group. I will find out what I already know about our breakfast food's journey, including the transport and the jobs that were needed to bring it to my table.
Success Criteria	I will listen carefully to others, share my own ideas and help the group members work together on the activity. I will be able to talk about what I knew about my breakfast food's journey and I will be able to say what I want to find out next.
Assessment	Self/peer/teacher review of posters' fitness for purpose; teacher observation; teacher questioning; self/peer/teacher review of presentations and what has been learnt during the topic.
Organising the Activity	The whole class will discuss and agree on what would make effective group work and agree to adopt the agreed criteria. The group needs to decide how to share out the group tasks. Each group has a different breakfast food (each food will need to have a country of origin indicated on the label), a sheet of flip-chart paper and marker pens. The teacher will explain that the purpose of the activity is to find out what we already know about the breakfast food's journey, and what we will need to find out or check. The groups need to know that the outcome of the activity is to have a poster from each group. The poster must be a map of their food's journey, with pictures or symbols showing the means of transport and jobs that were needed to bring the food from its source to the classroom. Reassure the children that it is OK not to know everything about the food's journey, encourage them to think about what they know about other foods and to share their ideas. Allow 15 to 20 minutes for the posters to be completed. Each group now reviews other groups' posters by walking around the room to view them. Alternatively, groups could present their posters to the rest of the class. This could be an opportunity to consider and develop presentation skills. Through the poster review, the pupils can begin to identify what they know and need to know about their food; how well they worked as a group; and what they want from their posters.

(p. 154). It is this pursuit of deeper learning that seems so well aligned with participatory approaches. However, it is not sufficient to dot the curriculum with more participatory experiential learning experiences. While Barnes (2007) recommends that 'experiences' are interpreted through the relevant skills and subject knowledge, curricular integration would also apply to participatory approaches. Making learning deep, meaningful and conceptual requires an open-minded and flexible approach to how we enable children to engage with the curriculum.

Reflective task

As a group or individually, using the format in Table 11.2 as a model, plan an activity for another subject (or based on a combination of two subjects), colour-coding opportunities where pupils can: participate by making choices under the guidance of the teacher; use enquiry methods; see where skills and concepts central to the subject are embedded in the activity; encourage discussion involving values.

The plan in Table 11.3 focuses on learning about the international transport of food, in ways which involve interactive group work and discussion of values.

Consider which areas of learning you think this activity would cover. Once you have captured your own thoughts, consider the findings in Table 11.4 which show student teachers' evaluation of the mapping activity. The headings used to evaluate the activity are taken from Oxfam's (2006 p. 4) model for Global Citizenship. According to Oxfam (2006), participatory approaches to learning can '[give] children the opportunity to develop critical thinking about complex global issues in the safe space of the classroom' (p. 2). The Oxfam scheme of work for Global Citizenship illustrates how values and attitudes can be integrated into the participatory learning activities. As teachers, we are expected to plan and assess learning in terms of understanding, knowledge and skills development, and maybe we consider the impact of learning on values and attitudes less frequently. We may assign these aspects of learning to RE and increasingly to PSHE – however, what if we deeply embed engagement with values and attitudes into our teaching and learning practices? What difference do we think this would make? Barnes talks about how schools seek to accommodate the 'all-encompassing sphere of shared values' (2007 p. 146) and notes the importance of values arising from 'genuine and sustained conversations'. Arguably, classroom practice provides regular and meaningful opportunities for these conversations which can in turn be facilitated through participatory activities.

Table 11.4 Evaluating potential and actual learning from the participatory activity: 'mapping the journey of a breakfast food'

Knowledge and Understanding	Skills	Values and Attitudes
Geography: map skills; relative distances; climate; landscapes; means of transport	Creating a meaningful map; demonstrating awareness of relative distances; transferring information from a globe or world map to own group map	Developing respectful awareness of similarities and differences between home and other places
Science: properties of materials (food and packaging); preserving foods; processing foods		Valuing food
Maths: understanding estimation and how to improve accuracy; knowing measures of distance and how they relate (metres/kilometres); knowing how to calculate	Estimating and calculating distances	Developing awareness of globalisation and how it affects us all
Literacy: understanding text has meaning; understanding how symbols can convey meaning	Reading labels for information; designing and using symbols; speaking and listening	Having an inclusive approach to sharing information through visual literacy
Group work: understanding how to contribute effectively to a group	Turn-taking; listening; critical thinking; negotiating; presenting own views; sharing ideas	Empathy; respect; cooperation
PSHE/AfL: developing self-awareness of what I already know and don't know	Identifying what I need to find out; listening to feedback	Self-awareness; being self-critical and receptive to critically constructive feedback
PSHE/Global Citizenship: understanding the contribution others make to my well-being; developing understanding of the work needed so I have food		Respect; empathy; self-awareness

The plan shown in Table 11.5 focuses on deepening understanding of a complex concept through dialogue. This plan uses as its stimulus a story by Raymond Briggs (*The Man* 1992). The approach for KS1 would be essentially similar though the stimulus choice would need to be more suitable. (See the final reflective task in this chapter which links to web pages supporting the choice of stimulus.)

In this case study, the children chose the question 'Who owns water?' It would be easy for a teacher to look at this question and see it as one which has an answer. It is, however, a rich question with lots of potential for dialogical enquiry.

The key concept chosen by the children was ownership, emerging presumably from the notion that water is owned by the utilities company from which we buy it. In practice, however, this dilemma offers an excellent way into a dialogue which raises many sub-questions. Is it really the water that the company owns or is it the cost of collecting, purifying and transporting it that we are paying for? Do I own the water

Table 11. 5 A Year 3 group studying where their water comes from

Learning Outcome	The ability to reflect more deeply on the meaning of a key concept, in this case that of ownership.
Success Criteria	I will be able to ask thoughtful questions and, in talking about one of those, I will begin to see how we might challenge each other's ideas.
Assessment	Self-assessment of my contribution to the discussion. Teacher assessment of responses to exercises carried out after the discussion.
Organising the Activity	A visit to the local water treatment works provided an excellent stimulus, but since the intention was to develop more philosophical questions we moved the children into the role of a group of 'little people' living on a fictional island. To do this, a story *The Man* by Raymond Briggs was used (1992). This story is particularly appropriate because it has embedded in it many questions. It involves a small man (he could stand on your hand) who arrives in a boy's bedroom. As the book progresses, various dilemmas become evident. Should the boy treat him in the same way that he would treat any man? Is it fair to treat him differently because of his size? After reading this book, the children were led into the fictional island where these small people depended upon the mainland for their water supply. The role of the book at this point had been both to introduce a fictional element which would distance the children a little from their own place and also to encourage a deeper level of questioning from them, modelled by the issues raised in the book. Gradually, these discussions were developed into a series of questions. At this stage, it is essential that the teacher understands the nature of a 'philosophical question', one which we could talk about together based upon our own experiences of similar yet different aspects of life. Such questions invariably encompass a range of concepts and it is these concepts (big ideas with rather fuzzy boundaries) that we want to develop different understandings of. Help in identifying and supporting children in creating this type of question can be found in numerous books on philosophy for children. Increasingly, I use the 'questions quadrant' developed in *20 Thinking Tools: Collaborative Enquiry in the Classroom* (Cam 2008). Once the question is chosen, the teacher manages a whole-class enquiry, exploring the meanings using philosophy for children techniques.

that falls upon my roof? If so, do I have responsibility for either storing it or paying someone else (another utilities company) to take ownership of it in removing it?

Children will often show remarkable creativity if encouraged to discuss in this way, providing the teacher understands the nature of the discussion. To do this, training in the nature of philosophical enquiry with children is needed and this can be found via the Society for Advancing Philosophical and Reflective Learning in Education (SAPERE).

There are many ways of developing further children's thinking on the concept of ownership. Our aim is not to write exercises which lead to an answer so much as exercises which promote deeper thinking around the nature of the concept.

In this example, there were certain moments in the dialogue which could be seen as 'critical events' in that they had a significant impact on the dialogue. (For more information on critical events, see Woods [1993] and further examples in Rowley and Cooper [2009 pp. 132–3].) Amy, for example, suggested that water 'belongs to the earth'. This was later challenged by Stuart who said that 'The Earth can't own something if I can't pick it up'. Stephanie then challenged Stuart with an example: 'But a tree can own water because it takes it up from the ground'. This shows how one statement (in this case by Amy) is often critical in dialogue and whether that is picked up and developed by other children can depend a lot on the teacher's handling of it.

These examples suggest that both participatory approaches and dialogue can, handled well, develop deeper learning through actively engaging the learner in a real enquiry.

Reflective task

We learn a great deal by trying out the activities we plan with children first: the advantages and pitfalls. In a group, at your own level, list key philosophical questions related to ownership. Decide on the question to be explored. One person records the ensuing discussion as a concept map. Following the discussion, consider what the concept map shows: ideas which led to further ideas; ideas which were contested; how through discussion the group has arrived at a deeper understanding of the concept of ownership than any individual had previously. Write individual self-assessments based on the learning objectives and success criteria of the lesson plan. (See also the web material for this chapter and consider this task alongside the discussion questions below.)

Summary

In this chapter, we have attempted to justify participation and enquiry methods as key elements of primary learning. We have argued that enquiry methods are often closely related to participation and that the method that we adopt has important implications for both the knowledge and value aspects of learning. We have further investigated dialogue as an essential aspect of enquiry and participation in primary classrooms, both potentially leading to deeper learning.

Questions for discussion

- How could you integrate participatory approaches to learning into a cross-curricular theme you would like to explore with your class?

- How would you define participatory approaches to learning? What would you say are its fundamental features?
- Do methods of enquiry differ in different subjects or in 'domains of knowledge' (as defined by Alexander 2008)?
- How important is dialogue as a method of whole-class enquiry?
- To what extent are primary children able to ask philosophical questions?
- What is the significance of the stimulus that you use to motivate children's enquiry? (See additional web materials for this chapter to help develop both this question and the reflective task on p. 237.)

Further reading

Berthelson, D., Brownlee, J. and Johansson, E. (2009) *Participatory Learning in the Early Years: Recent Research and Pedagogy*. London: Routledge.
This informative and thought-provoking book explores different ways in which the experiences and participation in learning of young children are explored and understood in theory and practice. It will encourage you to continue the discussion about infants' and toddlers' participatory learning in group settings.

Fisher, R. (2012) *Teaching Thinking: Philosophical Enquiry in the Classroom*. London: Continuum.
This book shows how to encourage children to think critically and creatively through dialogue. It is concerned with the kinds of talk we already have with children but 'doing it better', to develop their reasoning, moral thinking and social education. It shows how introducing children to a 'community of enquiry' through philosophical discussion can enrich thinking in any subject area. It is illustrated by examples of the author's work with teachers and children.

Mercer, N. and Hodgkinson, S. (2008) *Exploring Talk in School*. London: Sage.
Based on extensive research, this book interprets learning as social and cultural and classroom talk as the most important tool for guiding the development of understanding and jointly constructing knowledge. The research is firmly rooted in classroom teaching and in how effective classroom interaction may be undertaken in different contexts.

Roche, M. (2011) 'Creating a Dialogical and Critical Classroom: Reflection and Action to Improve Practice', *Educational Action Research* 19(3): 327–43.
An inspirational self study action-research enquiry by a primary school teacher who wanted to create a more critical and dialogical form of pedagogy.

Further resources

Chambers, R. (2002) *Participatory Workshops*. London: Earthscan.
This guide is written for facilitators of participatory workshops. It provides thorough and clear explanations of ways to engage participants in learning. Many of the activities are directly transferable to a classroom setting and others have the potential to be easily adapted for classroom and school use.

Global Dimension (available at: http://globaldimension.org.uk/) provides easy access to a wide range of websites, activities and resources to support participatory and interactive engagement, with thematic approaches to global education and other learning contexts.

Oxfam Education (available at: http://www.oxfam.org.uk/education/) provides a wide range of online and downloadable participatory activities and resources designed for Global Citizenship and are easily transferable to other learning contexts.

References

Alexander, R. (2006) *Education as Dialogue: Moral and Pedagogical Choices for a Runaway World*. Hong Kong: Hong Kong Institute of Education and Dialogas.

Alexander, R.J. (2008) *Towards Dialogic Teaching: Rethinking Classroom Talk*, 4th edn. York: Dialogos.

Alexander, R. (ed.) (2010) *Children, their World, their Education: Final Report and Recommendations of the Cambridge Primary Review*. London: Routledge.

Assessment Reform Group (2002) *Assessment for Learning: 10 Principles*. London: Assessment Reform Group. Available at: http://gtcni.openrepository.com/gtcni/bitstream/2428/4623/1/Assessment%20for%20Learning%20-%2010%20principles.pdf

Barnes, J. (2007) *Cross-Curricular Learning 3–14*. London: Sage.

Briggs, R. (1992) *The Man*. London: Random House.

Cam, P. (2008) *20 Thinking Tools: Collaborative Enquiry in the Classroom*. Camberwell: ACER.

Chambers, R. (2002) *Participatory Workshops*. London: Earthscan.

Cooper, H. (ed.) (2004) *Exploring Time and Place Through Play*. London: Fulton.

Craft, A. (2000) *Creativity Across the Primary Curriculum: Framing and Developing Practice*. London: Routledge.

Craft, A.R. (2005) *Creativity in Schools: Tensions and Dilemmas*. London: Routledge Falmer.

Dewey, J. (1902) *The Child and the Curriculum*. Chicago: University of Chicago Press.

Dewey, J. (1956) *The Child and the Curriculum*. Chicago: University of Chicago Press.

DfE (2013) *The National Curriculum in England Framework Document*. London: DfE.

DfES (2003a) *Every Child Matters*. Available at: https://www.education.gov.uk/consultations/downloadableDocs/EveryChildMatters.pdf

DfES (2003b) *Excellence and Enjoyment: A Strategy for Primary Schools*. Available at: http://webarchive.nationalarchives.gov.uk/20040722013944/http://dfes.gov.uk/primarydocument/pdfs/DfES-Primary-Ed.pdf

DfID (2005) *Developing the Global Dimension in the School Curriculum*. London: DfID/DfES.

Freire, P. (1970) *Pedagogy of the Oppressed*. Harmondsworth: Penguin.

Hicks, D. and Holden, C. (eds) (2007) *Teaching the Global Dimension*. London: Routledge.

Lipman, M. (1993) *Thinking Children and Education*. Dubuque, IA: Kendall/Hunt.

Nottingham, J. (2010) *Challenging Learning*. Berwick upon Tweed: JN Publishing.

Oxfam (2006) *Education for Global Citizenship: A Guide for Schools*. Oxford: Oxfam.

Pollard, A. (2008) *Reflective Teaching*, 3rd edn. London: Continuum.

QCDA (2010) http://curriculum.qcda.gov.uk/key-stages-1-and-2/2010https://orderline.education.gov.uk/gempdf/1849627851/QCDA-10-4937-Single-Equality-Scheme- 2010-2013.pdf

Rowley, C. and Cooper, H. (2009) *Cross-curricular Approaches to Teaching and Learning*. London: Sage.

Siraj-Blatchford, I., Sylva, K., Muttock, S., Gilden, R. and Bell, D. (2002) *Researching Effective Pedagogy in the Early Years* (Research Report 256). Annersley: Department for Education and Skills.

Tanner, J. (2007) 'Global Citizenship', in D. Hicks and C. Holden (eds) *Teaching the Global Dimension*. London: Routledge, pp. 150–60.

Woods, P. (1993) *Critical Events in Teaching and Learning*. London: Falmer.

Websites

Multi-stakeholder processes – Participatory Learning and Action (PLA): http://portals.wi.wur.nl/msp/?page=1275

SEAL (Social and Emotional Aspects of Learning) (2005): https://www.gov.uk/government/uploads/system/uploads/attachment_data/file/222231/DCSF-RR064.pdf

Society for Advancing Philosophical Enquiry and Reflection in Education (SAPERE): http://www.sapere.org.uk/

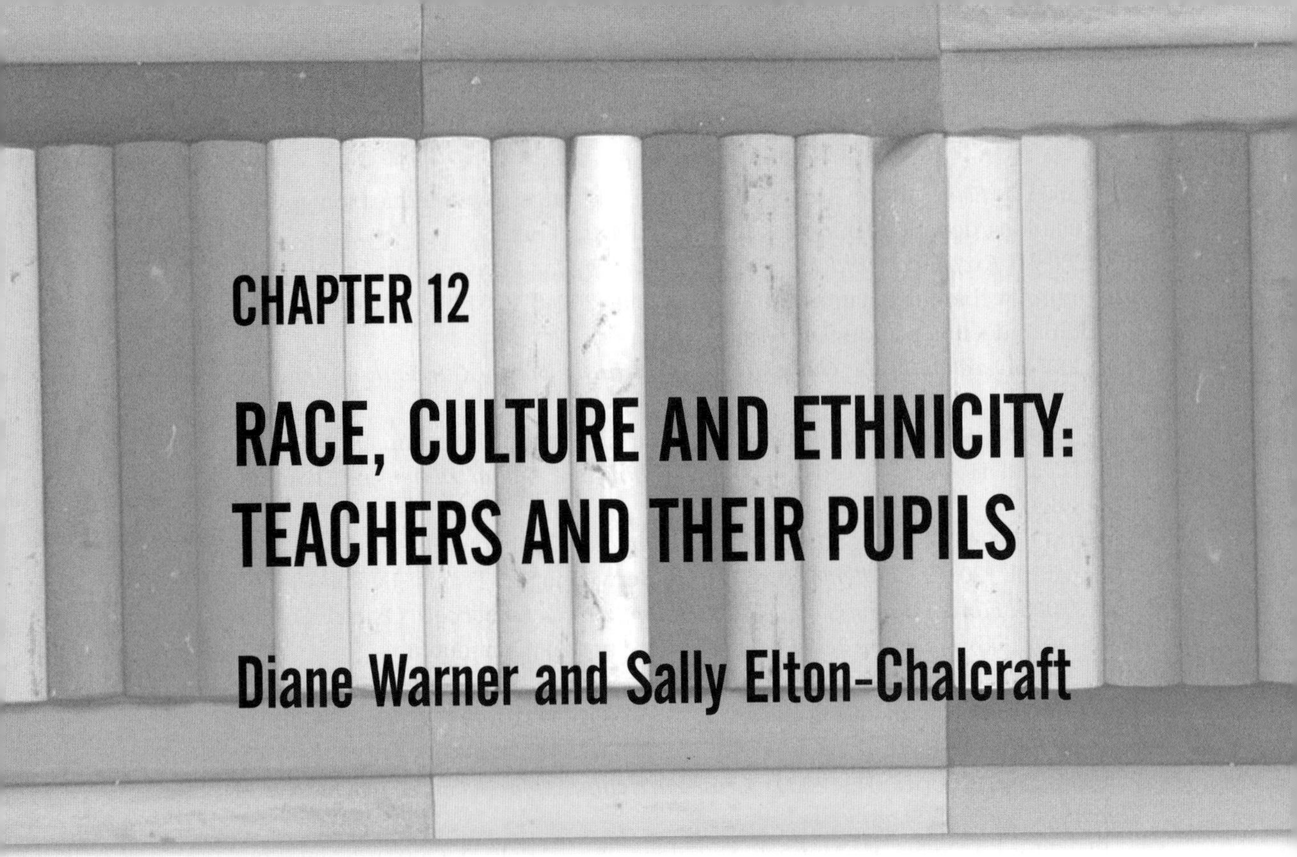

CHAPTER 12

RACE, CULTURE AND ETHNICITY: TEACHERS AND THEIR PUPILS

Diane Warner and Sally Elton-Chalcraft

By the end of this chapter, you should be able to:

- comply with (and seek to go beyond) the legal requirements that concern diversity and promote social cohesion
- understand the impact of your own ethnicity and attitudes towards diversity on your role as a teacher
- reflect on research which investigates cultural awareness among primary children and student teachers
- develop teaching and learning approaches which challenge intolerance and promote equality.

Introduction

This chapter will outline the current picture of racial and ethnic diversity in the UK for new and upcoming classroom practitioners, including statutory requirements and non-statutory guidance. Through consideration of your ethnicity and recent research into children's and student teachers' attitudes towards cultural diversity, you will be able to critically appreciate the importance of developing pedagogic approaches which are culturally responsive and challenging for you, your learners and the school community.

We are all racial and cultural beings, whether we belong to the majority or minority cultures, and this affects the way we think, act and interact with one another. Culturally responsive teaching understands this and also recognises that different racial and ethnic groups are vibrant and are to be valued and cherished. This type of teaching also recognises that all ethnic groups, including White British, are diverse within themselves, rather than being homogenous units. Therefore, recognising children as both individuals and inheritors of a particular cultural dynamic will promote positive self-esteem, racial equity and social justice.

UK classroom statutory requirements and national guidance for teachers

The UK has been an ethnically diverse group of countries for centuries but it is in the last few decades that large groups of peoples, from the Caribbean, Asia, the African countries and more recently from the European Union, have arrived. Varying reasons for this demographic change range from economic change to military and political unrest abroad, leading to the need for employment, refuge or asylum in the UK. The 2011 ONS Census identified a Black and Minority Ethnic (BME) population of 14 per cent which it mainly categorised into: Mixed/Multiple ethnicities, Asian/Asian British, Indian, Pakistani, Black/African/Caribbean/Black British groups.

There are currently 4.3 million children in maintained English primary schools, of which 28.5 per cent of pupils are classified as being of a minority ethnic origin (DfE 2013). This figure is reflected in the way BME populations are concentrated in urban areas; mainly London, the West Midlands, South Yorkshire and Leicester. Some schools in these areas have 100 per cent of minority ethnic children, and schools in rural or suburban areas of England have a handful or none at all. Most schools lie on the spectrum somewhere in between.

The main characteristics of ethnic and racial diversity in the UK are shown by cultural customs. These include: religion and forms of worship, language and dialect, food, music and dress. These differences embody the values, morals and outlook of groups and engender a strong sense of community and beliefs. However, it is important not to see groups as comprising individuals who all think, speak and live in exactly the same way. The 2011 Census alerts us to the fact that minority ethnic groups are varied within themselves:

> different groups share some characteristics but there are often greater differences between the individual ethnic groups than between the minority ethnic population as a whole and the White British people. (http://www.ons.gov.uk/census/index.html)

These differences reflect people's histories as well as current social phenomena. Pakistani Muslims in Lancashire, for example, may share many values and practices with Somali Muslims in West London, but there will be cultural and religious differences too, based on their past and how and where they live now. This will affect surface issues such as dress, food and daily customs, but more importantly members of these groups will have different views and opinions about deeper issues in life, based on the way they follow their religion and the way they are viewed and treated in British society. Alternatively, those whose heritage combines two or more racial backgrounds, such as a Caribbean-English or Irish-Chinese child, will embody both of these cultures, which they gained from their parents, but will also forge their own, new culture, which will develop as they express themselves in our rapidly changing society.

Schools and the law

Community cohesion

From September 2007, schools have been under a duty to promote community cohesion in three main areas:

- **Teaching, learning and curriculum** – to teach pupils to understand others, to promote common values and to value diversity; to promote awareness of human rights and of the responsibility to uphold and defend them; and to develop the skills of participation and responsible action
- **Equity and excellence** – to ensure equal opportunities for all to succeed at the highest level possible, removing barriers to access and participation in learning and wider activities and eliminating variations in outcomes for different groups
- **Engagement and ethos** – to provide a means for children, young people and their families to interact with people from different backgrounds and build positive relations, including links with different schools and communities locally, across the country and internationally. (DCSF 2007; DfE 2011)

Equality Act 2010

The Race Relations Amendment Act 2000 called for schools to eliminate unlawful racial discrimination and to promote equality of opportunity and good relations between people of different groups. This act has now been superseded by the

Table 12.1 The nine protected characteristics as outlined in the Equality Act 2010

Age	Gender	Race
Disability	Sexual Orientation	Religion or Belief (or a lack of belief)
Gender Reassignment	Pregnancy and Maternity	Marriage/Civil Partnership

Equality Act 2010 which still includes issues concerning race and ethnicity but also encompasses other characteristics. Schools must adhere to the Equality Act 2010 which outlines nine 'protected characteristics' (see Table 12.1).

The Equality Act 2010 makes it unlawful for direct or indirect discrimination, harassment or victimisation for anyone of three groups: those who *belong* to one of the nine protected characteristics, those who are *associated with* someone from one of the nine protected characteristics, or those who are *perceived to be a member*. Thus, everyone is, in fact, covered by this all-encompassing Act.

The role of the teacher is never straightforward and you may have already realised that some of these characteristics may be in conflict with each other – for example, some members of some Christian denominations and some Muslims, Hindus and other faiths may disagree, in principle, with the practice of homosexuality, but the Equality Act 2010 demands that homosexuals should not be victimised or discriminated against. Similarly, some women feel that some religious groups discriminate against women in their hierarchy. There are no easy answers to these dilemmas – but perhaps a healthy and open debate following the spirit of the law can assist children to see why the Equality Act 2010 was introduced, and the list below offers examples of how you can ensure you adhere to the law.

The implication of the Equality Act for schools, with particular reference to Race and Ethnicity, includes making sure you:

- draw on resources which are from a variety of cultures – e.g. authors outside the 'traditional canon' (not always using white, male and British authors)
- use images which reflect other perspectives – e.g. displays which show a variety of families from a range of different cultures, using maps with Australia at the top (whilst avoiding 'tokenism'– see Table 12.2 'Types of multiculturalism' on p. 254)
- seek opportunities for other voices to be heard – e.g. not always white, male, Christian, but rather a variety of views/opinions and not just the dominant standpoint in the catchment area of your school
- adopt a critical multiculturalist stance whilst avoiding tokenism (see Table 12.2 'Types of multiculturalism'), e.g. discuss why different dating systems exist, such as BCE (before the common era) and CE (the common era), the Christian BC (before Christ) and AD (Anno Domini), Muslim and Jewish calendars, etc.
- project appropriate 'institutional body language' (Dadzie 2000) – e.g. displays, ethos which celebrate a variety of cultures and viewpoints.

Requirements for gaining Qualified Teacher Status

You should now consider the Teachers' Standards which are requirements for all teachers to achieve before and after gaining QTS and PGCE. The selected standards, set out below, specifically relate to teachers working with children from minority ethnic backgrounds and impact upon becoming a culturally responsive teacher. The standards which relate specifically to diversity are listed below. In what ways do you think these standards can be synthesised (or not) with the duty to adere to the Equality Act 2010? For example, there is research currently underway to investigate teachers' and student teachers' responses to the complex issue of 'fundamental British beliefs' (Elton-Chalcraft et al. 2013).

An extract from the Teachers' Standards:

PART ONE: TEACHING

A teacher must:

1 **Set high expectations which inspire, motivate and challenge pupils**

i. establish a safe and stimulating environment for pupils, rooted in mutual respect

4 **Plan and teach well structured lessons**

v. contribute to the design and provision of an engaging curriculum within the relevant subject area(s)

5 **Adapt teaching to respond to the strengths and needs of all pupils**

ii. have a secure understanding of how a range of factors can inhibit pupils' ability to learn, and how best to overcome these

iv. have a clear understanding of the needs of all pupils, including those with special educational needs; those of high ability; those with English as an additional language; those with disabilities; and be able to use and evaluate distinctive teaching approaches to engage and support them

7 **Manage behaviour effectively to ensure a good and safe learning environment**

iii. manage classes effectively, using approaches which are appropriate to pupils' needs in order to involve and motivate them

8 **Fulfil wider professional responsibilities**

i. make a positive contribution to the wider life and ethos of the school

PART TWO: PERSONAL AND PROFESSIONAL CONDUCT

- Teachers uphold public trust in the profession and maintain high standards of ethics and behaviour, within and outside school, by:
  - treating pupils with dignity, building relationships rooted in mutual respect, and at all times observing proper boundaries appropriate to a teacher's professional position
  - showing tolerance of and respect for the rights of others
  - not undermining fundamental British values, including democracy, the rule of law, individual liberty and mutual respect, and tolerance of those with different faiths and beliefs
  - ensuring that personal beliefs are not expressed in ways which exploit pupils' vulnerability or might lead them to break the law.
- Teachers must have proper and professional regard for the ethos, policies and practices of the school in which they teach, and maintain high standards in their own attendance and punctuality.
- Teachers must have an understanding of, and always act within, the statutory frameworks which set out their professional duties and responsibilities.

What is your response to these standards?
Is it acceptable to question the standards?

While at face value these standards, particularly in Part Two, where you are asked to not undermine fundamental British beliefs, may seem innocuous, but research has found that many teachers feel uncomfortable and unsure about such an overtly political idea which has arisen as a 'result of the Home Office Prevent strategy for counter terrorism' (Elton-Chalcraft et al. 2013). This is a similar finding to Revell (2012) who investigated how some governmental initiatives such as *Prevent* and *Community Cohesion* have imposed new levels of intervention which are questionable and, as she suggests, a possible misrepresentation and manipulation of Islam.

Teachers' understanding of culture and ethnicity

The law promoting equality is an important framework, and the Teachers' Standards have to be complied with, but it is up to schools and teachers to create and practise in an environment which is educationally positive and affirming for its pupils. It is therefore important to develop a mindset which is broad and supportive (also see the section below headed 'Teachers seeing and understanding race and culture in the classroom'). If we belong to the majority culture and a comfortable social class, it is easy to expect certain privileges in life and not see how difficult and distressing it can be for those from minority groups who either have been settled here for two or three generations or are fairly new settlers. They will suffer indignities and hostilities, which can be violent but are more often subtle and 'hidden'. This means their daily lives are spent negotiating what happens to them, based on their colour, culture and religion.

'Cultural capital' is an idea which can influence the way in which teachers can understand and become more compassionate in their outlook and practice in the classroom. 'Cultural capital' was developed by sociologist Pierre Bourdieu in the 1980s and 1990s, who studied how people in a society have differing amounts of privilege and its consequent effect on their lifestyle, expectations and performances. (For access to Bourdieu's ideas try Grenfell 2012.) How much 'capital' or privileges people possess and use to their advantage depends on the type of employment, material wealth, family and education they encounter. Bourdieu called these areas 'fields' and understood them to influence personal life chances and social position; determining higher or lower status. The amount and acquisition of cultural capital can be positively or negatively influenced by performance in these fields. So, for example, a child who attends a primary school in an area where there is a high percentage of professional families, will be in an educative environment which prizes and extends academic, innovative and ambitious activities. The cultural capital in this type of school is high, leading to high-status outcomes such as university and professional employment for a higher proportion of the pupils. This is in contrast to a child from a minority ethnic group who may live in social housing and have parents in low-level employment or unemployment. This child's ability to engage well in school life is more negatively influenced. For teachers, trying to understand what a child 'brings' to school, will allow them to work more effectively with individual needs and a whole-school policy aimed at promoting well-being and life chances.

Another idea which is useful in developing educational understanding as a teacher is 'critical multiculturalism' (May and Sleeter 2010), which is noted in the 'Types of multiculturalism' table below. Critical multiculturalism embodies interaction, interchange and relationship between social groups and in education, and supports teachers gaining deeper and fuller knowledge of their pupils' ethnic and cultural needs, rather than staying only at the surface level of celebrating customs and festivals (tokenism). Further exploration of critical multiculturalism will be discussed in the section below headed 'Teachers and children: attitudes and approaches'.

Reflective task

Use the interactive map on the Guardian Education website to find out the ethnicity of primary school children in the area where you grew up, where you now study or work, and another part of the UK where you might have another personal or professional link (http://www.guardian.co.uk/news/datablog/interactive/2011/jun/22/english-school-system-interactive-map).

Also see: http://webarchive.nationalarchives.gov.uk/20080530183443/http://www.multiverse.ac.uk/viewarticle2.aspx?contentId=439&categoryId=262

1 What is your response and attitudes to the minority ethnic communities in these areas? Why do you think this?
2 How does this relate to the legal requirements stated in this chapter, your geographical position and your future plans?

Teachers and children: attitudes and approaches

Having considered the legal requirements and begun to think about cultural identity, we now invite you to consider the approaches to multicultural education you have seen in schools and begin to recognise good practice. We also ask you to consider your own mindset and evaluate how you can make a positive contribution to schools in the area of diversity. In this section, we draw on our own research to highlight how race, ethnicity, and attitudes towards these, can impact on teachers' and children's world views and behaviour. As you read, consider your own culture, those whom you might teach and the dominant cultural perspective expressed in the curriculum in primary schools today.

Children's awareness of race

Research in both predominantly white and also diverse schools found that the majority of 10-year-old children displayed anti-racist attitudes but nevertheless had internalised the prevailing Western white privilege mindset, whatever their own ethnicity (Elton-Chalcraft 2009). While recognising that the sample was comparatively small (about 80 children from four schools), it became apparent that most children in the multi-ethnic schools who were reasonably knowledgeable about their own culture and other cultures displayed anti-racist behaviour and attitudes (Figure 12.1, Quadrant A). Many children from all four schools were anti-racist even though they displayed limited knowledge (Quadrant B). A handful of children, mainly white boys from a low socio-economic background and in the low sets for maths and literacy, expressed racist comments. In this example, Bart, a white boy, and Kurt, a boy whose mother is white and whose father is of Jamaican heritage, discuss people of different cultures:

Kurt: They're ugly. [giggles]
Sally: They're ugly – so you think people who aren't the same culture as you are ugly?
Kurt: Yeah.
Sally: Why do you say that?
Kurt: Because they've got funny eyes and different to ours – ours are like that, theirs are bozeyed. [making facial gestures]
Bart: Yeah but Heidi [Kurt's girlfriend] is a different culture to you and everyone else in, and some people in, this thing, in this school, has [a] different culture to you but you like 'em – you're friends with 'em. So I don't know what you're pointing that for – ugly ... And so if Heidi's got a different culture to you are you gonna dump her?
Kurt: [embarrassed giggle] Nnooo.
(Elton-Chalcraft 2009 p. 114)

This interchange is interesting because Bart, who had himself expressed racist sentiments, was criticising Kurt's remarks. Thus, Bart and Kurt display racist attitudes towards a particular group but anti-racist attitudes towards a particular individual whom they dissociate from that group (Elton-Chalcraft 2009 p. 114; Troyna and Hatcher 1992). As a beginning teacher, are you aware of the stances towards different cultures held by the children in your placement schools? Is there an ethos of mutual respect or white Western privilege?

A small number of children in the research were deemed to be knowledgeable about their own and other cultures but still displayed racist viewpoints (Figure 12.1, Quadrant C). These children were either expressing disgust at an unfamiliar culture, while in the main expressing anti-racist sentiments towards numerous cultures, or they exhibited racist behaviour which they almost instantly regretted. Rachel, a girl of Caribbean heritage, also made a gesture with her eyes but instantly said, 'I shouldn't have done that', possibly because I asked her why she was making a gesture with the corner of her eyes. Many children from one of the multi-ethnic schools described one Muslim boy's racist name calling. However, Roy was described as a bully who dominated both Muslims like himself and other children (Elton-Chalcraft 2009 pp. 110–11).

Schools may attempt to be inclusive, refrain from stereotyping and promote community cohesion and anti-racism. Yet there may still exist within schools

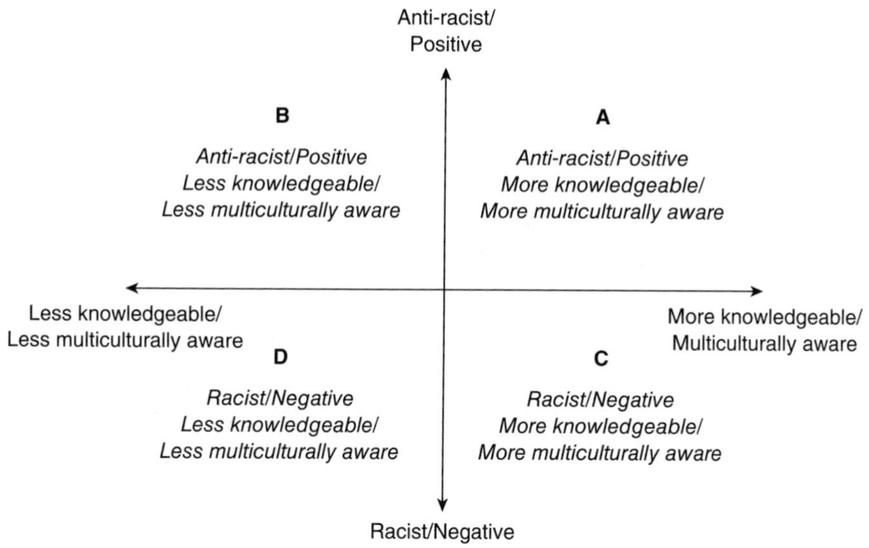

Figure 12.1 The range of children's attitudes and knowledge (Quadrants A, B, C and D)

Source: Elton-Chalcraft (2009).

a white Western privileged outlook which assumes that the dominant culture of white Western mindset is superior (Elton-Chalcraft 2009; Gaine 2005; Revell 2012).

Multicultural stances in schools

The previous section invited you to consider the children's awareness of race but there is a need to understand the school's 'institutional body language' too (Dadzie 2000).

Table 12.2 offers a rudimentary tool to consider how well a school, or class or teacher, approaches issues of diversity, ranging from tokenistic to critically multicultural. Where would you place yourself, schools you have visited or individual teachers?

The aim is for schools to adopt a 'critical multicultural' stance; however in their journey to this goal, many schools may still find themselves at the starting line – with a commitment to merely adhere to legislation. In practice, this could be the use of a limited range of multicultural resources such as a Welcome poster in different languages, an annual Hindu dance event or a Caribbean storyteller. The lesson ideas at the end of the chapter provide examples of anti-racist approaches which fulfil the critical multicultural stance.

Table 12.2 Types of multiculturalism (Elton-Chalcraft 2009 p. 82, adapted from Kincheloe and Steinberg 1997)

1	Conservative multiculturalists (mono culturalism)	are 'tokenist'. They attempt to address multicultural issues but, deep down, they believe in the superiority of Western (white) patriarchal (male dominated) culture. *This is a starting place for many teachers, but this stance is superficial – there needs to be genuine celebration of diversity.*
2	Liberal multiculturalists	are dedicated towards working to 'one race'. They attempt to gloss over differences in an attempt to make everyone equal and the 'same' ('they' are the 'same' as 'us' – they just happen to be a different colour). *Some teachers think this is 'equality in action' but actually they are adopting a 'colour blind' stance, denying that diversity exists.*
3	Pluralist multiculturalists	believe pluralism is a virtue, where diversity is pursued and exoticised. There is cultural 'tourism' where 'they' (as opposed to 'us') live in an exotic parallel world. For example, Hanukkah is the Jewish Christmas. *These teachers attempt to celebrate diversity but they use their 'own' cultural language to describe the 'other' (inferior) culture. There is not genuine equality.*
4	Left essentialist multiculturalists	are extreme in promoting the minority culture, to the extent that the dominant culture is seen as 'bad' and the marginalised as 'good'. *This stance is the opposite of pluralist – here the teacher elevates the 'other' culture and demotes the dominant culture. Again there is not genuine equality.*
5	Critical multiculturalists	believe in the promotion of an individual's consciousness as a social being. They promote an awareness (self-reflection) of how and why his/her opinions and roles are shaped by dominant perspectives. *This teacher appreciates that there are differences within, as well as between, cultures and there is open discussion of the dominance of one culture over another, while celebrating diversity and equality.*

Teachers seeing and understanding race and culture in the classroom

Research among 40 student teachers showed a deep desire to meet all children's needs alongside a lack of racial and cultural awareness (Warner 2010). This lack of awareness, in their thinking and attitudes, caused them to make automatic responses and assumptions that were based on their own cultural heritage. Reasons for this cannot be easily pinned down and neither would it be right to simplify what is a complex area, but the research identified factors which could be seen as useful starting points for everyone, whatever your cultural background. These were family, schooling and community and the social context of one's upbringing. Such factors can be seen as highly influential aspects of our identity formation and affect, in some way, how we see others.

Nearly all of the students in the study were of the majority ethnic group of the UK, i.e. White British. One had a part-European heritage. All had been educated and lived in white communities, and were currently studying at a mainly white university. It is pertinent to consider what values and assumptions they might have already formed about cultures, resulting from this mono-cultural focus of their backgrounds, and to think about how much this applies to all of us. Townsend (2002) describes this as a 'chain of entrenching, white-privilege practices', while Ambe (2006) speaks of 'deep-rooted patterns' which are part of our unconscious being.

Cultural starting points

The students acknowledged their mono-cultural backgrounds, with one stating, 'you simply draw on what you know'; while another, who had lived in the countryside as a child, explained:

> I'd never seen anybody of a different colour; you just knew people in the village. You didn't even think there was an outside world.

Commenting on the use of multicultural children's literature in the classroom, one stated:

> I understand why we have multicultural books because we have a multicultural society, so obviously we need to but I do feel sometimes that by making a book specifically for reading that is on an Asian subject matter, I think that can also make it more of an issue than it actually is.

Other students were worried about appearing ignorant of other cultures and religions, particularly while on placements in racially diverse schools. One commented:

> In 100% Asian school I might see it as more of a challenge because you are not as aware of the culture and beliefs; you're more of an outsider in some ways. Because you're not fully aware of their culture or beliefs I think I'd be more worried that I'd do something that'd offend them or be seen as wrong.

King (2004) suggests that a wariness of approaching cultural differences can result in following known attitudes and approaches, which only affirm the high status of the prevailing cultural majority, and the lower status of minority cultures. This 'avoidance' approach allows the side-stepping of the issue of how far we see minority cultures as subsidiary and unimportant, and therefore raises questions over teaching for equality of opportunity. Anti-racist legislation, community cohesion and school policies and curricula are important markers in this.

In contrast, the student teachers (all names are pseudonyms) in the research displayed and discussed areas of their lives which resisted a white privilege mindset and displayed a deep desire to teach with equity and understanding. Recognising his own cultural position and the desire to teach with equity, Will, part Ukrainian and part English, articulated his difference:

> My granddad was dark skinned and my mother was a single teenage mum, so although I did not know it at the time, I grew up understanding what it meant to be different.

His later employment in a firm which employed many Black and Asian peoples, also affected his outlook:

> You want school to reflect what's life. The reality is that you might grow up in a white area ... but that's not how the world is ... As educators we have the opportunity to make sure that children experience as many opportunities as they can and as diverse [sic] as they can.

Helena became more aware of societal attitudes towards difference and disadvantage because of her mother's job as a care worker with learning-disadvantaged people. As a teenager, seeking to become a teacher herself, Jessica often visited the school of her aunt, the head teacher of a multiracial West Midlands primary school, noting that the multicultural displays and signs in other languages provided important modelling of other cultures to the children. Lou, who lives in the white part of a racially segregated Northern town, has been able to hold on to her existing positive beliefs about racial diversity. While on placement at a white school, an incident involving the negative reaction of some parents about a new Asian child, jarred against Lou's sensibilities and understanding about teaching children equitably:

> We need to reduce ignorance and provide models to help children know they are important and reduce feelings of isolation. Some say 'teaching's teaching', but I think it's [racially-aware teaching] important ... It brings a different experience and that's important.

Becoming a culturally responsive teacher

The openness of these comments reveals that alongside personal cultural histories, the potential to re-shape attitudes is present. Participants in this research had begun to recognise that they did not exist in a cultural vacuum but that they were coming from the cultural majority and white privileged position. As both of these factors influence the way we teach, educators should aim for the 'critical-multiculturist' position, stated earlier, by questioning the underlying cultural assumptions of the curriculum and developing anti-discriminatory, inclusive pedagogies.

Initial teacher training and ongoing CPD are important catalysts in replacing entrenched ideologies and self-satisfied thinking and actions with challenging and transforming practices which reflect the complex and shifting nature of our multicultural society. Embracing more multi-faceted understandings, and encouraging this with children, dismantles blind simplicity and makes difference positive. Teachers need to present opportunities to replace unquestioned attitudes with informed, intellectual, reflexive and ultimately transformative beliefs and principles.

Reflective task

Consider a critical incident you have encountered in school which presents a challenge with reference to issues of diversity, e.g. racist name calling in the playground or the new arrival of a child who wears a prominent religious dress (turban, headscarf) at which the other children quietly poke fun.

1. What is the most appropriate initial response and why?
2. What is the 'institutional body language' of the school? Is this an isolated incident or a typical occurrence? What steps could a school take to ensure a critical multicultural approach?

Significant resources and information on issues of diversity in schools can be found on the Multiverse website at: http://webarchive.nationalarchives.gov.uk/20080530183443/http://www.multiverse.ac.uk/browse2.aspx?anchorid=17844&menu=17875

Teaching and learning for cultural and ethnic diversity

Being aware of ourselves as racial and cultural beings is an important position and enables an authentic and viable teacher–pupil relationship. This is a valuable attitude to foster in all schools to avoid a 'colour-blind' approach, an approach which comes from a failure to acknowledge race and ethnicity, or an uncertainty about how to notice it and then avoidance of the issue (Gaine 2005; Pearce 2005). Jones (1999) also suggests that there can be an attitude of professional indifference and lack of interest in the subject. This type of stance can lead to the formation of negative racist attitudes in children because, according to Pearce, 'unthinking racist insults and unintentional stereotypical racial references' are not linked to racism and therefore not challenged (2005 p. 35).

The following two examples of classroom practice will provide ideas and stimulate thinking for further teaching and learning in the area of valuing and raising awareness of racial and ethnic diversity.

Work in school 1: A Key Stage 1 approach

Using Persona Dolls: an early years foundation and KS1 approach

Brown (2001, 2008) gives practical advice on how to use Persona Dolls in the early years to combat discrimination. Her ideas can be extended for KS1 and KS2 children, particularly within RE lessons. Used alongside other approaches, Persona Dolls can provide a rich resource for learning 'about' and learning 'from' a particular religion/culture/way of life which is a requirement of many RE syllabi (QCA 2004).

Introducing Jeetinder

Introduce the Persona Doll and encourage your class to enthusiastically engage with the doll by asking lots of questions.

Name: My name is Jeetinder Singh. I am a Sikh which means ... *What's your name?*

Language: I speak Punjabi and English. *Do you speak other languages?*

Family: My sister's called Manjit Kaur. Girls often have Kaur after their name and boys often have Singh. But in this country that is sometimes a problem because of the use of first names and surnames so sometimes girls use Singh as a family name. Manjit is 14 and goes to secondary school. She is doing a GCSE in Punjabi (it's the language of many Sikhs who live in the Punjab – north-west India and south-east Pakistan where my grandparents came from). Manjit and Tejpreet, my brother, go to Punjabi school on Sundays; I'm going to go when I'm a bit older. *What are your brothers and sisters like?*

My family came to Britain in 1970, when my Dad was 10. (Show children where the Punjab is on the map.) Manjit and my elder brother, Tejpreet, who's 11 and I, were all born in this country. *Where were you born?*

Food: I like eating vegetable curry and dahl made from lentils. I also like fish and chips, especially from the chip shop round the corner from where we live. *What is your favourite food?*

Morning routine: In the mornings, I get up, wash, have breakfast and get ready for school. My mum used to help me tie my jurra (top knot) but I can do it myself now. (Children may ask *Why do you have a top knot?*)

In the Sikh religion, we believe it is important to keep our hair long. But actually my cousin Jagdeep and his dad have cut hair but they are still Sikh. In my family, the men have long hair and my dad wears a turban which takes him a while to put on! *How do you get ready in the mornings?*

Playground: On my way here, I went on the slide and swings at the playground just down the road from your school – my favourite is the slide. *What's yours?*

Religion: I sometimes get teased by older children for wearing a top knot. I don't get teased in the infants. *Have any of you been teased? What did it feel like? What did you do? What can I do?*

A problem, like the one above, would be introduced at the end of the first lesson or in the second, using the Persona Doll to demonstrate the problem-solving technique. For this and further ideas, visit the Sage website: www.sagepub.co.uk/cooper

Work in school 2: A Key Stage 2 approach

The Island by Armin Greder (2007)

This picture book provides an unusual and challenging resource and stimulus for teachers to enable children to engage with issues of cultural diversity and difference. The story follows a lost and desperate man, washed up on an island where he is confronted by forbidding walls and hostile islanders. He is allowed to stay but because he is different he is treated as an outcast. He is finally set adrift in his burning raft and the islanders return to their heavily fortified, narrow existence. It includes themes of:

- racial and cultural difference
- racism
- effects of immigration, including refugees and asylum-seekers
- human responses and the role of community.

The suggested teaching plan (full details on the adjoining Sage website www.sagepub.co.uk/cooper) covers five sessions, although it could easily be extended to cover a two-week period. This length of time allows for a development of

(Continued)

(Continued)

understanding of diversity through the effect and appreciation of the narrative and linked activities designed to draw learners towards greater awareness and knowledge of how we should live together. It uses a cross-curricular approach, which includes Literacy and PSHE, particularly providing significant time for children to share ideas and views and to know how to listen to and accommodate one another. When using the plan, teachers should also think about the cultural, linguistic and ability needs of their pupil groups so that it can be suitably adapted.

1 Preparatory activity

Ask children to think of between two and four aspects of their lives at home, school and in their communities that they really like and wouldn't want to be changed by anyone new coming in. Provide them with 'bricks' made from brown sugar paper to write their ideas on. Stick the bricks on a large display board, or hang them from a line suspended across the room, to symbolise a wall. This 'wall' will later be dismantled as the children discuss and discover positive ways of embracing change and difference.

2 Introducing the book

The book contains powerful black and white images which will elicit thoughtful discussion, so a good way of sharing it is to scan each page into a computer program to project onto a whiteboard. Look at the front cover; ask for predictions and responses. Read the first part of the story and talk about the children's initial feelings. Make links to their earlier feelings about wanting to keep things the same in their community. In pairs, children should now discuss the man and his feelings. Write these on one side of the wall. Discuss how there seems to be a contradiction between their feelings of things staying the same in their community and the predicament of new people coming in and new things happening. Leave it as an open dilemma at this point.

3 Beginning to explore the story and its messages

Use drama activities to explore this open dilemma by focusing on the actions and motives of the villagers. These could include:

- freeze frames – the children adopt the pose and view of a villager. You go round tapping different shoulders to allow them to appropriately voice their feelings. Do not allow the children to use inappropriate language however and have clear signs for going into and out of 'role', e.g. snapping your fingers.

- hot-seating – the teacher adopts the role of the man, taking questions from the 'villagers'. Place children in groups of 2–3 to think of questions which reflect how their village might feel. Encourage thoughtful questions and ensure there are no racially negative or inappropriate questions through giving some examples and by appointing a group leader to guide and monitor the others.
- conscience alley – this is a good point at which to show the children that not everyone would be hostile towards the man. Divide the class into two lines and choose a child to walk slowly down the middle, twice. On the first walk, one side should call out reasons why they do not like having him in their community. On the second walk, the other side should call out reasons why he could stay, what he has to offer, and to indicate how their minds have been changed since he came to their island.

4 Reflecting so far

Link the children's responses back to the wall, emphasising that although these early comments are natural responses, they may not be helpful and supportive. Discuss and take predictions about the ending of the story, including how a negative or a positive ending would affect the villagers and the man.

The complete plan continues the children's journey of understanding and can be found at: www.sagepub.co.uk/cooper

Summary

In this chapter, we have enabled you to begin to appreciate and understand what it means to be a culturally responsive and anti-discriminatory teacher. This includes the suggested ways in which you can adhere to, but also go beyond, the legal requirements for promoting equality by tackling racism and discrimination and valuing and celebrating children's cultural and racial heritages. You have been challenged to consider the impact of your own ethnicity and attitudes towards cultural diversity on your role as a teacher and have been offered the opportunity to engage with current research which discusses white privilege, colour blindness and a limited teacher mindset.

Teachers are always on a journey of discovery where constant re-evaluation of attitudes and ways of seeing the world become a key characteristic of their learning. This involves self-examination through questioning, observation and engagement in dialogue with colleagues, pupils and their families. It also involves monitoring one's thoughts and actions, noting new or recurrent prejudices, the effects on other people and ways of addressing them so that personal understandings and practice in the classroom change positively. Understanding your school's interaction with its community, through home–school events, visits and meetings with parents and carers will offer an important and welcome part of your role.

Even if the pupils in your school appear to be of a similar cultural position, for example they are mainly Indian and Pakistani Muslims or are all white, it is important for teachers to dismantle notions of perceived social norms of race and class, which may characterise children as 'cultural others', who don't quite 'fit in'. Teaching instead should centre on a more accurate picture of the existing pluralistic society of the UK and enable what Townsend (2002) calls 'culturally-responsive pedagogy'. Culturally-responsive pedagogy alters personal and professional behaviours, paradigms and judgements by trying to understand and see into the world of pupils from cultures different from your own. Teachers therefore need to draw on culturally plural modes of teaching which recognise, celebrate and raise the status of minority cultures; and on anti-racist modes which challenge the power imbalance experienced by minority-ethnic pupils. This involves engaging in teaching which develops identity and gives pupils a sense of playing an equal part in building and sustaining their school and community. These attitudes and practices, alongside a critical multicultural approach, should be adopted by teachers in both multi-racial and white schools, so that our pedagogies are transformed.

Questions for discussion

- Look at school policies on anti-racism, community cohesion, cultural diversity: how is policy demonstrated in practice? What could your contribution be at a whole-school level?
- Within your own classroom, what changes would need to be made to reflect a positive 'institutional body language'?
- What steps would you introduce to challenge children's thinking (through planning cross-curricular activities, through a story or poem) in adhering to a critical multicultural approach?

Further reading

Arshad, R., Wrigley, T. and Pratt, L. (eds) (2012) *Social Justice Re-Examined: Dilemmas and Solutions for the Classroom Teacher.* Stoke-on-Trent: Trentham Books.

This text is helpful for both new and student teachers because it covers issues of race and culture as well as other social justice issues which teachers face in their schools, including gender, poverty, class and religion. Insight into the subtle ways in which inequality often works are presented alongside classroom situations and strategies which can support teachers as they engage in constructive ways of working.

Knowles, E. and Ridley, W. (2006) *Another Spanner in The Works: Challenging Prejudice and Racism in Mainly White Schools*. Stoke-on-Trent. Trentham Books.
Suitable for teachers in both mono-and multicultural schools, this book aims to provide insight and ideas to challenge negative school and classroom attitudes caused by a lack of understanding and fear and help children develop respect for diversity.

Warner, D. (2010) 'Moving into the Unknown', *Race Equality Teaching* 28(3): 39–43.
This article presents research findings about white student teachers' understandings of racial and cultural diversity, through children's books.

References

Ambe, B. (2006) 'Fostering Multicultural Appreciation in Pre-service Teachers Through Multicultural Curricular Transformation', *Teaching and Teacher Education* 22(6): 690–9.

Brown, B. (2001) *Unlearning Discrimination: Persona Dolls in Action*. Stoke-on-Trent: Trentham Books.

Brown, B. (2008) *Equality in Action: A Way Forward with Persona Dolls*. Stoke-on-Trent: Trentham Books.

Dadzie, S. (2000) *Toolkit for Tackling Racism*. Stoke-on-Trent: Trentham Books.

DCSF (2007) *Guidance on the Duty to Promote Community Cohesion*. Nottingham: DCSF. Available at: http://webarchive.nationalarchives.gov.uk/20130401151715/https://www.education.gov.uk/publications/eOrderingDownload/DCSF-00598-2007.pdf

Department for Education (DfE) (2011) Community Cohesion and PREVENT: How Have Schools Responded? Available at: https://www.gov.uk/government/publications/community-cohesion-and-prevent-how-have-schools-responded

DfE (2013) Statistical First Release. Available at: https://www.gov.uk/government/uploads/system/uploads/attachment_data/file/207670/Main_text-_SFR21_2013.pdf (accessed 02.07.13).

Elton-Chalcraft, S. (2009) *It's Not Just About Black and White Miss: Children's Awareness of Race*. Stoke-on-Trent: Trentham Books.

Elton-Chalcraft, S., Lander, V., Revell, L., Warner, D. and Whitworth, L. (2013) 'Not Undermining Fundamental British Beliefs (2012 Teachers' Standards): "Right-wing government pandering", an "elusive set of values", or a welcomed "return to patriotism"'. Presentation to BERA (British Education Research Association), September.

Gaine, C. (2005) *We're All White, Thanks: The Persisting Myth about White Schools.* Stoke-on-Trent: Trentham Books.

Greder, A. (2007) *The Island.* Crows Nest, NSW: Allen & Unwin. This publisher's web page will provide further details on *The Island* and more teaching ideas: http://www.allenandunwin.com/default.aspx?page=94&book=9781741752663

Grenfell, M. (ed.) (2012) *Pierre Bourdieu: Key Concepts*, 2nd edn. Durham: Acumen Publishing.

Jones, R. (1999) *Teaching Racism or Tackling It: Multicultural Stories from White Beginning Teachers.* Stoke-on-Trent: Trentham Books.

Kincheloe, J.L. and Steinberg, S.R. (1997) *Changing Multiculturalism.* Changing Education Series. Buckingham: Open University Press.

King, J.E. (2004) 'Dysconscious Racism: Ideology, Identity and the Miseducation of Teachers', in G. Ladson-Billings and D. Gillborn (eds) *The Routledge Falmer Reader in Multicultural Education.* Abingdon: Routledge Falmer, pp. 71–83.

May, S. and Sleeter, C. (eds) (2010) *Critical Multiculturalism: Theory and Praxis.* London: Routledge.

ONS Census (2011) Available at: http://www.ons.gov.uk/ons/datasets-and-tables/index.html?pageSize=50&sortBy=none&sortDirection=none&newquery=ethnicity+data&content-type=Reference+table&content-type=Dataset (accessed 01.07.13).

Pearce, S. (2005) *You Wouldn't Understand: White Teachers in the Multi-ethnic Classroom.* Stoke-on-Trent: Trentham Books.

QCA (2004) *Religious Education: The Non-statutory National Framework.* London: QCA.

Revell, L. (2012) *Islam and Education: The Manipulation and Misrepresentation of Religion.* Stoke-on-Trent: Trentham Books.

Townsend, B. (2002) 'Leave No Teacher Behind', *Qualitative Studies in Education* 15(6): 727–38.

Troyna, B. and Hatcher, R. (1992) *Racism in Children's Lives.* London: Routledge.

Warner, D. (2010) 'Moving into the Unknown', *Race Equality Teaching* 28(3): 39–43.

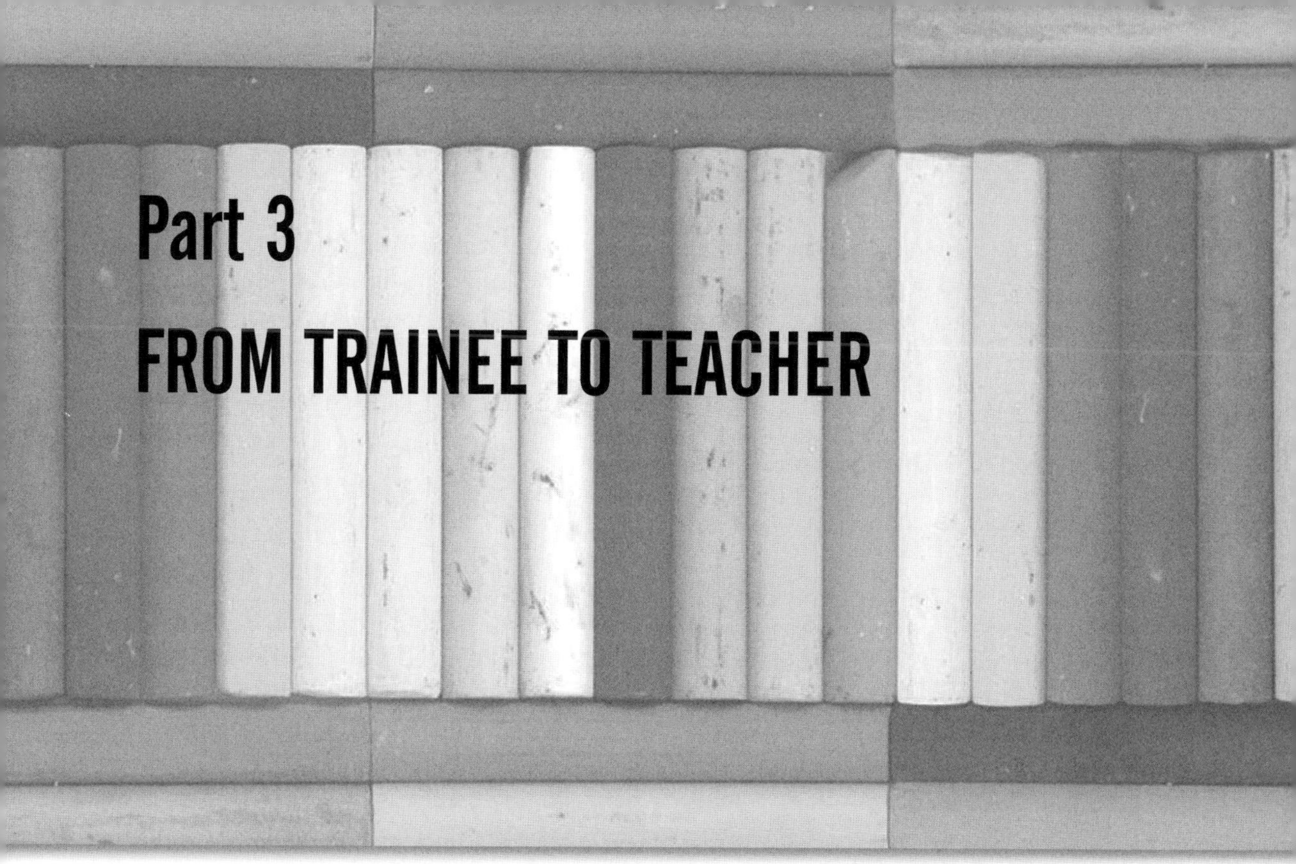

Part 3
FROM TRAINEE TO TEACHER

In reading Parts 1 and 2 of this book, you will have realised that complex, professional judgements are required in all aspects of teaching. You should have become increasingly aware of the kinds of questions to ask and evidence to consider in making them. There is rarely a single correct answer because there are so many variables to consider. By now, you should have developed, discussed and examined your personal educational philosophy which informs these judgements. In Part 3, Chapters 13, 14, 15 and 16 aim to show you, in practical contexts, how to take your professional thinking further, in reflecting on and thinking critically about educational issues. Chapter 17 reminds you of the statutory professional responsibilities you need to take into account in doing so. The final chapter gives an overview of the wide range of Teachers' Standards that have been addressed at increasingly advanced levels throughout the book, and suggests the ways in which you should be supported, as a qualified teacher, by networks of like-minded colleagues. It also shows how you are now in a position not just to be recognised as a qualified teacher, but also to take responsibility for your own continuing professional development and perhaps look towards taking a Masters degree in Education, and later a doctorate in Education.

CHAPTER 13

'LEARNING TEACHING' IN SCHOOL

Pete Boyd

By the end of this chapter, you should understand:

- that continued teacher learning is needed to maximise pupil learning
- that you need to be proactive in managing your work and workplace learning
- the importance of developing your professional identity as a teacher
- that you need to critically question both public (published) knowledge and practice
- that metaphors for learning are useful tools.

Introduction

Many practitioners working in the early years and primary age ranges may be heard to argue that 'you learn to teach by teaching'. This chapter broadly agrees with this view but argues that professional learning is most effective when the practitioner critically questions both public (published) knowledge and the practical wisdom of teachers within a particular setting. The chapter shows you how to maximise your professional learning while teaching in schools. It introduces seven workplace learning 'tools', which will enable you to plan, analyse and develop your practice, now and throughout your career. Each of the workplace learning 'tools' is a concise introduction to selected key ideas from workplace learning theory. Working through tools one to six will help you to understand the final, seventh tool which offers a metaphor for professional learning as 'interplay' between teachers' practical wisdom (what works in this school) and public knowledge (in the form of published theory, professional guidance and policy). However, each workplace learning tool can be selected and applied independently to a critical incident or issue that you have experienced. The final section of the chapter summarises the characteristics of effective professional development for teachers and challenges you to be proactive in making the most of your workplace learning opportunities.

Seven workplace learning tools

In proactively managing your professional development, it is important that you understand some key ideas about how teachers learn through their work. Teaching is a complex and challenging activity that requires a professional commitment to lifelong professional learning. In the short term the busy classroom teacher may claim to be prioritising the needs of the learners, but in the medium term the learners will benefit from the continued professional learning of their teacher. It is important to find time and space for your own professional development because your learning will enhance the learning of the children you teach. As proposed by John Hattie (2012) you need to continually ask the question 'what is my impact?', meaning what effect are you having on pupil learning? This teacher enquiry approach is the key to becoming and being an effective practitioner.

The seven teacher workplace learning tools proposed here for your practical use are:

1. Conceptions of an 'outstanding teacher'
2. Teacher enquiry
3. Pedagogical content knowledge
4. Teacher identities
5. Learning communities
6. Expansive workplace learning environments
7. A situated metaphor for teacher learning.

Workplace learning tool 1: Personal conceptions of an 'outstanding teacher'

One of the initial problems with becoming a teacher is that all of us have experienced a mix of school, college and university as learners. That adds up to thousands of hours of observing teachers at work. Many of us will have at least one lasting memory of a really outstanding and inspirational teacher. Of course, this experience is of value as we seek to become great teachers ourselves, but we are likely to have built up conceptions of an 'outstanding teacher' based on fragile assumptions and with ourselves positioned as 'the learner'. These personalised conceptions of teaching and learning are 'folk pedagogies' and need to be questioned (Bruner 1996). Learning to teach also means that we need to shift attention away from our 'performance' as a teacher onto the experience of our learners. As a beginning teacher you will have opportunities to observe teaching and learning in classrooms. It is important that you focus on the learning outcomes of the learners and that you are prepared to question the underlying assumptions you may have about what makes a good teacher. This kind of 'unfreezing' of existing ideas is very challenging and may lead to a period of uncertainty for you, but it is essential if you are to develop as a teacher.

Even when you have gained experience as a teacher in one or more schools, your own practice history will be both a support but also a potential limitation when you attempt to improve practice or when you move to a new school workplace. Awareness of your history, your identity as a teacher and your current repertoire of teaching and learning strategies, will help you to be a critically aware practitioner who is able to keep on learning.

To become a great teacher it is not sufficient to merely mimic the approach of other teachers. You need to gain some insight into what they are doing and why. This is because classrooms are varied, complex and dynamic workplaces involving relationships, and you will need to respond to your own classroom and develop your own personal approach to working with learners and other adults (Bauml 2009). The effective teachers that you observe may find it difficult to explain what they are doing; much of their practical wisdom is held as tacit, instinctive and hard to explain to others. Teachers' professional learning may be understood as a social 'interplay' that involves identity, relationships and emotions, as well as knowledge of subject content and pedagogy. It is a personal and career-long rewarding and challenging journey, through which you will be continually *becoming* a teacher.

Being prepared to continue your professional learning requires resilience and this is all about your emotional experience of teaching. Teacher 'resilience' means the ability to bounce back and may be defined as the ability to 'recover strengths of spirit quickly in the face of adversity' (Gu and Day 2007: 1302). Based on their large study of over 300 teachers, Gu and Day argue that resilience is closely connected to your sense of vocation as a teacher and to your self-efficacy. In relation to vocation they mean your sense of commitment to improving children's learning and lives and by self-efficacy they mean your belief that you can continue to improve as a teacher and make a positive contribution. Early in your career you will need to respond to both positive and negative experiences within your school workplace. Based on your own educational experiences you may have an idealised view of what kind of teacher you wish to be and you may need to make compromises in the face of the reality of your school workplace and the wider educational policy framework.

Reflective task

What kind of teacher do I want to be? What kind of teacher do my learners need? What kind of teaching maximises their learning? How are my conceptions of good teaching shaped by my prior experience and my current workplace context? What kind of teacher could I become? How do my personal ambitions as a teacher fit into my current school workplace and the wider educational policy framework?

Workplace learning tool 2: Teacher enquiry

Teacher enquiry is a broad term covering critical questioning of practice at different levels, from everyday evaluation of lessons through to a full practitioner research project. Enquiry-based teacher learning will involve some level of data collection and analysis, including observation, gathering and analysing pupils' voices or pupils' work, and analysing data on pupil progress. It may also involve engagement with different perspectives such as sharing practice with other teachers or with published texts and research journal papers. Through your initial teacher training and continuing professional development, you will come across a range of different enquiry-based activities, including some of the following:

- Evaluation of teaching: based on assessment of children's work and/or test scores
- Observation of teaching: followed by professional conversation
- Student voice: gathering and analysing the views of children
- Action learning: a group of teachers sharing issues and supporting each other
- Lesson study: collaboratively plan, teach, evaluate and re-teach a specific lesson

- Achievement data analysis: using grades or other measures of student progress
- Practitioner research: systematic collaborative research projects.

The most ambitious activity proposed, a systematic collaborative practitioner research project, is a powerful way to lead change in practice and drive school improvement (Lankshear and Knobel 2004). Most initial teacher education programmes will include an introduction to practitioner research. In order to become a confident and skilful practitioner researcher, for example capable of leading a challenging whole-school project, many teachers will initially take part in a collaborative research project or will complete a practitioner research focused Masters in Education award. Many qualified teachers choose to study towards a Masters award after gaining some experience in the classroom. A suitable programme will help you to develop research and leadership skills in addition to building an in-depth understanding of educational issues in your chosen area of specialism.

For teacher enquiry to reach the highest level of 'practitioner research', a key requirement is that the investigation is 'systematic' (Lankshear and Knobel 2004 p. 20). Characteristics of teacher 'research' identified by Lankshear and Knobel are:

- a carefully framed research question or issue that is manageable
- a research design that matches your research question
- an analytical framework ... a concept or theory used as a lens to study the problem
- a feasible and ethical approach to gathering data
- systematic analysis and interpretation of the data
- a research report or presentation that draws conclusions, identifies implications for practice and is subject to peer review.

The level of teacher enquiry you are able to pursue will depend on your work situation and the support available.

Reflective task

To what extent are you regularly adopting a teacher enquiry approach in your work? Which enquiry activities might be of use to you in handling current issues in your practice? How might you strengthen your approach to enquiry by collecting and analysing data, sharing practice with other teachers or engaging with relevant published guidance texts and research papers?

Workplace learning tool 3: Developing pedagogical content knowledge

There are conflicting views about what is meant by the professional knowledge of a teacher and it is a contested area of theory. However, one well-established idea is that the teacher brings at least two kinds of knowledge together. These are 'content knowledge' and 'pedagogical knowledge'. The 'content knowledge' means the curriculum subject being taught, for example geography or mathematics, and the 'pedagogical knowledge' means how to teach. The overlap of these two areas of teacher knowledge are sometimes referred to as pedagogical content knowledge (PCK) and this means the teacher's grasp of key concepts in the subject and how to teach them effectively, including knowing the most powerful explanations, metaphors, demonstrations and practical examples to make the subject comprehensible to learners (Shulman 1986; Banks et al. 2005). This relationship is shown in Figure 13.1.

It is possible to introduce new content or pedagogical ideas in a lecture or seminar but really developing 'professional content knowledge' requires work-based learning through being a teacher in your own classroom. Your teaching and professional learning will be shaped by ideas, rules and objects that seem commonplace and taken for granted in your workplace, for example a 'scheme of work' or the school's idea of 'excellent work' will affect your decisions and approaches. Your understanding of a key concept within a curriculum subject will shape your approach to teaching the lesson, but so will the view of how to teach that concept held by your teaching team or mentor teacher. However, do not forget that as a recent graduate you will have new knowledge to bring to the school. A useful way to focus on pedagogical content knowledge is to step back from the planning or evaluation of a lesson and ask 'what are the big ideas or key concepts, within the subject, underpinning the purpose of this lesson?'

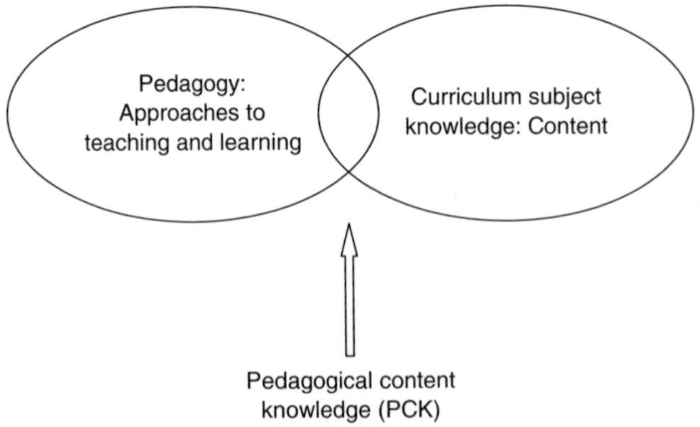

Figure 13.1 Illustrating the concept of pedagogical content knowledge

Reflective task

How well do I understand approaches to teaching and learning? How well do I really identify and understand the key concepts that form the content of my lessons? How are resources in the school or the views of other teachers influencing my teaching?

Workplace learning tool 4: Professional identity

It is necessary to 'become a teacher' through gaining teaching experience and critically reflective learning on that experience. It is not effective to simply 'tell' someone how to teach. Becoming a teacher means building a professional identity, a developing story that you tell about yourself, concerning the kind of teacher you are. As an individual you will have multiple identities, interweaving professional identity with other aspects of your life, and these develop over time to form trajectories of identity, as illustrated in Figure 13.2.

Your identity as a teacher may have different strands within it, for example from your first degree you may have an identity associated with a subject discipline, such as 'historian' or 'physicist'. You may be an enthusiast in a hobby or leisure activity that helps to define you and influences your practice as a teacher, such as 'movie critic' or 'mountaineer'. Within your workplace you should try to identify one or two identity role models – these will be teachers who you might model yourself on. It may just be a particular characteristic of a teacher that you admire and seek to develop. It is also worth considering what teacher identities are highly valued within your workplace and how closely they align to the kind of teacher you want to be. Your professional identities will develop in negotiation with your practice, meaning

Figure 13.2 Showing trajectories of identity: multiple interwoven stories about self developing over time

that the story you tell about yourself as a teacher is related to your approach to classroom teaching (Wenger 1998). This means that 'practice and identity' can be added to the teacher knowledge diagram, as in Figure 13.3.

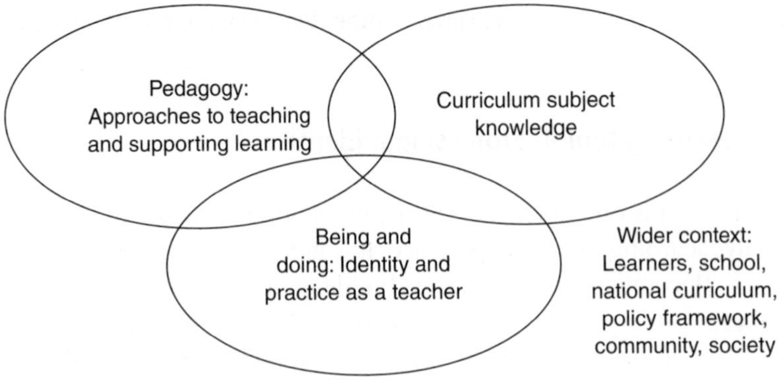

Figure 13.3 Illustrating how your teacher knowledge, identity and practice are related

This more complex diagram suggests that your practice and identity are overlaid with content and pedagogical knowledge to make your professional knowledge more personal and more grounded. The surrounding rectangle represents the wider context of your teacher knowledge, including the school in its community and wider society, within an often rapidly changing educational policy framework. This diagram emphasises the interrelationship between the cognitive, emotional and social aspects of being a teacher. The central overlapping area represents great lessons when everything comes together to promote effective learning. It is important for teachers to do 'identity work' as part of their ongoing professional learning. This means reflecting on your development as a teacher, using one or more collaborative activities with other new teachers, such as writing and sharing narratives, using short talking head video clips and using metaphors.

Reflective task

What are the strands that I bring together to form my identity as a teacher? What kind of teacher am I? What teachers or combination of teacher characteristics provide a role model for development for me as a teacher? How effectively do my lessons reflect the teacher identity that I wish to develop?

Workplace learning tool 5: Professional knowing in learning communities

From a situated learning perspective, teachers working within a school may develop a shared sense of purpose and form a 'community of practice', by developing a collaborative repertoire, for example, of teaching strategies and ways of working. A student or beginning teacher will hopefully be welcomed as a newcomer and through negotiation will gradually build a sense of belonging and eventually become a full member of the group (Lave and Wenger 1991; Wenger 1998). Teacher expertise from this perspective becomes more about professional *knowing* than knowledge (Blackler 1995). This teacher 'knowing' is dynamic, situated, social, contested and shaped by the tools, rules (sometimes unwritten rules), values and key ideas within the school as a workplace.

As a newcomer teacher it is important to understand the history of the group of teachers you are joining, to acknowledge the unwritten rules in force, to recognise that you bring something new and can aim to participate and also to contribute. You will need to appreciate the power involved in any community of practice, with some teachers in the group claiming status, for example by long membership or by holding a promoted post. The newcomer will need to be resilient and determined to learn from setbacks as well as successes, and to handle disappointing learner behaviour, challenging feedback, and even occasional knock-backs from more established teachers in the school. This is close to the kind of resilience we would hope to develop in our learners.

The concept of 'communities of practice' has been developed through the study of apprentices (Wenger 1998). Arguably the teachers' workplace is more complex and the practice of teaching is more contested than many apprentice crafts (Fuller et al. 2005). The concept of a 'learning community' combining elements of situated learning with organisational and change literature has underpinned school improvement efforts internationally. More recent thinking on communities of practice (Wenger 1998) takes account of modern, complex professional workplaces by considering a workplace as a 'constellation' of overlapping communities of practice. The overlapping communities or networks that you might experience or seek to develop include: a formal teaching team or department in your school; a less formal group of colleagues in school that you find you can relate to and tend to share and collaborate with; some teachers in a partnership school; a subject specialist network of teachers (for example, the Geography Association or the Association for Science Education); one or two colleagues that you trained with and keep in touch with; an informal mentor teacher you use occasionally for informal support; a group of teachers that are completing a part-time Masters programme with you … and so on. These examples range from networks both within and external to your school and from more formal professional arrangements to more informal social contacts. Some networks will be face to face and others will be blended or fully online. You will need to be personally proactive in developing such networks as they will support your professional learning and career development. If you fail to get promotion or a particular post in the future, it is no good reflecting back and blaming the head teacher or the school for not providing sufficient opportunities or training. Much professional learning is informal and can be pursued whatever your work situation; even formal professional development programmes requiring fees will mainly provide a framework to provoke or support your workplace learning.

Reflective task

Is there a shared purpose and repertoire within my school workplace? What are the unwritten rules and who holds different kinds of power within the team, department or school? How am I gaining membership of the community and what might I contribute? Who are my current mentors and am I managing those relationships and making the most of their support? What other communities or networks do I belong to and how might I strengthen and develop my professional networks?

Workplace learning tool 6: Expansive workplace learning environments

The concept of an expansive workplace learning environment was applied in a study of secondary school teachers and developed a continuum of expansive to restrictive workplace environments, shown in Table 13.1.

Even if you are fortunate to work in a school with a more expansive workplace learning environment, you will require resilience – an ability to sustain your commitment and manage tensions between your personal and professional identities (Gu and Day 2007). In considering your workplace learning environment it is important to bear in mind that we all have agency; we are able to shape our workplaces as well as experience them. By acting with integrity, being willing to openly share our practice with trusted colleagues, and by maintaining an ethical code, we can help to influence our workplace learning environment. Even in a restrictive workplace environment, it will be possible to form a community of practice with like-minded colleagues in or beyond the school. This is a key point of this chapter; the onus is on you, as a learning professional, to be proactive in pursuing your professional learning and career development. Some teachers claim that they are too busy to pursue their own learning and that they prefer to focus on the needs of their learners. But you need to prioritise your professional learning for the benefit of your pupils because you will soon be of little use to

Table 13.1 Illustrating the workplace learning environment expansive–restrictive continuum for teachers (Hodkinson and Hodkinson 2005)

<<<EXPANSIVE	RESTRICTIVE>>>
Close collaborative working	Isolated, individualist working
Colleagues mutually supportive in enhancing teacher learning	Colleagues obstruct or do not support each other's learning
An explicit focus on teacher learning, as a dimension of normal working practices	No explicit focus on teacher learning, except to meet crises or imposed initiatives
Supported opportunities for personal development that go beyond school or government priorities	Teacher learning mainly strategic compliance with government or school agendas
Out-of-school educational opportunities, including time to stand back, reflect and think differently	Few out-of-school educational opportunities, only narrow, short training programmes
Opportunities to integrate off-the-job learning into everyday practice	No opportunity to integrate off-the-job learning
Opportunities to participate in more than one working group	Work restricted to home departmental teams within one school
Opportunity to extend professional identity through boundary crossing into other departments, school activities, schools and beyond	Opportunities for boundary crossing only come with a job change
Support for local variation in ways of working and learning for teachers and work groups	Standardised approaches to teacher learning are prescribed and imposed
Teachers use a wide range of learning opportunities	Teachers use a narrow range of learning approaches

pupils if you do not continue to learn. You may one day be an expert teacher with 10 years of experience *or* a beginner teacher with one year of experience repeated 10 times.

A particular issue in schools is the often very high levels of accountability (for example, pressure for high test or exam results) and the high-risk quality review process (in the UK that means Ofsted inspection). At least three of the 'restrictive' characteristics in the continuum seem relevant to those schools where responding to review body expectations, post-inspection action plans, and review body criteria seem to dominate professional development activity. It is an important element of professional integrity that the learners' needs, in their broadest sense, are the number one priority for all teachers and schools. This is a dilemma that you will come across and need to handle carefully, understanding the pragmatic priorities of school leaders in response to review bodies but also working to go beyond those requirements to achieve excellence in terms of outcomes for learners.

The continuum in Table 13.1 helps to show how professional learning is situated and social, and the issue around review bodies and school inspection highlights the contested nature of teachers' professional knowing.

Reflective task

How does your current school workplace learning environment seem to fit into the expansive–restrictive continuum? How are you contributing to your workplace learning environment? How are you proactively seeking learning opportunities within your workplace? To what extent does your workplace environment encourage teachers to move beyond review body requirements and strive for excellence in responding to learner needs and maximising their potential?

Workplace learning tool 7: A metaphor for professional learning

In our everyday talk as teachers we use metaphors, linguistic representations, as a powerful method of capturing the experience of learning (Lakoff and Johnson 1980). For example, two important metaphors for student learning have been proposed as 'acquisition' and 'participation', reflecting in turn transmissive and social constructionist theories of learning (Sfard 1998). As an example, language used by a teacher such as 'I delivered the topic' may reveal the underlying use of the acquisition metaphor for learning.

Despite their apparent usefulness, some popular metaphors may be misleading and we would argue that an example of this is the flawed metaphor of a 'gap between theory and practice'. The theory–practice gap metaphor is very widely used in teacher education and development. It is often used subconsciously and underpins statements such as 'we need to apply that theory to practice' or 'all that theory is irrelevant because we know in practice what works in our school'. The theory–practice gap presents professional knowledge or knowing as either one or the other, either abstract theory or what works here, whereas these kinds of knowledge are interwoven within the complexity of the successful classroom teacher's approach.

An alternative metaphor is that teachers' professional learning is an 'interplay' between vertical public (published) knowledge and the horizontal practical wisdom of teachers (Boyd and Bloxham 2013) illustrated by Figure 13.4.

In this metaphorical framework public knowledge is seen as foregrounding published work, including theory texts, research papers, professional guidance books or other resources and also policy documents. This public knowledge is seen as a vertical knowledge domain because of the way it is hierarchically structured and holds power because of its published status. The horizontal domain of practical wisdom of teachers foregrounds 'ways of working' in particular classrooms and educational workplaces. This knowledge is situated and socially held by teaching

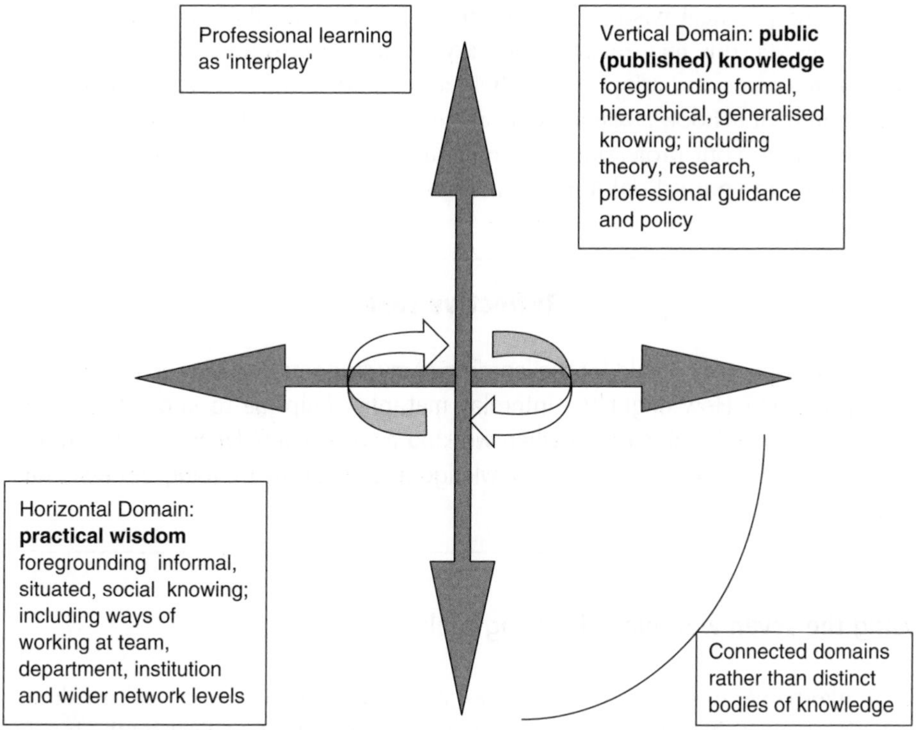
Professional learning as 'interplay'
Vertical Domain: **public (published) knowledge** foregrounding formal, hierarchical, generalised knowing; including theory, research, professional guidance and policy
Horizontal Domain: **practical wisdom** foregrounding informal, situated, social knowing; including ways of working at team, department, institution and wider network levels
Connected domains rather than distinct bodies of knowledge

Figure 13.4 A situative metaphor for teacher learning (Boyd and Bloxham 2013)

teams and includes tacit knowledge and unwritten rules, although it is also likely to include elements whose origins could be traced back to forms of public knowledge.

Professional learning may be considered as an 'interplay' between these two domains. The metaphorical term 'interplay' helps to capture the complexity, dynamism and element of power involved in this learning. It is important for teachers to critically consider the metaphors they hold and use, for their own professional learning and for the learning of their students (Martinez et al. 2001).

The metaphors we hold for our own professional learning and for children's learning are important because they shape our practice. In this case we propose that you consider your professional learning as a teacher to be an interplay between the vertical public knowledge domain and the horizontal practical wisdom domain. When considering critical incidents or your general progress as a teacher, this metaphor recognises the high value of local, socially held ways of working but challenges you to also critically question and engage with relevant public knowledge, policy, professional guidance and learning theory. Teachers are busy professionals and are usually embedded in their particular school. Clearly they will place high value on the practical wisdom held by the teachers and other staff in their workplace. However, this may make it too easy for teachers to limit their repertoire of teaching strategies and adopt locally held assumptions and expectations about the children in their school. Engaging critically with public knowledge adds an element of externality to your professional learning and helps to avoid circular thinking and conservatism in your school improvement efforts.

Reflective task

What metaphors do I hold for the learning of my students and how do they shape my approach? How might the interplay metaphor help me to understand and plan my professional learning when working as a teacher? How will I maintain critical engagement with public knowledge as part of my ongoing professional learning?

Using the seven workplace learning tools

As an alternative to considering one tool at a time to review a critical incident or issue that you are handling in your work, you might prefer to reflect on the incident or issue using all of the tools. Table 13.2 provides a framework for this approach.

Table 13.2 Showing how the seven workplace learning tools may be applied to a particular critical incident in your work

Workplace learning tool	Key idea	Key question
1 Conceptions of an 'outstanding teacher'	We all hold conceptions of a good teacher and good teaching based on our personal experiences.	What beliefs have I brought to this incident or issue from my personal history?
2 Teacher enquiry	Teacher enquiry is a necessary process in order to interpret and use policy, guidance, research evidence and theory in our classrooms.	What data have I collected and analysed and how do my findings relate to policy, guidance, research evidence and theory?
3 Pedagogical content knowledge	Curriculum subject knowledge must be combined with knowledge of teaching, learning and assessment.	In this topic what are the key curriculum subject concepts and what teaching strategy am I using to engage students with them?
4 Teacher identities	Teachers develop multiple trajectories of identity–beliefs about themselves as a teacher which are in negotiation with their classroom practice.	What kind of teacher do I want to be and what are the implications for my response to this incident or issue?

Workplace learning tool	Key idea	Key question
5 Learning communities	Collaboration with other teachers, staff, parents and wider networks is an essential element of a teacher's workplace.	How is collaboration with colleagues helping me to resolve this incident or issue?
6 Expansive workplace learning environments	Expansive workplace learning environments encourage teacher learning, collaboration, experimentation and boundary crossing.	How does my workplace environment support or restrict my response to this incident or issue?
7 A metaphor for teacher learning	My learning as a teacher is an interplay between the vertical public knowledge domain and the horizontal practical wisdom of teachers in my workplace.	How am I engaging with relevant knowledge from vertical and horizontal domains to inform my response to this incident or issue?

The following scenario illustrates how the seven workplace learning tools might apply to one scenario involving a student teacher, Phil, following a visit from his university tutor.

Work in school

Phil: I was really pleased with the way my teaching placement was going. I have good control of my Year 5 class and I have taken care to implement the class teacher's schemes and routines. She's so pleased with me that she has given me a considerable level of independence. So I was surprised and disappointed when my school-based mentor observed my literacy lesson and was very critical of a lack of challenge and of assessment.

University tutor: Perhaps my feedback has challenged your conceptions about what good teaching looks like (Tool 1). You need to gather evidence of children's learning through formative assessment strategies and analyse the level of challenge in your lessons (Tool 2). Identify the key concepts that the lesson is focused on and consider how they are best taught and assessed (Tool 3). Perhaps you should reflect on the value you place on achieving a quietly busy classroom through good behaviour management? You seem to admire the 'strict' teachers in the school but need to decide if you want to be the kind of teacher that manages behaviour or that nurtures learning (Tool 4).

Phil: I do agree that in this school there is a big emphasis on behaviour management. However, the other Year 5 teacher seems very interested in

(Continued)

(Continued)

experimenting with innovative learning activities so maybe I should ask to observe some of her teaching (Tool 5)? I am not sure if that is what student teachers in this school normally do, but I guess it will not hurt to ask (Tool 6).

University tutor: I also think that you might go back to read again about some of the principles of assessment for learning with its emphasis on creating opportunities for formative assessment and the development of a positive classroom learning climate where it is OK to make mistakes and to struggle with challenging tasks (Clarke 2008). You might experiment with some challenging learning activities and consider how your children respond (Tool 7).

Phil: I agree that seems to be a good next step but I must admit it might be a bit awkward if I start to change some of the classroom routines that the class teacher has in place. I guess I need to go one step at a time, negotiate with the class teacher, and see if I can involve her in my enquiry by observing or helping to assess the children's work.

Analysis

This final modest action plan by Phil reflects the influence of several of the tools introduced in this section but above all it shows that he is willing to be proactive in terms of his professional learning and in terms of influencing his workplace. Making a contribution to the development of children's learning, appropriate to his current situation, is part of being a professional teacher and of becoming a member of a learning community. It is also important to recognise that each of us is able to shape our workplace and help to make it more expansive.

Reflective task

Select a critical incident or issue that you are currently dealing with in your classroom teaching and use one or more of the workplace learning tools to help to critically reflect on what happened and what action you will take in response.

Effective professional development for teachers

Extensive review of research has identified the key characteristics of effective continuing professional development for teachers (Cordingley et al. 2003). Effective continuing development involves:

- sustained engagement by the teachers with an issue or new approach
- collaboration and good levels of trust between the teachers involved
- external input and challenge from engagement with new information or evidence
- an element of classroom coaching, putting ideas into action with peer feedback
- perseverance because change in classrooms takes time to become embedded.

Within these characteristics the requirement for some 'external input and challenge' might come from an online resource, a professional guidance or research text, and/or an external consultant or programme. This externality means that your professional learning does not simply consist of copying the practice you find in your current school. Teaching is a dynamic and contested practice and your professional learning must engage you in questioning the evidence base beyond your workplace boundaries.

Managing workload and priorities

Teachers work hard – in the UK primary teachers work on average around 50 hours per week during term time (OME 2008). To remain effective and healthy it is important that you manage your workload and maintain a sense of control and of confidence in your impact as a teacher.

Teachers have experienced intensification of their work over the last 20 years; they are handling increasing pressures from the external policy framework, from parents and from school leaders (Apple 1986). A useful study of Belgian primary teachers found that when they experience 'calls for change', they are motivated by their commitment to children's learning to filter these demands and use professional judgement in implementing new top-down initiatives (Ballet and Kelchtermans 2009). The study showed that the mediating effect of school leaders, the quality of the collaborative workplace environment and the strength of individual teachers' professional identity were all important factors in controlling intensification. A study in Canada highlighted the importance to new teachers of social support from colleagues to create a feeling of all 'being in this together' (Pomaki et al. 2010). This study suggests that it is important for new teachers to find ways to interact with colleagues and build informal alliances, as well as using the more formal support offered such as a formal mentor and your programme teaching team.

Much of the general guidance on time management for busy professionals focuses on prioritising tasks and making lists. However, it is important to clarify your personal mission before time management is likely to become effective (Covey 2004). You need to be clear on what kind of teacher you want to be and what your career ambitions are. Once these are identified then they form a basis for planning work effort. It is all too easy to become distracted by seemingly urgent but actually unimportant tasks and to ignore important non-urgent longer-term goals. Long- or medium-term planning, building long-term relationships with colleagues, and making steps towards being the kind of teacher you want to be are the kind of mission-critical activities that you need to prioritise (Covey 2004). By planning your work on a weekly basis, including personal, family and social priorities, you should be able to plan some time to devote to your strategic priorities, including your continued professional learning.

Children are entitled to support from teachers who maintain their continuing professional development, who experience a reasonable work–life balance and who have collaborative support from their colleagues. Despite the undoubted constraints in some schools, teachers have some autonomy and ability to influence workplace culture and to prioritise their own work effort.

Managing your mentors

Some kind of formal mentoring is likely to be part of the support provided for you as a new teacher. If the formal arrangements are not in place then you should do your best to find an informal mentor yourself. Identify a colleague that you respect and trust – usually they will be within your school but that may not always be possible. Having a mentor is potentially a very positive and useful resource but in itself it does not represent an enquiry-based strategy. You should aim to use the workplace learning tools proposed in this chapter in collaboration with your mentor so that you have a useful framework and data to consider. It is very important that you are proactive in managing your relationship with your mentor in order to make the best use of the opportunity. If you are wary of your formally appointed mentor then work to build trust but also draw your own boundaries concerning what you are willing to share with them and seek another informal mentor with whom you feel able to share practice honestly. This issue of being proactive in managing your own professional learning is an important message on which we can close this chapter. School workplaces vary enormously as learning environments. Rather than relying on the school or blaming colleagues, it is for you to take charge. Decide what kind of teacher you wish to become and then start the work of achieving that goal. Many experienced teachers will claim that being a great teacher is a natural gift. Some of them are in senior positions and really should know better. There are many very effective teachers with a wide range of styles and you will need to work hard and with a proactive approach to your own learning to develop your own style and become the teacher you want to be.

Summary

This chapter emphasises the importance of teachers planning proactively for their professional learning while teaching in schools, in order to develop their teacher identity and their capacity to make decisions about their practice, rather than being clones of a particular policy or context. In order to do this the notion of seven 'workplace learning tools' was introduced and you were encouraged to use these to analyse critical incidents in school. This chapter argues that the seventh workplace learning tool, the metaphor for professional learning as the interplay between public knowledge and the practical wisdom of teachers, is the key to your continued professional development.

Questions for discussion

- To what extent do working conditions, resources and the culture of schools support teacher enquiry with critical questioning of both the practical wisdom of teachers and public knowledge?
- How proactive are you being in planning for your professional development? What are your next steps in prioritising your workplace learning?

Further reading

Eaude, T. (2012) *How Do Expert Primary Class Teachers Really Work? A Critical Guide for Teachers, Headteachers and Teacher Educators.* St Albans: Critical Publishing.

If you are interested in workplace learning theory then this concise and accessible guide will be of interest. It introduces key ideas around the nature of expertise and then discusses how some primary teachers use their expertise to maximise children's learning.

Hodkinson, H. and Hodkinson, P. (2005) 'Improving Schoolteachers' Workplace Learning', *Research Papers in Education* 20(2): 109–31.
This is a useful study that used the expansive–restrictive workplace learning environment framework to investigate the workplaces of school teachers. The paper will help you to consider what kind of school workplace you currently work in, how you might be proactive in enhancing that environment, and what kind of school you would like to work in.

Lankshear, C. and Knobel, M. (2004) *A Handbook for Teacher Research: From Design to Implementation*. Maidenhead: Open University Press.
Teacher practitioner research is a powerful approach to enhancement of your practice and of your children's learning. This text provides a thorough overview of research design, ethics, data collection and analysis. It will help you to complete formal research assignments as part of your initial teacher education and Masters programmes and to use a collaborative practitioner research project as a driver for change in your school.

Twiselton, S. (2004) 'The Role of Teacher Identities in Learning to Teach Primary Literacy', *Educational Review* 56(2): 157–64.
This is a very useful paper for new teachers. It focuses on the professional learning of student teachers as they develop from holding identities as 'classroom managers', through to 'curriculum deliverers' and in some cases to 'concept builders'. You might consider which of these apply to your own practice and how you are progressing. You might also consider to what extent we perhaps all revert to classroom manager approaches on a wet and windy Thursday afternoon in November!

References

Apple, M.W. (1986) *Teachers and Texts: A Political Economy of Class and Gender Relations in Education*. London: Routledge.

Ballet, K. and Kelchtermans, G. (2009) 'Struggling with Workload: Primary Teachers' Experience of Intensification', *Teaching and Teacher Education* 25(8): 1150–7.

Banks, F., Leach, J. and Moon, B. (2005) 'Extract from New Understandings of Teachers' Pedagogic Knowledge', *The Curriculum Journal* 16(3): 331–40.

Bauml, M. (2009) 'Examining the Unexpected Sophistication of Preservice Teachers' Beliefs about the Relational Dimensions of Teaching', *Teaching and Teacher Education* 25(6): 902–8.

Blackler, F. (1995) 'Knowledge, Knowledge Work and Organizations: An Overview and Interpretation', *Organization Studies* 16(6): 1021–46.

Boyd, P. and Bloxham, S. (2013 in press) 'A Situative Metaphor for Teacher Learning: The Case of University Teachers Grading Student Coursework', *British Educational Research Journal*.

Bruner, J. (1996) *The Culture of Education*. London: Harvard University Press.

Clarke, S. (2008) *Active Learning Through Formative Assessment*. London: Hodder Education.

Cordingley, P., Bell, M., Rundall, B. and Evans, D. (2003) 'The Impact of Collaborative Professional Development (CPD) on Classroom Teaching and Learning', *Research Evidence in Education Library*, London: EPPI-Centre, Institute of Education. Available at: http://eppi.ioe.ac.uk/EPPI Web/home.aspx? page=reel/reviews.htm.

Covey, S.R. (2004) *The 7 Habits of Highly Effective People: Powerful Lessons in Personal Change*. London: Simon and Schuster.

Day, C.W., Stobart, G., Sammons, P., Kington, A., Gu, Q., Smees, R., et al. (2006) *Variations in Teachers' Work, Lives and Effectiveness*. Final report for the VITAE Project, DfES.

Evans, K., Hodkinson, P., Rainbird, H. and Unwin, L. (2006) *Improving Workplace Learning*. Abingdon: Routledge.

Fuller, A., Hodkinson, H., Hodkinson, P. and Unwin, L. (2005) 'Learning as Peripheral Participation in Communities of Practice: A Reassessment of Key Concepts in Workplace Learning', *British Educational Research Journal* 31(1): 49–68.

Gu, Q. and Day, C. (2007) 'Teachers' Resilience: A Necessary Condition for Effectiveness', *Teaching and Teacher Education* 23(8): 1302–16.

Hattie, J. (2012) *Visible Learning for Teachers: Maximising Pupil Learning*. New York: Routledge.

Hodkinson, H. and Hodkinson, P. (2005) 'Improving Schoolteachers' Workplace Learning', *Research Papers in Education* 20(2): 109–31.

Lakoff, G. and Johnson, M. (1980) *Metaphors We Live By*. Chicago: Chicago University Press.

Lankshear, C. and Knobel, M. (2004) *A Handbook for Teacher Research: From Design to Implementation*. Maidenhead: Open University Press.

Lave, J. and Wenger, E. (1991) *Situated Learning: Legitimate Peripheral Participation*. Cambridge: Cambridge University Press.

Martinez, M.A., Sauleda, N. and Huber, G.L. (2001) 'Metaphors as Blueprints of Thinking about Teaching and Learning', *Teaching and Teacher Education* 17(8): 965–77.

Office of Manpower Economics (OME) (2008) *Teachers' Workloads Diary Survey: March 2008*. London: Office of Manpower Economics. Available at: http://www.ome.uk.com

Pomaki, G., DeLongis, A., Frey, D., Short, K. and Woehrle, T. (2010) 'When the Going Gets Tough: Direct, Buffering and Indirect Effects of Social Support on Turnover Intention', *Teaching and Teacher Education* 26(6): 1340–6.

Sfard, A. (1998) 'On Two Metaphors for Learning and the Dangers of Choosing Just One', *Educational Researcher* 27(2): 4–13.

Shulman, L.S. (1986) 'Those Who Understand: Knowledge Growth in Teaching', *Educational Researcher* 15(2): 4–14.

Thomas, L. and Beauchamp, C. (2011) 'Understanding New Teachers' Professional Identities Through Metaphor', *Teaching and Teacher Education* 27(4): 726–69.

Wenger, E. (1998) *Communities of Practice: Learning, Meaning, and Identity.* Cambridge: Cambridge University Press.

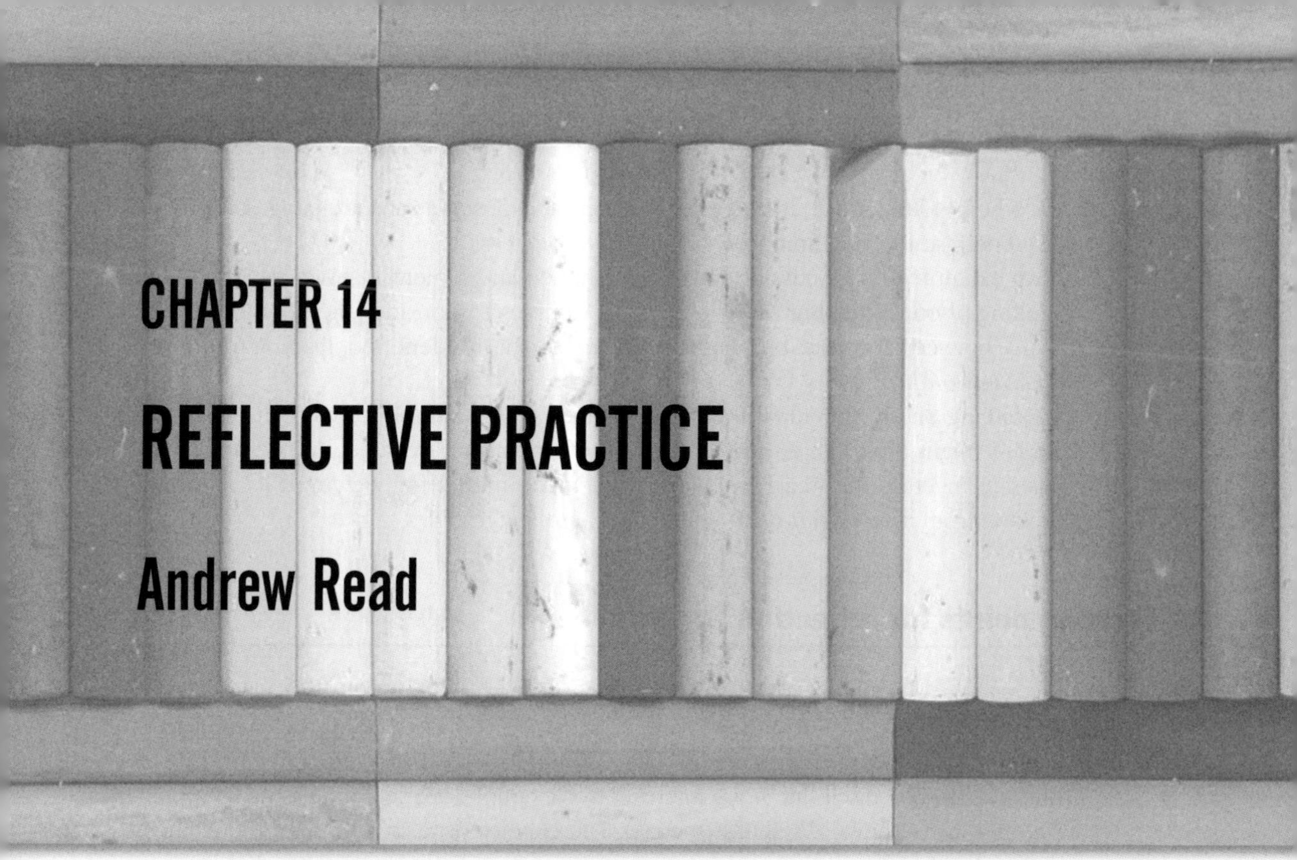

CHAPTER 14

REFLECTIVE PRACTICE

Andrew Read

By the end of this chapter, you should be able to:

- reflect on descriptive accounts of your own practice
- plan for and provide evidence of your own reflective practice
- begin to establish an overview of your own developing reflective practice.

Introduction

Chapters and books on reflection and reflective practice tend to open with a section describing various theories and frameworks. But theory can distance us from the process of reflection itself: it is the *application* that makes the difference, to your own primary practice and to your written accounts of this. So this chapter begins with an example of a trainee's descriptive lesson evaluation and identifies some potential starting points for reflection (including dealing with *unforeseen situations* and recognising *theories in use*), putting these in a theoretical context. Questions to ask when looking back at lesson evaluations and observations are suggested: these may energise the beginning of the reflective process.

An example of a discussion between a trainee and a mentor serves as a basis for thinking about reflecting on values. Opportunities to consider the *cognitive dissonance* between *theories in use* and *espoused theory* are identified, leading to *critical reflection-on-practice.*

Drawing on an individual trainee's experience, an example of what the *reflective process* might look like is provided. Ways of organising evidence in order to demonstrate meeting the Teachers' Standards, and a model for viewing this reflective process from a *meta-reflective* perspective, are suggested.

Starting points for reflection

Put simply, reflection involves thinking about something. But we think about things in different ways: we recall (for example, what we were told about behaviour management in a lecture), we consider (for example, what the lecturer meant by the phrase 'assertive discipline'), we interpret (for example, we settle, perhaps temporarily, on what 'assertive discipline' means). The characteristic of reflection, the element that makes it different from other ways of thinking, is that it is thinking that leads to a 'useful outcome' (Moon 1999 p. 4). In the context of the classroom, this is thinking that leads 'towards higher-quality standards of teaching' (Pollard 2005 p. 17). The case study below shows how Anna thought about her lesson early in her first placement.

Case study

Anna, Placement A, Day 7. Year 2 class, 28 pupils. Written lesson evaluation

Today I read the text we will be using this week to the class. I made sure all the children were listening before I started by reminding them of my rules. I gave J and R a sticker each because they had their arms and legs crossed first and I wanted to see good listening. I asked G to sit on the carpet by my feet so I could keep an eye on him. I read the story with a clear voice and all the children were engaged because they were looking at me. I had to stop once because B started talking to his neighbour. I wrote B's name on the board and drew a sad face next to it. B said he couldn't see the pictures. I told him to put his hand up next time he had something to say. B remained quiet for the rest of the story. When I had finished reading the story I asked the children to put their thumbs up if they had enjoyed the story. All the children put their thumbs up so this was a successful lesson.

This is the beginning in two senses for Anna: it is the beginning of her experience in school within the context of her course; this is also, potentially, the beginning of a process of reflection. Her evaluation is descriptive: the term *descriptive* sometimes implies a need for further analysis – this is the case when the phrase 'too descriptive' is written by tutors on student essays. However, description can be a positive starting point, providing context and a basis for exploration (Ghaye and Ghaye, 1998). In addition, the evaluation is the result of an experience: Kolb argues that 'immediate personal experience is the focal point of learning' (1984 p. 21). But something is missing from Anna's evaluation, at least on the surface, preventing it from leading into a reflective process: it is a recollection, an account of something that happened. What sets reflection apart is that it leads to a *useful outcome*. In a sense, Anna's evaluation is complete in itself.

Having said this, there are several aspects within this piece of descriptive writing that suggest opportunities for reflection. For a start, it is packed with theory. Brookfield argues that 'most workers ... are theorists': 'they are constantly testing out hunches, intuitions, and guesses about what will work against their own reality' (1987 p. 152). When one of these approaches is effective in one particular context, it is put aside to be used again when a similar situation arises. Brookfield argues that these effective approaches are similar to Schön's *theories in use* (1987): an effective approach is identified, some explanation is provided for why the approach is effective, and the theorist demonstrates an openness to change in the light of shifting circumstances (Schön 1987). Such *theories in use* may also evolve from what we observe or from what we understand to be the accepted model in the particular situation. *Theories in use* may stem from our own prior experience as pupils: we think back to our favourite teachers, or perhaps to those with the strategies we feel in retrospect were the most effective – these strategies may form the basis of our theories. These theories form what we know about 'good practice': we might talk about 'what works well with these pupils'.

Reflective task

Look at Anna's lesson evaluation.

What theories does Anna bring to her lesson? What effective approaches does she identify? What does she see as 'good practice'?

What explanations for these approaches does Anna provide?

What evidence for the effectiveness of these approaches is there in Anna's evaluation?

Anna's lesson evaluation also indicates that parts of the lesson presented her with responses from the pupils that she had not anticipated. Schön talks about the element of surprise, where 'something fails to meet our expectations' (1987 p. 26). Brookfield suggests that these 'unforeseen situations' trigger the need for us to 'question our habitual ways of working' (1987 p. 151). Tripp states that, when introducing the idea of critical incidents, 'we have to ask both what happened and what allowed or caused it to happen' (1993 p. 9). Schön uses the notion of *surprise* as the basis for a discussion of 'reflection-in-action' (1987). Schön argues that reflection-in-action occurs when we are in the middle of doing something (for example, in the middle of reading a story) and 'our thinking serves to reshape what we are doing while we are doing it' (1987 p. 26). Anna's evaluation suggests that surprise, reflection-in-action and some reshaping took place: 'I had to stop once because B started talking to his neighbour. I asked him to share what he had to say with the rest of the class.' This is complicated, however, because Anna's lesson evaluation is written *after* the event – it would, of course, be very difficult to write it at the time – and in part is a recount of her reflection-in-action. She may, indeed, be unaware of her reflection-in-action. A next step could be for Anna to explore the ways in which she responded to the unexpected within the lesson, or, as Schön puts it, to 'reflect *on* our reflection-in-action' (Schön 1987 p. 31).

Reflecting on reflection-in-action

One of the challenges of this is that it may be difficult to see where and when something unexpected has happened. When we write a lesson evaluation after the event, we are already filtering and editing the experience, summarising what happened and quite possibly missing important details. Descriptive writing in this context can be very useful: a detailed statement of what happened during the course of the lesson,

Table 14.1 Anna, Placement A, Day 7. Year 2 class, 28 pupils. Lesson observation by mentor

3.15 –	Anna has all pupils on carpet – some quiet talking from pupils; Anna waits for 10 seconds, folds her arms; gives stickers to J and R – says, 'Well done, good sitting'. Anna continues to wait – looks at G, raises her eyebrows, puts finger to her lips – G continues to talk to his neighbour. Anna says, 'G, come and sit next to me – I want to be sure you're listening'. G moves. Anna raises her eyebrow at other pupils, says, 'I can't see anyone else who deserves a sticker' – the talking stops. Anna shows the front cover of a picture book – *Not Now Bernard.*
3.18 –	Anna asks, 'Does anyone know this story?' Most of the pupils raise their hands. B says, 'I like the bit when ...'. Anna says, 'B – you must remember to put up your hand'.
3.20 –	Anna reads the story – holding the book to her right, the pages are open towards the pupils, Anna looking around the book to see the text. Most pupils are engaged – M and N are playing with something on the carpet; B is whispering to his neighbour – M, N and B are sitting to Anna's left.
3.22 –	Anna notices B, stops reading. Anna writes 'B' on board and draws a sad face. B says, 'But I can't see the pictures'. Anna says, 'I've already told you – you must put up your hand'.

without any interpretation or analysis, can support the writer in identifying key moments. A lesson observation by a peer or mentor can provide this descriptive detail; an audio recording might provide a useful and more manageable alternative. Table 14.1 shows a lesson observation by Anna's mentor.

Even where the lesson is recounted in detail, it can still be hard to spot where reflection-in-action has taken place. It can be harder still to know what to do with the reflection-in-action once you have spotted it. However, spotting it can be the start of a reflective process. There are lots of models of reflective processes. When reflecting, people 'recapture their experience, think about it, mull it over and evaluate it' (Boud et al. 1985 p. 19). The *recapturing* might be a descriptive account recorded in a journal, or part of a lesson evaluation or a lesson observation; the *thinking/mulling* is where the process becomes potentially reflective. *Evaluating* involves making some kind of judgement. When we judge something, we compare it, often subconsciously, with a set or sets of criteria. These criteria are external (for example, the Teachers' Standards) or internal (i.e. our own set of values and beliefs, our own personal philosophy). It could be argued that Boud et al. (1985) miss the crucial next step in their simplified definition: when reflecting, people evaluate then *respond* in some way that moves the process towards a *useful outcome* (Moon 1999). Table 14.2 shows an example of how Anna might move from the descriptive to the reflective.

Table 14.2 Shows how Anna might move from describing her practice to reflecting on it

Descriptive		Reflective (reflecting on reflection-in-action)	
Recapturing experience		Thinking about it/mulling it over	Evaluation
Unforeseen situations	My response/ reflection-in-action	Questioning my response	Identifying an aspect to develop – leading to an outcome
B is whispering to his neighbour.	Anna writes 'B' on board and draws a sad face.	Why did I draw a sad face on the board? Where does this approach come from? What was my aim? How did B's whispering make me feel? What was my aim in writing B's name and drawing the sad face? To what extent was my response a reflection of my needs? What impact did drawing the sad face on the board have on B's behaviour?	How does my response fit with my values? To what extent did I achieve what I wanted to (short term/long term)? To what extent did I understand and address the needs of the pupil/s? How else could I have handled this unforeseen situation?
B says, 'But I can't see the pictures'.	Anna says, 'I've already told you – you must put up your hand'.	Why did I repeat the rule? Where does this approach come from? What was my aim? How did B's objection make me feel? To what extent was my response a reflection of my needs? What impact did the repetition of the rule have on B?	

The questions in *questioning my response* could be generalised and applied to any descriptive account of practice in order to step into a reflective process: Why did I act in this way? What led me to this approach? What did I aim to achieve by acting in this way? How was I feeling when I did this? How did this approach relate to the needs of the pupil/s? What impact did my action have?

The *evaluation* column specifically addresses the trainee's own values. Closer thinking about how our practice in the classroom relates to our values provides a further opportunity to enter a reflective process.

Reflecting on values

Table 14.3 shows an excerpt from a dialogue between a trainee, Khadija, and her mentor.

Khadija has a rationale for how she has organised the groups. This is her *theory in use*. The discussion with the mentor begins to challenge this. Khadija hesitantly suggests an alternative arrangement but comes up against a barrier: 'we put the pupils in literacy groups for history'. This is in line with Ghaye and Ghaye's notion of *critical reflection-on-practice* (1998 p. 33) in which the status quo, in this case the 'accepted routine' of children working in literacy groups for history, is challenged. By

Table 14.3 Khadija, Placement A, Day 9. Year 4 class, 27 pupils. Lesson focus: History. Discussion with mentor

Mentor :	Tell me about how you organised the pupils today.
Khadija :	They were in their ability groups with the less able group at the table at the back where the TA can work with them – they were labelling the pictures – they needed something simple to keep them on task. The most able group were with me – I wanted to challenge them, get them to think about how they could use the artefacts to build up a picture of what life was like during the War. The middle-ability groups had the worksheets – I wanted them to work in silence so that the noise level in the classroom was kept down.
Mentor :	What information was the ability grouping based on?
Khadija :	I had the pupils in their literacy groups. The most able group are all working at Level 4c in reading and writing.
Mentor :	How did their reading and writing skills support them during the discussion work with the artefacts?
Khadija :	Well, one of them needed to scribe down the ideas they came up with on the paper. But ... I suppose it was really more about the discussion ... asking questions ... suggesting what the objects could have been used for.
Mentor :	How might you have organised the groups differently?
Khadija :	I guess more of the pupils could have been involved in this kind of activity. The TA could have supported the less able group – she was doing that anyway. The middle groups would struggle though: they're not very good at collaborating or getting their ideas down on paper and I couldn't scribe for them all. I could have put them into mixed-ability groups but that would be tricky to manage because we put the pupils in literacy groups for history.

bringing it closer to the surface Khadija has an opportunity to clarify her understanding and to question 'assumptions made about effective teaching'. It is important to recognise that 'critical' here, as Ghaye and Ghaye make clear, is *not* a synonym for cynical, destructive or negative: *critical reflection-on-practice* is not an invitation to Khadija to lay into practice at the school; it 'has the intention of being creative and constructive' (Ghaye and Ghaye 1998 p. 34).

However, the challenge to accepted routine is only implicit in the mentor's questions. The mentor could suggest to Khadija that she puts the pupils in mixed-ability groups for the next history lesson. But, as Dewey (1926) argues, the student 'can't see just by being "told", although the right kind of telling may guide his seeing' (in Boydston 1984 p. 57). Reflection is significantly about ownership, and it is important that Khadija works through this and understands for herself that a *shift* in her idea of 'good practice' could be beneficial for the pupils.

Within this discussion, Khadija's *theory in use* clearly implies a set of values that underpins her practice. But these values are not necessarily the values she shares publically. We may all do this at various points: we tell our friends or colleagues that we live by one set of values but in practice we may be less consistent. For example, we may tell our friends that we are committed to re-using plastic carrier bags at the supermarket but then find ourselves taking fresh plastic carrier bags at the checkout because we have forgotten to bring the ones we have at home. This is linked closely to the idea of *theory in use* (what we do in practice) and *espoused theory*, which Brookfield describes as 'the theories that people claim to follow, even when their own actions contradict this claim' (1987 pp. 152–3). Before starting this placement, Khadija shared her theories with her peers; these *espoused theories*, shown in Table 14.4, imply a set of underlying values.

Brookfield describes the friction 'between what we say we believe and what we privately suspect to be true' as *cognitive dissonance* (1987 p. 153). While it can be uncomfortable to recognise that our thinking may be inconsistent and that *cognitive dissonance* is present in our own dealings with theory and practice, this does provide a springboard to reflection. Dissonance demands resolution, and this resolution represents the *useful outcome* that is central to reflection. However, it would be misleading to suggest that the reflective practice model, *in practice*, is a simple one.

Table 14.4 Khadija's *espoused theories*

Pupils need to discuss their ideas in order to construct new knowledge and understanding.
All pupils need to be challenged in order to achieve to the best of their ability.
It is important to support pupils in their development of independence and autonomy.

Reflective task

Look at the discussion between Khadija and her mentor and the list of Khadija's *espoused theories*.

What values underpin Khadija's *espoused theories*?

What *theories in use* are evident in Khadija's comments? What values do these suggest?

What *cognitive dissonance* might there be between Khadija's theories in use and her espoused theories?

Work in school

Trainee question: After reflecting on the lesson I think it would be useful to group the children in a different way, but it was made very clear to me that school policy is to group the children as I am currently doing. How can I act on the conclusions I have reached?

Mentor response: We think that the way we organise children here has had a very positive impact on outcomes over the last two years. How certain are you that changing the way you group children will have a positive impact? What evidence do you have? What is it about the way that children are grouped that you think is not working? How could you get the children to work differently *within* the familiar grouping context? What else could you change (e.g. the planned activities, your questions, the use of talk, etc.) that might impact positively while keeping the grouping arrangements consistent?

The reflective process in action

Table 14.5 shows how Khadija's practice in history lessons developed over several weeks.

Khadija adapts her practice, emerging with an alternative *theory in use*. She tries out a number of strategies: the 'discussion time', the mixed-ability grouping, the distribution of roles. The strategies she experiments with are not new to the world of teaching and learning, but this is not a problem. Pollard (2005) makes it clear that *reviewing* work published in the area of practice concerning us and *gathering* models of 'good practice' from other teachers are key elements in the reflective process (2005 pp. 17–23). Indeed, it could be argued that there is nothing new in education:

Table 14.5 Shows how Khadija's practice in history lessons developed over several weeks

Khadija's practice (i.e. what she does in class)	Khadija's rationale	Khadija's evaluation (sometimes after mentor observation and discussion)	The reflective process
Day 9: All pupils work in 'ability groups' Some pupils work in silence	'We put the pupils in literacy groups for history'. Manages noise level	'The lesson worked well because the pupils who find collaboration difficult did the worksheets and the noise level was kept down'	*Descriptive reflection-on-practice* (Ghaye and Ghaye 1998) in Khadija's account of lesson to mentor Opportunity for *critical reflection-on-practice* (Ghaye and Ghaye 1998) with possible challenge to routine identified *Cognitive dissonance* between Khadija's *espoused values* and *theories in use* recognised (Brookfield 1987; Schön 1987)
Day 14: Introduces 5-minute 'discussion time' at the start of group work	'... to help pupils clarify with each other what they have to do'	'The most able group seemed to use "discussion time" most effectively'	*Collecting/analysing evidence* (Pollard 2005) *Perceptive reflection-on-practice* (Ghaye and Ghaye 1998), drawing links between descriptions and Khadija's 'personal feelings' (Ghaye and Ghaye 1998 p. 29) A new *theory in use* emerging. Khadija hypothesising and 'deducing new implications for action' (Kolb 1984 p. 21)
Day 19: Introduces mixed-ability grouping in history lesson	'I thought the more able pupils could model discussion'	'Some of the less able pupils were just sitting there – not taking part at all – it was frustrating' (*reflecting on reflection-in-action*, Schön, 1987)	
Day 19: Stops the lesson – gives each group six roles (manager, scribe, time-keeper, etc.) to distribute	'I needed to do something to get them all joining in' (*reflecting on reflection-in-action*, Schön 1987)	'It worked quite well. There was more participation although the more able pupils tended to dominate – they often took the manager role'	
Day 24: Introduces group activity where outcome is collaborative – focus in lesson introduction on different roles	'They knew they had to talk about what their own role was'	'It was all about talking – some of the less able pupils had quite a lot to say – they were quite articulate in front of the class. We still need to do some work on collaboration, though'	*Cognitive dissonance* resolved to some extent – discussion of ideas integrated into practice *Useful outcome* (Moon 1999) achieved *Higher-quality standards of teaching*? (Pollard 2005)

it has all been tried out before. However, the strategies Khadija introduces during her placement are *innovatory* because they are *new to Khadija's practice* and may also be *new to the pupils* or *the learning context* (i.e. that classroom, that subject, that time of day). Khadija is reflecting 'systematically on the effectiveness of lessons and approaches to teaching' (Teachers' Standard 4), and introducing, in response to her reflections, 'approaches which enable pupils to be taught effectively' (Teachers' Standard 5). She is taking 'responsibility for improving teaching' and drawing effectively on interaction with her mentor (Teachers' Standard 8).

However, when we try something new in the class, it may often initially 'fail' because of our own uncertainty and the pupils' unfamiliarity with the novelty. It is important, however, to use this 'failure' to move forward. In order to improve practice, we need to refine and try again, rather than return to the safe ground of the status quo. Reflective practitioners are, essentially, learners and risk-takers. The experience of trying something out and finding that it does not quite work involves risk: this parallels the experience of pupils. By participating in the reflective process, practitioners can become a role model to 'guide pupils to reflect on the progress they have made and their emerging needs' and 'encourage pupils to take a responsible... attitude to their own... study' (Teachers' Standard 2).

Work in school

Trainee question: I want to try something new but I'm worried that if it doesn't work I could fail this placement. What should I do?

Mentor response: Introduce one new element at a time, maintaining everything else that has worked previously. If I'm going to observe you, let me know what the new element is and ask for feedback on it. (This demonstrates that you know what you are doing and are taking responsibility.) Be clear about the purpose of the innovation: What do you want to achieve by introducing this new element? I could feed back specifically on how well the innovation met this objective. Think about what is likely to go wrong and ensure you have addressed these potential slips in your plan – with an 'escape route' in place if the lesson seems to be falling apart. In the worst case scenario you'll return to a tried and tested (and successful) formula in the lesson and need to rethink the introduction of this innovation. In the best case, you'll introduce the innovation without any hiccups and see a positive impact on pupils' learning. Either way, you are demonstrating the capacity to take responsibility for improving your teaching.

Providing evidence of your own reflective practice

As part of your teacher training course, induction year or further professional development, you may be required to assemble a portfolio of evidence demonstrating that you have met or are in the process of meeting the Teachers' Standards. But how might you provide evidence of taking responsibility for improving teaching, of your effective relationships with colleagues (Teachers' Standard 8), and of your capacity to adapt to meet pupils' strengths and needs (Teachers' Standard 5)? Table 14.6 lists Teachers' Standards which relate explicitly or implicitly to reflective practice.

Table 14.6 Teachers' Standards (TS) relating to the process of reflection on practice

A teacher must

TS4	reflect systematically on the effectiveness of lessons and approaches to teaching
TS5	know when and how to differentiate appropriately, using approaches which enable pupils to be taught effectively
TS8	take responsibility for improving teaching through appropriate professional development, responding to advice and feedback from colleagues
	develop effective professional relationships with colleagues, knowing how and when to draw on advice and specialist support

One way of demonstrating in a portfolio that you have taken on this responsibility is through *organisation*: evidence needs to be organised in a way which implies the reflective process that has taken place and suggests impact or *shift* in practice or *in thinking*. Returning to the example of Khadija's developing practice (pp. 296–7), evidence could be provided through an appropriately sequenced selection of lesson plans, lesson observations, lesson evaluations and reflective journal entries, as suggested in Table 14.7. The evidence here is for both the existing practice and the new practice: without acknowledgement of existing practice the shift would not be evident.

Published work may also have had an impact on Khadija's thinking. She may have read articles or chapters on encouraging pupils to work collaboratively, or on enabling participation in group work. However, when constructing your portfolio, a photocopied chapter, article or excerpt on either of these only evidences your ability to photocopy. The links between theory and practice, between what you have seen or read and what you do, need to be explicit.

This reflective process can be made more explicit through *annotation*. However, annotation needs to be brief. The word implies 'notes' rather than an essay. If these notes become lengthy, the annotation may become too descriptive. Overly descriptive annotations may suggest that the examples you give do not provide sufficient

Table 14.7 Suggests ways in which Khadija might provide evidence of taking responsibility for improving teaching

Khadija's practice (i.e. what she does in class)	Evidence indicating shift (from Day 9 to Day 14)
Day 9: All pupils work in 'ability groups' Some pupils work in silence	Lesson plan: *ability groups* Lesson evaluation: 'the lesson worked well' Reflective journal: recognition of *cognitive dissonance* following discussion with mentor
Day 14: Introduces 5-minute 'discussion time' at the start of group work	Lesson plan: *discussion time* Reflective journal: *rationale* ('to help pupils clarify...') Lesson evaluation: *discussion time* worked for *some* pupils

evidence. A simple set of conclusions to draw from this is that you need to *welcome* observation and discussion, retain *all the evidence*, *keep it organised* in a way that is easy for you to explain, and *maintain a reflective journal*.

Maintaining a reflective journal

A reflective journal may be a requirement or a recommendation. What it can do is remind you about how you used to think and how and why this thinking has shifted. However, writing 'Reflective Journal' on the cover of an exercise book will not ensure that the contents are reflective. By interrogating *yourself* about the source or location of the evidence you are drawing upon, opportunities to evaluate and analyse evidence (Pollard 2005) emerge, leading to thinking about *innovatory* ways

Table 14.8 Examples of starting points for interrogating your own thinking

Location/source	Interrogating yourself
My thinking	What experience leads me to think this? What other philosophies are there? What barriers are preventing me from thinking differently?
Plans	To what extent does this represent what actually happens/happened? To what extent did this lesson meet the objectives I sought? (Teachers' Standard 4) To what extent did *all pupils* develop understanding/skills/knowledge/values? (Teachers' Standards 5 and 6) How effective were the different elements of the lesson: differentiation, assessment, resources, etc.? (Teachers' Standards 4, 5 and 6)
Lesson evaluations	How effectively did I teach? How appropriate were my approaches in the context of this lesson? (Teachers' Standard 4) What did pupils learn? (Teachers' Standard 6) How do I feel about this? How could I have done this differently ... in a way that reflects my developing personal philosophy? (Teachers' Standard 4)
Written lesson observations	To what extent does this reflect my own thinking about the lesson? How clear am I about my strengths and the areas I need to develop? (Teachers' Standard 8) What questions does this raise about my practice? (Teachers' Standard 8)
Annotated examples of pupils' work	What does this show about pupil learning? (Teachers' Standard 6) What does this show about *my understanding* of pupil learning? (Teachers' Standards 3, 5 and 6) To what extent does this work provide evidence that my practice echoes my developing philosophy?
Records of discussions with mentors and tutors	What was the purpose of this discussion? To what extent was my own learning enhanced by this discussion? (Teachers' Standard 8) What do I need to do now? (Teachers' Standard 8)
Reflective journal	Why is this passage particularly descriptive? Why did I choose to write about this particular event? What incident/s caused me to reflect on my reflections-in-action or on my values?

of doing things, active experimentation (Kolb 1984) and useful outcomes (Moon 1999). Table 14.8 gives examples of questions you could use as a starting point for interrogating your own thinking.

You can also interrogate your thinking about the reflective journal itself.

The process of reflecting on reflection has already been touched upon in relation to reflecting on reflection-in-action. However, by extending this, taking it from the micro to the macro, opportunities to engage in meta-reflection emerge. These can form the core of thinking and writing about reflective practice and can be supportive when working at Masters level.

Meta-reflection

At its simplest level, reflection is about finding a solution: you identify a concern, think about it, try something out, and, when it works, refine your practice accordingly. Khadija's reflective experience sees just such a change in practice. Once this outcome is achieved, you start again: a new reflective cycle kicks off when a new concern is identified.

However, there are problems with this model. One is that, as a trainee or as a teacher, you will encounter several concerns, simultaneously or on successive days, all of which require some kind of resolution. As a reflective practitioner, several reflective cycles will be running at the same time.

Another more complex issue is that the reflective process is not really circular, although the simplified visual models (Kolb 1984; Pollard 2005) may suggest this, and it is not an 'evenly progressive sequence' (Illeris 2006 p. 151). Once a solution has been found, you will not, as a reflective practitioner, re-enter the process at the same starting point. You will have acquired a new set of reflective skills, new understanding around the role of the teacher, and have refined the values that underpin your thinking; you will be drawing on a broader range of experience. Your re-entry into the reflective process will be deeper than your previous entry. So rather than a cycle, the process is a *reflective spiral*. This, in essence, is similar to Bruner's spiral curriculum model (1960): Bruner argues that 'any subject can be taught effectively in some intellectually honest form to any child at any stage of development' (1960 p. 33). If we consider reflection to be a spiral process, then the reflective practitioner might return repeatedly to the same element of practice (for example, behaviour management) but each visit would involve a deeper response, acknowledging the practitioner's *stage of development*.

When looking at this spiral in a meta-reflective way, you need to step back. You can create your own analogy for this stepping-back. *Helicoptering* is one that serves as an example: as you rise above the reflective process, the details of the reflective landscape (e.g. what you said to the class, how the pupils responded, how well you thought the lesson went) become less clear; the overall geography (e.g. the way your values shifted from the beginning to the end of a placement, the kinds of concerns that occupied your thoughts) becomes clearer. Meta-reflection is about reflecting on the whole reflective process, identifying themes and patterns, recognising changes in depth and breadth.

Take Anna, for example. Her initial concerns focused on pupils following the rules and ensuring that pupils were quiet. By the end of Placement A, she had developed a range of strategies to *manage classes effectively, using approaches which are appropriate to pupils' needs* (Teachers' Standard 7). She became much more aware that different pupils had different requirements, so by the beginning of Placement B her focus was on *adapting teaching to respond to the strengths and needs of all pupils* (Teachers' Standard 5), particularly those with English as an additional language. This in turn led her into developing her knowledge of approaches to assessment (Teachers' Standard 6). Her confidence in using formative assessment strategies developed but she became conscious that she tended always to initiate opportunities for self- and peer-assessment. By the beginning of Placement C, Anna's focus was on guiding learners to *reflect on the progress they had made and their emerging needs* (Teachers' Standard 2).

Looking at this from a meta-reflective perspective, Anna might argue that her initial reflections were about getting the pupils to do what she told them. She was focused on establishing her authority, but was less aware of (or concerned about) the pupils as individuals. As her confidence in her presence in the classroom increased, she began to acknowledge pupils' individual needs, adapting her practice accordingly. In her final placement, her attention shifted to enabling pupils to operate independently. Anna could think about this process as a meta-reflective continuum:

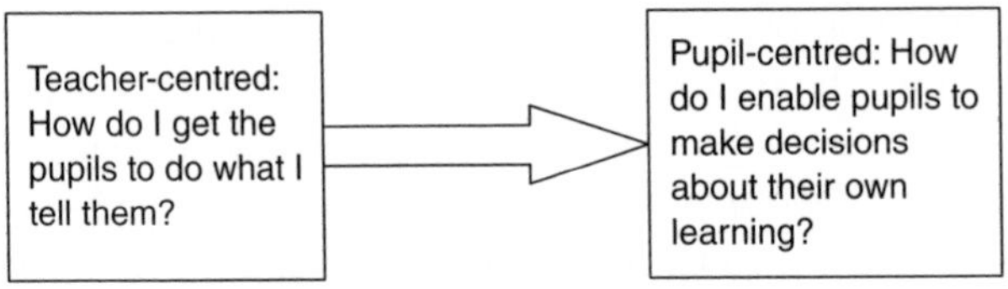

Figure 14.1

Summary

Descriptive accounts of your practice such as lesson evaluations and observations form a practical starting point for the reflective process. By questioning these accounts, concerns related to practice may emerge. Sometimes these concerns will relate to the cognitive dissonance between what you say you believe and what you do in practice. Resolution of this dissonance, in which *critical reflection-on-practice* (Ghaye and Ghaye 1998) plays a part, is at the heart of the reflective process. As you gain experience and confidence, your engagement with reflection will become deeper and broader: a reflective spiral. By retaining a broad bank of evidence, and by organising and questioning this appropriately, you demonstrate reflective development. By stepping back from the evidence, a broader perspective emerges and opportunities to reflect on your own reflective development arise.

Questions for discussion

- How do you respond to unforeseen situations in the classroom? Why do you respond in this way?
- What are your *espoused theories* and what *cognitive dissonance* is there between these and your *theories in use*?
- What were your key concerns about practice at the start of your training? To what extent have these shifted as your experience has broadened?
- Where do you stand on the teacher-centred to pupil-centred continuum?
- What would a continuum which more effectively represented your own reflective development look like?
- What are the obstacles to your engagement with reflective practice? How might you overcome these?

Further reading

Boud, D. (2001) 'Using Journal Writing to Enhance Reflective Practice', *New Directions for Adult and Continuing Education*, 90. Available at: http://sydney.edu.au/education_social_work/groupwork/docs/Reflection.pdf

Boud discusses *occasions of reflection*, the ways that journal writing can be used, and identifies some of the barriers to journal writing.

Hansen, A. (ed.) (2012) *Reflective Learning and Teaching in Primary Schools*. London: Learning Matters.

Hansen presents a range of approaches to improving teaching and learning, including chapters on encouraging children's reflectiveness and on using children's talk.

Illeris, K. (2006) *How We Learn: Learning and Non-learning in School and Beyond*, 2nd edn. Abingdon: Routledge.

Illeris discusses models of learning and suggests versions which might better reflect reality.

Moon, J. (2001) *Reflection in Higher Education Learning: PDP Working Paper 4*. Learning and Teaching Support Network: Generic Centre. Available at: www.york.ac.uk/admin/hr/training/gtu/students/resources/pgwt/reflectivepractice.pdf
Moon summarises some key theoretical approaches to reflection and discusses the relationship between reflection and learning.

Roche, M. (2011) 'Creating a Dialogical and Critical Classroom: Reflection and Action to Improve Practice', *Educational Action Research* 19(3): 327–43.
Roche chronicles her journey, as an experienced teacher, from a silent, passive classroom to one in which children have the confidence and capacity to participate fully. She notes that children's questions led her to 'critique practices and norms'.

References

Boud, D., Keogh, R. and Walker, D. (eds) (1985) *Reflection: Turning Experience into Learning*. Abingdon: RoutledgeFalmer.

Boydston, J. (ed.) (1984) *John Dewey: The Later Works Volume 2: 1925–1927*. Carbondale, IL: SIU Press.

Brookfield, S. (1987) *Developing Critical Thinkers: Challenging Adults to Explore Alternative Ways of Thinking and Acting*. Milton Keynes: Open University Press.

Bruner, J. (1960) *The Process of Education*. Harvard: Harvard University Press.

Ghaye, A. and Ghaye, K. (1998) *Teaching and Learning through Critical Reflective Practice*. London: David Fulton.

Illeris, K. (2006) *How We Learn: Learning and Non-learning in School and Beyond*, 2nd edn. Abingdon: Routledge.

Kolb, D. (1984) *Experiential Learning: Experience as the Source of Learning and Development*. Englewood Cliffs, NJ: Prentice-Hall.

Moon, J. (1999) *Reflection in Learning and Professional Development*. Abingdon: RoutledgeFalmer.

Pollard, A. (2005) *Reflective Teaching*, 2nd edn. London: Continuum.

Schön, D. (1987) *Educating the Reflective Practitioner: Toward a New Design for Teaching and Learning in the Professions*. San Francisco: Jossey-Bass.

Tripp, D. (1993) *Critical Incidents in Teaching: Developing Professional Judgement*. Abingdon: Routledge.

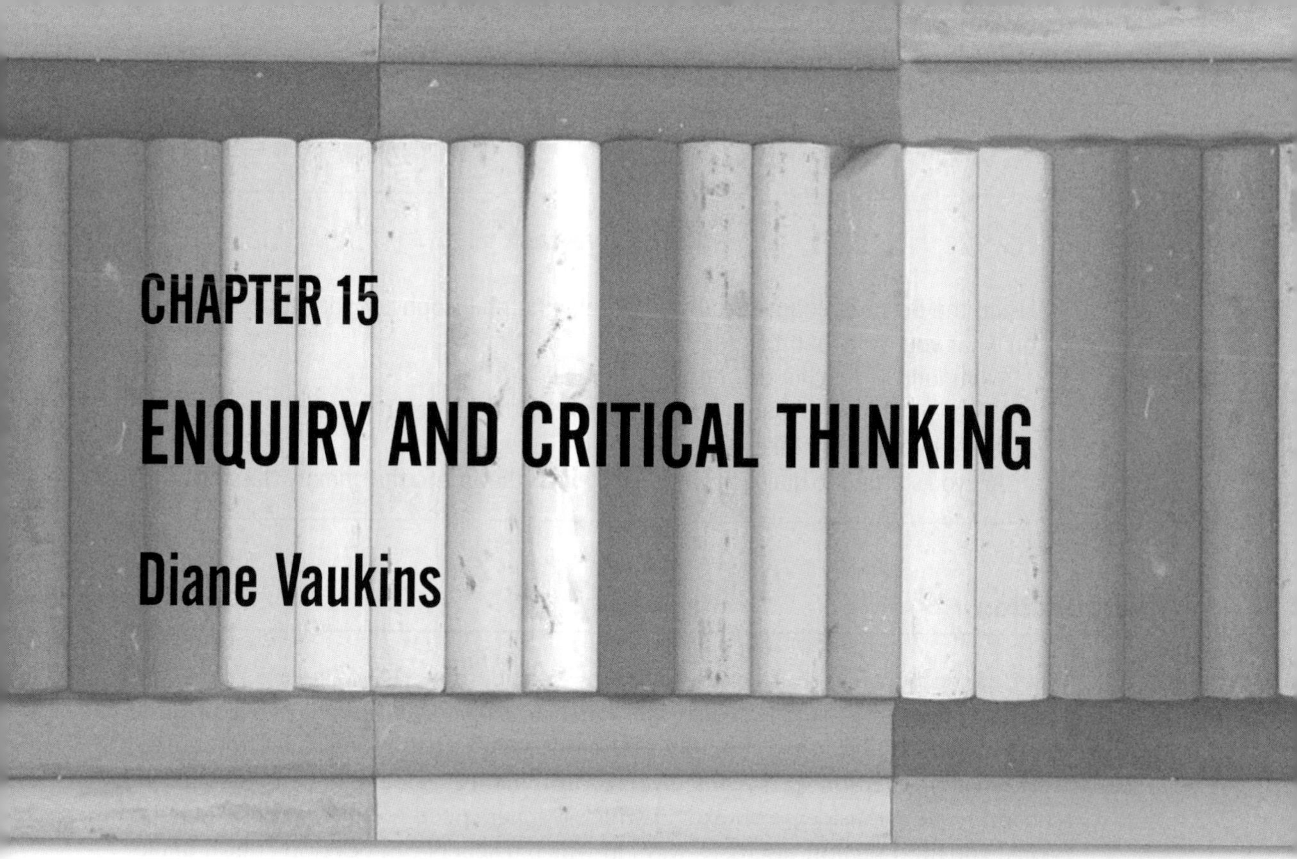

CHAPTER 15

ENQUIRY AND CRITICAL THINKING

Diane Vaukins

By the end of this chapter, you should be able to:

- understand what is meant by enquiry and critical thinking
- understand why it is an essential skill for both teachers and pupils to learn
- understand the personal disposition you need to develop, in order to become a critical thinker
- develop a personal philosophy, in order to manage your own professional development and communicate your thinking to other professionals and stakeholders in education.

Reflective task

Using the previous chapter and your developing philosophy of education, reflect on what you have learnt so far.

What kind of teacher do you think you will be?

Have you changed your mind as you have studied different modules and completed school-based placements?

Are you starting to question why things are as they are in the primary classroom?

Introduction

The first section of this chapter begins by considering what is meant by critical thinking and why it is an essential skill for both teachers and pupils to learn. Next, the personal disposition you need to develop in order to become a critical thinker is discussed. Then the processes involved in thinking critically are explained. The second section considers contexts in which teachers need to apply critical thinking skills. The third section discusses ways in which teachers can develop critical thinking skills in children throughout the primary school.

What is meant by critical thinking?

Thinking is something we all do subconsciously, but there are times when it is necessary to focus our thoughts in order to deal with specific situations. Moore and Parker (2009) refer to this as 'thinking about thinking'. They refer to truth and the application of reason while Cottrell (2005) suggests that it involves the use of skills and attitudes. Dewey (1909) offers the idea that it involves active participation and often creates further thought as a result of conclusions reached.

Before you can begin to offer opportunities for children to become critical thinkers in the classroom, you must first decide what your own interpretation is and if indeed you are a critical thinker. For many people, it is a natural process. Chaffee (2009), a key writer on critical thinking in education, claims that it is his philosophy of life and how he defines himself, and that what we believe in has to stand the test of evaluation.

However, for many, it is a completely new idea, something that needs to be learned and practised. Critical thinking essentially means reasoned, disciplined thinking, which informs your decisions about what to think and how to behave. Reading, writing, speaking, observing and listening can all be done critically – or uncritically. There is no single definition of critical thinking. Paul (1988) calls it the ability to reach sound conclusions based on observation and information. Beyer (1983) describes it as assessing the authenticity, accuracy and worth of claims about knowledge, beliefs or arguments. Norris (1985) says that critical thinking enables you to apply everything you know and feel, to evaluate your own thinking and especially to change your ideas or behaviour. It is a skill which everyone can improve but it does not necessarily develop with maturity. Therefore, it should be learned at all ages (Lipman et al. 1980).

Reflective task

Consider what has been discussed regarding the definitions of critical thinking.

Do you consider yourself to be a critical thinker?

If you do – how will you begin to transfer these skills to the teaching profession?

If not – what will you need to do in order to develop these skills ready to enter the teaching profession?

Why is critical thinking essential for teachers and pupils?

Qualifying as a primary teacher is just the beginning. Like driving a car, once you gain your licence, then you really begin to understand how to drive, adapting your style to suit the needs of the vehicle that you are driving. This is also the case once you qualify to teach. You need to adapt all that you have learned in your training to the needs of the school, the curriculum, but most importantly the children in your class. As you do this, you will be developing and forming a personal philosophy of education and establishing the kind of teacher you will ultimately become.

One purpose of critical thinking is to ensure that delivery of the curriculum is as effective as possible. Many factors can help you to become a critical thinker. Amongst these is the desire to want to learn and delve deeper into the learning of others, creating independent learners with enquiring minds ready to become effective members of the community in which they live.

Another is to enable the process of reason and justification of ideas once discussion has taken place and all viewpoints have been considered. This can then lead to effective and significant change reflecting new ideas.

It should be clear by now that teachers, and we hope their pupils, are constantly asking questions, making judgements and decisions, often about issues involving values and contradictory viewpoints. Therefore, critical thinking is not an isolated skill unrelated to other skills in education. It is a seminal skill that permeates everything teachers do. It is essential to playing a responsible part in a democratic society. This theme runs throughout this book, particularly in Chapter 1 which describes constant changes in educational legislation, Chapter 2 on educational philosophy and learning theories, Chapter 7 on reflective practice in the early years, Chapter 11 on dialogical enquiry and philosophy for children, Chapter 14 on reflective practice and in the following chapter which explores educational issues. However, this chapter looks systematically at what the process of critical thinking involves and how you can practise and develop it in a variety of school contexts.

What personal disposition is necessary to develop critical thinking skills?

Critical thinking requires intellectual empathy and intellectual humility. First, it is important to want to ask questions and to recognise and be prepared to engage with problems. In order to be well informed, it is important to seriously consider other people's points of view, to listen to other people's reasons and to be reflectively aware of your own beliefs. Look for alternative hypotheses, explanations, sources and plans and be open to them and only take up a position if this is justified by the information available. For critical thinking to be a valuable process, it is important to communicate well with others, not to intimidate or confuse others, taking into account their level of understanding and also their feelings. Critical thinking requires a willingness to be clear, precise and accurate and to think in terms of breadth and depth and to be fair. It is also essential to be honestly willing to criticise yourself, for example to admit that you do not have all the information, or it cannot be known or that your inferences are unjustified. A lack of these dispositions can lead to self-deception and closed-mindedness. It is helpful in developing these qualities to sometimes argue in support of a case for which you have no real sympathy, and to identify your own ignorance about a subject, admitting that you 'thought you knew but merely believed'. It takes time, practice and commitment to learn to become less biased and more broad-minded, through intellectual empathy and humility. This involves personal and intellectual development. The basis for critical thinking then is that you are rational rather than emotional, that you are self-aware and able to recognise your own motives, bias and assumptions, are honest and not deceiving yourself, open-minded and disciplined.

How to learn to think critically

Although contexts for critical thinking in education are numerous, the underlying processes are the same. They need to be learned and practised, for developing sound, critical judgement is an ongoing goal. If you are studying for your teaching qualification at a teacher training establishment then you will have been challenged in your face-to-face sessions and in your assignments to be critically analytical using research and theory to support your developing views. On school placements you will have been able to observe classroom practice and learning taking place and then been able to reflect on this and think critically about issues that may have occurred in a calm way, away from the school environment. If you are studying for your teaching qualification by completing a School Direct programme of study then you may have been in a school setting for most of the time and therefore able to follow issues through to their conclusion and have been able to practise these critical thinking skills first hand. Whichever route you have taken, this thought process should not end once you qualify. Rather, it should be the basis on which you build and develop your professionalism. However, alongside the views of research and theory, when you are in post as a teacher you now need to take into account wider issues that affect the school you are in.

Reading critically

A lot of information you will want to use as evidence to support or criticise an argument will be from your reading of newspaper articles and professional and academic books and journals. It is important to be aware of the hidden techniques which writers (or speakers) may use to try to persuade you. It is still possible, even in a free and open society, to try to indoctrinate by only presenting one side of a case or omitting prejudicial material.

Reflective task

Read the Secretary of State for Education, Michael Gove's response to a question about his free schools policy, in the House of Commons (21.06.10) on the companion website (www.sagepub.co.uk/cooper). Then consider the following points:

- Re-read the text to find evidence that he is trying to persuade the reader of the rightness of his policy through appeals to emotions or through offering sound evidence.
- What evidence is there to support his free schools policy?
- Fact and opinion are often confused. Go back to the text to find examples of this confusion.
- Highlight in the text the emotive language. Why do you think this has been used?

(Continued)

(Continued)

- Try to pick out from the text any 'persuader words' used to persuade you of what is being said.
- What makes the statistics that are used reliable or unreliable?
- As you were reading did you feel that you should have known what he was saying?
- Look back through the text to find assertions which are not supported by arguments.

Try this interrogation of some other texts and avoid using these hidden techniques yourself!

Analysing competing perspectives

There is growing interest in the concept of 'community cohesion' and also in faith schools. In discussing the following question, you will develop your ability to analyse competing perspectives and develop your own informed perspective. You will need to read the following articles:

Grace, G. (2003) 'Education Studies and Faith-based Schooling: Moving from Prejudice to Evidence-based Argument', *British Journal of Educational Studies* 51(2): 149–242.

Short, G. (2002) 'Faith-based Schooling: A Threat to Social Cohesion', *Journal of Philosophy of Education* 36(4): 559–72.

Reflective task

As you read the articles above, make notes on the following questions:

- What were the key claims advanced?
- Were the key claims supported by reference to research evidence?
- Could the key claims be counteracted by reference to any research evidence?
- Did the articles support or counteract the claim that faith schools enhance community cohesion?

Then, if possible, work in two groups, one in favour of the emergence of growing numbers of faith schools and one opposed to this development. Each group should identify and present some key arguments to support the allocated position, followed by a debate of the issues.

You may wish to deepen your understanding by visiting the websites of the Citizenship Foundation, Multiverse, or Runnymede Trust.

There is no single definition of critical thinking processes but the following sequence is a basic guide or checklist for evaluating your developing critical thinking. Do you:

- recognise the problem then identify and formulate a question, about which there are different points of view to explore?
- gather the information from different perspectives (what you have read, heard, seen, done)?
- analyse the evidence from different perspectives? Develop arguments from different viewpoints?

Here are some of the questions you may want to ask: How valid is the evidence? Is it justified by the proponent's expertise? Do people have conflicting interests? Do the sources agree? Are the reasons given sound? Were hypotheses justified? How? Was minimal inference involved? Is the report based on the proponent's experience or that reported by someone else? Are there any records? Is data reliable? Is there a breadth of evidence? Are claims made about people's beliefs and attitudes reliable? Are claims that certain things happened valid? Is that the author's intended meaning? Is there evidence and counter evidence? Are there any other explanations? Are there unstated assumptions and values? Balance, weigh and decide if any value judgements made are acceptable:

- Compare similarities and differences between arguments from different perspectives.
- Then identify different conclusions reached, the reasons given for reaching them and unstated reasons for reaching them. Dispose of anything which is irrelevant.
- Ask and answer questions clarifying or challenging each viewpoint (e.g. Why? What do you mean by…? Give me an example. But what if…? What are the facts? Is this what you are saying? Can you say a bit more about that?) Look at the structure of the argument from different perspectives and summarise it.
- Synthesise the argument from different perspectives.
- Reach a personal conclusion. (It may not be possible to reach a group consensus.) Reconstruct your own thinking on the basis of wider experience. Is the proposed conclusion consistent with all the known facts?

Contexts in which teachers apply critical thinking skills

Classroom management and organisation

Once you have established what critical thinking is, the next thing to consider is how to facilitate and develop this in your classroom. At first, you will be experimenting with all sorts of different teaching styles to find what best suits both yourself and the children in your class. Your placement experience should have given you an insight into the type of teacher you are, and your targets for your induction year will help to focus on areas of pedagogy that you need to develop further. If you have studied on a School Direct programme then perhaps you will have been involved with one class for a substantial part of the training and so have developed clear ideas about the ethos of your classroom. How should your classroom be set up? What resources will you need if you are going to facilitate the type of learning that involves critical thinking? If learners are to be able to weigh up the pros and cons of any situation, they will need access to all the relevant information to allow for a balanced judgement to be made. This might involve the use of books, the internet, interviewing different people, making time to discuss, mull things over, ask questions, and much more.

Reflective task

Read the descriptions below and decide which best describes the kind of teacher you are at present:

Didactic

Teachers with this approach generally see themselves as deliverers of information, informing children of the knowledge that they need through instruction and expecting them to remember it. There is little room, if any, for children to explore ideas for themselves or offer any ideas of their own.

Facilitator

Teachers with this approach focus on activity-based learning. They expect children to use their initiative and learn in an active rather than a passive way. Collaboration forms part of this style of teaching.

Learner

Teachers with this approach see themselves as part of the learning process, working together with the children to discover answers and solutions to problems.

Consider your response to this task and decide whether you may need to begin to adapt the way you teach in order to be able to achieve a classroom where children are inspired to want to learn and encouraged to make enquiries and ask questions. It may be that you need to settle on a combination of all three styles or use a different style for different areas of the curriculum.

Curriculum planning

Critical thinking and the National Curriculum

The Preamble to the Teachers' Standards requires teachers to be self-critical and (Standard 3) to develop a critical understanding of developments in the subjects and curriculum areas they teach. Throughout the National Curriculum (DfE 2013) children are required to think critically. In English they must learn to discuss and evaluate. In mathematics they must be assisted in making their thinking clear to themselves as well as to others and use discussion to probe and remedy misconceptions. In science pupils must be encouraged to understand how science can help to explain what is occurring, to predict and to analyse causes. In design and technology they must develop critical understanding of its impact on the modern world. In geography they must analyse and communicate data gathered. In history children should ask perceptive questions, think critically, weigh evidence, sift arguments and develop perspective and judgement.

It is also necessary to think critically about how you select contexts for teaching the statutory curriculum, about time management, cross-curricular links, differentiation, groupings, assessment, and professionals and stakeholders in education.

Having begun to establish your own philosophy, you may discover that this does not always sit well within the constraints of the primary education system you are working in. However, as a qualified teacher, you are working within the constraints of a given curriculum and primary school system that involves being accountable to other professionals and stakeholders. Important among these are parents and governors.

Parents

Today more than ever, parents are expected to be involved in the education of their children. As a class teacher, you are responsible for reporting on the progress of children both throughout the year, at parent evenings and at the end of each year when a full written report is required. You will be required to make complex judgements about pupils' attitudes, relationships, attainment and progress based on evidence and to convey this in appropriate ways through discussion with parents. What sort of evidence do you collect? How? How do the different kinds of evidence connect? How does it relate to what parents tell you? How can you work in partnership with them to support their child's learning? Children and families are different and this needs to be taken into account in considering these questions.

Governors

Although the head teacher is ultimately responsible for managing a school, it is the governing body that sets the strategic framework that is to be implemented. Within this framework will be objectives, targets, policies and strategies for monitoring and evaluating progress across the school. The governing body also acts as a critical friend to the head teacher, in order to ensure that the children are receiving the most effective education.

As a class teacher and subject manager, it will be necessary for you on occasion to write reports about the attainment and progress of the children in your class ready to deliver to the governors. This will involve careful analysis of results and justification of your actions. As previously mentioned in this chapter, you will need to have thought critically about your teaching methods and future development in order for this report to play an effective part in school development.

Developing children's critical thinking skills

Enquiry

When children begin school, they are natural enquirers, full of imagination and brimming with questions. The introduction of the Creative Curriculum and the increased importance of the role of play in KS1 strived to nurture and develop this natural enquiry and channel it towards the prescribed levels of achievement set down in the National Curriculum.

This type of enquiring mind is not exclusive to children in early years settings and KS1, but can become lost or repressed as children move through the primary years. As a newly qualified teacher, it is all too easy to become so involved in the everyday running of your classroom and ensuring that you are delivering the required content of all subjects, that you begin to forget the importance of taking time to consider questions such as: Why am I doing this? What is the purpose of...? How can I improve this? Is there another way to approach this? Is this relevant to the children in my class? If you are not an enquirer or critical thinker, how can you facilitate, develop and encourage this in your classroom?

Teaching for thinking

Is it really possible to teach children to think and what does teaching for thinking really mean? As previously mentioned, in order to develop enquiring minds, children need to be encouraged both to ask and answer questions. The type of questions that are asked and the follow-up to the answers are paramount to the success and effectiveness of this pedagogical style.

There are several types of question to consider when trying to encourage and teach children to be active thinkers. These are typically: closed, open and probing.

- **Closed questions**: usually require a yes or no answer or there is just one answer. For example – What is your name? Would you like a cake?
- **Open questions**: can usually be answered in more than one way. For example – What did you think of…? How would you do that?
- **Probing questions**: are usually used to encourage thinking as they require the questioner to listen to the answer and direct their questioning in an investigative way in order to elicit as much information as possible from the child being questioned, and hence ascertain the level of knowledge and understanding. For example – when assessing the ability level of children in your class, it is important that they are able to explain and demonstrate their knowledge in various ways including discussion. Use of probing questions will allow children to develop their thought patterns and ideas.

Reflective task

As a class teacher, it will be your responsibility to assess the level of achievement of children in your class. In some cases, you may have the added task of administering government tests and ensuring that the children in your class are prepared both academically and mentally for such requirements. In order to do this effectively, you will need to think carefully and develop different strategies.

- How will you arrange the children – friendship groups, ability groups?
- How do you question?
- How do you record and act on any assessment outcomes?

Critical thinking across the curriculum

From the beginning, children need to understand the enquiry processes. While Owen and Ryan (2001) argue that 'enquiry is taught, not just caught, and needs to be modelled carefully by the teacher', the Cambridge Primary Review (Alexander 2010 p. 24) refers to the need for children to learn how to approach electronic media, including film and television, with the same critical awareness as reading and writing. 'If language unlocks thought', it says, 'then thought is enhanced and challenged when language is pursued with purpose and rigour' (p. 25) and children learn how language is used in different ways in different disciplines.

An example of an activity where children combine these skills might be creating an account of the past, whether it is written, given in role play or a display or involves asking questions about sources. These may be written, oral, buildings, sites or artefacts. Often there is no single correct answer because sources are incomplete, and for other reasons. It is necessary to make inferences, supported by reasoned arguments, to listen to the arguments of others, and perhaps change your own view. Accounts and interpretations of the past are constructed by selecting, interpreting and combining sources to create a reasoned argument; there may be different but equally valid interpretations.

These skills of reasoning, inference, interpretation and justification are transferable across many curriculum subjects and children need to be encouraged to make the links between the learning in one subject and that in another. In order to do this, the teacher will also need to use similar skills in planning, evaluating and assessing.

Faith and belief

The Cambridge Primary Review (Alexander 2010 p. 24) considers that non-denominational schools should teach about religious beliefs, respect and understanding, but that they should also encourage children to discuss the validity of religion itself.

Citizenship and ethics

The Cambridge Primary Review (Alexander 2010 p. 24) emphasises the importance of this area of the curriculum in terms of widespread concern it found about material greed and the aims of education to encourage respect and reciprocity, interdependence, sustainability, celebration of culture and community, exploring, knowing and common sense. The Review sees dialogic teaching as essential in doing this in a 'domain which has global and national components and includes values, moral codes, customs and procedures by which people act'.

Work in school

Student: I certainly have tried to teach children to become critical thinkers. I think it's essential, in personal lives and as citizens in a democracy. But I'm not sure how well I have succeeded so far.

Mentor: Neither teachers nor the children they teach become critical thinkers overnight! But I think you have both made a good start. You asked me whether you could arrange the classroom differently to make group and class discussion more relaxed, for example. Look back over your lesson plans. Highlight each time you have identified an open question, asked children what they think about something, in different subjects. Did you allow time for them to express different ideas and create a respectful atmosphere in which they could take turns to discuss them? If you did this it is a considerable achievement. Check your evaluations to see how you might build on what you have achieved.

Student: Yes, it's true I have worked hard insisting on turn-taking and courtesy in the discussions. And children have had some amazing ideas. I'd really like to collect them as evidence for assessments and records because they can always explain more aurally than in writing. How could I do this?

Mentor: That is a very good point. Critical talk precedes extended critical writing, and ideas expressed in writing do not usually reveal the sophistication of a child's thinking. Why not help the transition by making writing part of the discussion process. For example, you might record ideas (with initials) on the whiteboard – maybe as a diagram or concept map, showing how children develop each other's ideas. Or children might work with partners and jot down their ideas on Post-its, which can be put on the wall for everyone to share and comment on in a class discussion. Or sometimes you might try a television discussion, perhaps in a *Newsnight* format or as a debate between two contrasting organisations and video record it. This would give you lots of data – but don't do it too often. It's time-consuming to analyse!

Summary

This chapter has briefly outlined what is meant by enquiry and critical thinking, in order for you to grasp the ideas and begin to develop your own skills in these areas. The use of different methods of enquiry and questioning will help to improve both your own thinking and that of those for whom you will be facilitating learning in the future. Government policies, teaching approaches and philosophies, scholarly literature and educational debates in the media will continue to change and will always have influence over the education of future generations. All these things should enable you to effectively develop a personal philosophy in order to manage your own professional development and communicate your thinking to other professionals and stakeholders in education. Qualifying to teach should be just the start of a journey of enquiry and thought, both for yourself and for all the children you will share learning with in the future. Perhaps the most important thing of all for you is to encourage and embrace the idea that in order for children to become critical thinkers and enquirers, they will need to challenge *your* ideas and ways of thinking. However, as Rice (1985) points out: 'To really ask is to open the door to the whirlwind. The answer may annihilate the question and the questioner'. How you manage this is something you will need to decide for yourself.

Questions for discussion

- What is my personal philosophy of education and learning? Has it changed since I read Chapter 2? How?
- Am I a critical thinker?
- How am I going to facilitate critical thinking for the learners in my classroom?
- What are my teaching approaches/styles?

Further reading

Chilvers, D. (2013) *Creating and Thinking Critically: A Practical Guide to How Babies and Young Children Learn*. London: MA Education Ltd.

This looks in depth at what is meant by creative and critical thinking in *young* children, the developmental theory behind this and how it links to good practice.

Cottrell, S. (2011) *Critical Thinking Skills: Developing Effective Analysis and Argument*. New York and Basingstoke: Palgrave.

This book shows you how to understand critical thinking skills and, through activities, to develop your own critical thinking, in relation to media, written, audio and televisual material.

Cox, S. and Robinson-Pant, A. (2008) 'Power Participation in Decision Making in the Primary Classroom: Children as Action Researchers', *Educational Action Research* 16(4): 457–68.

This paper explores the constraints experienced by both children and teachers in sharing decisions and carrying out action research. Teachers struggled with their need to mediate the project aims in the context of the changing nature of their professional role and in the context of the current- target-driven nature of the school culture.

Larkin, S. (2010) *Metacognition in Young Children*. London: Routledge.

Metacognition, 'thinking about thinking', in both adults and children is explored, as well as its role in Accelerated Learning and why it should be developed; for example, it is argued that metacognition mediates between subject boundaries in cross-curricular learning.

Website

Independent Thinking: http://www.independentthinking.co.uk/default.aspx

This website promotes and offers ideas for developing independent thinkers. It offers interesting ideas to change the way you may have thought about learning in the past and offers new ideas to encourage independent thinking.

References

Alexander, R. (ed.) (2010) *Children, their World, their Education: Final Report and Recommendations of the Cambridge Primary Review*. London: Routledge.

Beyer, B. (1983) 'Common Sense about Teaching Thinking Skills', *Educational Leadership* 41: 4–6.

Chaffee, J. (2009) *Thinking Critically*, 9th edn. Boston, MA: Houghton Mifflin Harcourt.

Cottrell, S. (2005) *Critical Thinking Skills*. Basingstoke: Palgrave Macmillan.

Dewey, J. (1909) *How We Think*. Boston, MA: D.C. Heath and Co.

DfE (2013) *The National Curriculum: A Framework*. London: DfE.

Lipman, M., Sharpe, A.M. and Ofskanyoy, F.S. (1980) *Philosophy in the Classroom*. Philadelphia, PA: Temple University Press.

Moore, B. and Parker, R. (2009) *Critical Thinking*. New York: McGraw-Hill.

Norris, S.P. (1985) 'Synthesis of Research on Critical Thinking', *Educational Leadership* 42: 40–5.

Owen, D. and Ryan, A. (2001) *Teaching Geography 3–11: The Essential Guide.* London: Continuum.

Paul, R. (1988) 'Critical Thinking in the Classroom', *Teaching K–8* 18: 49–51.

Rice, A. (1985) *The Vampire Lestat.* New York: Ballantine Books.

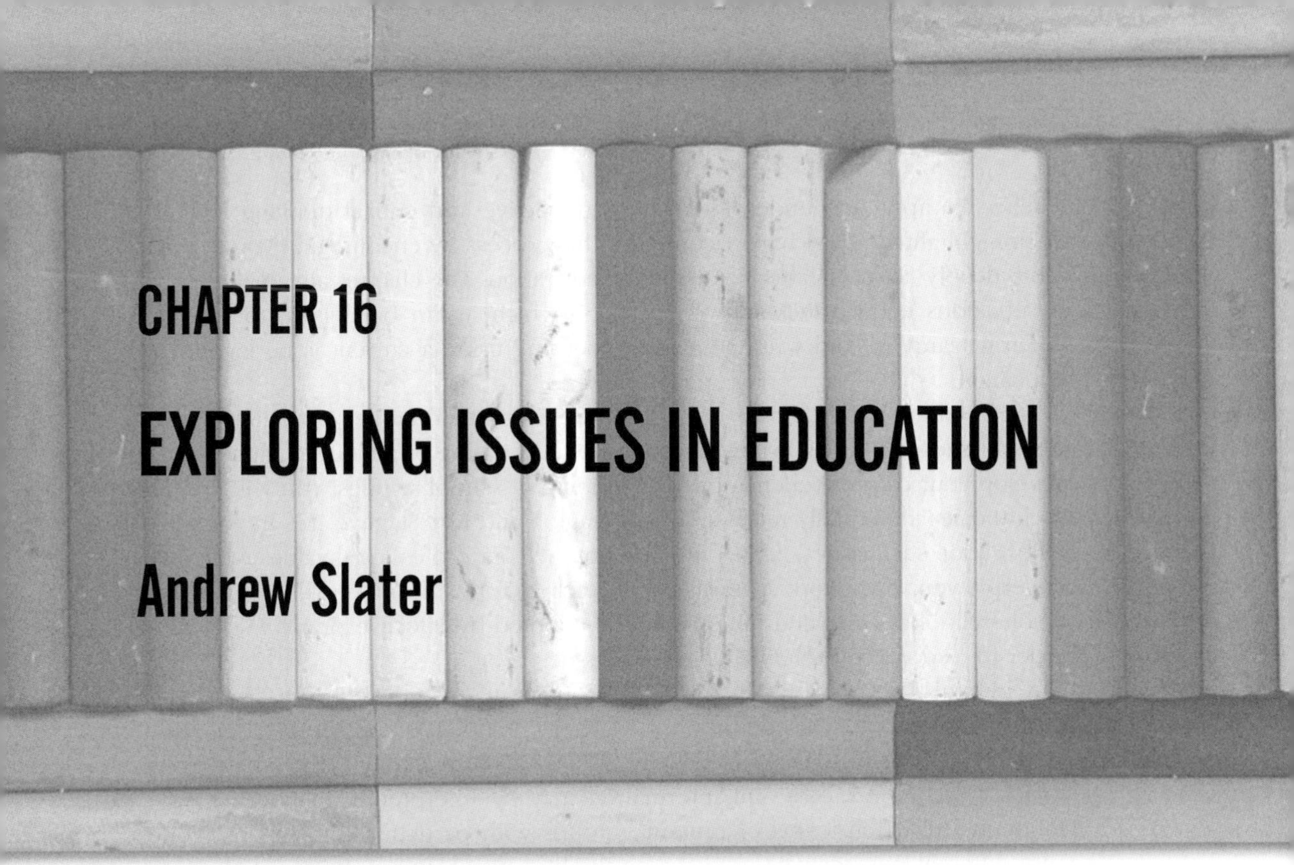

CHAPTER 16

EXPLORING ISSUES IN EDUCATION

Andrew Slater

By the end of this chapter, you should be able to:

- understand what is meant by topical educational issues, and their impact on children, schools and society, by using frameworks to explore competing perspectives
- find related, relevant literature, both professional and academic, in journals, books and on the internet
- investigate and evaluate the relationship between your own professional experience and the competing perspectives
- engage in professional debate about contentious issues in education and develop your own argued viewpoint, supported by evidence.

Introduction

In reading and engaging with the different chapters in this book, you will have gained a deeper understanding of a range of professional demands. The value of a reflective approach underpinned by constructive and critical thinking has also been highlighted. This chapter continues this process by encouraging you to think more deeply about themes and issues in education. The chapter also makes some observations about the kinds of questions which it can be helpful to consider when researching and writing an essay focusing upon a current issue in primary education.

The debating points and issues highlighted within this chapter are mainly whole-school issues such as bullying, promoting healthy eating or gender equality. As you develop your own experience through training in school settings, you will see that such themes are equally relevant in Key Stage 1 and Key Stage 2. It is important to reflect upon such issues, taking into account the core professional values which will underpin your own work as a classroom teacher. You will also need to be aware of whole-school policies and other strategies adopted by effective primary schools in order to respond to such challenges and issues.

A helpful starting point in thinking about issues in education is *The Shorter Oxford Dictionary*. This defines an 'issue' as 'a point or matter of contention' (Little et al. 1959 p. 1051). Where there are issues there is inevitably debate. Some issues are complex. Relevant information may be interpreted in differing ways. Influential research teams or pressure groups with particular interests may offer very different perspectives or views on the best way forward. It is seen as essential that student teachers and teachers are equipped to explore and engage with such debates.

The process of writing an essay which explores a current issue in primary education can be challenging. Essays of this kind sometimes feature in training courses because they provide a rewarding opportunity to consider an issue in depth. This process is helpul because it creates an opportunity to consider recent policy developments. At the same time you can explore your own ideas whilst taking into account other perspectives.

The capacity to write in a clear and concise way is an important background skill which is helpful in professional life. It is likely that in your training you will find that this skill is consolidated in a range of ways, including the preparation of essays or other assignments. You may find that you are required to write a reflective essay which provides an exploration and critical analysis of a selected current issue in primary education. Some examples of the kinds of titles which may be used for such essays are provided in Table 16.1.

This chapter begins by showing you how to identify different perspectives on an educational issue through analysis of wide reading, linked to your personal experience in schools. Then it helps you to identify the kinds of questions to ask about a variety of current issues. The questions raised can assist you when discussing or reflecting upon an issue as part of your professional development. The questions may also be helpful when writing an essay which examines a whole-school issue

Table 16.1 Essays focusing upon current issues in primary education

General: a focus which you select, taking into account your own areas of interest
Identify a current issue in education which affects primary schools. Develop a critical exploration of the issue you have chosen, noting relevant implications for parents, pupils and teachers. Your essay should be informed by your reading of recent and relevant research.
General: an essay which enables you to select your own focus, taking into account the underlying theme of community cohesion
Focus upon a current issue in primary education which has implications for community cohesion. Provide a rationale for your selected issue. Drawing upon a review of relevant research, develop a critical review of the issue. You will need to offer a conclusion which takes into account your own school-based experience and suggests potential ways forward.
An essay with a specific theme: Bullying – an ever-changing problem?
Drawing upon your own reading, consider the question of whether or not bullying remains a problem which primary schools need to address. Review recent research relating to this theme, highlighting key implications for primary schools and trainee teachers.
An essay with a specific theme: Gender – the need for a balanced approach?
Drawing upon your reading, explore the relationship between gender and attainment. Review recent research highlighting aspects of good practice which enhance the progress of boys and girls. Taking into account your own school-based experience, highlight some priorities for your own future professional development.
An essay with a specific theme: Promoting healthy eating
'The quick way to ensure that all children develop the habit of healthy eating is to make school dinners compulsory in the primary sector'. Assess this claim, supporting your analysis through reference to your own reading and relevant aspects of your experience in school. Present a reasoned case for alternative ways forward.

in depth. Next, the chapter considers how to explore widely used concepts such as 'community cohesion', and concludes with a framework for systematically analysing the different dimensions of educational issues, for example local, national and global dimensions.

Current issues, competing perspectives, questions and evidence

When writing essays there is sometimes a risk that broad educational themes (e.g. standards in primary education or accountability in education, 'personalised learning' or 'healthy eating') may be presented in a predominantly descriptive way. Such presentations can obscure the underlying issues and questions which demand fuller analysis and discussion. It is here that your reading is important. It creates a platform for deeper and more reflective consideration, which displays more adequately your emerging qualities as a developing professional who can grapple with challenging issues. This reading and related reflection will enhance your understanding of differing perspectives. In turn, this will lead to a clearer appreciation of positive ways to address the identified problems. The preamble of the Teachers' Standards (DfE 2013a) requires you to 'act with honesty and integrity'; probing an issue and weighing different perspectives about it will enable you to honestly clarify where you stand in interpreting statutory requirements and advice and other statements about education you may encounter both in research and in the media. This is what entitles you to hold an informed, professional opinion and contributes to your ability to be self-critical (Standard 3) and is part of your ongoing 'appropriate professional development' (Standard 8). Understanding how to explore and have an informed view about issues also enables you to develop critical thinking in your pupils, as discussed in Chapter 15 and required by the National Curriculum, for example to help children to discuss critically in English, to critically understand the impact of technologies, to gather, 'analyse and communicate data' in geography, and to 'ask questions, think critically, weigh evidence, sift arguments and develop perspective and judgements' in history (DfE 2013b).

Identifying competing perspectives

Reading and research

Exploration of competing perspectives is not easy. It may require consideration of the perspectives of influential organisations or groups with vested interests. The views of organisations may reflect deeply held values or a priori commitments. In addition, pressure groups sometimes commission independent research, which helps to shape key policy commitments. Teaching associations, for example, often have clearly thought-through stances and policies in relation to a wide range of work-related issues. In practice, a range of factors may shape the policy adopted by teaching associations with regard to specific issues such as the remodelling of the workforce. Formal policy positions may be informed by reference to independent research. But at the same time, they may also draw upon perceptions relating to the interests of the association's members, evidence gleaned from surveys or evaluations and the underlying value commitments of the association.

One of the main challenges in focusing upon the competing perspectives relating to a current issue is to develop a dynamic appreciation of how arguments are developing, taking into account the subtle ways in which key parties utilise data from research. It is also important to appreciate that sometimes organisations change their policies and approaches in response to changing circumstances.

Where an organisation has a strong commitment, you may feel that there is a need to be prepared to reflect upon the ways in which relevant information is employed to support or reinforce key arguments and claims. It is arguably here that your own independent reading is particularly important.

More generally, it should be noted that the status of research should always be of interest to the reader. In exploring some current issues, it is likely that you will find that you need to engage with relevant research studies prepared by teachers or other independent researchers. The theme of bullying is a case in point. The theme has been explored by many independent researchers, including teachers preparing action research projects located in individual schools. The evidence available from international studies is also of considerable interest (Cowie and Jennifer 2007; Roland and Munthe 2001; Smith 2003). A balanced coverage of bullying or aggression in school requires some engagement with research of this kind. It also requires careful consideration of major studies and significant government reports which address emerging issues. For example, the theme of cyber bullying has attracted growing attention in recent years. It is important to be aware of reports and guidance provided by the government and other key agencies which focus upon this problem (DCSF 2007a).

As you develop your reading you may sometimes wonder about the relevance of your sources, taking into account your core interest in the primary sector. In preparing an essay it is likely to be research which relates to primary school contexts which will be of particular interest.

In exploring research evidence, it is important to ask key questions. How reliable is the research? What is the nature of the link between separate studies? Remember that reference to peer-reviewed journals provides real assurance about quality.

Table 16.2 provides a framework which you may find useful when you begin to develop your own reading, focusing upon a selected theme. It is sometimes helpful to keep a concise record of this kind as you develop your reading. The comments made in each column are simply indicative of the kinds of points which may begin to emerge from this process.

Personal experience

Your exploration of research relating to a selected theme will help as you begin to explore an issue in greater depth. However, it is also important to recognise the relevance and value of the experience you have gained when in school. It is, after all, in the dynamic context of school-based training that a sharper appreciation of the impact of problems such as bullying and obesity emerges. Moreover, this promotes greater understanding of the impact of such issues upon children, schools and families. It is also when you are in school that you have an opportunity to gain more meaningful insights about effective strategies to address areas of concern.

Formal research studies are not the sole source of meaningful knowledge and understanding. Helpful insights which lead to a more subtle understanding of an issue may emerge from a process of active reflection upon relevant aspects of

Table 16.2 A framework for recording reading about a selected issue

Status of source	Key points and findings	Implications for debate and discussion relating to the selected current issue
Recent large-scale research study completed by a team from a major university	A range of recommendations. The key recommendations are: ...	This appears to be an important study ... The scale of this study is one factor which may suggest that there is a need to explore the recommendations carefully However, there may still be some grounds for caution. Interestingly, this is a point which the research team also appears to recognise
A recent DfE report Such a report is not a piece of academic research; however, it provides some important insights into significant recent developments which are relevant to my area of interest	Key recommendations are: ... Reference to a range of case studies which appear to highlight aspects of best practice	Highlights important recent developments ... Provides a timely overview which offers some clear guidance, drawing upon case studies
Action research project completed in one school setting	Detailed suggestions made re. areas for progress in one school setting	Possible implications for other similar contexts. However ...

school-based experience. A capacity to be reflective has consistently featured in the QTS training standards. Standard 4.4 (DfE 2013a) refers specifically to systematic reflection. Through developing the skills of reflection, you begin to challenge your own thinking and so develop a more profound appreciation of the opportunities and challenges which particular current issues present.

Identifying key questions

It is helpful to have some key questions in mind when you begin to focus upon a new whole-school issue. An issue which attracts debate is likely to be a theme which has important implications for a range of interested groups:

- What are the implications of this issue for teachers and learners?
- What are the implications of this issue for schools, families and the wider community?
- What are the implications of this issue for the student teacher?

It is particularly important that you are prepared to ask your own questions when focusing upon a current issue. The questions which you feel are most pertinent are likely to reflect the experience that you have gained in school. You will also find that your questions reflect your reading and any related discussion with other students.

Table 16.3 Current issues and related questions

Educational inequality

- Is there evidence that educational inequalities are being reduced?
- Is there any evidence that educational inequalities can be tackled through the redistribution of resources?
- Is there research evidence which shows the best ways to tackle educational inequalities?

Bullying

- Is a consistent whole-school approach the best way to tackle bullying?
- Is there evidence that the problem of bullying is becoming more serious?
- Do some teachers miss warning signs of bullying problems because they have too many commitments?

Testing and standards

- Is there evidence that standards in primary schools are currently rising?
- Is there evidence that the current approach to assessment has resulted in rising standards?
- Which forms of assessment are most closely associated with rising standards?

Education and community cohesion

- Do strong school communities have a wide impact upon a locality?
- Is parental involvement the best way to build strong school communities?
- Does the formal school curriculum or the 'hidden curriculum' have the greater impact upon cohesion at school level?

Creativity and standards: tensions and debates

- Do schools which place an emphasis upon creativity achieve high standards?
- Is there evidence that a lack of creativity leads to low standards of attainment?
- Do children vary in their responses to creative approaches in the classroom?

Table 16.3 highlights a number of important current themes. It also identifies some of the kinds of questions that it may be helpful to consider when focusing upon each of these issues. But you will see that only three questions are raised in relation to each selected theme. You may feel that this is grossly inadequate. In practice, there are likely to be many more debating points relating to each topic. As you look at each section in Table 16.3, consider whether there are any other questions which are worthy of attention in relation to each of these issues.

Work in school

Student 1: I have decided on an educational issue (x) which I want to investigate further. I have read quite a lot about (x) already. It seems there are a number of different views about it. I need to find out

(Continued)

(Continued)

more, based on my own experience, and perhaps develop some ideas about how I think (x) should be dealt with. How can I go about this in school?

Mentor: This (x) is certainly an area of concern. I suggest that first you re-read your notes on your reading and list the different viewpoints which emerged. Then explore how each of these relates to your experience in school. This will help you to develop your own perspective. The experiences of practitioners like you and how they respond to issues are very important.

Student 1: Yes, listing the key arguments will give me a good framework for developing a discussion. Thanks. But where can I find the school information?

Mentor: Talk to colleagues in school about their views, experiences and strategies to address (x). You can also observe how (x) impacts on the lives of specific children and families – but be very sensitive in how you do so! You will probably find our school policies relevant too. You also have the opportunity to consider (x) and its impact on our local community through observations in the locality. Observation in the playground and children's parents' and teachers' casual chat can give you interesting insights. You need to be very sensitive and discreet about anything you write though. I suggest you keep these notes at home. But make a habit of writing your own reflections as you collect your notes. This is a complex issue with no simple solutions so don't be surprised if you struggle with finding your own position on it. You may find it raises further questions in your mind.

Student 1: That's really clarified things for me. Thank you. May I start by interviewing you?

Mentor: Of course – and do share your data collection with me. I'm fascinated!

Student 2: I've been reading about global/central/local perspectives on educational issues. What on earth is this about? For example, I'm very interested in issues related to the school curriculum, because of all the control there is from central government these days, but how can this help me?

Mentor: If you are thinking about an educational issue, you develop a deeper understanding of it if you look at it from different perspectives. In this case I suggest you consider the question from the perspective of all the stakeholders. Who has a right to some say in what is taught and learned – how much – why? Are there tensions between them and how are they resolved? Write notes on your thoughts about each of these questions concerning curriculum control from different perspectives: the international community, central government and Ofsted, the local education authority, the head teacher, the school governors, welfare agencies, teachers, parents, children. I think you might change your mind about central control...

Questions and resource implications

Some important questions have begun to come into focus as this section has considered current issues in primary education. But, so far, no attention has been given to an important underlying issue: namely, that of fair resource allocation. How adequate then is this approach? On the surface, the issue of resource allocation may seem to be far removed from the experience of the student teacher visiting classroom contexts for limited periods of time. But for the foreseeable future, it is likely that issues relating to resource allocation will assume growing significance. It is arguable that the debate about class sizes is a case in point. Over the years, this debate has attracted considerable attention. The benefits of small classes have been consistently noted (Blatchford and Basset 2003). Yet it is likely that it will be increasingly difficult to sustain meaningful dialogue relating to this theme without significant reference to economic considerations. In short, small teaching groups are particularly expensive. There are significant opportunity costs in teaching small groups. It is arguable that meaningful debate relating to the best way forward has to grapple with this unfortunate reality.

The current educational context is one in which the underlying issue of resource allocation is likely to be a growing preoccupation. Its relevance for major themes such as inclusive education and curriculum content and delivery is obvious. This raises a further point which is worth consideration. How will key decisions which relate to life chances and equal opportunities be made? In the years to come, important questions will inevitably be raised about policies and priorities. It will be important that such debates are underpinned by a genuine commitment to social justice and fairness (Rawls 1971).

Where the issue of resourcing is raised, other questions inevitably begin to demand attention. Who should exercise control when resources are allocated? Who is entitled to make key decisions? Who ensures that resources are used in responsible and cost-effective ways? Such questions shift attention to an important and related theme: namely, the question of how accountability systems operate to ensure that resources are used effectively.

On the basis of the points highlighted within this section, it may now be possible to identify some further generic questions which it is helpful to raise when focusing upon a current issue. The questions are as follows:

- Are resources currently used well?
- Is it clear that policy changes and innovations are leading to progress?
- Does current research highlight best practice?
- Is there a growing consensus about the best way forward?

What do you feel about this list? Do you feel that these questions take into account the need to be prepared to consider the relevance of resource allocation? Are there questions which you would delete or add to this list? In developing a framework to support exploration of a chosen current issue in primary education, you may find that is helpful to develop your own list of such questions.

Reflective task: Research evidence and your own school experience

This task is designed to help you as you continue to think about the process of exploring educational issues. It raises a series of questions relating to the broad theme of behaviour management. The task should remind you of the need to:

(a) read widely, taking into account relevant recent research
(b) reflect upon experience gained in school
(c) focus upon competing perspectives, taking into account key insights and implications.

Assess the following questions:

- Is there research evidence to show that behaviour management is less challenging in classrooms where teaching is good?
- Is there evidence that all children respond well to positive behaviour management strategies?
- Are there ever times when it is appropriate to utilise behaviour management strategies which undermine established whole-school approaches?

- How can an appropriate balance be maintained between provision for the needs of individuals and groups?
- Is high-quality teaching the best way to tackle the problem of poor classroom behaviour?
- Is there research evidence to show that poor short-term memory is a factor which leads to behaviour problems for some children?

Consider the following points as you assess the questions:

(a) How can my own reading help in the process of developing my thinking relating to each of these questions?
(b) How does the experience that I have gained in school influence my responses to these questions?
(c) What other questions would I raise in order to develop a thorough exploration of an issue relating to effective behaviour management?

A generic framework to support exploration and analysis, based on core concepts

When writing essays, or working on other assignments, it is important to express your thoughts clearly. In order to do this it is helpful to have a clear grasp of the key concepts which are relevant in focusing upon a selected theme. You need to be clear about the core meaning of the terms or concepts which you encounter when reading about and researching particular themes. You also need to be clear about the way in which you use terms in your own writing.

There are useful texts which can provide some support here. For example, Brighouse and Woods (2013) note a range of relevant terms which relate to the process of school improvement.

Within this section, attention focuses briefly upon some important concepts.

Clarifying widely used concepts

'Poverty'

The term 'poverty' is widely used in the social sciences and is an example of a concept which may require further clarification. The word 'poverty' is commonly used in everyday discussion and its core meaning is widely understood. But the concept of 'poverty' may need to be used more precisely when writing an assignment. Some clarification may be required to establish and draw out the distinction between its absolute and relative dimensions. For some analytical purposes, this distinction is particularly helpful: it opens up the possibility of more meaningful analysis of a whole range of issues relating to social inequalities. Indeed, one influential dictionary of sociology suggests that the term 'relative poverty' 'is used to demonstrate the inadequacy of definitions of absolute or primary poverty by referring to the cultural needs of individuals and families within the context of the rest of society' (Jary and Jary 1991 p. 489).

Equally, there is a need to exercise care in the use of other concepts. Concepts such as 'social class', 'social mobility' and social capital may sometimes need to be explained. For example, when analysing the impact of 'social capital', it may be necessary to draw out the distinction between 'bridging' and 'bonding' social capital.

'Community cohesion'

There are times when a concept gains a particular significance or resonance. It is therefore important to be alert to this tendency. The concept of 'community cohesion' is a relevant example here. The broad question of how schools may play a role in promoting 'community cohesion' has received a great deal of attention in recent years. It is likely that there will continue to be lively debate about the real meaning of the term 'community cohesion'. In this context, it is important to note that the recent DCSF guidance (2007b) provides a helpful starting point in understanding the core meaning of the term:

> By community cohesion we mean working towards a society in which there is a common vision and sense of belonging by all communities; a society in which the diversity of people's backgrounds and circumstances is appreciated and valued; a society in which similar life opportunities are available to all; and a society in which strong and positive relationships exist and continue to be developed in the workplace, in schools and in the wider community. (DCSF 2007b)

New or re-visited concepts may also sometimes become relevant when focusing upon particular themes. For example, Cantle (2012) focuses upon 'interculturalism', teasing out its relevance for the formation of cohesive communities.

'Surveillance'

'Surveillance' is another concept which offers scope to gain intriguing insights relating to some current issues. It is arguable that the theme of surveillance has increasingly featured in social research in recent years (Hier and Greenberg 2007; Hope 2009). Its growing significance may reflect the fact that the overt use of techniques for surveillance has been one of the most striking social developments of the modern or, perhaps more accurately, post-modern era. Nowadays in town centres, surveillance cameras keep a watchful and paternal eye upon members of the public. Motorists drive with care because of the presence of hidden cameras on busy roads. Speed cameras act as a constraining mechanism, encouraging motorists to be watchful and at the same time reducing accidents.

The processes of surveillance which characterise today's society do not merely operate through obvious monitoring systems such as these. The work of the French thinker Foucault, for example, provides an important reminder that subtle forms of surveillance have actually featured in schools for many years (Foucault 1977). Moreover, it is arguable that reference to the theme of surveillance can offer important insights about the psychological impact of current systems for monitoring and accountability. Sometimes there may be a rather fine line between positive processes designed to support monitoring and accountability and potentially less desirable processes of surveillance. *In some essay tasks, you may need to tease out such distinctions.*

A wider question is perhaps whether the impact of surveillance is always necessarily negative. Reference to the issue of school violence, for example, provides a timely reminder that sometimes surveillance can have positive as well as negative effects. School-based bullying is perhaps more likely to occur in contexts where monitoring systems are weak. Equally, school-based bullying can all too easily occur in contexts far removed from adult supervision. Adult 'surveillance' may play an important role in preventing such bullying. Yet, somewhat paradoxically, it is also arguable that the concept of surveillance can be employed in making sense of an apparently growing phenomenon: bullying via mobile phones and computers is particularly unpleasant and serious in its consequences, precisely because it employs techniques of surveillance which cause enduring pain (DCSF 2007a).

Basic conceptual dimensions to support analysis of issues

Basic conceptual dimensions which provide a framework for analysis of current issues form relatively straightforward contrasts. These are the *local/global* and *local/central* divisions; the division between *public* and *private* spheres; and the split between *representation* and *reality*. The local/central divide is an addition to three pairs of terms which you may have already encountered on some social science courses (Anderson and Ricci 1994; Open University 1996). Each of these divisions will be examined in more detail below. However, before focusing attention on these concepts, it may be helpful to pause to reflect upon the way in which the education system in England and Wales has changed over the last 30 years.

During this era, education has become a major priority for central government, and spending on education has risen dramatically. Government priorities have been embedded in a constantly developing legislative framework which has seen the development and revision of a National Curriculum and a constant drive for improvement and effectiveness. New systems for testing, monitoring and accountability have become important during this period (Bartlett and Burton 2012; Chitty 1998; Maclure 1988).

In this era of innovation one constant has remained. It is still the case that it is in local contexts that the policies of central government are implemented. Moreover, the independent, or interconnected, actions of local authorities, governing bodies, head teachers and class teachers all affect the relative success or failure of policies from the centre.

Local/global and local/central

The local/global and local/central conceptual themes are each relevant precisely because they open up the possibility of examining such links. Through attention to the interface between the 'local' and 'central', some sense can be made of the way in which the policies of central government impact in the regions. Interestingly, when developing an analysis of such policies, there is no need to suggest that all power is held in the centre. Nor is there any need to assume that communication simply flows in one direction. Some of the most significant questions to raise and examine may indeed relate to the ways in which the actions of central government reflect and respond to developments and innovations in local contexts.

The issue of 'healthy eating' can serve to illustrate the utility of the local/global and local/central themes. In recent times, and in part as a response to external pressure, central government has pushed for improved standards of diet and nutrition. Yet even though this approach has apparently been in response to public demand, it has run into difficulties in some local contexts. In this case, analysis of the interplay between local and central factors may help to shed some light on the challenges which central government faces when seeking to ensure that a widely supported social policy is implemented effectively. More broadly, it should be noted that research has consistently shown that local factors are of major importance when exploring key issues relating to health education (Mayall et al. 1996).

The division between local and central dimensions is an important conceptual theme which may illuminate a whole range of major or minor issues in relation to which decisions from the centre have impacted in local contexts. Moreover, its relevance is not merely confined to an examination of the ways in which the decisions of central government are implemented at school level. The real area of debate may sometimes be the link between the school and the local authority. For example, a local authority may seek to ensure that secondary schools adopt a particular procedure with regard to the disclosure of examination results. Yet individual schools may seek to implement this policy in differing ways which actually undermine standardised practice.

The notion of a division between the local and the global can also be applied to the link between international bodies and national governments. Once again, the conceptual distinction between the local and the global opens up a potentially rewarding framework to support discussion, debate and analysis.

You will have noticed that in focusing upon the issue of healthy eating, I have tended to focus upon the local/central conceptual division. You may also wish to reflect upon whether there are any local/global dimensions to this debate. For example, issues of sustainable development, food supply and related ethical questions may also require attention within the context of unfolding debate relating to this issue.

Reflective task: Local/global and/or local/central?

Is it helpful to highlight two separate conceptual divisions here? Or are these two strands actually separate dimensions of an underlying local/global divide?

Public and private

The division between public and private spheres is an important characteristic of our society. It is far from surprising then that the *public/private* divide can be highlighted as a third conceptual dimension which may shed light on some current issues in primary education. For example, the issue of whether or not it is appropriate for some children to be educated at home raises important questions which relate to children's rights and entitlements. There is currently significant interest in the contexts in which children benefit from opportunities to participate in society (Hart 2009). But it is arguable that where education is provided at home, some of these opportunities may be missed. Reference to the public and private divide may help in the formation of questions to enhance debate relating to the issue of whether or not it is appropriate to provide education at home.

An enduring feature of the education system in England and Wales is that there is an influential independent sector which is in significant ways less subject to government control and regulation. The fact that some independent schools are still known as 'public' schools should not obscure the underlying point: schools in the independent sector are private institutions, albeit institutions which are increasingly run by companies and trusts running families of similar schools (Ball 2007).

Attention to the public/private division can help in making some sense of a whole series of underlying questions. The issue of what independent schools contribute to the public good in return for charitable status currently deservedly attracts attention. Somewhat less obviously, the issue of whether children in the private sector are afforded the same protections and privileges as state-sector pupils is worthy of attention now that we live in an era when it is claimed that 'every child matters'. The public/private conceptual theme can underpin exploration of both of these questions.

On the surface, the division between public and private sectors is precise. Yet, reflection upon some of the most significant changes since the 1980s suggests that this is by no means entirely the case. The creation of grant-maintained schools and the subsequent development of colleges and academies under a range of guises have to some extent blurred this distinction, although the position of academies is not quite the same as that of fully independent schools. The Education and Inspections Act (2006) also had significant implications with regard to the role of local authorities. It paved the way for the emergence of a new generation of 'trust schools' (Parker et al. 2007). Such schools – 'liberated' from some aspects of local authority control – could work closely and collaboratively with a range of outside sponsors. This development had significant implications which related to the areas of democratic accountability, finance and public interest.

A further significant policy initiative has seen new opportunities for parent groups to create free schools. Over time, it will be interesting to see whether there are tensions between this development and other policy priorities, including the need to form and maintain cohesive communities. It is arguable that there is scope to raise important questions about this theme, drawing upon the public/private divide. Key areas for consideration may relate to children's rights. In time, questions relating to the participatory entitlements of children who attend free schools may also command attention. Reference to the public/private conceptual theme may well prove rewarding in the process of making some sense of this policy development.

Representation and reality

The relevance of the fourth major conceptual theme – namely, the division between *representation* and *reality* – is perhaps less immediately obvious, given the underlying nature of many of the core issues in primary education. But attention to wider political debate in recent times highlights the way in which processes of presentation and representation impact upon the 'real' world. The representation/reality divide offers one route to begin to get beneath the surface of debates which concern trust and spin. It opens up a line of analysis which has the potential to contribute to an informed exploration of current issues with a political dimension by focusing attention on the gap between claims and underpinning realities.

This division is helpful for a second reason. It draws attention to the need to explore some of the ways in which stereotypes, images and ideas impact upon social life. Media images may play a key role in shaping perceptions of particular groups. Such images may create tensions and sharpen divisions. Stereotypical images can work to close off opportunities and thereby may contribute to continuing inequalities. An analysis focusing upon the gulf between representations and realities is likely to have a heightened sensitivity to such injustices.

The process of developing an analysis which raises questions about the links between representation and reality is by no means simple. Yet images, stereotypes and perceptions may influence choices, lines of action and an underlying sense of identity.

Of course, media-driven images may not always be passively absorbed. The representation/reality theme is helpful precisely because it opens up the possibility of asking searching questions about responses to images and stereotypes. Further, it opens up the possibility of asking questions about the ways in which a sense of identity may be constituted and re-constituted. Reference to the representation/reality theme may therefore provide a helpful framework to support analysis of some current issues, including perhaps most notably issues which relate in some way to identity.

Table 16.4 Concept divisions and issues

Divisions and distinctions to prompt the process of asking questions	Examples of possible areas for which the distinction is relevant
Local and central dimensions	Issues which raise questions relating to fair allocation and effective use of resources
	Decision making with regard to curriculum content
	Assessment systems
	Monitoring systems and accountability arrangements
Local and global dimensions	Issues relating to sustainable development and responsible use of resources
	Issues relating to the impact of new technologies
	Issues relating to the role of government in education
	School starting age
Representation and reality	The presentation of information relating to academic performance
	Policies and strategies relating to behaviour management
	Policies and approaches which relate to bullying and associated problems
	Gender stereotypes and academic attainment
Public and private spheres	The role and responsibilities of family units
	The boundary between the responsibilities of families and schools
	Accountability issues relating to independent schools
	School organisation and control

Table 16.4 returns to the concepts introduced at the beginning of this section. The table highlights some debating points or issues which each pair of concepts may help to analyse. Sometimes, when identifying questions relating to a selected current issue, you may find that a pair of concepts is particularly helpful. However, it is also likely that you will find that there are times when it is appropriate to refer to each dimension. For example, there may well be times when reference to the 'public/private' dimension proves helpful when considering issues relating to the fair allocation and use of resources. An illustration would be a debate relating to the issue of whether families should be required to contribute towards the cost of school trips.

Reflective task: Concepts and current issues

This creates an opportunity to reflect more fully upon the utility of the concepts discussed in this section. As you focus upon each of the concepts, you may wish to reflect upon relevant aspects of your own professional experience.

Take a look at each of the concepts highlighted below. Discuss what you feel is the core meaning of the term. Consider whether you feel that the concept is likely to be helpful when discussing a selected current issue. Working with a discussion partner, decide upon three issues which you feel it will help you to analyse. You may also wish to think about whether the concepts create scope to gain fresh insights relating to any new issues which currently require particular attention.

Table 16.5

Concept	Possible areas of relevance
Inclusion	Exploration of special needs
	Exploration of good practice in the classroom
	A highly relevant concept for debate relating to community cohesion
Surveillance	Possible relevance to aspects of discussion relating to systems for accountability, including ...
	Possible relevance when focusing upon forms of bullying, including ...
Social capital	A concept which will be helpful when exploring ...
	A concept which can be divided into ...
Social mobility	A concept which is vital for discussion focusing upon inequalities, including ...
Social class	A concept which is vital for exploration of many themes, including ...
Equal opportunities	A concept which is vital for discussion of many themes, including ...

There is one further point to note when reflecting upon some of the concepts which may support analysis of selected current issues in primary education. The concepts which assist here can in some respects be seen as family members. The concepts of 'choice' and 'parental power', for example, form part of a network of interconnected concepts relating to the notion of a 'market'. Equally, it is arguable that the concept of 'surveillance' forms part of a wider network which relates to the theme of power and control. You will find that it is rewarding to prepare concept maps of relevant and interconnected terms when you begin to focus upon a new issue. Reference to such terms helps when identifying key questions. Appropriate reference to concepts also helps when preparing a carefully focused analysis of a selected theme.

Preparing written assignments

This chapter has explored some points which are helpful when analysing or exploring current issues in primary education. The points raised may be useful when working on essays or other assignments which require you to explore an issue in depth. The focus in this chapter has been upon wider issues rather than themes which relate directly to the process of teaching in the classroom. Nonetheless, some of the factors which assist when writing essays about current issues may be equally relevant for some other tasks.

First, the value of reading recent and relevant research has been noted. This is important because developments in education can happen quickly. Moreover, it is in part through reading journal articles which focus upon such research that you will gain a deeper understanding of the good practice which contributes to school improvement. Equally, research may provide a warning sign of emerging issues or challenges.

In focusing upon reading, a related point was noted: namely, the need to be clear about the quality and status of your sources. This is an important point to take into account in the process of evaluating your sources and so weighing your arguments.

Second, the chapter has encouraged you to think carefully about the concepts which may inform your exploration of a selected theme. This has included attention to some conceptual frameworks which may help to alert you to key questions or dimensions which need to be taken into account when exploring specific issues. The chapter has also highlighted the need for clarity when utilising concepts such as 'poverty', 'community cohesion' or 'surveillance' in the process of teasing out the impact of selected current issues in primary education.

When preparing assignments, it is always important to try to support key claims through reference to your own reading. As you focus upon selected sources, you will no doubt need to develop a constructively critical approach. But it is most important to be critical when focusing upon our own work (Fairbairn and Winch 1996).

Above all, it is important to recognise that many issues are highly complex. In preparing assignments which focus upon selected issues, there is a need to be somewhat cautious when offering suggestions about the best way forward. Clearly, carefully considered reference to research evidence is likely to be helpful. But a tentative rather than dogmatic approach may well provide a stronger platform for discussion which notes salient points and provides genuine insight.

Summary

This chapter has emphasised the importance of exploring and evaluating current issues in education. The enhanced understanding which emerges from this process will be informed by your reading. It will also reflect your own experience. The chapter has noted that you will need to make sense of competing perspectives – a process which implies that you can assess the claims and motivation of relevant stakeholders. The chapter has provided frameworks which enable you to do this by reading systematically and critically. It has also recognised the value of reflecting on your professional experience. The importance of identifying key questions to support the exploration of current issues has been stressed. It has also been seen that you will need to analyse what is meant by widely used concepts, taking into account tensions between different dimensions. A heightened awareness of relevant concepts will provide a secure platform for informed analysis and debate. It will also enable you to take a constructively critical approach to innovation.

Questions for discussion

- How can awareness of current issues enhance your own practice in the classroom?
- How can awareness of current issues enhance your capacity to relate effectively to parents and pupils?
- How can awareness of current issues enhance your capacity to relate effectively to professional colleagues?
- How important is it to continue to take an informed interest in current issues during your professional career?
- Are some current issues more important than others?

Further reading

Bartlett, S. and Burton, D. (2012) *Introduction to Education Studies*, 3rd edn. London: Sage Publications.

A wide-ranging book which provides a broad introduction to key areas within the field of education studies. A strength of this book is the fact that it adopts a multi-disciplinary approach.

Cross, D. et al. (2011) 'Three-year Results of the Friendly Schools Whole-of-school Intervention on Children's Bullying Behaviour', *British Educational Research Journal* 37(1): 105–29.

A major Australian study which evaluates the effectiveness of whole-school intervention programmes in primary schools. The research focuses upon data relating to a large number of schools involved in the intervention programme and some additional comparison schools. The study makes a range of important observations, including some which relate to factors supporting the successful implementation of whole-school interventions.

Kassem, D., Mufti, E. and Robinson, J. (eds) (2006) *Education Studies: Issues and Critical Perspectives*. Maidenhead: Open University Press.

A book which provides a carefully focused and critical exploration of a range of important issues.

Mellor, D. and Delamont, S. (2011) 'Old Anticipations, New Anxieties? A Contemporary Perspective on Primary to Secondary Transfer', *Cambridge Journal of Education* 41: 301–46.

This British study focuses upon primary to secondary transfer. It includes references to research conducted at different points in time, noting persistent fears and concerns which some children have relating to secondary transfer. In addition, the study identifies features of secondary schools which are anticipated in a more positive way.

Sharpe, J., Ward, S. and Hankin, L. (eds) (2006) *Education Studies: An Issues-based Approach*. Exeter: Learning Matters.

This book is informed by a clear recognition of the key areas that feature in education studies courses. The book helps to situate themes which require discussion and analysis.

References

Anderson, J. and Ricci, M. (eds) (1994) *Society and Social Science: A Reader*. Milton Keynes: Open University Press.

Ball, S. (2007) *Education plc: Understanding Private Sector Participation in Public Sector Education*. London: Routledge.

Bartlett, S. and Burton, D. (2012) *Introduction to Education Studies*, 3rd edn. London: Sage Publications.

Blatchford, P. and Basset, P. (2003) *The Class Size Debate: Is Small Better?* Maidenhead: Open University Press.

Brighouse, T. and Woods, D. (2013) *The A–Z of School Improvement: Principles and Practice*. London: Bloomsbury Education.

Cantle, T. (2012) *Interculturalism: The New Era of Culturalism and Diversity*. Basingstoke: Palgrave Macmillan.

Chitty, C. (1998) *The Education System Transformed*. Tisbury: Baseline Books.

Cowie, H. and Jennifer, D. (2007) *Managing Violence in Schools: A Whole-school Approach to Best Practice*. London: Paul Chapman Publishing.

DCSF (2007a) *Cyberbullying. Safe to Learn: Embedding Anti-bullying Work in Schools*. Nottingham: DCSF.

DCSF (2007b) *Guidance on the Duty to Promote Community Cohesion*. Nottingham: DCSF.

DfE (2013a) *Teachers' Standards*. London: DfE.

DfE (2013b) *The National Curriculum: A Framework*. London: DfE.

Fairbairn, G. and Winch, C. (1996) *Reading, Writing and Reasoning: A Guide for Students*. Maidenhead: Open University Press.

Foucault, M. (1977) *Discipline and Punish: The Birth of the Prison*. London: Allen Lane.

Hart, R. (2009) 'Charting Change in the Participatory Settings of Childhood', in N. Thomas (ed.) *Children, Politics and Communication*. Bristol: The Policy Press.

Hier, S. and Greenberg, J. (2007) *The Surveillance Studies Reader*. Maidenhead: Open University Press.

Hope, A. (2009) 'CCTV, School Surveillance and Social Control', *British Educational Research Journal* 35(6): 891–907.

Jary, D. and Jary, J. (1991) *Collins Dictionary of Sociology*. London: HarperCollins.

Little, W., Fowler, H. and Coulson, J. (1959) *The Shorter Oxford Dictionary*. Oxford: Clarendon Press.

Maclure, S. (1988) *Education Re-formed*. London: Hodder and Stoughton.

Mayall, B., Bendelow, G., Barker, S., Storey, P. and Veltman, M. (1996) *Children's Health in Primary Schools*. London: Falmer Press.

Open University (1996) *Block 7: Social Science and Society*. London: Open University Press.

Parker, A., Duncan, A. and Fowler, J. (2007) *Education and Inspections Act 2006: The Essential Guide*. London: NFER.

Rawls, J. (1971) *A Theory of Justice*. Oxford: Oxford University Press.

Roland, E. and Munthe, E. (eds) (2001) *Bullying: An International Perspective*. London: David Fulton.

Smith, P. (ed.) (2003) *Violence in Schools: The Response in Europe*. London: RoutledgeFalmer.

CHAPTER 17

STATUTORY PROFESSIONAL RESPONSIBILITIES

Nerina Díaz

By the end of this chapter, you should understand:

- the differences between statutory and non-statutory legislation, how they inform school policies and the implications for you as a teacher
- how statutory and non-statutory legislation is made and how it is changed
- that interpreting professional values can involve ethical dilemmas requiring discussion and reflection and examination of your personal values.

Introduction

This chapter explains what is meant by statutory responsibility. It explores the implications of statutory legislation. The examples cover employment, the curriculum, race relations, inclusion, and safeguarding children's health and well-being. The chapter explores the implications of statutory legislation through scenarios and examples of events you may encounter in school. As you will by now be aware, education is integrally connected with politics and has become increasingly so. Therefore, changes in governments are frequently accompanied by changes in educational legislation, which are inevitably value-laden and controversial. As a professional educator and a citizen, it is important that you have an informed view about proposed changes and are prepared to participate in debates about them. This chapter will raise your awareness of these issues.

Legislation, statutory instruments and non-statutory guidance

Education in the United Kingdom is the responsibility of devolved national governments: the Northern Ireland government, the Scottish government and the Welsh Assembly government. Education in England is the responsibility of the UK government. Teacher's professional duties are framed by legislation, statutory instruments, and statutory and non-statutory guidance. The latest Education Act to receive Royal Assent was in 2011. It amended parts of the Education Act 2002, but statutory legislation still refers to areas of this act which remain applicable.

Legislation

Legislation, statutory instruments (which provide the necessary detail that would be considered too complex to include in the body of an Act) and statutory guidance are all legal documents which teachers should comply with. Schools and local authorities must follow statutory guidance unless they can show they are doing something just as good or better. The Special Educational Needs Code of Practice and the Code of Practice for Schools on the Disability Discrimination Act 1995: Part 4, are examples of statutory guidance. Statutory guidance is indicated within the first few pages of a government report and is available on the government websites.

Non-statutory guidance

Non-statutory guidance does not require a legal duty for schools to have regard to it. Schools may, however, find it helpful in understanding their duties and in deciding how they should implement the statutory requirements. For example, the pamphlet, 'Religious Education in English Schools: Guidance, January 2010', is non-statutory. However, there is a statutory requirement for a head teacher and governing body to establish a behaviour policy for a school, and there is non-statutory guidance to help in this process.

Legislative procedure

Legislative procedure consists of several stages in both the elected House of Commons and the unelected House of Lords before being enacted by royal consent and becoming an Act of Parliament. This Act is binding, even if, after a general election, the governing party does not support the policies enshrined. It requires a new Act of Parliament to supersede any existing Acts. When a general election is announced, the government needs to decide which Bills to proceed with before parliament is dissolved – this is called the 'wash-up'. Some Bills do not survive the 'wash-up', even though the Act has been anticipated and potential statutory information has been made available in the public domain. The incoming government may then withdraw the proposed legislation. This happened with the Rose Review of the National Curriculum for England and Wales which was published in 2009. Many schools were creating strategies for implementing the new curriculum, which was withdrawn by the Conservative/Liberal-Democrat Coalition Government in 2010. Consequently, the National Curriculum framed in the Education Act 2002 remained statutory in England until replaced with new legislation on the curriculum by the incoming government or by the Welsh Assembly.

Statutory frameworks within which you work

Qualified teacher status

Teaching in England

Anyone wishing to work as a qualified teacher in a maintained school or non-maintained special school in England, including a maintained nursery school or a Pupil Referral Unit, must have qualified teacher status (QTS) and have completed an induction period equivalent to three school terms. The Induction Arrangements for School Teachers (England) Regulations 2012 are effective from September 2012 with revision in September 2013. A significant element of the induction regulations is that newly qualified teachers (NQTs) may only complete induction in relevant institutions. Normally, these would be in the maintained sector, including some FE colleges. Independent schools (including academies, free schools, British Schools Overseas) may choose to offer statutory induction to their NQTs, but if they do so, must adhere to the regulations and statutory guidance. If you are considering applying for your first job in a setting other than a maintained school, you are advised to check whether you are able to complete your induction year there. If you are considering taking a post in a nursery setting you are also advised to find out whether the post is suitable for induction.

Note though that, while NQTs are encouraged to start their induction as soon as possible after gaining qualified teacher status (QTS), there is no requirement to complete induction within a certain time frame. Once you have attained QTS you can undertake short-term supply work of less than one term in relevant schools for a maximum period of five years. This is a fixed time limit with no discretion to extend. Short-term supply placements of less than one term, or equivalent, cannot count towards induction. It is not possible to backdate the start of an induction period if a short-term supply contract is extended beyond one term.

Schools requiring special measures are not able to offer induction, except in cases where Ofsted have judged a school, or part of a school, to be suitable to host induction. However, if you have already started your NQT year before the school entered special measures you may continue with the induction.

Head teachers and principals have the responsibility to ensure that an NQT has an appropriate induction programme, provided by a nominated induction tutor, and make a recommendation to the local authority (LA) on whether the NQT has met the Teachers' Standards. In turn, the LA has responsibility to monitor the school's recommendation, and to communicate the decision to those involved. Overseas trained teachers can choose to be assessed against the Teachers' Standards at the same time as QTS standards. If they choose not to, or do not meet these standards, they will be required to undertake induction like any other NQT.

An NQT has only one chance to complete statutory induction. An NQT who has completed induction, and is judged to have failed to meet the relevant standards at the end of their induction period, is not permitted to repeat induction (although they may appeal against the decision). This does not, however, result in a loss of QTS, but they cannot be employed in a maintained school and their name is included on the list of persons, held by the Teaching Agency, who have failed satisfactorily to complete an induction period.

There is no legal requirement to complete satisfactorily an induction period if an NQT intends to work solely in the independent sector including an academy, a free school, an independent nursery school or an FE institution.

An NQT cannot start their induction until their appropriate body has been agreed (see Table 17.1).

If you obtain a post in a teaching school it is important to note that a teaching school that is an accredited ITT provider cannot be the appropriate body for an NQT for whom it recommended that the award of QTS should be made, nor can a teaching school be the appropriate body for an NQT whom it employs, or who has served any part of their induction at that school.

The duties assigned to the NQT and the conditions under which they work should be such as to facilitate a fair and effective assessment of the NQT's conduct and efficiency as a teacher against the relevant standards.

The head teacher/principal of the institution and the appropriate body are jointly responsible for ensuring that the supervision and training of the NQT meets their development needs. As an NQT you must be provided with the necessary employment tasks, experience and support to enable you to demonstrate

Table 17.1 Types of institution in which an NQT may be employed, and the body responsible for managing the induction process, in each type of institution

Type of institution	Appropriate body
Community, foundation or voluntary schools Community or foundation special schools	A local authority with which the school reaches agreement
Maintained and non-maintained nursery schools or children's centres	A teaching school (subject to the conditions outlined)
Non-maintained special schools Pupil Referral Units (PRUs)	The local authority in which the school is situated (if agreement cannot be reached between the school and one of the above)
Academies, free schools or city technology colleges	A local authority with which the school reaches agreement
Other independent schools including independent nursery schools	A teaching school (subject to the conditions outlined)
British Schools Overseas	The Independent Schools Teacher Induction Panel (ISTIP) (for their members and associates or additional members only)

satisfactory performance against the relevant standards throughout and by the end of the induction period:

- You should have an induction tutor with QTS.
- You should have a reduced timetable to enable you to undertake activities in the induction programme. This should consist of no more than 90 per cent of the timetable of other mainscale teachers in the school. This is in addition to the timetable reduction in respect of planning, preparation and assessment time (PPA) that all teachers receive. NQTs in independent schools, including academies and free schools, independent nursery schools and FE colleges must also have a reduced timetable on a comparable basis, but it is important to note that independent schools are not obliged to provide PPA time.
- You should not be subject to unreasonable demands; including not normally being required to teach outside the age range and/or subject(s) for which you have been employed to teach.
- You should not be expected to deal, on a day-to-day basis, with discipline problems that are unreasonably demanding for the setting.
- You should be regularly teaching the same class(es).
- You should be involved in similar planning, teaching and assessment processes to those of other teachers working in similar posts.
- You should not be expected to be involved in additional non-teaching responsibilities without the provision of appropriate preparation and support.
- You should receive a suitable monitoring and support programme, personalised to meet your professional development needs. This must include:

  - Support and guidance from a designated induction tutor who holds QTS and has the time and experience to carry out the role effectively
  - Observation of your teaching and follow-up discussion. Observations may be undertaken by your induction tutor or another suitable person who holds QTS from inside or outside the institution.

- You should meet with the observer to review any teaching that has been observed. Feedback should be prompt and constructive. Arrangements for review meetings should be made in advance and a brief written record made on each occasion. It should indicate where any development needs have been identified.
- You should receive regular professional reviews of progress which is informed by evidence from your teaching. Objectives should be reviewed and revised in relation to the relevant standards and your needs and strengths. You should record evidence of progress towards objectives and agreed steps to support you in meeting your objectives. Evidence should come from practice. You will have three formal assessments during the year, and formal assessment forms completed for the first two assessments. The final assessment is at the end of the induction period and will form part of the induction report. Interim assessment is required if you leave a post during the induction year.
- You should have the opportunity for observation of experienced teachers either in your own institution or in another institution where effective practice has been identified.

The length of time required to complete NQT is normally one school year, with the minimum time contributing to the NQT one school term, either full-time or part-time pro-rata. Extensions to the induction year may be agreed with the appropriate body for absence during the year or other reasons.

The Teaching Agency keeps records of teachers who have completed or part-completed induction and these are available to employers. The Teaching Agency also keeps records of all appeals. It is recommended that assessment reports are retained by both the institution and the appropriate body for a minimum of six years. You are advised to retain the original copies of your assessment reports.

Teaching in Wales

The present induction arrangements were applicable from 2012. All teachers are required to register with the General Teaching Council of Wales (GTCW).

NQTs are required to complete an induction period of three school terms or the period of time equivalent to 380 school sessions (one session is equivalent to a morning or afternoon of teaching), and NQTs without regular employment can accrue school sessions until 380 sessions have been completed.

NQTs will be assessed against the Practising Teacher Standards (PTS) at the end of the induction period and will be required to gather evidence of how their practice meets the PTS. The support and supervision of the NQT will be carried out through a partnership between the school(s) where the NQT works and an external mentor working on behalf of the appropriate body.

There is also the introduction of an optional Masters in Educational Practice (MEP) for NQTs commencing their induction period from September 2012, which is intended to run concurrently with the induction period and provide the basis for early professional development beyond the end of the induction period.

Teaching in Scotland

It is a legal requirement for any teacher teaching in a Scottish state school to be registered with GTC Scotland. If you qualified outside Scotland you must apply for registration and be assessed against 'Registration and Standard Rules and the Statement of Principles and Practice'. All graduating ITE students are guaranteed a one-year training contract with a reduced maximum class commitment time, the remaining time being available for professional development. Probation will be limited to one year and permanent employment restricted to fully registered teachers.

Teaching in Northern Ireland

In Northern Ireland, public (state) education is administered centrally by the Department of Education Northern Ireland (DENI), locally in controlled schools by five Education and Library Boards (ELBs) and in maintained schools by the Council for Catholic Maintained Schools (CCMS).

Northern Ireland does not have requirements for new teachers to complete a probationary year, although there is an induction year and a subsequent two-year professional development period. In Northern Ireland, you must register with the General Teaching Council Northern Ireland (GTCNI). The requirement to fully register applies to full-time, part-time and substitute teachers.

Employment

Teachers' pay and conditions

England and Wales There is a statutory document published by the government which refers to England and Wales. The *School Teachers' Pay and Conditions Document* (STPCD) (which may also be known as 'the blue book') outlines the standards and pay for the different grades of professional staff employed by the school. It is a requirement that pay scales are reviewed annually. All schools maintained by the Local Authority are legally subject to the STPCD. Schools with independent funding are not subject to the STPCD, and neither are state-funded academies nor free schools. Advice concerning pay and conditions for work in academies and free schools is available from teaching unions.

Wales Whilst the conditions for pay are negotiated through the same body as England, other conditions of service are administered through The General Teaching Council for Wales (GTCW) which is the independent, self-regulatory professional body for teachers in Wales. It undertakes, on behalf of the Welsh Government, tasks in relation to the administration and confirmation of Qualified Teacher Status (QTS), administering induction including hearing Induction Appeals, Early Professional Development (EPD) and Masters in Educational Practice (MEP) programmes, and undertaking Disclosure and Barring Service (DBS) Checks for NQTs wishing to register with the GTCW for the first time.

Scotland In Scotland, negotiations about teachers' pay and conditions are dealt with by the Scottish Negotiating Committee for Teachers (SNCT), chaired jointly by representatives of teaching organisations, local authorities and the Scottish government. The *SNCT Handbook of Conditions of Service* gives full details of current agreements.

Northern Ireland In Northern Ireland, terms and conditions of employment and pay scales are contained within the Teachers' (Terms and Conditions of Employment) Regulations (Northern Ireland) 1987. There are several categories of school in Northern Ireland:

- Controlled Schools: these come under the control of the ELBs.
- Maintained Schools: these come under the control of the CCMS.
- Voluntary Grammar Schools: these come under the control of the school's board of governors.
- Grant-maintained Integrated Schools: these come under the control of the school's board of governors.
- Irish-medium Schools: these come under the control of the school's board of governors. These schools educate pupils through the medium of the Irish language.

There is a Committee for Education to advise and assist the Minister for Education. The Committee undertakes a scrutiny, policy development and consultation role with respect to the DENI and plays a key role in the consideration and development of legislation.

However, in the whole of the UK, the teachers' pay and conditions legislation is subject to changing policies. In England, national pay agreements may be impossible to retain under the government's academy programme and their encouragement of the establishment of free schools. The principle that any primary or secondary school judged outstanding by Ofsted can be fast-tracked to academy status, or that failing schools are mandatorily transformed into academies, could destroy the unions' ability to negotiate pay and conditions centrally and, in doing so, make it virtually impossible to retain any cohesive national England and Wales pay agreement.

Fitness to teach

In **England**, statutory regulations concerning fitness to teach are detailed in The Education (Health Standards) (England) Regulations 2003. The regulations indicate the prescribed activities that teachers should be fit for, and the procedure to be followed if a teacher is no longer considered fit for the job. However, employers also have a duty to have regard to the provisions of the Disability Discrimination Act 1995.

In **Wales**, there is currently no specific guidance provided by the Welsh Government regarding the capability of teachers, and schools largely rely on guidance from local authorities and/or unions, although new guidance is being drafted in 2013. However, capability procedures (i.e. discipline and potential dismissal) for teachers can be instigated at any time. Governing bodies in Wales are required (by Regulation 7 of The Staffing of Maintained Schools (Wales) Regulations 2006/873) to establish procedures to deal with teacher capability and competence issues.

Schools must also take into account other statutory requirements such as the Employment Act 2002. The Employment Act requires that the following three steps are completed in all cases which may lead to dismissal:

- a statement in writing of what it is the employee is alleged to have done
- a meeting to discuss the situation
- the right of appeal.

In **Northern Ireland**, fitness to teach is determined by the employer, and there is an appeals procedure.

In **Scotland,** you will demonstrate fitness to teach against the Scottish standards, detailed in the 'Framework on Teacher Competence' published by GTC in March 2012.

Work in school

Student 1: My sister developed epilepsy in her twenties. I fear that this could happen to me. If it did would I have to give up my career as a teacher?

Mentor: If you did develop epilepsy there should be no barrier to working as a class teacher or head teacher. Some people have faced barriers in getting the support they need but this is disability discrimination and is unlawful; however, decisions to continue to teach must be made on an individual basis. To support a person to carry out their duties safely, risk assessments, re-definition of role and reasonable adjustments might be needed. Depending on your support

(Continued)

(Continued)

needs, your employer might want to talk about the job role. This will include possible 'reasonable adjustments' that can be made to the job. Reasonable adjustments can be made to help you to do the job effectively and to help keep you and the people in your care safe, should a seizure occur.

Student 2: I understand that, as a teacher, I am responsible for the safety of the children in my care. But accidents do happen – and children should be allowed to take risks. So where do I stand if someone has an accident?

Mentor: You would need to demonstrate that all reasonable care had been taken, with regard to the age of the child, to prevent an accident in which a child is injured. For example, make sure a climbing frame is not too high for the children who use it, and that there is a surface beneath it which will cushion a child's fall. If a floor is slippery find a way to prevent children walking on it. Otherwise you could be considered legally responsible for a child being injured.

Teachers' conditions of service

The statutory requirements for teachers' conditions of service for maintained schools in England and Wales, which schools and Local Education Authorities must abide by, are set out in the *Conditions of Service for School Teachers in England and Wales*, commonly referred to as 'the burgundy book'. The burgundy book represents the national agreement between the six teacher associations and the local authorities and contains sections about:

- appointment, resignation, retirement
- sick pay scheme
- maternity scheme
- other leave
- grievance and disciplinary procedures
- miscellaneous conditions.

It also includes information concerning the following:

- premature retirement compensation
- memorandum of agreement for the release of teachers

- agreement on facilities for representatives of recognised teachers' organisations
- relations between teachers' organisations and LEAs: collective dispute procedures
- insurance and travelling allowances
- teachers and the school meals service.

However, if large numbers of schools choose to become academies, the unions (and Local Education Authorities) are unlikely to have the concerted power to agree teachers' conditions of service.

Contractual entitlements to leave

Under the burgundy book, all teachers have the following contractual rights to leave of absence:

- for examinations
- for jury and other public service
- for accredited representation of recognised teachers' organisations.

Leave for other purposes

Although there are no national agreements for leave with or without pay for other purposes, such as participation in Parliamentary elections or as a national representative in sport, an authority shall make known to their teachers any provision they may have.

Leave of absence agreements and policies

It is important to distinguish between agreements which give rise to contractual entitlements and school policies which merely assist in the interpretation of the application of the contractual provision.

Leave of absence agreements established at local authority or diocesan levels may give rise to contractual entitlements for teachers. This occurs if an agreement is expressed in such a way as to give individual entitlements to teachers rather than giving 'advice' to governing bodies, and the teacher is employed by the local authority, or employed by a governing body which has accepted that such agreements are incorporated into the contracts of teachers at their school. There is no power for contractual agreements which have been established at local authority or diocesan level to be undermined at school level.

The following categories of absence are included in agreements and are usually taken as paid leave:

- hospital, GP, clinic and dental appointments
- compassionate leave for bereavement and illness of close relatives where there is a caring responsibility
- moving house
- accompanying children and close relatives to hospital or GP appointments
- domestic emergencies such as a gas leak or flood
- attendance at children's milestone celebrations, for example graduations or school performances.

There may also be provision for leave for religious observance and celebration of festivals.

Discretionary leave arrangements

There is a potential for difficulty when diocesan or local authority policies contain certain categories of leave granted at the discretion of the head teacher and/or the governing body.

Professional conduct

England

The Teaching and Higher Education Act 1998 established the General Teaching Council (GTC) as the independent regulatory body for teaching in England. It was tasked to contribute to improving standards of teaching and the quality of learning, and to maintain and improve standards of professional conduct among teachers. It was also the awarding body for Qualified Teacher Status (QTS). Following the election of the Conservative/Liberal-Democrat Coalition Government in 2010, the GTC was abolished.

Wales

Wales continues to support a general teaching council (GTCW) whose function is to ensure teachers are properly qualified and to maintain high standards of conduct and practice. It also advises on teaching and learning and administers government funding for teacher development.

Scotland

Scotland has an independent GTC, conferred in 2012. This is the world's first independent professional, regulatory body for teaching.

GTC Scotland's general functions are to:

- keep a register of teachers
- establish and review the standards of education and training appropriate to school teachers
- establish and review the standards of conduct and professional competence expected of a registered teacher
- investigate the fitness to teach of individuals who are, or are seeking to be, registered
- keep itself informed of the education and training of individuals undertaking courses for the education and training of teachers
- consider and make recommendations to Scottish Ministers about matters relating to teachers' education, training, career development and fitness to teach as well as the supply of teachers
- keep such registers of other individuals working in educational settings as it thinks fit
- maintain a scheme of Professional Update for teachers.

Northern Ireland

The GTCNI does not currently have a remit with respect to competency or discipline. However, if you are dismissed by your employer or resign in circumstances where you would have been dismissed, for example for misconduct or incompetence, you will be referred to the GTCNI and may be summoned to attend a hearing conducted by council members, who will determine whether you should remain on the register.

The GTCNI has the power to investigate criminal sanctions, which are now automatically referred to it. You are therefore advised to inform your employer if you have been convicted of or cautioned for a criminal offence just prior to taking up a new appointment.

If you are removed from the register, you will be unable to work in a maintained school.

The cases below came before GTCs and are examples of what is generally regarded as unacceptable professional behaviour.

Reflective task

1 Consider the case of a teacher who accesses the internet and emails excessively during lesson times. Is this acceptable?

Combined with knowledge of another action involving shoplifting, this teacher was given a reprimand (of two years).

(Continued)

(Continued)

What are the implications of this case for teachers and trainee teachers?

2 Consider the case of a teacher having an evening out with friends and having a few drinks. The evening was cold and the teacher needed to use the toilet. As there were bushes nearby, he used those. The teacher was caught by police and cautioned for a public order offence.

The GTCE found the teacher guilty of unacceptable professional conduct in that while a registered teacher he was cautioned for committing an act outraging public decency by behaving in an indecent manner.

Legislative framework guiding practice in maintained schools

The curriculum

England

Prior to 1988, there was no national curriculum for England and Wales. Provision for the National Curriculum is found in the 1988 Education Reform Act. Originally comprising of large detailed documents, by 1995 the National Curriculum was reduced and simplified and became a manageable point of reference for teachers. A new National Curriculum was published (DfE 2013) which is statutory for all pupils of school compulsory age in community and foundation schools, including community and foundation special schools, voluntary-aided and voluntary-controlled schools. At Key Stages 1 and 2 it gives programmes of study, setting out the matters, skills and processes to be taught at each stage, in core subjects (English, mathematics and science) and in eight foundation subjects, with notes and non-statutory guidance. During 2013 the previous curriculum for the core subjects in years 3 and 4 and for all the foundation subjects at Key Stages 1 and 2 was disapplied, to enable teachers to prepare for the introduction of the new curriculum in 2014. Schools will have freedom to develop their curricula within this framework.

This document is the statutory document for the National Curriculum in maintained schools in England. Academies, free schools and private schools are under no obligation to follow this curriculum.

Wales

The National Curriculum for Wales was issued in 2008. It consists of a Framework for Children's Learning for 3–7-year-olds, called the Foundation Stage. It has seven areas of learning and a subject-based curriculum for Key Stage 2 (7–11 years).

Scotland

Scotland implemented the 'Curriculum for Excellence' from 2010 onwards. The curriculum supports learning at 3–18 years. There are eight curriculum areas supporting four aspirations of knowledge and understanding, skills, capabilities and attributes.

Northern Ireland

There is a statutory curriculum for Northern Ireland, introduced in 2008, consisting of six areas of learning and religious education. It applies to the 12 years of compulsory schooling.

Reflective task

What do you consider the advantages and disadvantages of a national curriculum?

What might be the consequences for the concept of a national curriculum if the majority of school provision is outside state provision?

What would your ideal curriculum consist of?

Early years

In 2006, the Childcare Act made provision for statutory requirements for children aged 0–5 years cared for in any setting other than the home. This is known as the Early Years Foundation Stage (EYFS). It details three elements considered necessary for learning and development and six areas to be covered. Early years education takes place in a variety of settings including state nursery schools, nursery classes and reception classes within primary schools, as well as settings outside the state sector such as voluntary pre-schools, privately run nurseries and childminders.

In 2006, Sir Jim Rose published his final report of 'The Indēpendent Review of the Teaching of Early Reading', (DES, 2006) which made the recommendation that the teaching of phonics incorporated into early reading should be taught using synthetic phonics. Following the acceptance of the review recommendations, the National Curriculum was amended. The National Literacy Strategy and the National Numeracy Strategy, launched in 1998, were integrated into the National Primary Strategy, named 'Excellence and Enjoyment' in 2003, followed by a renewed Primary Framework in 2006. All these documents were for guidance and did not include any statutory requirements.

The revised Statutory Framework for the Early Years Foundation Stage (EYFS) was published in April 2012, (DfE 2012)coming into effect in all early years settings and school-based early years provision which is inspected by Ofsted from September 2012. The EYFS Framework and supporting guidance documents can be found at http://www.foundationyears.org.uk/early-years-foundation-stage-2012/

In **Wales**, children are entitled to a free part-time early years place the term following a child's third birthday until they enter statutory education. These places can be in a maintained school or a non-maintained setting such as a voluntary playgroup, private nursery or childminder which is approved to provide education. The Foundation Phase is a holistic developmental curriculum for 3–7-year-olds based on the needs of the individual child to meet their stage of development.

In **Scotland**, local authorities have a duty to secure a part-time funded place for every child starting from the beginning of the school term after the child's third birthday. Pre-school education can be provided by local authority centres, or private and voluntary providers under a partnership arrangement. In Scotland, early years education is called ante-pre-school education for those who start receiving their pre-school education in the academic year after their third birthday until the end of that academic year (note: depending on when the child turned 3 years of age, some children may only receive part of an academic year's worth of ante-pre-school education (e.g. 1 term), whereas other children may receive an entire academic year of pre-school education). All children are entitled to receive a full academic year's worth of pre-school education in the academic year before they are eligible and expected to start primary school.

The commitment in the **Northern Ireland** Executive's Programme for Government is to 'ensure that at least one year of pre-school education is available to every family that wants it' (Perry 2012). Funded pre-school places are available in statutory nursery schools and units and in those voluntary and private settings participating in the Pre-School Education Expansion Programme (PSEEP). Places in the voluntary/private sector are part-time, whilst in the statutory nursery sector, both full-time and part-time places are available. Pre-school education is designed for children in the year immediately before they enter Primary 1. Taking into account the starting age for compulsory education in Northern Ireland, this means children are aged between 3 years 2 months and 4 years 2 months in the September in which they enter their final pre-school year.

Head teachers are responsible for the implementation of statutory curricula, including assessment and reporting. (The assessment and reporting element does not apply to hospital schools.)

Assessment and Reporting Arrangements (ARA)

Assessment and reporting procedures differ for the four countries of the UK.

England

In June 2013 the Secretary of State indicated that the system of 'levels' used to report children's attainment and progress will be removed and not replaced. However, National Curriculum tests will remain as statutory end of Key Stage assessments. Ofsted's inspections will be informed by whatever pupil tracking data schools choose to keep. Schools will continue to benchmark their performance through statutory end of key stage assessments, including national curriculum tests.

Schools will use their own approaches to formative assessment to support pupil attainment and progression. The assessment framework should be built into the school curriculum, so that schools can check what pupils have learned and whether they are on track to meet expectations at the end of the key stage, and so that they can report regularly to parents.

Children in early years settings When a child is aged between 2 and 3, practitioners must review their progress, and provide parents and/or carers with a short written summary of their child's development in the prime areas. This progress check must identify the child's strengths, and any areas where the child's progress is less than expected. If there are significant emerging concerns, or an identified special educational need or disability, practitioners should develop a targeted plan to support the child's future learning and development involving other professionals.

In the final term of the year in which the child reaches age 5, and no later than 30 June in that term, the EYFS Profile must be completed for each child. The Profile must reflect: ongoing observation; all relevant records held by the setting; discussions with parents and carers, and any other adults whom the teacher, parent or carer judges can offer a useful contribution. Each child's level of development must be assessed against the early learning goals. Practitioners must indicate whether children are meeting expected levels of development, or if they are exceeding expected levels, or not yet reaching expected levels ('emerging').

Wales

In 2013 the Welsh Government published the *Statutory Assessment Arrangements for the End of Foundation Phase, and Key Stages 2 and 3*. Learners will be assessed soon after entry to school, and at the end of the Foundation Phase (age 7 years) and at the end of Key Stage 2.

Scotland

In 2011 the Scottish government published *Curriculum for Excellence. Building the Curriculum 5: A Framework for Assessment.* Assessment focuses on the application of standards and expectations of each learner's progress and achievement in knowledge and understanding, skills, attributes and capabilities. Assessment is quantified via a system of levels for the primary age-group: Early (pre-school and P1), First (to end of P4), Second (to end of P7).

Northern Ireland

Statutory assessment arrangements were revised for 2012–13. Schools are required to assess pupils' progress in cross-curricular skills with reference to incoming levels and focus on communication, mathematics and ICT.

Reflective task

What could the consequences be for schools if they are no longer using levels to indicate children's progress?

What might be the consequence of a statutory testing regime?

A wider strategy for improving children's lives

Safeguarding children

England Statutory guidance entitled *Working Together to Safeguard Children* was published by the DfE in March 2013. Following on from the Children Act 2004, which considered that collaboration both between schools and other agencies was considered essential to achieving objectives of an Every Child Matters agenda, the guidance details methods of working partnerships across all public services children may come into contact with.

All schools, state or privately funded, and further education institutions, have a duty to safeguard and promote the welfare of pupils. They are required to create and maintain a safe learning environment for children and young people, and identify where there are child welfare concerns and take action to address them, in partnership with other organisations where appropriate.

The Early Years Childcare Act 2006 also makes it clear that all registered providers, except childminders, must have a practitioner who is designated to take lead responsibility for safeguarding children within each early years setting and who should liaise with local statutory children's service agencies as appropriate. Early years services include children's centres, nurseries, childminders, pre-schools, playgroups and holiday and out-of-school schemes.

It is deemed the responsibility of the employers to ensure their employees are confident and competent in carrying out their responsibilities, and are aware of how to recognise and respond to safeguarding concerns.

Scotland The Scottish government has framed guidance entitled *Getting It Right for Every Child* published in 2012 which draws from a number of guiding documents of policies and strategies. The values and principles are built from the Children's Charter 2004, and it also promotes inter-agency working.

Wales The Welsh government refers to section 175 of the Education Act 2002, issuing guidance entitled *Safeguarding Children in Education: The Role of Local Authorities and Governing Bodies under the Education Act 2002* in 2010. Schools and education settings have a duty to safeguard and promote the welfare of children and young people. The guidance provides advice about protecting children and young people in Wales from the potentially devastating impact of domestic abuse.

Northern Ireland The Safeguarding Board (Northern Ireland) Act 2011 ('the Act') was passed in February 2011. The Act provided the legislative framework for the creation, in 2012, of a new regional Safeguarding Board for Northern Ireland (SBNI). The Act consolidates the concepts of multi-agency working and provided for the establishment of Safeguarding Panels, which will support the work of the SBNI.

Reflective task

What are the benefits and potential difficulties involved in multi-agency working?

Consider a situation in which a child's behaviour is causing you concern. You have, over the course of approximately six weeks, exhausted your repertoire of strategies to help the child, and the situation only appears to be getting worse. What are the next moves for an inexperienced teacher?

(a) Ask for the child to be moved to another class?
(b) Phone the parents?
(c) Discuss the situation with a trusted colleague, possibly the child's previous teacher?
(d) Discuss the situation with the pastoral team?

The ultimate answer should be (d). It is unwise to phone the parents without knowledge of the child's background, and without the sanction of senior staff to support you. Option (c) is an intermediate step. It is important that you do not lose confidence in your abilities as a teacher, and if you feel that you are disclosing your own inadequacies as a teacher to senior staff, it may be easier to discuss the situation with another colleague initially. Nevertheless, the child's needs are the priority. Once it is established that the child is at risk, there is a hierarchical procedure which should be followed, and the potential for a number of professionals to be involved.

Health and safety

Responsibility for health and safety derives from the 1974 Health and Safety at Work etc. Act 1974. It places overall responsibility for health and safety with the employer. For maintained schools, this is the Local Education Authority; for other schools, it is usually the governing body or the proprietor. As well as the health and safety of children, staff, visitors and volunteers to the school, education employers also have duties to the health and welfare of pupils and associated adults involved with off-site visits. The employer may delegate responsibility for health and safety to an employee, but retains ultimate responsibility.

Employees also have duties. They should take reasonable care of their own and others' health and safety, informing the employer of serious risks, and cooperate with their employers by carrying out activities in accordance with training and instruction. Although the employer is responsible for health and safety, the employee can be implicated if they have failed to take notice of instructions and procedures.

Reflective task

When taking children on a school trip, what situations may require you to be aware of the health and safety regulations? Consider issues that may arise when:

- taking children to public toilets
- a child or accompanying adult has an accident
- an accompanying adult behaves inappropriately.

Race relations

Human rights

The Universal Declaration of Human Rights (UDHR) set out, for the first time, fundamental human rights which are to be universally protected.

There are 30 Articles in the UDHR describing fundamental human rights and Art. 26 is the right to education. After the UDHR the UN went on to develop specific Conventions to cover a range of issues, for example disability, racism, women's rights.

The Race Relations (Amendment) Act (2000) places three general duties on all schools and other public bodies:

- to eliminate discrimination
- to promote equality of opportunity
- to promote good race relations.

All schools are required to:

- actively promote 'race' equality
- prepare a 'race' equality policy
- monitor attainment by ethnicity, using new, electronic data systems
- monitor exclusions by ethnicity
- monitor progress and make such information publicly available.

Schools have a legal responsibility to monitor and record any racist incidents. Inexperienced teachers may feel bound by the school's practices. The school's anti-racist or 'race' equality policy should set out suggestions for a response, but you are within your rights to point out that you think the response is inappropriate.

Reflective task

Consider the consequences of advice to ignore a racist comment overheard in the playground, with the view that the children 'don't mean anything by it'.

There are many factors which might determine your response, but consider whether ignoring the comment is a dereliction of your legal duty. Overt ways of responding might include involving the senior management team to talk to the perpetrators, contacting parents/carers to discuss the school's concerns, talking to the victims of the name-calling, and, ultimately, if the name-calling persists, seeking advice from the local authority.

Pre-empting the situation could reflect a wider school ethos. How could this be achieved through the curriculum planning? Would this planning be suitable for mono-cultural schools?

Residential and boarding schools also have to comply with Ofsted National Minimum Standards (NMS) intended to safeguard and promote the welfare of children who live (board) at a boarding school.

In Northern Ireland, equality and human rights are mainstream responsibilities for the Department of Education.

Community cohesion

As a result of the Education and Inspections Act 2006, a new section 21(5) was inserted into the Education Act 2002, introducing a duty on the governing bodies of maintained schools to promote community cohesion as from September 2007. Non-statutory guidance was published in 2007, and Ofsted was required to report on schools' performance from September 2008.

Legislation relevant to community cohesion includes the Equality Act 2006, the Race Relations (Amendment) Act 2000 and the Children Act 2004.

> Community cohesion is defined in the guidance as: working towards a society in which there is a common vision and sense of belonging by all communities; a society in which the diversity of people's backgrounds and circumstances is appreciated and valued; a society in which similar life opportunities are available to all; and a society in which strong and positive relationships exist and continue to be developed in the workplace, in schools and in the wider community. (DCSF 2007)

The *Guidance on the Duty to Promote Community Cohesion* (DCSF 2007) is grouped under three headings:

- teaching, learning and curriculum
- equity and excellence
- engagement and extended services.

Reflective task

Use these headings as a guide. How could you create a learning environment that will ensure your class community is cohesive? Consider issues such as valuing diversity, the concept of citizenship, human rights, removing barriers to participation, links with other communities, and opportunities for families and the wider community to take part in activities.

Think about your physical classroom environment, yourself as a role model, your approach to the curriculum, and your contact and relationship with parents and the wider community.

The guidance acknowledges that schools cannot compensate for all societal tensions. What are the potential barriers when planning activities encouraging community cohesion and how can these be mitigated?

Understanding children's rights

The UK ratified the Convention on the Rights of the Child (UNCRC) on 16 December 1991. All children, without exception, have entitlements to over 40 specific rights. (See http://www.unicef.org/crc/ for more information.)

The Children's Commissioner for England, responsible for promoting awareness of children's views, interests and other rights guaranteed by the Convention, must make an annual report to Parliament.

A horrific case of neglect leading to the death of Victoria Climbiè, led to the passing of the Children Act 2004, providing a legislative spine for developing more effective and accessible services focused around the needs of children, young people and families. *Every Child Matters: Change for Children* (ECM) was published in November 2004, and is concerned with the well-being of children and young people from birth to age 19.

The government's aim was for every child, whatever their background or their circumstances, to have the support they need to:

- be healthy
- stay safe
- enjoy and achieve

- make a positive contribution
- achieve economic well-being.

Under the new arrangements for Ofsted inspections, schools are required to complete a self-evaluation form (SEF) which forms an integral part of the inspection process. Schools are asked to refer to how they are actively promoting the five aims of ECM.

Inclusion

The National Curriculum states that schools should provide relevant and challenging learning for all children. There are three principles set out in the statutory inclusion statement:

- setting suitable learning challenges
- responding to pupils' diverse learning needs
- overcoming potential barriers to learning and assessment for individuals and groups of pupils.

Reflective task

Take each of the five aims of the ECM agenda and consider how you can ensure that you fulfil the five aims for *all* the children in the school. This could be through whole-school activities, class-based activities, out-of-school activities or individual actions. Consider how you can incorporate these into daily activities.

Summary

This chapter has explained the legislation against which teachers' employment and professional duties are framed. It has outlined the differences between statutory and non-statutory guidance, and the implications of legislation for changes in government policy. Teachers' conditions of employment were explored from both the employers' and employees' perspectives. Statutory professional responsibilities for the curriculum, assessment and reporting, the Every Child Matters agenda, including understanding about children's rights, inclusion, safeguarding children, community cohesion, health and safety and race relations were also explained.

For current legislation and guidance, visit the relevant government websites. For commentary and explanation of legislation and guidance, visit the union websites. The largest unions for England are the NUT (http://teachers.org.uk) and the

NASUWT (http://www.nasuwt.org.uk). Other teachers' unions are Voice (http://www.voicetheunion.org.uk/) and ATL (http://www.atl.org.uk).

Questions for discussion

These questions ask what you know about your responsibilities as an employee (guidance for answering these questions can be found in the chapter):

- Do you know how to access the school's risk assessment documents?
- Are you sure that every child in your class is treated equally, free from discrimination and any sort of bullying?
- Does every child in your class experience challenging activities suitable for their abilities?
- Do your activities involve and respect the community you serve?
- Are you aware of the school procedure if you are concerned about a child's health and well-being?
- Are you keeping records that will enable you to write a constructive and comprehensive report for the children's parents?

These questions ask what you know about your employer's responsibilities to you (guidance for answering these questions can be found in the chapter):

- Are you aware of the terms and conditions of your employment if you are not in a mainstream state school?
- Do you know the pay scales and possible progression you could make through them?
- Are you aware of what you should do if you think you require time off? Will there be tensions between family or cultural expectations and your conditions of employment? How can you resolve these?
- Are you aware of who can help you if you have a dispute with your employer?

Further reading

Children and Young People Act (2008). London: HMSO.

References

Department for Children, Schools and Families (DCSF) (2007) *Guidance on the Duty to Promote Community Cohesion*. Nottingham: DCSF. Available at: http://webarchive.nationalarchives.gov.uk/20130401151715/https://www.education.gov.uk/publications/eOrderingDownload/DCSF-00598-2007.pdf

Department for Children, Schools and Families (DCSF) (2009) *Independent Review of the Primary Curriculum: Final Report*. London: DCSF. Available at: http://www.educationengland.org.uk/documents/pdfs/2009-IRPC-final-report.pdf

Department of Education and Skills (DES) (2006) *Independent Review of the Teaching of Early Reading*. Department for Education and Skills. Available at: https://www.education.gov.uk/publications/.../0201-2006pdf-EN-01.pdf

Department for Education (DfE) (2012) *Statutory Framework for the Early Years*. Available at http://www.foundationyears.org.uk/wp-content/uploads/2012/07/EYFS-Statutory-Framework-2012.pdf

Department for Education (DfE) (2013) *The National Curriculum in England*. London: DfE. Available at: https://www.gov.uk/government/uploads/system/uploads/attachment_data/file/244223/PRIMARY_national_curriculum3.pdf

Department for Education (DfE) (2013a) *Working Together to Safeguard Children* (2013) Department for Education. Available at http://www.workingtogetheronline.co.uk/documents/Working%20TogetherFINAL.pdf

DfEE and QCA (1999) *The National Curriculum: Handbook for Primary Teachers in England Key Stages 1 and 2*. London: HMSO.

Perry, C. (2012) *Programme for Government Pre-school Commitment*, Northern Ireland Assembly.

Scottish Executive (2004) *A Curriculum for Excellence: the curriculum review group*. Scottish Executive: Edinburgh. Available at: http://www.gov.uk/Resource/Doc/26800/0023690.pdf

Scottish Government (2011) *Curriculum for Excellence. Building the Curriculum 5: A Framework for Assessment*. A summary is available at: http://www.educationscotland.gov.uk/Images/BTC5_tcm4-605259.pdf

Scottish Government (2012) *Getting it Right for Children and Families: a guide to getting it right for every child*. Available at http://www.scotland.gov.uk/Resource/0042/00423979.pdf

The Welsh Government (2013) *Safeguarding Children and Education: the role of local authorities and governing bodies under the Education Act 2002 in 2010*. Available at http://dera.ioe.ac.uk/18167/2/270813-draft-guidance-en.pdf

The Welsh Government (2013) *Statutory Assessment Arrangements for the End of Foundation Phase, and Key Stages 2 and 3*. Available at http://wales.gov.uk/docs/dcells/publications/130219-statutory-assessment-arrangements-2012-13-booklet-en.pdf

CHAPTER 18

MOVING INTO NEWLY QUALIFIED TEACHER STATUS AND BEYOND

Hilary Cooper

By the end of this chapter, you should:

- have reflected on what you have learned from this book
- have an understanding of what is meant by professional studies in education and that this is a fundamental, although 'fuzzy' concept
- have developed and be articulate about your personal philosophy of education and how to apply it in your teaching, within evolving statutory requirements and guidance
- be aware of the ways in which subject and professional associations can enable you to remain in contact with networks of like-minded colleagues, in your first teaching post
- understand the nature of a Masters-level degree in education and the ways in which you have a good foundation for studying at this level and how this relates to doctoral study.

Introduction

This chapter will review the aims of the book and the theme which underlies it: that you should mediate changing statutory requirements and non-statutory guidance through your personal philosophy. It will consider the book as a whole and help you to reflect on what you have learned through reading and interacting with it. It will reinforce your awareness of why 'professional studies' should underpin all your teaching. It will encourage you to articulate your personal educational philosophy, which, it is hoped, has developed through reading the book, and demonstrate the ways in which you are well prepared to undertake further study at Masters level.

The aims of this book

Throughout this book, you should have become increasingly aware that teachers are constantly responsible for making professional decisions related to teaching, planning and assessment, classroom organisation, behaviour management, and individual and diverse pupil needs, in order to provide equal opportunities which enable all children to reach their potential. You have been encouraged to reflect on and develop your practice and to make links between theory and practice through a raised awareness of controversial issues and by developing your ability to inform yourself about these, from relevant literature and contemporary comment. The book has aimed to promote practice informed by value judgements, promoting the educational development of the whole child: social, emotional and cognitive. It has aimed to encourage innovative and creative teaching and learning.

Statutory statements about professional attributes are inevitably succinct and prescriptive and can be interpreted in simplistic ways, if students are unable to appreciate the judgements and decisions which underlie them. If you are not able to bring informed professional judgements to bear on your work, your teaching across the curriculum will be the transmission of government requirements rather than being informed by a unique set of personal skills and understandings. If you are not able to analyse, reflect on and take responsibility for your practice, it will remain static rather than develop. And, finally, you will be vulnerable to constant political manipulation. This book has aimed to enable you to meet current and future government requirements within a broad and deep interpretation of the concept of 'professional studies'.

It is to be hoped that you are becoming aware of the ways, and many contexts, in which, as a primary school teacher, you need to think critically, make informed judgements and take responsibility for your own developing professional expertise.

But do not worry if you feel overwhelmed by the proposition that you should do so. Since you are still at the beginning of your professional journey, it could not be otherwise. The Cambridge Primary Review (Alexander 2010) has a section on 'Expertise and Development: Ways of Thinking' (pp. 416–20). It recognises that experience shapes us differently, as people and as professionals, and that by the time you retire you can expect to have a 'richly elaborated knowledge about curriculum, classroom routines and pupils that allows you to apply with despatch what you know to particular cases'.

The Review was critical of the framework by which this development was assessed by the Training and Development Agency UK (TDA 2007), saying that this was unhelpful since teachers may demonstrate their expertise in different ways. The Review suggests that teachers' development is tracked better by evidence than government policy, which has implied that teachers use the same basic repertoire at each stage of their careers and that this depresses rather than raises standards. Development is seen by the Review as progress from novice, through competence, to expert, recognising that excellence includes such concepts as artistry, flexibility and originality, which are difficult to define precisely but instantly recognisable. So accept that you will gradually become expert by using the approaches suggested throughout this book. This criticism has been addressed subsequently in the Teachers' Standards (DfE 2013), which see professional development as interpreted in terms of role and context, whereas the Standards for Wales, Ireland and Scotland define it more specifically.

Overview of the concept of professional studies

Having read this book, you should understand that 'professional studies' in education means a body of knowledge, understanding and skills, based on consideration of the values and aims which underpin the many decisions that each lesson requires. Professional studies encompass the pedagogy which brings educational aims and values to life, and translates the curriculum into learning and knowing which engages, inspires and empowers learners – or not. This body of knowledge and skills involves:

- communication, collaboration and relationships with pupils, colleagues and parents
- understanding how children learn and how to progress their learning, responding in a supportive way to individual differences between children
- provision of a learning environment in which all children can reach their potential
- taking responsibility for your own professional development through reflection on and evaluation of your experience and practice, your reading and interpretation of policies.

Professional attributes

These four themes are a synopsis of the professional attributes required for achieving qualified teacher status, which run throughout this book. Table I.1 (pp. 6–11) showed you how this book reflects the Professional Standards for England, Wales, Scotland and Northern Ireland and invited you to use them to monitor your development as you read the book. You need to consider the significance of these themes in relation to your more detailed learning of how to teach each of the subjects of the curriculum.

However, it is important to remember that research (Alexander 2010 pp. 450–1) suggests that there is no single definition of teacher professionalism because the concept is fluid, plastic and dynamic and fails to recognise the 'more nuanced and dilemma-conscious private conversations of primary teachers … where feelings matter … and where subtlety and realism puncture the notions of "one-size-fits-all" and "good primary practice"'.

Reflective task

Take the plan for a lesson you have taught and the related evaluation. Highlight any of the Teachers' Standards which are reflected in the lesson plan. List the Teachers' Standards which you demonstrated as an integral part of your practice but did not need to state in the plan or evaluation. Are there any which, on reflection, you could have demonstrated but did not?

Analysis of the professional standards addressed in this book

It is clear from Table I.1 that professional attributes are not discrete. Most of them run through several chapters of this book. Analysis of the table shows that the professional attributes which are addressed most frequently in the book are personal qualities (the ability to work collaboratively and communicate effectively and to take responsibility for your own professional development) as well as personal values and beliefs (particularly in relation to behaviour management and equal opportunities).

Teachers' personal responsibility for developing their practice is referred to in Chapters 2, 3, 4, 15 and 16. The importance of constructive criticality is discussed in Chapters 1, 2, 9, 11, 14, 15 and 16 and provision of equal opportunities for children with diverse learning needs is covered in Chapters 5, 11, 12 and 14.

Personal educational philosophy

It was suggested in Chapter 2 that, while reading this book and relating it to your experience and other reading, you develop, review and adjust your personal educational philosophy statement. If you have done this, it will be helpful, as a personal statement is generally required as part of an application for a teaching post.

Reflective task

If you have not revised your statement of educational philosophy over time, write it now, drawing on discussions throughout this book. You might choose to use the following headings:

- My interpretation of the aims of primary education
- How I apply them in the following contexts
- Subject knowledge
- How children learn and how I support their progress
- Planning, monitoring and assessment
- Inclusion, individual differences and special educational needs
- Behaviour management
- Children's personal and social development.

However you decide to structure your statement, keep it brief. There may be a hundred applicants. And do relate it to the advertisement for each particular post and school. The interviewers need to know that you are the one person they are looking for! Therefore, it is important to give a flavour of your personality and experience; what you have actually done in school in a variety of curriculum areas and with specified age groups. This will show you can make connections between theory and practice and will give the interviewers a good idea of the things to talk to you about. Be prepared to critically evaluate what you tell the interviewers about your work in schools.

Reflective task

Read 'What is Primary Education For?' (Alexander 2010 Chapter 12 pp. 180–200). Do you want to revise your statement after reading this?

Networks of like-minded colleagues

Subject associations

This book has been about critical reflection on practice in order to develop your own philosophy and resist manipulation. But although you may feel that you have developed and can defend a robust personal philosophy, you may not be fortunate enough to find a school where this is shared by everyone. Teachers come from different backgrounds and are of different ages. In my experience it can be extremely frustrating when a belief in strategies and values you are convinced are sound is not shared by colleagues. Although the standards require teachers to continually develop their practice through reflection, research and collaboration, this is difficult to achieve. The standards also require us to work together with colleagues and parents. This too is often treading a tightrope! You want to fit in. You also want to fulfill your ideals – indeed your potential. So the pressure to compromise, or even to give in, is very great. You want to continue with your professional development but there is little funding for this, so where do you turn?

The answer is by joining and taking an active part in a professional and/or a subject association (membership can be set against tax!). Here you will find the support of like-minded and idealistic people, opportunities to meet and work with others or to do so online, and receive up-to-date information and advice in dealing with issues and finding good resources. Subject associations provide a link with universities and research and best practice – offering a source of advice and a feeling of being part of a large and vibrant intellectual community, which may be missing when you are no longer in a university environment. Examples are given below.

Mathematics

The National Centre for Excellence in Mathematics (NCETM) (https://www.ncetm.org.uk) is funded by the DfE (you can register online). It provides high quality continuing professional development (CPD) resources and encourages collaboration amongst staff, by sharing good practice locally, regionally and nationally, through courses, regional networks and online, and supports teaching in schools. It also funds, supports and disseminates research. The personal learning section includes a professional learning framework, self-evaluation tools and a personal learning space for anyone who has registered. Partners include:

- Association of Teachers of Mathematics (http://www.atm.org.uk)
- Children's Mathematical Network (http://www.childrens-mathematics.net)
- Further Mathematics Support Programme: provides support for students and teachers' CPD (http://www.furthermaths.org.uk)
- Mathematical Association (http://www.m-a.org.uk)

English

- The National Council of Teachers of English (http://www.ncte.org) aims to support work with pupils and families to promote life-long literacy, to help with resources and materials and with confronting issues.
- The National Association for the Teaching of English (http://www.nate.org.uk) provides national and regional courses, and continuing professional development resources.

Science

- Primary Engineer (http://www.primaryengineer.com) works with schools to provide courses which develop technology, science and mathematics.
- The Association for Science Teacher Education (http://theaste.org) provides regional and national networks and resources and is a forum for debate and promoting excellence.

History

- The Historical Association's resources include the journal, *Primary History*, online continuing professional development modules, lessons and exemplars, as well as conferences and forums and opportunities to comment on policies (http://www.history.org.uk).

Geography

- The Geographical Association (http://www.geography.org.uk) supports teachers and students through journals, publications, training events, websites and lobbying government about the importance of geography (incorporating the performing arts).

Music

- The Schools Music Association (http://www.schoolsmusic.org.uk) organises events, awards, training, grants and resources.

Sport and PE

- The Association for Physical Education (http://www.afpe.org.uk) develops PE-related policy and offers professional support for members through high-quality professional development opportunities, journals and national working parties.

Art

- The National Society for Education in Art and Design (http://www.nsead.org) promotes and defends art, craft and design across all age phases, defines and reassesses policies, disseminates new ideas, research and good practice, and provides a forum for discussion.

Professional associations

These are non-profit-making associations seeking to further the interests of pupils, teachers and lecturers in primary education.

- The National Association for Primary Education: this is concerned with the learning of children from birth to 13 (http://nape.org.uk). It works with teachers, parents, governors and schools, through sharing good classroom practice, conferences and the journal, *Primary First*. It brings groups of like-minded colleagues together, enables discussion about innovative strategies and issues and participates in discussions at the highest level with other organisations.
- The Association for the Study of Primary Education: ASPE (http://www.aspe-uk.eu) was founded on the belief that one of the best ways to advance primary education is through professional collaboration and action. Members are early years and primary practitioners, advisors and consultants, Local Education Authorities and university teachers. The journal *Education 3–13* reports on cutting-edge research. The emphasis is on collective study, collaborative activity, theoretical study, scholarship and informed debate.

Teachers' unions

You may not be sympathetic to all their campaigns but, as my father, a committed member when unions were less activist, always said: 'when one of your pupils is involved in a serious accident while you are in loco parentis, you need all the support you can get'.

- The National Union of Teachers (NUT) (http://www.teachers.org.uk) offers legal advice and insurance and also provides learning opportunities for newly qualified teachers, and for continuing professional development.
- The National Association of School Masters and Union of Women Teachers (http://www.nasuwt.org.uk) offers legal and professional services, and guidance on dealing with employment issues.

Work in school

Student: Goodness knows I'm not work shy – although I do think a consideration of work/life balance aids good teaching! But I have friends who have been expected to work on Saturdays (maths and language workshops for parents) and on a Sunday (performing a class play in the local church) and even to supervise school journeys in holiday time. Is this reasonable?

Mentor: The School Teachers' Pay and Conditions Document (STPCD) applies to maintained, foundation and voluntary-aided schools. It specifies that a teacher must be available for work for 195 days, or 1265 hours in any school year, at such times and places as specified by the head teacher, but should not be required to work on Saturday or Sunday. You should be given a calendar at the beginning of each calendar year setting out all your commitments. Usually there can be flexible and amicable negotiations about these. But if you suspect that you are being asked to work for longer than the STPCD specifies, you should discuss this with your NUT representative – assuming you have joined!

Student: I'd really like to join all the subject associations but couldn't possibly afford to.

Mentor: Most have a school membership, so ideally persuade your head teacher and subject coordinators of its advantages. Or you might share the cost of membership with friends, or each join your own specialist subject association and share resources. I think it's really important to be part of a larger professional network outside your school.

Moving from qualified teacher status to a Masters degree

Many teachers told the Cambridge Primary Review (Alexander 2010) that they wanted more time to reflect, research and study. This echoes the need for continuing professional development and for teachers who take responsibility for this. Most Masters degrees in education involve a research study, usually based on enquiry into your own practice. Throughout this book, you have been encouraged to think reflectively and critically.

Part 3 focused on this process in more structured ways, through chapters on reflective practice, enquiry and critical thinking and exploring educational issues in order to prepare a small research study. The later chapters in this book should help you to move through this continuum of level criteria. This will put you in an ideal position for study at Masters level. This usually requires a sustained investigation of a question of your choice, based on a critical analysis of the relevant literature, theory and previous research. It will include modules on how to collect and analyse data and present

Table 18.1 Shows the progression in knowledge, skills and understanding from qualified teacher to Masters and doctoral level research

Requirements for the award on an Honours degree in Education Studies (Benchmark standards Level 7) QAA (2007) (http://www.qaa.ac.uk)	Descriptor for a Masters degree (level 7) taken from the Framework for Higher Education Qualifications for England, Wales and Northern Ireland (QAA 2010; Appendix 2a, England, Wales and Northern Ireland; Appendix b, level 11, Scotland) (http://www.qaa.ac.uk)	Doctoral Degree Characteristics (2011) Descriptor for a higher education qualification at doctoral level (level 8) Framework for Educational Qualifications in England, Wales and Northern Ireland (QAA 2011) (htttp://www.qaa.ac.uk)
Knowledge and understanding Demonstrate a critical understanding of: • the underlying values and principles relevant to education studies and a developing personal stance which draws on personal knowledge and understanding • the diversity of learners and the complexities of the education process • the complexity of the interaction between learning and contexts, and the range of ways in which participants (including learners and teachers) can influence the learning process • the societal and organisational structures and purposes of educational systems • the possible implications for learners and the learning process	To achieve the award of a Masters degree students should demonstrate **a systematic understanding of knowledge, and a critical awareness** of current problems and/or new insights, much of which is at, or informed by, the forefront of their academic discipline, field of study or area of professional practice	For the award of a doctoral degree students must have demonstrated the creation and interpretation of new knowledge, through: • original research or other advanced scholarship, of a quality to satisfy peer review, extend the forefront of the discipline, and merit publication • a systematic acquisition and understanding of a substantial body of knowledge which is at the forefront of an academic discipline or area of professional practice • the general ability to conceptualise, design and implement a project for the generation of new knowledge, applications or understanding at the forefront of the discipline, and to adjust the project design in the light of unforeseen problems
Application Demonstrate the ability to: • analyse educational concepts, theories and issues of policy in a systematic way • identify and reflect on potential connections and discontinuities between each of the aspects of subject knowledge and their application in educational policies and contexts	Demonstrate a comprehensive understanding of techniques applicable to student's own research or advanced scholarship	Students must have demonstrated a detailed understanding of applicable techniques for research and advanced academic enquiry and a detailed understanding of applicable techniques for research and advanced academic enquiry

(Continued)

Table 18.1 (Continued)

• accommodate new principles and understandings • select a range of relevant primary and secondary sources, including theoretical and research-based evidence, to extend personal knowledge and understanding • use a range of evidence to formulate appropriate and justified ways forward and potential changes in practice		
Reflection Demonstrate: • the ability to reflect on personal and others' value systems • the ability to use knowledge and understanding critically to locate and justify a personal position in relation to the subject • an understanding of the significance and limitations of theory and research	Demonstrate: • originality in the application of knowledge, together with a practical understanding of how established techniques of research and enquiry are used to create and interpret knowledge in the discipline	Students continue to undertake pure and/or applied research and development at an advanced level, contributing substantially to the development of new techniques, ideas or approaches
Communication and presentation		
Students should be able to organise and articulate opinions and arguments in speech and writing using relevant specialist vocabulary Students should be able to use ICT in their study and other appropriate situations Students should be able to: • collect and apply numerical data, as appropriate • present data in a variety of formats including graphical and tabular • analyse and interpret both qualitative and quantitative data	Demonstrate conceptual understanding that enables the student: • to evaluate critically current research and advanced scholarship in the discipline • to evaluate methodologies and develop critiques of them and, where appropriate, to propose new hypotheses	Communicate their ideas and conclusions clearly and effectively to specialist and non-specialist audiences

Students should have the ability to collaborate and plan as part of a team, to carry out roles allocated by the team, take the lead where appropriate, and fulfil agreed responsibilities	Demonstrate how to deal with complex issues both systematically and creatively, make sound judgements in the absence of complete data, and communicate their conclusions clearly to specialist and non-specialist audiences	
Improving own learning and performance		
Students should be able to articulate their own approaches to learning and organise an effective work pattern including working to deadlines	Demonstrate self-direction and originality in tackling and solving problems, and act autonomously in planning and implementing tasks at a professional or equivalent level	Continue to undertake pure and/or applied research and development at an advanced level, contributing substantially to the development of new techniques, ideas or approaches
Students should be able to process and synthesise empirical and theoretical data, to create new syntheses and to present and justify a chosen position having drawn on relevant theoretical perspectives	Continue to advance their knowledge and understanding, and to develop new skills to a high level. Holders will have the qualities and transferable skills necessary for employment, requiring: • the exercise of initiative and personal responsibility • decision-making in complex and unpredictable situations • the independent learning ability required for continuing professional development	Doctoral degrees are awarded for the creation and interpretation, construction and/or exposition of knowledge which extends the forefront of a discipline, usually through original research Holders of doctoral degrees will be able to conceptualise, design and implement projects for the generation of significant new knowledge and/ or understanding Holders of doctoral degrees will have the qualities needed for employment that require both the ability to make informed judgements on complex issues in specialist fields and an innovative approach to tackling and solving problems

and evaluate your findings. Table 18.1 shows the progression from Qualified Teacher Status to a Masters degree and how you could build on this at doctoral level.

So make a habit of reading, keeping up to date with critical professional thinking. Make it a regular habit to engage with the wide-ranging, challenging and thought-provoking papers in the *Journal of Philosophy of Education*. Recent papers deal, for example, with such debates as: What is fairness in assessment? What are educational rights? The subservience of liberal education to political ends. What does it mean to be educated? What is meant by religious education? Race, schools and the media and the relationship between research and practice and the kinds of educational research we should value. I hope this has whetted your appetite for further study! Good luck – and here's a final quotation from Alexander (2010 p. 512):

> Abandon the discourses of derision, false dichotomy and myth and strive to ensure that the education debate at last exemplifies rather than negates what education should be about.

Summary

This chapter has considered the aims of the book in developing critical and reflective practice and cautioned that, while you should understand the process, this must be seen as an area of continuing professional development. The importance of articulating your personal educational philosophy, exemplified by your experience in school, when you apply for your first teaching post was discussed. Information was given about national organisations which will offer you professional support networks and opportunities for continuing professional development. The chapter concluded by illustrating the ways in which engagement with this book and some experience as a teacher can place you in a confident position to apply for a higher professional qualification.

Children's experience of primary school in the future is in your hands. It is an exciting prospect – and a great responsibility.

References

Alexander, R. (ed.) (2010) *Children, their World, their Education: Final Report and Recommendations of the Cambridge Primary Review*. London: Routledge.

Department for Education (DfE) (2012) (updated 2013) https://www.gov.uk/government/publications/teachers-standards

DfE (2013) *The National Curriculum: A Framework*. London: DfE.

QAA (2007) *Education Studies*. Mansfield: QAA. http://www.qaa.ac.uk/Publications/InformationAndGuidance/Documents/Education07.pdf

QAA (2010) *Masters Degree Characteristics*. Gloucester: QCA. http://www.qaa.ac.uk/Publications/InformationandGuidance/Documents/MastersDegreeCharacteristics.pdf

QAA (2011) *Doctoral Degree Characteristics*. http://www.qaa.ac.uk/Publications/InformationAndGuidance/Documents/Doctoral_Characteristics.pdf

Training and Development Agency UK (TDA) (2007) *Teacher Professional Development in England*. http://webarchive.nationalarchives.gov.uk/20111218081624/http:/tda.gov.uk/

INDEX